I received a card from a patient I had for several years who had been severely traumatized in early childhood. The card had a picture of a swan on the cover and inside was the following message:

> **"But what do you think she saw when she looked down into the water? Her likeness, but how changed! She was no longer a dark, gray bird, ugly to look at, but a beautiful swan.... The poor swan was so happy she did not know what to do, but she was not at all proud. She heard them say that she was the most beautiful of all the birds....I never dreamed of such happiness when I was an ugly duckling,"**
> Hans Christian Anderson.

Thank you Dr. Scott, for helping me to change from being a lost ugly duckling to a person of value and worth."

Since that time the swan has been the symbol in my office to remind me of what can be done for those who feel as the ugly ducklings of our society. Deep inside there is a person of value and worth, created in the image of God, if we can just help them out of the mire and into the beauty of their potential.

THE HANDBOOK OF BRIEF PSYCHOTHERAPY BY HYPNOANALYSIS

John A. Scott, Sr., Ph.D.

authorHOUSE®

AuthorHouse™
1663 Liberty Drive
Bloomington, IN 47403
www.authorhouse.com
Phone: 1-800-839-8640

First published by AuthorHouse 3/15/2011

ISBN: 978-1-4567-1792-6 (sc)
ISBN: 978-1-4567-1791-9 (e)

Printed in the United States of America

Any people depicted in stock imagery provided by Thinkstock are models,
and such images are being used for illustrative purposes only.
Certain stock imagery © Thinkstock.

This book is printed on acid-free paper.

Because of the dynamic nature of the Internet, any Web addresses or links contained in
this book may have changed since publication and may no longer be valid. The views
expressed in this work are solely those of the author and do not necessarily reflect the
views of the publisher, and the publisher hereby disclaims any responsibility for them.

Rapport
Relax

Realize → Diagnosis

Re educate → (regress to baby)

DEDICATION

To my parents, Ruby Register Scott, and Clarence E. Scott, who provided a loving, consistent and stable environment for us three children, conducive to the kind of family we strive to achieve with our clients.

Rehab (Rehearsal)

Reinforcement

As we build Rapport, Relax and
we will realize the cause of your
issue, then we will reeducate (regress)
to the origin of issue
Finally we will Rehabetate (A belief)
+ Reinforce all work done

CONTENTS

ACKNOWLEDGEMENTS

I am deeply indebted to William J. Bryan, Jr., M.D. and Richard Rubottom, M.D. who initiated my interest in hypnoanalysis and who were my mentors.

Marvin Koven, Ph.D., Leo Weisbender, Ph.D., and Jordan Packer, Ph.D., of the California Graduate Institute read early drafts and freely gave helpful advice and counsel.

My colleagues in the American Academy of Medical Hypnoanalysts have contributed much through clinical experience and have provided a forum for presentation and discussion of the various aspects of this study.

I must express my deepest thanks to my wife, Jo. It takes an unusual woman to tolerate a husband who spends most of his adult life going to school and working while she tends to the various needs of three children; then, when the children are gone and the nest is empty, for him to be tied up in research and writing once again. Jo has done it superbly. Furthermore, as an English teacher in the public schools, she has offered much help in all of my writing by proofreading and making many valuable suggestions.

It is with pleasure that I also give credit to my children for their help. My son, John, Jr., Ed.D. (a partner in my profession) has made valuable contributions in thought and editing as well as sharing in the writing of Chapter 7 on age regression to birth. My daughter, Emily Scott-Lowe, Ph.D., and husband Dennis Lowe, Ph.D., have also made helpful suggestions. My son, David R.T. Scott, A. I. A., did the art work.

Ms. Jerry Blair, a friend and former colleague from the staff of Harding Graduate School of Religion, was very helpful as a proofreader.

Finally, I must thank my friend, Hugh McHenry, Ph.D., Professor of Mathematical Sciences at Memphis State University, who took my original disks and somehow assiduously transferred them to an up-to-date computer which could give birth by laser printer to this document.

FORWARD

The American Academy of Medical Hypnoanalysts is pleased to offer the second edition of this handbook that is our textbook. In it is explained the tenets of our methodology which has been refined through more than 60 years of scrutiny and practice. This is the only book that fully explains this unique body of theory and technique. The Academy is continually proactive in its efforts to develop research evidence to demonstrate the strengths of this method but we are mostly practitioners. Therefore this book explains the art of our practice and how it compares to and differs from those others that provided the context within which it was developed.

When the author, Dr. John Scott, Sr., first went to Los Angeles to study under Dr. William J. Bryan, Jr., only medical doctors were deemed qualified to undergo this training. Dr. Scott saw the potential that this methodology held for all mental health practitioners. That was 1971. He persuaded Dr. Bryan that as a minister, counselor and seminary professor he could advance the interests of the American Institute of Hypnosis. However, Dr. Scott was the only non-medical person that Dr. Bryan trained. Partly due to this issue as well as the perceived need for freedom to grow the method and the practitioners, a group of eight of Dr. Bryan's trainees separated in 1974 to form a new organization, the Society of Medical Hypnoanalysts. Dr. Scott became the ninth member. The Society of Medical Hypnoanalysts is now The American Academy of Medical Hypnoanalysts. The Academy is now proud to be a multidiscipline group. All practitioners who are licensed as therapists in their state of residence are eligible for membership and training. While appropriate training, ethics and credentials are necessary we recognize that being a healer is as much a condition of spirit as of training.

Many perspectives in society have changed since this book was written and first published. Hypnosis and Medical Hypnoanalysis have evolved as well. As you read these pages you will notice that this book reflects much from a previous time. Dr. Scott did most of the writing of this book in the 1980s. His wordings, citations and illustrations are expressive of his time and his training. We ask that you overlook these to see the beauty and opportunity expressed in the theory and practice of this unique modality. These perspectives are just as fresh and exciting in today's world as they were when Dr. Bryan and his colleagues were developing them in the 1950s. In fact, listening to the subconscious will seem new and exciting in every generation. For just as good taste is never the common standard, so also, listening to the deep meanings of life and living will never be the common mode of communicating. Healing requires that we find those deep conflicts and resolve them so that life may rediscover its purpose. It is our hope that you find the enduring content of this work. We have found these principles to offer real answers in both our practices and our lives.

John A. Scott, Jr., Ed.D.

For the editorial board, AAMH.

PREFACE

A THERAPY WHOSE TIME HAS COME
THE AGE OF HYPNOSIS

In the last ten years there has been a surge of interest in hypnosis. Its techniques and procedures have become so widely familiar that such terms as hypnotherapy, autohypnosis, hypnology, analytical hypnotherapy, clinical hypnosis, therapeutic hypnosis, Ericksonian hypnosis, hypnobehavior, New Hypnosis, hypnogogic images, neuro-linguistic programming, hypnosynthesis, Medical Hypnoanalysis and others have found their way into, at least, the recognition vocabulary of the general public. The interest is so great that a growing number of organizations are promoting hypnosis in one form or another. On any given weekend, one need not travel very far to find a class, seminar, or lecture being held on the subject.

Furthermore, I would venture to say that the number of books published on Hypnosis in the last ten years far exceeds the total output of all such subject-related material printed during the past fifty years. Certainly recent publications have been more scientific, and have taken into consideration the progress that has been made in related fields such as behavior modification, metapsychology, biofeedback and relaxation control. The subject has also been approached from a variety of perspectives, including the diagnostic, therapeutic, experimental, and analytical, not to mention the vernacular quest.

Personal Frustrations With Therapy

Frankly, by 1971 I had become frustrated and discouraged with both individual psychotherapy and marriage counseling. As I look back, in spite of the fact that part of my time was spent teaching at the graduate level and part in private practice, I probably was suffering from burnout. A part of the problem, as I saw it at that time, was that not enough patients in individual therapy were having the degree of success that I had anticipated they would, or achieving that success as quickly as I thought they should. Perhaps my standards for them were too high. Perhaps my standards for myself were too high. Perhaps my techniques were not what they should have been.

Preface

Another issue was financial. Were the fees which I collected for the services rendered justified? In analyzing my situation, I found I had a certain amount of guilt, a certain amount of frustration, a touch of obsession-compulsion mixed with a mild case of fatigue and monotony. It was at this time that I first became acquainted with Medical Hypnoanalysis.

Medical Hypnoanalysis As A Solution

My theoretical background, which includes psychoanalytically oriented psychotherapy, psychiatry and a mixture of Rogerianism and TA, made me a receptive candidate to this new procedure. I had had a speaking acquaintance with hypnosis, but, like many professionals, I used it only in exceptional circumstances, and, as I think now, not very effectively. After a few years of training and practice, I inaugurated Medical Hypnoanalysis into my private practice as a treatment modality for neurotic disorders. I was so highly gratified by the successful results achieved with this method of therapy that I made plans to discontinue marital therapy as such and concentrate on hypnoanalysis with individuals in psychotherapy.

Basically, the procedure was directed, short term, and analytically oriented. And the results with patients were gratifying. I could see more patients, achieve more positive results in a shorter period of time, and thus have a greater degree of satisfaction within myself.

SHARING THE PROCEDURE

The time has come to share the procedure with a broader segment of the professional community than those who appear at weekend seminars. Yet, in order to share this procedure, it becomes necessary to start with a description of Medical Hypnoanalysis as a modality used in individual therapy. In so doing I provide this with the expectation that my professional colleagues will have an opportunity to verify my own conclusions, and at the same time, I am confident, to make adaptations and improvements which will be profitable to society at large.

Unfortunately objective research is currently minimal. Only one comparative study has been completed (Scott, Jr., 1991). But with the publication of this material there will surely be others who will take up the challenge and produce for the professional community further studies and experiments which will aid all of us in our joint quest for improvement in individual and couple psychotherapy.

A DEFINITION OF MEDICAL HYPNOANALYSIS

Since there is diverse terminology used in the literature on hypnosis it will perhaps be helpful to the reader to have a working definition of Medical Hypnoanalysis presented early. The following was formulated by the Society of Medical Hypnoanalysts (Now called the American Academy of Medical Hypnoanalysts).

"The practitioner of Medical Hypnoanalysis requires a training background in the basics of psychology, developmental psychology, psychopathology, and psychotherapy as well as in hypnosis.

"Medical Hypnoanalysis is dynamic, short term, and directed. It is dynamic in that the treatment approach emphasizes causes rather than symptoms, explanations rather than descriptions, and unconscious forces rather than conscious forces as being the ultimate origin of the psychopathology. It is short term in that in most of the situations thirty or less sessions are required for the completion of treatment procedure. It is directed therapy in that the psychotherapist, upon making a diagnosis, follows a medical model of psychotherapy aimed at alleviating the symptoms by means of resolving underlying unconscious causes.

"Medical Hypnoanalysis first examines the presenting symptoms of the patient by means of a case history, observing verbal and nonverbal communication, while seeking unconscious clues to the ultimate causes of the symptoms in order to make a psychodynamic diagnosis. After the patient is introduced to hypnosis, the majority of the therapeutic sessions are conducted with the patient in the hypnotized state. The therapist investigates the unconscious by using the following procedures: 1. A specifically designed word association test, 2. Dream analysis, 3. Age regressions directed at crucial periods earlier in the patient's life.

"Such procedure allows identification and re-interpretation, adjustment or re-evaluation and desensitization of the specific causal events. This procedure is directed at correcting the symptoms and the unwanted behavior which causes suffering and disease. For example, depressions, phobias, obsessions, psychosomatic disorders, self-destructive and anti-social behavior and other emotional and psychological problems can be relieved.

"There are a variety of methods and procedures of applying the basic hypnoanalytical method. Individual varieties are based on the specific training and treatment circumstances of the clinician."

Hypnoanalysis is therefore receptive to various theoretical approaches but is best viewed as a truly eclectic modality.

THE "MEDICAL HYPNOANALYSIS" TITLE

An additional word is necessary regarding the use of the word "Medical" in the title "Medical Hypnoanalysis" since there are some who could be confused by its use. The Society of Medical Hypnoanalysts was given birth by a group of physicians meeting in Chicago in 1975 (now called the "American Academy of Medical Hypnoanalysts") and there the name of the procedure was debated. Inasmuch as all present were physicians who utilized hypnosis in their practice, and followed a "medical model" of treatment, they felt the name was appropriate. Their hope was to distinguish this procedure from all other procedures and systems and give it a name which evidenced this individuality.

When men with Ph.D.'s were qualified to join the group there was some sensitivity to their membership because of the use of "Medical" with regard to their status. Thus Category II in the membership roster was added, and they were permitted to practice "Medical Hypnoanalysis" as a psychotherapeutic procedure. This is without any intention of implying that those without medical degrees are practicing medicine in the literal sense of that word.

In recent years the term "medical" has been more generally applied. Actually, the term is based on a Latin root meaning "to heal" and this is without regard to the use of medications. Since it is becoming more widely accepted that the most important system of health is the brain itself, the line of demarcation between the influence of the physician and influence of psychology gets thinner. Barber (1984) bluntly states, "ideas can effect the physiological activities of the cells in the human body." And Rossi (1986) and Rossi & Cheek (1988) are making bolder statements than ever, backed by scientific evidence, concerning the mind-body interrelationship and the vast healing powers of the mind. Ornish's program for reversing heart disease claims to be "scientifically proven" and much of it is based on mental-emotional processes (Ornish, 1990).

Lewith, in The British Medical Journal (1985), referred to people seeking treatment by "alternative medicine" and included such treatments as acupuncture, manipulative medicine, homoeopathy, clinical ecology, biofeedback, psychotherapy, the Alexander technique, and hypnosis. Thus it is clear that "medical" includes a broad spectrum of healing or treatment modalities for the curative process.

More and more schools of medicine and schools of psychology are including departments or chairs of "behavioral medicine." Courses and books are taught and written on the interdisciplinary characteristics of physiology, medicine and the psychological components of the curative process and health. It is common knowledge that the foremost medical problem in our culture is the adverse influence of stress which is as much, or more, psychological than physiological, but in any case is medical. This brings us to another facet of this interesting subject.

Eniatric healing concerns "healing within the self". Just as the body tends to heal itself while the physician acts as a facilitator, director and helper so as to speed the process, likewise, the mind tends to heal itself (and protect itself with a myriad of defense mechanisms), while the psychotherapist acts as facilitator, director and helper.

Thus the term "Medical Hypnoanalyst" does not imply, per se, that the therapist has a medical degree or dispenses medications. Rather, it is the title of a particular process of psychotherapy, duly defined and registered, utilizing hypnosis in a specified manner. Training is provided for those who already have completed their education in social work, psychology or medicine.

The major purpose of this work is to describe the use of hypnosis for the clinician, rather than to stimulate laboratory and experimental work on the phenomena of the trance. Therefore, I have avoided becoming involved in discussions on susceptability of persons to the trance state as well as "depth" levels etc. These details along with subjects of motivation for hypnosis and whether or not the hypnotic state can be emulated are details which are fascinating for the theoretician and researcher, but not apropos to my purpose here. As is characteristic of the Hilgards, they tell the relationship story beautifully in a few words: "the experimental findings will undergird the work of the clinician" (Hilgard & Hilgard

1983,xi). See Barber (1958); Chaves (1968);Dalal (1966); Hilgard (1979); Orne (1971) Spanos (1970)

OVERALL PLAN OF BOOK

It is the aim of Volume One to describe Medical Hypnoanalysis clearly enough for the experienced psychotherapist, who has a background in dynamic psychology, to apply the method in his clinical practice with a minimum of additional training. Volume Two will describe the modification of hypnoanalysis for the treatment of marital dysfunction.

I have used a variety of terms in reference to the practitioner of hypnoanalysis in order to cover the range of professionals who employ it in their practice, as well as to prevent monotony to the reader. Such terms are: therapist, analyst, hypnoanalyst, clinician.

Out of respect for the policy of fair treatment of individuals and groups, I have made an effort to avoid writing in a manner which reflects role prejudice or sex bias. Yet I have endeavored to avoid awkwardness in using pronouns; consequently, "he," and "she," are used in a variety of ways. But unless there is a specifically named antecedent, ambiguity of gender is implied.

August 1996
Memphis, TN

CHAPTER 1

HISTORY OF HYPNOANALYSIS

INTRODUCTION

Obviously, in delving into the use of the term "hypnoanalysis," a history of hypnosis is implied. But, because there are so many excellent summaries of the history, it does not fall into the province of this chapter to repeat what has already been done by so many capable scholars. Rather, the purpose of this section is to narrow the historical quest to the particular use of hypnosis as an adjunct to analytical therapy. In 1968, Klemperer observed that "it is still too early to determine" whether one day the modality of psychotherapy, known as "hypnoanalysis," will grow from an adjunctive role to a special and autonomous form of treatment. I believe that day has now come. Like the converging of many streams and rivulets, the theoretical input and clinical experiences of many scholars and clinicians have been merging and the confluence of these experiences serve as a foundation which may now be laid for recognizing hypnoanalysis as not just an "adjunct" to another form of therapeutic procedure, but as a specialized and autonomous form of therapy.

"Hypnoanalysis" as a term, historically has been loosely used. It has been applied to the generalized use of hypnosis in direct suggestion for symptom removal on one extreme and as an adjuvant in psycho-analysis at the other extreme (Brenman & Gill, 1947). Buckley (1950) refers to a process of "hypnotic analysis as a relatively untried technique." Conn (1949a) used the term "hypno-synthesis" in reference to the use of hypnosis with psychoanalysis. Then Lifshitz and Blair (1960) refer to the resurgence of "abreactive therapy" by which they mean the use of hypnosis as it was used in the treatment of war neuroses. Kline (1955) published a book on Hypnodynamic Psychology in reference to the use of hypnosis "within the framework of psychoanalytic treatment." "Hypnoidal psychotherapy" is used by Steger (1951); Schneck (1954) alludes to "scientific hypnosis." And of course, there is the *British Journal of Medical Hypnotism*, with frequent use of "medical hypnosis." One of the latest and finest works on the subject is Barnett's *Analytical Hypnotherapy* (1981), in which a system of combining analytical principles together with hypnosis is very skillfully done.

Such a state of affairs can only lead to confusion. It depends on "which newspaper one reads" as to what meaning one derives from the practice or use of "hypnoanalysis." In view of such confusion it is no wonder that Gill and Brenman (1959) came to the conclusion that "hypnotherapy" was a misleading term and "should be abandoned"; and "the term 'hypnoanalysis' is sufficiently lacking in specificity as to be useless" (p.355f).

In the last 15 years a growing number of clinicians have gravitated to the practice of hypnosis, in an analytic context, as a full time specialty called "Medical Hypnoanalysis." While the theory and practice has been dynamic in that it has been evolving and developing, it has also been crystallizing as an "autonomous" psychotherapeutic procedure. An organization of professionals interested in such a specialty has now been functioning since 1975. It is my purpose in this chapter to summarize the history of the use of hypnosis as an adjunct in analytic psychotherapy, thus enabling us to get a more objective perspective on where we are currently.

Admittedly, the task I have set before me is no easy one. Since scholars who specialize in the use of hypnosis cannot even agree on a definition, and greatly differ among themselves on what takes place when one is hypnotized - and even question if such a state exists - it is not going to be simple to bring order out of such confusion. However, I do not expect this work to achieve completely such a high goal. Rather, I am sending up a trial balloon which may, perchance, serve as a basis for further investigations and contributions from others in the field. At a time when "short-term" therapy is the order of the day, it is certainly apropos to utilize a procedure which all authorities recognize as being a means to shorten psychotherapy. Yes, "hypnoanalysis" is a procedure whose time has come.

HISTORY OF THE USE OF "HYPNOANALYSIS"

The prefix "hypno-" was apparently used for the first time for a number of words describing what we now call the hypnotic state in 1821 by a Frenchman, Entienne Felix d'Henin de Cuvillers (Gravitz & Gerton, 1894).

As far as I can determine, Brenman and Gill (1947) are accurate in attributing to Hadfield the origin of the hyphenated term "hypno-analysis." Hadfield verified this in a personal communication to Crichton-Miller stating that he invented the term in the First World War to describe the method of using hypnosis as a means of reviving forgotten and repressed experiences, mainly in amnesia cases. However, he also used it as an alternative method to free association and dream interpretation (Ambrose & Newbold, 1958). But this refers to the use of the term "hypno-analysis". The history of hypnosis in analysis goes back much further than this.

THE FREUDIAN PERIOD

In Mesmer's pioneering efforts he, of course, made many mistakes in a trial and error procedure, but he must be given credit, as Chertok does (1978a), for a "scientific" approach to the study of hypnosis. He maintained that the "magnetic fluid" which he supposed people to have, was not due to divine or evil influences. It was for Mesmer's pupil, Marquis de Puysegur, to make the first "analytic" discovery, and as Conn (1982) states, "mark the emergence of dynamic hypnotherapy." In 1784 de Puysegur hypnotized a shepherd named Victor, who, when he awoke, did not remember the events which occurred during his session. De Puysegur concluded that we have two independent memories. Thus, the unconscious was recognized for the first time (Chertok, 1978a). The concept of the unconscious continued development in nineteenth century French discourse and had an influence on Freud (Chertok, 1978b).

The use of hypnosis during this early period was primarily for suggestion, which prompted Bernheim in 1888 to observe that "all was suggestion" (Bernheim, 1888).

The process, whatever it may be called, of using hypnosis in a general framework of psychoanalysis was used by Breuer and Freud by 1895. Breuer had discovered that hypnosis could be used to enable an hysterical patient to recall the events which were the ultimate cause of her hysteria. Thus the case of Anna O. became the basis for what Freud later called

3

the "cathartic method," and which, of course, became the foundation for later psychoanalysis. Breuer and Freud (1893,1939) introduced periods of hypnosis at intervals during analysis and soon conceived the mechanism of repression, another fundamental principle of psychoanalysis. Gruenewald (1982) points out that Freud recognized hypnosis as a means to assist in the revival of memories of the past while the patient was in a state of increased suggestibility.

In addition, the use of hypnosis led to Freud's discovery of transference. He observed that in hypnosis there is a real encounter between two persons. When Breuer and Freud hypnotized women, Mrs. Breuer and Martha (Freud's fiancee) were jealous. It is assumed that, because of the libidinal aspects of hypnosis, Freud dropped its use in favor of developing psychoanalysis (Chertok, 1968; Gruenewald, 1982). Undoubtedly there was more to the decision than that, but Kline (1958) verifies that Freud was sensitive to the fact that hypnotic behavior involved an intense emotional relationship between the hypnotist and the patient. And he (Freud) admitted some confusion and ambivalence regarding hypnosis. But Kline sees Freud's abandonment of hypnosis for reasons that are more complex. He sees "subjective motives" and "objective motives."

The subjective motives include: (a) Freud's involvement in non-hypnotic psychoanalysis and the extension of free-association technique; (b) he felt a sense of failure in being unable to obtain a somnambulistic state in enough patients; (c) he was sensitive to the development of a libidinal relationship between therapist and patient.

The objective grounds for Freud's discarding the use of hypnosis are: (a) hypnotic suggestion failed to produce lasting results; (b) "hypnosis conceals all insight into the play and interplay of mental forces and psychodynamic interaction; (c) hypnosis covers over the patient's resistances and thus inhibits effective psychotherapy; (d) hypnotic techniques give the patient the impression of a laboratory experiment and in this respect interfere with the setting for psychotherapy" (Kline, 1958, p. 5). In Kline's evaluation he rightly observes that Freud's subjective reasons are understandable and justified. But his objective reasons have not proved to be valid.

Kline (1958) observes that since Freud abandoned the use of hypnosis, it fell into disuse in the formal psychoanalytic movement simply because Freud was looked upon as an authority figure. Yet the reasons he rejected its use are no longer valid.

Freud does give credit to his contemporaries, Charcot, Breuer, and Bernheim, ... and acknowledges their effective use of hypnosis. There is, however, no evidence that hypnosis was used more than occasionally in their treatment. This proved to be the case for many years to come. Thompson (1950) makes an interesting observation in pointing out that in the evolution of Freud's clinical practice, psychoanalysis grew out of the use of hypnosis, then hypnosis was dropped from his practice in preference for free association.

Except for a few allusions to the analytic use of hypnosis (for example, Sidis, 1902, who appears to be one of the earliest to utilize it in the study of the dynamics of personality) its use at the turn of the century was primarily confined to direct suggestion. It is as if the psychoanalysts went their way and the hypnotists went their way. (*The International Journal of Psycho-Analysis* does not have a single full length article on the use of hypnosis in an analytical context through 1982. There are a few references to hypnosis and some book reviews, but the subject is largely ignored.)

The dichotomy present between psychoanalysis and hypnosis at the turn of the century is reflected in the writings of Ferenczi (1926). In 1913 he stated that "hypnosis is nothing else than a temporary return to this phase of infantile self-surrender, credulity, and submission. At any rate the analysis of such cases usually exposes mockery and scorn concealed behind the blind belief." In 1915 he bluntly said, "I think the difference between hypnotism and analysis is this: hypnotism is like the beater that beats the dust farther into the clothes, but analysis is like the vacuum cleaner; it sucks out the symptoms." It is said of Freud that he compared hypnosis and analysis to the technique of painting and sculpture as characterized by Leonardo da Vinci (Ferenczi, 1926).

Ferenczi appears to reflect the general view of hypnosis by psychoanalysts at the time (1908) when he states (Ferenczi, 1926, pp.27f):

I will only touch briefly here on the question of hypnosis and suggestion, and remark forthwith that some successes are to be achieved by these means. Charcot already explained that hypnosis is a kind of artificial hysteria, and psycho-analysis further supported this by confirming that suggestion, whether employed during hypnosis or in the waking state, merely suppresses the symptoms, i.e. it employs the method in which the hysteric failed in his wish for self-cure. The ideational group occasioning the disease remains untouched by the treatment in the unconscious of the neurotic whose symptoms we strangled by hypnotism. Indeed in a certain sense it is enlarged, that is, the hitherto existing symptoms are now joined by a new one that can certainly, for a time, prevent the expression of pre-existing symptoms. When the force of the suggested prohibition weakens [and for this it suffices that the patient leave the doctor's environment], the symptoms may immediately man themselves again. I regard hypnosis and suggestion as usually safe and harmless methods of treatment, but as holding out little promise of success, and their employment, moreover, is much circumscribed by the fact that only quite a small number of people can really be hypnotized.

These issues, as bases for controversy, were to continue for decades to come.

In another context, Ferenczi, in 1921, makes an analytical observation which is not without merit. He states that in

father-hypnosis the subject performs all that one asks him to do, as by that means he hopes to escape from the danger threatened by the dreaded hypnotist; in mother-hypnosis he does everything to ensure to himself the love of the hypnotist.

Meanwhile Keller (1917) is given credit by Brenman and Gill (1947) for one of the early attempts to combine hypnosis with the techniques of psychoanalysis.

Thus, at the turn of the century there were, for the most part, two camps. In the one were the hypnotists who dealt with direct suggestion for symptom removal; and in the other were the psychoanalysts who, as a group had not yet utilized hypnosis in therapy. Some analysts had enough of a professional curiosity to observe or practice hypnosis on occasion and as a result voiced some opinions and began to formulate theoretical concepts; but too little was known about the possibilities of hypnosis at that time to utilize it effectively enough for it to be widely accepted and practiced in psychotherapy. Nevertheless, the foundation had been laid. As the dark clouds of war spread over Europe, so the discoveries in psychotherapy were broadening and were finding new impetus with the onset of war.

THE PERIOD OF WORLD WAR I

Reference has already been made to the fact that Hadfield first used the term "hypno-analysis" as a process of using hypnosis in treating amnesias in war shock cases. The procedure, which had been used in earlier cases, was to revive forgotten and repressed experiences in hypnosis as an alternative method to free association and dream interpretation (Ambrose & Newbold, 1958).

The period of World War I gave some stimulation to the uncovering techniques available with hypnosis. The pressure on the army hospitals was to treat the patients in the shortest possible time. Traumatic war experiences, which frequently involved amnesia, lent themselves particularly well to treatment by hypnosis (Hadfield, 1920; Brown, 1921; Simmel, 1921). Take note that Brown is the first to call attention to the fact that usually more than one event of a similar type was involved as the traumatic basis for the production of the patient's symptoms. His point was that frequently it took more than one traumatic event to weaken the psyche and precipitate the neurosis. Wingfield (1920) had already demonstrated the value of going back to some earlier period in life in seeking the ultimate source of symptoms.

Paul Schilder and Otto Kauders (1927) are given credit for writing the first book of its kind attempting to explain the phenomenology of hypnosis from the psychoanalytical point of view (Bryan, 1928, p. 05). Their statement appears to be the best summary available at this time:

We consider this method (psycho-analysis) to be a royal remedy in the treatment of serious neurotic troubles, regardless of whether they result in organic symptoms or not. Hypnosis is the only method for easy and medium cases and so may have great symptomatic value even in the treatment of serious cases.

There is no indication of a widespread interest during the period prior to World War II, but there are glimpses of individuals who manifested some curiosity about the use of hypnosis in an analytical setting. And, if the publication of a journal is any evidence, the place of greater interest seems to be Great Britain. For examples see Speyer and Stokvis (1938), Bramwell (1921), Hadfield (1919, 1920). Others of this era were Hull (1933), Janet (1925), Platonow (1933), Eisenbud (1937). Of course, the "grand old man" of hypnosis, M.H. Erickson, was the leading figure in hypnosis during this period. Although he did not practice psychoanalysis with it, he utilized analytical principles along with hypnosis and in so doing laid the groundwork for a more advanced utilization later (1933, 1938a, 1939b; Erickson & Kubie, 1939, 1940).

Erickson (1937) demonstrated that, at least in some cases, apparent unconsciousness could develop while reliving a traumatic experience in hypnosis.

Kubie, as an analyst, must be given great credit for pioneering work at his time (1939, 1943a, 1943b etc.). He made many contributions in conjunction with Erickson, in demonstrating, for example, that it is even possible to alter memories in hypnosis (1941).

It was a significant disclosure when Kubie observed (1939) that the essence of all neurosis was that a command had been repeated many times in the child's mind by an authority figure. Such repetitions must occur because of the resurgent instinctual demands. This appears to be the substance of what we now call negative hypnotic suggestions related to what Araoz (1981) calls "negative self-hypnosis." Kubie (1943b) also recognized that hypnogogic reverie could produce and clarify unconscious material.

Another example (in addition to Erickson) of a non-psychoanalyst utilizing psychoanalytical methods at this time was Berg (1941). He gave a popular description of the psycho-analytical method for the lay public.

The challenge had been thrown by now and the cudgels of debate had been taken up. For example, Young (1940) discusses the issue of whether age regression was "fact or artifact." And Winn (1940) thought it necessary to attack psycho-analysis in order to provide a scientific foundation for the study of hypnotism.

Zenkin (1948, p. 54) gives an apt summary for this early period. He states:

Freud's refusal to continue his investigations with this method (hypnosis) caused it to fall rapidly into disrepute. Although on the continent many psychiatrists and physicians continued to employ it, in our country it was relegated to the limbo of stage tricks, cracks and cranks.

Before going further it will be helpful to summarize some of the psychoanalytic principles which had been utilized with hypnosis by the period immediately preceding World War II. 1. Hypnosis was used to revive forgotten and repressed memories. 2. Hypnosis was used in dream interpretation. 3. It was possible to produce post-hypnotic amnesia. 4. Hypnosis led to an awareness of a subconscious mind in addition to the conscious mind. 5. When hypnosis was used in regression to previous traumatic experiences, catharsis could be produced, and this was extremely helpful in curing the patient. 6. The use of hypnosis led to the recognition that the mind may repress unpleasant experiences from the consciousness. 7. Hypnosis led to the discovery of the principle of transference. 8. The use of hypnosis led to the recognition that a plurality of events of a similar nature make up the etiology of the symptoms.

These discoveries were made over a period of some 50 years and by therapists in scattered environments. There is no evidence that any one utilized all or even most of these principles in clinical practice during this time.

It took the trauma of the Second World War to bring about a

true resurgence in the use of hypnosis as an adjunct to analytical psychotherapy.

THE PERIOD OF WORLD WAR II

Erickson and Kubie (1941) further stress the value of abreaction in the recall of childhood experiences by the use of hypnosis in describing the cure of a case of acute hysterical depression. The patient was first deeply hypnotized and then given some "protective suggestions" concerning hypnosis, and, it was noted, that the hypnotist had a permissive attitude. It was clear to the therapists that the patient had several previous traumatic experiences, severe enough so that, in order to soften the readjustment and to avoid guilt or fear, post-hypnotic amnesia was produced. This was destined to become a procedure used later by some therapists.

Erickson and Kubie recognized that there was some repression of insight from the age regressions, but otherwise they refer to the treatment as "the usual psychoanalytic technique." For example, many repetitions were used. An observation was made that the patient was cured with "only rudimentary insight," that is, there were insights, conscious and unconscious, which were never understood or clarified to either patient or therapists. These two authors further observe that the patient's behavior in age regression corresponds to the functioning during an earlier phase of its maturation.

Such reports undoubtedly furnished the basis for the heightened popularity of hypnosis in age regressions for the cure of war neuroses. For example, Grinker and Spiegel (1943) used a "dramatic" technique in their treatment. Buckley (1950) describes in some detail a year's experience in the neuropsychiatric clinic of an Army general hospital. There were 22 cases showing symptoms of headache following head trauma with alteration of consciousness, "of these, 9 cases were treated by hypnotic analysis." All had preconcussive amnesia and were in treatment 1 to 15 weeks. At the beginning, Buckley stated to the patients that this was a relatively untried technique, but he desired to use hypnosis for age regressions in order to recall the trauma. He reported remarkable success. By now Erickson (1945) had already observed that any really co-operative individual could be hypnotized, though this idea was open to dispute.

Kubie (1943a) was among the earlier psychoanalysts to go to print with a program for the treatment of war neuroses by the use of hypnosis to produce abreactions. Since most of the war neuroses were acute traumatic reactions, the use of hypnosis was particularly effective. Frequently the cure would be dramatically short. Barnett (1981) is probably right in observing that the reason for such short term cures was that the trauma was recent and took place during adulthood.

Kubie and Margolin (1944) stress that hypnosis is a regression to a partially infantile state, in which ego boundaries become partially blurred to both the hypnotist and to the subject, so that time and sensory perceptions are dislodged from their anchorage in outside reality. These authors also refer to facilitating hypnosis by relative immobilization and low-intensity, monotonous, or rhythmical stimulation. With regard to transference, Kubie and Margolin (1944, p.618) postulate that:

If the hypnotic state could be produced without the use of any...prehypnotic maneuvers the... subject's thought content would then arise solely out of the depths of his own personality.

Treatment of war neuroses stimulated more experimentation due to the desire to shorten the psychotherapeutic procedure. Consequently, as with numerous scientific endeavors, war provoked progress in the use of hypnosis in the psychiatric clinic (Conn, 1949b; Kubie, 1943a; Masserman, 1941; Rosen & Myers, 1947; Watkins, 1949; and many others).

Although Watkins (1949) does not claim to practice hypnoanalysis as such, he used hypnosis in an analytic environment, recognizing that the "job in the army hospital is minor, not major psychological surgery." Motivated by the need to treat war neuroses as quickly as possible, he utilized hypnosis with a number of techniques which fostered insight. Some of the techniques were: dissociated handwriting, several projective procedures, analysis of transference reactions, abreaction, teaching under trance, and others.

In what he calls the "in-and-out method," Watkins would take the patient in and out of hypnosis 12 or 15 times in one hour for the purpose of helping the patient to reintegrate concepts at both the conscious as well as the unconscious level. He stresses that this is important to achieve a permanent cure.

Watkins states that in achieving insights for some patients the therapist may prefer to go slowly, suggesting that the insight or understanding "will emerge a little at a time" over a period of two weeks. His general rule was to start with the more superficial manifestations and later attack the deeper problem.

As a result of these endeavors, a number of prominent clinicians, some of whom were psychoanalysts, came forward with a combination of hypnotic techniques with psychoanalysis, or at least with analytical procedures stimulating insight. When one looks back on this state of events concerning hypnosis and in-depth therapy from the vantage point of the present, one can see a kind of search going on (by a few pioneers) for a shorter, in-depth, procedure to cure psychosomatic and psychoneurotic disorders. But there was a lack of system and organization. There were a number of loose ends regarding hypnosis (for example, what it was, were its "cures" lasting, what was the relationship between the hypnotist and the patient, etc.).

There were more loose ends concerning psychoanalysis (should an analyst have a medical degree? Disagreement on procedures from the physical position of the analyst to the method of handling transferences, in addition to the most obvious problem of an open-ended, extended period of time for the analysis, etc.) A search was going on, consciously for some individuals, and unconsciously, I think, for the profession as a whole, for a shortened and improved form of the analytical procedure. There were a number of prophets crying in the wilderness for solutions. Several of these will be summarized in the following pages. Here we see the "conception" of hypnoanalysis taking place.

THE CONTRIBUTIONS OF R. M. LINDNER

An outstanding contribution was made by R. M. Lindner. As a psychoanalyst he was going against the mainstream of his colleagues by his procedures. He wrote a number of articles, introductions to books (written by others) and his own book as well (1944). In laying the foundation for describing his method of hypnoanalysis, he gives us an eye witness account of the status of affairs in 1944 in the quest for bringing about systematization and harmony in the field of hypnosis and analysis. He states (1944, p.15):

In no place, and at no time, though, has [hypnoanalysis] been subjected to careful scrutiny as a respectable procedure warranting the serious and unprejudiced consideration of clinicians engaged in the study and treatment of mental or behavior disorders.

Lindner refers to the fact that hypnoanalysis, a technique composed of psychoanalysis, hypnoanalysis and hypnosis, was at that time still in the formative stage. He states that he made his first tentative experiments with it in 1939 and was, by the time of the writing of his book, more organized, but still unfinished. "It did not spring up full blown and armored. Its growth was independent, painful. Its application cautious and hesitant" (p.15). He makes an impressive point when he observes that the very fact that it has been necessary to call hypnoanalysis into existence is a proof of the inadequacy of both psychoanalysis and hypnosis. Take note, however, that basically "hypnoanalysis" at this period meant that hypnosis was used on occasion in psychoanalytic procedure to achieve a specific point such as overcoming a persistent resistance, nothing more.

In summarizing the contribution of both the fields of psychoanalysis and hypnosis to hypnoanalysis, Lindner states (p. 5):

From psychoanalysis it has extracted certain procedural modes and the interpretative core. It validates beyond question the data of analysis. It provides a fixative means for the therapy without which analysis is no more than an exercise in diagnosis. From hypnosis it has drawn a probe for penetration into the darkest recesses of human performing.

In addition he points out certain weaknesses in both psychoanalysis and hypnosis as these procedures had been practiced in the majority of cases. Specifically psychoanalysts had objected to the use of hypnosis because; 1) not all patients could be hypnotized; 2) it was said that although a specific symptom could be cured through the emotional catharsis during the trance, the cure would be temporary; 3) that hypnosis influences those "unconscious factors" which have been striving for expression and does not affect the prohibiting "forces" responsible for their exclusion. Lindner takes care to answer these objections.

Furthermore, he is emphatic in building a case for the advantages of using hypnosis in psychoanalysis. He asserts that hypnoanalysis shortens the period of treatment and should not last longer than three or four months (using daily sessions). During this period "the cathartic and abreactive processes are just as complete and the therapeutic yield as rich as that claimed for any other given psychotherapeutic tool." Hypnoanalysis can raise to awareness quickly the repressed, often emotionally surcharged material. By reconstructing the individual history of the patient, the process provides for the development of self-knowledge to the patient by analytic interpretations shared by both the analyst and the patient. In addition, it aids in the implementation of healthy attitudes and approaches to life by imbedding these understandings firmly into the personality.

Lindner's Procedures and Techniques

The first phase of Lindner's treatment, apparently lasting about one week, consists of daily sessions in which the patient is taught to go quickly into hypnosis, and deeply enough so as to recall accurately, or forget completely, what has transpired during the session. During this period a workable and manipulable transference is also developed.

The second phase (also lasting one week) deals with recall under hypnosis. While in a deep trance the patient should be able to revert to earlier periods of life and verbalize events from that period. The patient is also expected to be able to carry out posthypnotic suggestions.

The third phase is the actual hypnoanalysis. Observe that much of what Lindner now does (as other contemporaries did) is to use psychoanalytic procedure except that the patient is hypnotized.

The patient is seen daily, having been instructed in the method of free association, and begins each session with whatever topic he brings to the hour. Hypnosis is resorted to only when it is apparent that the patient is resisting by withholding crucial material. It is stressed that the patient must review the last few associations and recollections that he produced prior to the hypnosis session. Then the hypnotic session is held, in which the patient is to recall material pertinent to the last few associations wherein there was such resistance. Complete amnesia for these hypnotic events is produced.

At the following sessions the key associations, i.e. those which had been given by the patient immediately before he was made to sleep, are again presented. The reason for this is that it gives evidence of the validity of analytical material and also is a weapon for the literal disintegration of resistances. The aim is to have the material, which had resisted disclosure, flow smoothly after hypnosis, as if there had never been reluctance to produce it. Lindner feels this benefit of hypnoanalysis saves half the time of typical psychoanalysis. It also removes the primary objection that many psychoanalysts have had to the use of hypnosis, namely, that the total personality rarely, if ever, participates in the disclosures made while in hypnosis. In this way the total personality does participate in hypnosis. Of course the transference is dissolved and displaced and redirected into the practical application in the life of the patient.

Lindner recognized the two forms of hypnotic memory recall, one in which the patient influences his recollections by the sum of his experiences since the actual events took place. And in which the patient actually lives again the time of which he is telling and it exists now uninfluenced by the accumulation of life since that event.

Lindner points out that the analyst must make the following decisions in hypnoanalysis: 1) When to employ hypnosis. 2) When to encourage free association. 3) When to employ revivification or regression. 4) When to demand abreaction in the waking state. 5) When to engraph the interpretation and significances directly onto the personality. (This last is the most delicate and requires the most skill.)

Lindner feels so strongly about the effectiveness of this form of analysis that he maintains that for the first time there is, by hypnoanalysis, a method of penetrating to the core of the psychopathic personality. Not only may the process be applied to a wide range of diagnostic entities but, as its principles are more fully comprehended, he predicted the procedure would be improved.

In his book, Lindner presents a case in which the patient is a psychopath and gives an hour by hour report illustrating his process. He states that the inability of the psychopath to come into rapport with anyone evidences the need and value of hypnoanalysis. He states:

This case needed a technique of sufficiently active incisiveness to plunge into the farthest reaches of awareness and extract from therein, in total, the historical scenes that were too painful to be faced without preparation.

He further reports that in the past five years there were six cases of psychopathology plus one male hysterical somnambulist, one sexually frigid woman, one feebleminded psychotic boy, two male anxiety neurotics, one male bronchial asthmatic, three male homosexuals, one male alcoholic, and one male kleptomaniac. None of these analyses exceeded four months. He reports that in some cases symptoms entirely disappear, in others the patient learns to live with the condition, and in others there is an "alteration, permanent and deep-seated, of the patient's life style."

In conclusion Lindner evaluates the methodology by a comparison to psychoanalysis in which he states what in essence others of this period do, namely, that "nothing new in the way of interpretation of behavior results from hypnoanalysis: that it tends rather to verify and substantiate the insights into behavior-dynamics which the psychoanalytic approach affords."

In reviewing Lindner's book in *The International Journal of Psycho-Analysis*, W. Clifford M. Scott (1946) tersely comments, "This unique factual report of a new type of experiment in psychotherapy should interest all analysts..."

I have devoted a large amount of space to summarizing Lindner's procedure because he was one of the few who clearly presented the methodology by this time and followed it by case examples. As he states, at this stage in the development of hypnoanalysis, it was largely dependent on the backbone of psychoanalysis. This presentation will be used as a base for comparison of other modalities which appeared later in this same period.

THE CONTRIBUTIONS OF LEWIS R. WOLBERG

Another clinician who wrote extensively, giving case material, was Lewis R. Wolberg. At this period he had two prominent works dealing with the subject of hypnoanalysis (1945, 1948). Instead of writing from a prejudiced point of view against hypnotherapy while upholding psychoanalysis (as some contemporaries did), he not only acknowledges that "palliative psychotherapy reinforced by hypnosis" has a place in successful treatment, but writes extensively in teaching how this may be done. In my opinion, this leveling influence is significant. He clearly delineates the type of cases that can respond to such palliative therapy, and emphatically cautions against endeavoring to use such procedures where an analytic approach should be made. Such an understanding can greatly benefit therapists and, obviously, be a blessing to patients receiving their treatment.

Wolberg acknowledges his predecessors who demonstrated that hypnosis could facilitate the psychoanalytic process. He repeats previous assertions that the greatest value of hypnosis lies in its effectiveness in overcoming resistances to uncovering unconscious material. Like Lindner, he cites, and answers, the traditional objections to the use of hypnosis in the analytic process. They had to do with hypnotizability, the validity of the material revealed in hypnosis, and the effect of hypnosis on transference. With regard to the latter point, Wolberg observes that an "innovation" in hypnoanalysis is that the patient's transference feelings can be analyzed as they develop before they have a chance to be repressed.

In dealing with the objection that by using hypnosis the patient is too passive for the therapy to be effective, Wolberg presents a positive case for the active participation of the patient in the therapeutic process.

Wolberg verbalizes a drawback with hypnoanalysis which, in my opinion, continues to some extent today (unless adjustments in procedure obviate such a problem). The point is that some patients, not seeing the value or necessity of analytic procedure, will expect the therapist to take an authoritarian position while they take a role of passivity. They reject a nondirective procedure. These and other factors (such as the patient with a weak ego) will have to be taken into account in preparing the patient properly for hypnoanalysis.

John A. Scott, Sr., Ph.D.

Wolberg's Procedures In Hypnoanalysis

Wolberg follows Lindner's lead in taking one to two weeks of daily sessions to prepare the patient adequately for hypnoanalysis. He feels that a somnambulistic trance is essential and that the patient must be capable of going into a trance immediately at a signal. Further, he observes that a one and one half hour session is preferable to the traditional one hour period. That each session starts with the first fifteen or twenty minutes spent in traditional free association, with the subject matter being the basis for later hypnotic suggestions. After this, hypnosis is induced so that the hypnoanalytic procedures may be utilized.

Hypnoanalytic Procedures

Free association is recognized, at this time, as being the foundation for the entire analytic process. It will be observed that whereas Freud had dropped hypnosis in favor of free association, some analysts were now able to combine the two procedures effectively. In the event that there are resistances to waking free association, hypnosis may be used to overcome this.

Dreams play an important role in both psychoanalysis and hypnoanalysis. In hypnosis the patient may be encouraged (and trained) to dream about the problem either then, while in trance, or in a typical night dream later. The author points out that dreams which take place under hypnosis may be interpreted by the patient while hypnotized, but should not be interpreted in the waking state.

Automatic writing and hypnotic drawing, as utilized by Wolberg in the hypnoanalytic procedure, are described. As with dreams, the patient is encouraged to interpret the cryptic messages of both.

Another means to soften resistances is the use of play therapy, which may be utilized in both the adult or regressed stages in hypnosis. Of course directions for its use must be given by the therapist and may have to be repeated.

Dramatization (apparently first designed by Moreno, see Wolfe and Rosenthal, 1948) is an effective procedure wherein the patient is asked to act out certain scenes. This was a particularly effective procedure in treatment of the war neuroses. The therapist may play a passive role, encouraging the patient to act out the scenes, or the therapist may actively participate by taking the role of a participant.

Crystal and mirror gazing are recommended by Wolberg. A mirror may be made to be blank (like the crystal) by angling it so that it reflects the blank space of the ceiling. The patient is encouraged to visualize or hallucinate by looking into the blankness of the crystal or mirror and report on what is seen.

The two forms of age regression, as previously described by Kubie and Erickson, followed by others, are well outlined by Wolberg. Age regression is induced when the suggestion is accepted by the patient that a previous period in life be recalled. It is a state in which the patient simply remembers the past, with language and attitudes from the present contaminating the past experiences.

Revivification is the regressed state wherein the patient mentally actually returns to the earlier event and relives it as if going through it again. Wolberg points out that the regression procedure can be used in combination with other hypnoanalytic techniques, of dream induction, play therapy, drawing, dramatics, automatic writing and mirror gazing. This is a good example of how Wolberg builds on the work of his predecessors (both in psychoanalysis and hypnotherapy) and makes his own contribution to the improvement of the therapeutic procedure. The following is another example.

Apparently Eisenbud was the first to use the induction of an experimental or artificial conflict into the hypnotic session with the patient (see Eisenbud, 1937, Wolf, 1948). Wolberg very clearly explains the technique as an advantage to a patient whose resistances prevent gaining insight that should be clear. In the case where unconscious conflicts or drives are producing, for example, a somatic response and the patient does not comprehend this, the therapist can contrive an incident, in hypnosis, which demonstrates the pattern. The patient is told that upon awakening from hypnosis he will understand the cause and effect in the contrived situation (which may be based on a factual event from the patient's past or on a fictional event) and then be able to apply that principle to the situation at hand in the therapy.

Wolberg, in his usual lucid style, points out the practical applications of hypnoanalysis and devotes many pages to clarification of the process (including case verbatims), viz., 1) in keeping with traditional psychoanalysis, hypnoanalysis permits the development of a transference neurosis with its analysis; 2) hypnoanalysis is used to desensitize the patient, allowing the repressed elements of his personality to be brought to recognition; 3) the patient is reeducated by means of psychoanalytic insights.

It is obvious that both Lindner and Wolberg, as psychoanalysts, deserve a great deal of credit for breaking with strict psychoanalytic tradition in organizing and synthesizing analytical concepts and hypnosis. Wolfe (1948), as a contemporary colleague, gives them recognition accordingly. It is as if they saved hypnosis from ineffectual or inappropriate use and gave it a dignity which enabled others to join their ranks with further improvements and refinements.

Wolfe and Rosenthal (1948) have a chapter on "Hypnoanalysis, the New Therapy" in which they give Erickson, Kubie, Wolberg, and Lindner a great deal of credit and summarize their procedures. The book is an excellent presentation and is aptly titled, *Hypnotism Comes of Age*.

THE WORK OF GILL, BRENMAN, KNIGHT AND MENNINGER

The war had drawn such attention to the need for shorter and more effective therapy that many prominent members of the American Psychiatric Association, meeting in May 1946, called for a scientific inquiry and study of the possible psychotherapeutic value of hypnosis (Zenkin, 1948). Perhaps it was such attention that prompted Margaret Brenman, Ph.D., Merton Gill, M.D., and Robert P. Knight, M.D. to begin a research project on hypnosis at the Menninger Foundation. It was sponsored by the U. S. Public Health Service and the Austin Riggs Foundation. The entire field of psychotherapy and hypnoanalysis benefited greatly from their research.

Gill regards hypnosis as a state of altered ego functioning in which the defenses are not obliterated, but are altered. He maintains that the integrative function of the ego remains relatively unimpaired, and suggests utilization of transcribed playbacks when amnesia for the hypnotic state occurs in order to aid the integrative function of the ego (Gill, 1951).

Gill and Menninger (1946, Brenman & Gill, 1947) give us insight into their technique of hypnoanalysis as of 1946. A specific case of a 36 year old housewife with a series of somatic complaints and illnesses is given in some detail. One element of the procedure which I did not see specifically listed by either Lindner or Wolberg was the emphasis placed on taking a complete history and diagnostic study prior to treatment recommendations. In the case of this patient there were a series of death-like experiences to her and/or other family members over her life time. She was diagnosed as a psychoneurotic with neurasthenic hysterical and depressive features.

Technique

The patient was seen in 50 minute interviews five times a week for a total of 133 sessions. It is immediately apparent that the core of the therapeutic procedure was psychoanalysis and that hypnosis was a state utilized to facilitate the analysis. It is significant to the ongoing controversy regarding basic hypnotizability of subjects, that this patient was observed to be capable of only a slight depth in hypnosis at first, whereas after a period of time she was capable of a deep state.

In each session she would come in, lie down on the couch, and go into deep hypnosis and begin talking. Although the therapist sat in view of the patient (rather than behind her), her eyes were closed during the interviews.

Dream interpretation and free association were the basic procedures in which hypnosis was used, with the patient actively intervening in the interpretation. The patient always remembered the material of the interviews except one time when amnesia was produced.

The complete analysis fell into four distinct periods. The first period of 60 hours resulted in the disappearance of all the symptoms. She was told that she had made rapid progress, but if she was to have a lasting recovery, more work should be done. She reluctantly agreed to stay and almost at once many of the symptoms returned.

The second period covered hours numbered 61 through 100. The third period hours 101 through 119, and the fourth period covered hours 120 through 133, at the conclusion of which, she was free of all her symptoms except a slight tremor. Follow-up indicated the patient continued to make progress in gaining in self-understanding, and a fuller acceptance of her femininity. Such an acceptance coordinated with an increase in the size of her breasts, a condition which happens with many women as a result of the mind modulating the biochemical functions within the cells of all the major organ systems. [I, personally, have had some female patients who had the Ponce de Leon Syndrome, and during the course of age progression to maturity in hypnoanalysis, had a noticeable increase in breast size. See also, Erickson, (1960/1980); Rossi, (1986); Williams, (1974).]

In another case reported by Gill and Brenman (1943) about this same time, a patient, because of particular circumstances requiring abbreviated treatment, was seen for 67 interviews lasting one to one and one-half hours each, six days a week. In this latter case several innovative and specialized techniques were used. For example, the patient was told that, on the count of a particular number, certain specified thoughts would come to her mind as a single significant word, or a series of letters would appear which would spell a revealing word, or a picture would emerge. She was also told she would have a dream pertaining to her problem, which was almost always successful.

The authors made several observations concerning the process. Regarding the material of the content of hypnoanalysis, they observed that there was nothing unusual. The advantage of using hypnosis was, then, as had been anticipated, that the entire process had been shortened over what it would have been without the use of hypnosis. There were no long periods of resistance and digression as there likely would have been in psychoanalysis alone. Furthermore, the authors felt that in this period (133 sessions) more deep material was brought out by using hypnosis.

Regarding work with dreams it was felt that hypnosis aided in recalling the forgotten elements, clarifying the obscure details, returning to the main theme of the analysis if distracted, and the patient could re-dream a dream in hypnosis if it was advantageous.

Two approaches were employed in age regressions. One was to reproduce the initial appearance of a symptom. Another was to strengthen insight by reproducing a time at which ideas deduced from the material were consciously present in their original form.

The use of specialized techniques, made possible by the use of hypnosis, enabled the therapists to participate more actively in the analysis and to use more direction than usual. Thus the therapists were free to decide which trend they desired to explore further. This freedom to be more directive was destined to become a key factor later in the refinement of hypnoanalysis.

In addition to the above modification of psychoanalysis, a new technique was used for the first time. The patient was told to envision a blackboard in her mind and to write on it but without being able to read it until it was entirely written. The rationale is that automatic writing is a means to let significant material bypass censorship while being produced, but once written it can be presented to consciousness for interpretation.

Another innovation for psychoanalysis is the use of hypnosis for direct suggestion for temporary relief of symptoms while analysis proceeds. Direct suggestion for symptom removal had long been an objection made by analysts against the use of hypnosis. It is now bravely, and wisely, used as an analytic procedure by these pioneers.

In order to move forward more quickly in this case (Gill & Menninger, 1946), the patient, through fantasy, realized a masochistic sexual surrender to her father figure, which was an expression of one of her leading conflicts.

As a result of this case, the researchers made significant progress in advancing theory in hypnoanalysis by answering objections. One objection was that by abbreviating analysis in using hypnosis the patient's problem in all of its current and conscious manifestations would not be sufficiently resolved. This was not the case. Follow-up with the patient revealed that attitudes that had not been worked through in the treatment gradually disappeared.

Another traditional objection was that hypnoanalysis can effect only very incomplete insight because it eliminates defenses instead of enabling them to be analyzed. Neither did this prove to be true in this case. Hypnosis did not eliminate defenses; it can, and sometimes does, weaken them. Defense mechanisms can be analyzed in hypnosis. (It is assumed that it is necessary to analyze defense mechanisms for analysis to be complete.)

Parenthetically, I would like to inject here an observation regarding hypnosis and defenses. We observed that some scholars rely on hypnosis because it shortens therapy time by bypassing the patient's defenses. Others feel that the defenses need to be recognized and analyzed, and that this can be done by using hypnosis. If both sides are right then it means that the therapist, being in control, can use the process with which he feels most comfortable, taking into account the type of patient he has. It would appear that there are two variables here. One, the personality of the patient, as it fits in the therapeutic relationship, will determine the number and strength of the defenses. Two, the personality and method of the therapist will determine what defenses are recognized and how important they are, at any given time, to the ongoing progress of the therapy.

Brenman and Gill answer another objection popular in the literature, namely, if repressed material is forced to consciousness it is not desirable, because the unprepared ego would be unable to tolerate the anxiety thus provoked. The answer to this by these clinicians is that the technique of direct suggestion is a means of counteracting this anxiety (see also Gill and Menninger, 1946). Furthermore, the hypnotic relationship itself is reassuring to the patient. Note that Lindner (1944), in order to brace himself against this objection, used to suggest to the patient, with almost every age regression, that posthypnotic amnesia would take place. This enabled him to bring the repressed material to the surface at the most opportune time.

Another objection to forcing repressed material into consciousness is that even though there is intellectual acceptance, emotional conviction is lacking. Brenman and Gill point out that profound emotional affect accompanied the recovery of repressed material in their cases.

With regard to the question of hypnotizability, the authors distinguish between the underlying basis of hypnotizability in a particular person and the meaning of hypnosis to that person. In hypnoanalysis (presumably because of the frequent and constant use of hypnosis) one can discover the individual view or meaning of hypnosis for that particular patient. We can assume that this observation has a direct bearing on the issue of whether every individual has a fixed potential for being hypnotized or not. Ambrose and Newbold (1958) and others were destined later to build on this in demonstrating that trance ability can be improved.

Brenman and Gill (1947) in their excellent book reviewing the literature on hypnosis at that time, aptly reflect the disorder of the professional world on hypnosis and hypnoanalysis. The latter term had been "loosely employed" for a wide variety of therapeutic techniques. This further indicates that hypnoanalysis, rather than being an organized system of therapy of itself, was still simply another variation of procedure in the psychoanalytic frame of reference. However, the position of these analysts (p.86) was that hypnoanalysis

...holds the greatest promise for a shortened method of psychotherapy which, nevertheless, retains the crucially important factor of 'insight' as a mechanism of cure.

In drawing contrasts between hypnoanalysis and other methods of hypnotherapy, Brenman and Gill stress that in hypnoanalysis the therapist is generally more passive, the technique is uncovering, the time span is longer, and the training background of the therapist must be in the problems of psychodynamics.

THE CONTRIBUTION OF L.M. LECRON
AND JEAN BORDEAUX

LeCron and Bordeaux (1949) in a chapter entitled "A System of Brief Hypnoanalysis" open with what has now become a watchword and stated aim of hypnoanalysis, viz., "to secure complete and permanent results as quickly as possible." The procedure, summarized, came basically from non-orthodox psychoanalysis, plus some points taken from other schools of psychotherapy, plus the supplement of hypnotism.

The authors bring up a certain specificity concerning treatment time

that I have not found in the literature up to this period, (although it could be there), and that is the ability to place certain broad time limitations on different types of cases for treatment. They state that a few cases may terminate in five or six sessions, while mild cases could take ten to thirty or more, and severe cases up to a hundred hours of treatment. Based on work by Alexander and French (1946), they stress that a careful study of the patient's personality and a written case history within the first two sessions should give the therapist a treatment plan and some idea of the rate at which he can proceed.

Although LeCron and Bordeaux, like many predecessors, strive for a deep trance by teaching the patient at the beginning, there are significant innovations for which they should be given credit. They begin by giving strong suggestions of eventual cure to the patient. They also frankly admit that, on occasion, symptoms sometimes flare up and temporarily become worse as a result of undertaking treatment. Thus, from the beginning the therapists strive to break down resistance and establish confidence.

In dealing with the ultimate causes of the symptoms, these analysts review the traditional psychoanalytic view of how repressed conflicts and memories generate energy, and this energy may be discharged as a part of the cure when the actual causes of the neurosis are learned. Although many psychoanalysts consider it unwise for the patient to have much knowledge of psychoanalytic theory, the authors feel that the sooner the patient obtains a correct understanding of his condition the quicker a cure can be effective.

It is clear that LeCron and Bordeaux, as they themselves state, primarily follow a procedure of modified psycho-analysis with the inclusion of hypnotism for brevity, as their form of hypnoanalysis. Their goals of insight, understanding, comprehension of instincts, reeducation and the like are traditional; and the procedures include age regression, dream induction and analysis, automatic writing and drawing, crystal and mirror gazing, and direct inquiry in hypnosis.

In reviewing the book by LeCron and Bordeaux, Zenkin (1948) cites the terrible need for brief methods of therapy for the great number of people in need of help, and for this reason, therefore, professionals cannot neglect the instrument of hypnoanalysis as a brief therapy. But Zenkin criticizes LeCron and Bordeaux, stating their "details are never full enough, never detailed enough for those who want to apply the methods described" (p. 355).

John A. Scott, Sr., Ph.D.

HYPNO-SYNTHESIS: THE METHOD OF J. H. CONN

Conn (1949a, Gindes, 1951) apparently coined the term "hypno-synthesis" and applied it to the use of hypnosis in synthesizing the insights and understandings in a reeducation process after psycho-analysis had taken place. He outlined the basic procedures of grafting hypnosis onto a framework of psycho-analysis utilizing free association without directing the patient and stresses that hypnosis can be used with active patient participation as a "creative, unifying interpersonal experience and therefore can be classified as a form of dynamic psychotherapy" (p. 10).

Although Conn does not here introduce new procedures, he does make significant contributions to theory. For example, he observes that the so called trance depth does not necessarily indicate the degree of involvement of the patient's personality in the hypnotic state. In agreement with Erickson, he states, "one individual in the somnambulistic stage may be essentially little involved in the hypnotic state, whereas another individual in a light state of hypnosis may be deeply involved" (Conn, 1949a, p. 10). He further emphasizes his point:

What becomes of the traditional levels of the 'depth' of hypnosis? They remain as phenomenological, descriptive terms without pertinence for the dynamic problems of personality structure and function with which the modern psychotherapist is most concerned. For the latter purpose, a different conception of 'depth' has been developed, more particularly concerned with motivation.

BERNARD C. GINDES AND NEW CONCEPTS OF HYPNOSIS

It was time for a book entitled, *New Concepts of Hypnosis* (Gindes, 1951). Surprisingly, Lindner was laudatory in the introduction to this book. He states (pp. xi, xii):

the book represents a valiant effort to insure the rehabilitation of hypnosis. One of the few such books likely to succeed. . . it is a sober and balanced survey... unique among many volumes . . . in this third great wave of concern with hypnosis as a therapeutic agent..

Ostensibly, Gindes was endeavoring to prove a point, to persuade colleagues of the value of hypno-analysis and hypno-synthesis.

In one chapter, (pp.208-246), Gindes reviews the principles of psychoanalysis. There doesn't appear to be anything new or different in this list. Gindes' review of these principles sets the stage for his bold

statement that hypno-analysis was a major innovation to psycho-analysis and Freudian techniques. He then proceeds to the issues.

He is specific in the ways hypno-analysis improves the therapy. In drawing a contrast between psycho-analysis and hypno-analysis he states that the usual analytic method must, of necessity, wade through the extraneous material before significant items appear in the free association period. Many patients stall for weeks avoiding a point they do not want to face. Hypnosis enables the patient to face the reality of such difficult thoughts. And it does so by taking the patient back to the original experience that caused the trauma and to the precise emotional reaction of that time, rather than a rationalized emotional reaction tacked onto it by years of living.

Gindes conceives of two stages in the therapy. The first stage, "hypno-analysis" in which hypnosis is used while following the traditional psycho-analytic techniques, such as free association, dream analysis and the like. One procedure we have not seen in the techniques of preceding analysts is the use of a word association test. He makes the point that words produced in hypno-analysis apparently lie closer to the affective life and lead more directly to the unconscious material. This and the other methods enables the patient to make contact with the repressed material.

Stage two, "hypno-synthesis" constitutes the moral, physical, mental, and emotional adjustment to the material presented in Stage One. Direct suggestions are given to the patient during hypnosis, to exert independence, self-reliance, and serenity upon awakening, thus abandoning the transference relationship. In order to promote and maintain recovery, explanations are made to the patient so as to connect the symptoms and the material of the analysis. Thus the word "synthesis," which signifies a combination.

The patient must understand how the various associations and connotations of the illness conform to the experience which was revealed in analysis. Further, the therapist should demonstrate how all fringe symptoms are related to the one, main symptom which is connected with the particular experience. The point is, if the analysis is well done, it won't be necessary for the patient to receive specific suggestions for the amelioration of the symptoms. The symptoms will vanish.

In conclusion it should be said that Gindes calls attention to the work of his outstanding predecessors, Lindner and Wolberg. I get a feeling from Gindes that I did not get from the analysts previously listed, that he has a more "directive" attitude with his patients than they do.

John A. Scott, Sr., Ph.D.

Incidentally, Gindes' book is not devoted exclusively to hypno-analysis. The bulk of it is devoted to other aspects of hypnosis.

THE CONTRIBUTIONS OF JEROME M. SCHNECK

Schneck apparently had a broad interest in hypnosis and had written extensively on the subject. His first publication (known to me) was in 1947, and his first title on hypno-analysis was in 1951.

This author was quite frank and open in his efforts to bridge the gap between the symptom removal school and the analytic school with regard to the therapeutic use of hypnosis. I think we could see this coming in the work of Gindes. Now, two years later, Schneck states the obvious, that the professional thinking and bias of the therapist plays a big part in the method of using hypnosis, but its use is not basically inconsistent with most of the well known psychotherapeutic and psycho-analytic orientations. As an example he cites two well known controversial subjects, viz., resistance and transference.

The approach to these items is dependent on the desires and judgment of the therapist. The hypnoanalyst may undertake the elucidation of resistances and their resolution, and may embark on an analysis of the various aspects of the transference relationships if he so desires. The overall therapeutic approach will be the determining factor in whether the therapist chooses to ignore the nature of transference relationships or circumvent resistances. But this issue is not peculiar to hypnotherapy. Schneck believes that the best results with hypnotherapy will be obtained by those therapists who are most flexible in their overall therapeutic approach and in their use of hypnotic techniques.

There are other variable factors to be considered in the therapeutic approach, such as the nature of the disability, the personality of the patient, the abilities demonstrated by the patient as a hypnotic subject, time available for treatment, environmental pressure on the patient during treatment and during the period of readjustment, and the relationship between patient and therapist. By citing these various factors, and showing flexibility on other issues, Schneck demonstrates a certain open-mindedness concerning the therapy regimen which was not evidenced by most of his predecessors.

Schneck, like his predecessors, deals with the issue of the inter-personal relationship between the patient and therapist on a pre-hypnotic and hypnotic level. And he deals at length with the use of hypnosis in testing procedures.

Of course, he gives much attention to the hypnoanalytic techniques, but without describing any innovative procedures. However, he does expound on the use of a word association test and on creating dual and multiple personalities in hypnoanalysis.

Kline and Schneck (1951) worked with a word association test which had been compiled by Orbison and used by Rapaport. In a controlled experiment, they concluded that such a technique as a word association test would have its greatest value with patients in hypnotherapy and hypnoanalysis.

Schneck describes how dual and multiple personalities may be induced artificially in some patients so that the induced personalities function as representatives of unconscious processes in the patient himself. Such an induced personality may find expression in speech, through automatic writing, or in other apparently ego-alien behavior patterns during hypnosis. Integration of data is clearly essential, however, for ultimate insights and personality change.

Schneck clearly makes a contribution to the ongoing progress of hypnoanalysis as a system. Different approaches are outlined here and in subsequent publications by him. A number of problems are clarified, such as those mentioned in the preceding paragraphs, but others as well. For example, he alludes to forms of apparatus to be used in hypnotic induction, and engages in a discussion with Orne on age regression.

In concluding a chapter on hypnosis in psychiatry, Schneck refers to progress that has been made in the use of hypnosis in psychotherapy, yet "not much more is known today about the basic issues of the hypnotic state itself and hypnotic phenomena than were quite well known to earlier workers..." (1953, 182). Thus the areas for future investigation "...have virtually no bounds" (183). And Schneck, himself, continued to have a part in that future investigation.

OTHER CONTRIBUTIONS

The Annual Survey of Psychoanalysis edited by John Frosch (1951) has several contributors stimulating thought and clinical procedure on the analytical use of hypnosis. For instance, Mazor sees little or no difference in the hypnotically induced dream and the sleep dream, but the former provides more reliable and objective evidence of the nature of the dream work than is possible with analysis alone. Mazor also questions the universality of dream symbols. These concepts were later to be used in hypnoanalysis.

Moss (1967) builds on the work of Erickson and Kubie with a fuller description of hypnosis in dream interpretation.

Ehrenreich, quoted in this same volume (Frosch, 1951), makes another important point regarding hypnotizability, namely, that it is "not a stable trait which is either present or absent, and that hypnosis is experienced in a highly personal fashion by each subject." The author "questions the meaningfulness of general criteria for hypnotizability which are based on an assumption that all subjects in hypnosis will behave in a uniform fashion." (See also Ehrenreich, 1951.)

Hilgard (Frosch, 1951) recognizes the promise that hypnosis holds for the study of psychodynamics, but he states that "its results have to be interpreted with extreme caution."

Attention was called to the effect of hypnosis on the function of the ego by Fisher (1953). The author stresses that the induction process changes the ego function in that consciousness, motility and perception are manipulated, and any time this takes place it involves the fantasy systems and the attendant risk of raising anxiety. This was destined to become a big issue later.

Bellak (1955) represents the kind of research that was going on with hypnosis in the analytic context. This researcher is not writing directly on the subject of hypnoanalysis, but his work makes a contribution in stimulating further study on theory. In stead of looking on hypnosis as a "state of narrowed consciousness" as had been asserted previously, Bellak suggests that it be viewed as a "state of partial self-exclusion of the ego similar to the process of falling to sleep, but not identical with it." He compares it to having an orgasm in which there is an awareness only of the orgastic process.

Ambrose and Newbold (1958) have a chapter on "Hypnoanalysis" which apparently is intended to report on the current conditions. Although nothing really new is presented in the chapter, I refer to them because here is another work, as of this date, which indicates a continuation of the basic psychoanalytic procedure as the framework of hypnoanalysis. The authors agree that a case history is necessary, that direct suggestion may be utilized, and rely on the usual techniques employed with hypnosis for the analysis. One point that is different from the usual list of techniques is that they suggest a technique of taking the patient back to birth by counting backwards from the patient's current age to zero.

Freytag (1959) presents a specific case of a man having anxiety hysteria who was treated by her with hypnoanalysis. The process was essentially as has been presented in the previous descriptions which are basically psychoanalytic in their nature. At the beginning of each day the patient was asked what the main feeling of that day was and then was asked to regress to the time when this same feeling started. Usually, after the session was over, the therapist suggested that the patient would have amnesia for the events recalled in the session. Presumably this was to protect the ego of the patient from suffering the consequences of trauma. In spite of the fact that the patient did not achieve a deep trance, many age regressions brought to light situations of great fear.

In this case, the concept of negative hypnotic suggestion came out, though it was not called by name as such. The patient had lost faith in a doctor because of feeling like a helpless victim, further, a priest had expressed no hope for him, and then to make matters worse, some gypsies said he had been bedevilled or bewitched, and that their incantations were useless.

Both therapist and patient felt that the total time of the analysis (72 sessions in all) was shortened because of the patient's effective use of self hypnosis at home as well as its use in the office sessions. In addition, direction suggestions were used on occasion. The patient, at one time, went for many months without any symptoms, then there were one or two brief periods of anxiety which were recognized at session #45. In all, such a case presentation clarifies the discussion of theory which occupies much of the literature. B. Stokvis (1955) reports on the use of hypnosis and psychoanalysis in the Leyden Psychiatric Clinic. His understanding of "hypno-analysis" is that it is a combination of hypnotic catharsis and re-educative suggestions, as Hadfield had used it (Hadfield, 1940), and he distinguishes between that procedure and one which combines hypnosis with psychoanalysis. The process used in the Leyden clinic is that in certain cases a patient in the waking state is treated by a cathartic-analytic procedure, "while endeavoring to re-enact repressed psycho-traumatic events of the past, in the hypnotic state" (p.253). Later those experiences are discussed with the patient.

This brief, pithy article by Stokvis illustrates how the discussion, even controversy, continues among psychoanalysts on the use of hypnosis and how this becomes entangled with in-house conflicts over what is the process of true psychoanalysis. Stokvis states, "In 'classical' psychoanalysis it is the transference neurosis that should be first of all analyzed; and it is obvious that it would be considerably complicated by the application of hypnosis" (p. 253). He goes on to assert that when the patient goes through hypnosis it alters his personality as well as his view of the analyst, and these alterations have their traces in the conscious mind, which alterations would then have to be analyzed. Since the analyst must maintain neutrality, hypnotic procedure is not consistent with psychoanalysis.

If I understand Stokvis' position, he accepts the occasional use of hypnosis to reenact repressed psycho-traumatic events, but any further use of it, as some contemporary analysts were doing, becomes "short therapy" and should not be called orthodox psychoanalysis.

His analysis of the situation among clinicians using hypnosis appears to be accurate and timely. The use of hypnosis as a cathartic method combined with analytic viewpoints was indeed headed for "short therapy" and was destined in time to be accepted as a separate procedure.

King (1957) makes a point that is worth mentioning with reference to the analytic view of hypnosis. He asserts that hypnosis brings basic changes to the ego or critical faculty. He also observed that there is a decrease in the subject's ability to read and do arithmetic when in a trance. More importantly, he maintains the mechanism for developing schizophrenic symptom formation is analogous to the induction of hypnosis, inasmuch as schizophrenia is a suggestive phenomenon, resulting from unconscious forces within the personality. Their constant action from within finally overwhelms the critical faculty, in the same manner as suggestion by the therapist overwhelms the critical faculty in hypnosis.

This is not the place to discuss such profound issues, but it occurs to me that in an incidental way he anticipates the left brain right brain inquiry, namely, when a subject is in a trance, he is functioning primarily from the right brain, but it is the left brain which functions primarily when a person is doing arithmetic.

Rhodes (1957) is a good example of how further progress was being made in understanding responses of the patient to hypnoanalysis. We should keep in mind that as hypnosis was practiced with persons who were not suffering from serious emotional disturbances, there would not likely be the same responses to hypnosis as there would be to those who suffered an emotional disorder. One would expect that the subject with a fragile ego would need to be dealt with in a different way from one who had a strong ego. Accordingly, Lindner and others induced post-hypnotic amnesia as a protective measure, not knowing, due to a lack of accumulated experience, what might be the consequences otherwise. The work edited by Rhodes makes some contributions to these issues while describing the process of hypnoanalysis. Erickson's contribution to this volume is such an example (pp.164-180).

He cautions that when the patient's unconscious understandings are allowed to become conscious before a conscious readiness exists, they will result in conscious resistance, rejection, repression or even loss of the unconscious gains. In order to prevent this he points out that in hypnotherapy an advantage is to be able to work independently with the unconscious without being hampered by the reluctance of the conscious mind to accept the unconscious material. The therapist, therefore, by working with the unconscious, can "temper and control the patients rate of progress and thus effect the reintegration in the manner acceptable to the conscious mind" (p. 171).

Many others were doing research at this time, but only a few can be mentioned. Bowers and Brecher (1955) observed the emergence of multiple personalities during hypnosis. Klemperer, to be referred to in more detail later, describes changes in body image in hypnoanalysis (1954). Chertok and Kramarz (1959) report that the hypnotic state manifests itself sometimes more on the physiological level and at other times more on the psychological level. Gill and Brenman published the results of their further progress in the use of hypnosis in 1959. This monumental work, truly a milestone, is the result often years of careful research, and anything I say about it here will be woefully inadequate. This book is all inclusive, dealing with induction, the hypnotic state, regression and hypnoanalysis. It is here that they state (p. 356):

The term "hypnotherapy" is misleading and should be abandoned, so do we feel the term "hypnoanalysis" is sufficiently lacking in specificity as to be useless.

These researchers go on to review the views and techniques of the analytic use of hypnosis which they previously had described, and crystalize a kind of negative statement regarding hypnosis. Particularly, they state (p. 357):

that "hypnosis" is not and should not be considered an independent "kind" of psychotherapy nor a procedure which should be "engrafted" to any therapeutic relationship mechanically. Rather it should be regarded as a special sort of interpersonal relationship which may be used in countless ways and with utmost flexibility as a tool in the course of psychotherapy, the precise time and mode of application to depend on the nature of the problem, the current psychodynamic balance and the therapeutic aims being pursued.

Gill and Brenman and their collaborators use penetrating insight in facing the gap between academic psychologists (with learning theory),

hypnosis uses

and psychoanalysts (with psychoanalytic theory), not only in defining "hypnosis" but in its practical application in therapy. They recognize the emergence of ego psychology as a kind of middle ground and accept and elucidate the consequences.

These astute researchers betray careful clinical study which should be read by all practitioners of hypnosis. Among other things they conclude that the use of hypnosis for direct suggestion and for abreaction of traumatic experiences may be effective; that the "use of dreams in hypnosis is probably the most fruitful" of specialized hypnotic techniques; that the adjuvant use of hypnosis to analysis may facilitate the process with some, in other cases it may make no difference, and with some cases it may be a deterrent.

Obviously, key factors are the personality of the patient as well as that of the therapist (plus his theoretical and clinical background), not to mention the nature of the emotional disorder. Thus, there are strengths and hazards in the use of hypnosis in an analytic therapy.

Of course, we must keep in mind that this group of researchers, as fine as they are, are reporting from where they were at the time (1959), and there is enough subjectivity to their psychoanalytical point of view, as well as their point in time, as to bias some of their conclusions. But this does not keep their work from being a milestone in the development of hypnoanalysis.

CONTRIBUTIONS SINCE 1960

Articles in the professional journals indicate the ongoing interest in advancing the analytic use of hypnosis: Conn (1960) reports research on the psychodynamics of recovery under hypnosis. Kline (1960) refers to hypnotic age regression as being "experimental psychotherapy." Baron (1960) writes on levels of insight and ego functioning in relation to hypnoanalysis. Schneck (1960) has an article on "Incest Experience During Hypnoanalysis." Raginsky (1961) brings in a new element with the use of plasticine in hypnoanalysis.

Of course, there are articles and reports in the journals from this period which bear on the subject either directly or indirectly, such as Kubie (1961, on hypnotism and psychoanalytic investigations), Fromm (1965,1970, on age regression), Fromm and Shor (1979), O'Connell, Shor, and Orne (1970) etc. These reports, and others like them, represent the ongoing interest and research in hypnosis and analysis, each contributing something to the field, though not always referring to "hypnoanalysis" as such.

Kline (1963) stresses the significance of regression in hypnosis:
in this rather primitive, or prelogical interaction, the patient makes available
aspects of his own self concept and body image which may now be influenced
and directed through the regressive experience, and while symbolic of earlier
developmental experiences, has within it the uniqueness of the therapeutic
relationship which previously was lacking.

The regression is thus an "intense dynamic experience" (rather than a mere technique in therapy) "within which the patient's world of reality may, for the first time since his own childhood, be touched and influenced in a constructive manner." Kline's view, while not revolutionary, represents enough of a variation to be significant and was destined to play a part in the theoretical concepts of what hypnosis is, and what transference is, in hypnosis (cf.Brown & Fromm, 1986).

Lifshitz and Blair (1960) make a contribution on the handling of abreaction. They point out that both physical and emotional alterations take place in the patient during an abreaction, and in order to effect a change in the patient, a particular abreaction may have to be repeated, and even when a change does take place, it may not last. Their report indicates that with succeeding repetitions of the abreaction there is a gradual decrease of respiration, GSR, heart rate, frontalis muscle activity, etc. Thus the body reflects what is taking place in the emotions with the abreactional release.

Cheek, (a diplomate with the American Board of Obstetrics and Gynecology), and LeCron, (a certified psychologist), reflect their non-psychoanalytical background in a critique of Freudian analysis. They point out that psychoanalysts treat only five patients a year, and by contrast, hypnotherapy, with their uncovering techniques, will require at most 15 to 20 sessions. They play down dream analysis and free association, but do recommend giving a specific dream suggestion to save time, and free association with hypnosis. They recommend, as uncovering techniques, automatic writing, use of ideomotor movements for answers to questions, and certain projective techniques. Even though they do not refer to "hypnoanalysis" as such, they are utilizing the principles of dynamic psychology with the use of hypnosis.

John A. Scott, Sr., Ph.D.

THE LATER WORK OF LEWIS R. WOLBERG

In 1964, Lewis Wolberg issued a revision of his earlier work entitled *Hypnoanalysis*. He is a prolific writer of great clarity and lucidity, who, in my opinion, is unequaled by others in this field. Furthermore, his broad experience in psychotherapy, and his seemingly unprejudiced manner with regard to any one therapeutic modality, make him an unusual teacher. Of course, he makes it clear that his therapy of choice is psychoanalysis, but this does not prejudice him against other forms, which he acknowledges and describes.

In the work alluded to (1964), he takes the time and space (424 pages) to clarify the subject. Although basically hypnoanalysis is nothing more than "psychoanalysis performed in a controlled setting" (p.251), he gives sufficient detail as to the nuances of differences as to be most helpful. Wolberg carefully describes the requirements for the therapist, conditions for accepting a patient for hypnoanalysis, the types of patients most responsive to therapy, methods of hypnotic induction, and description of hypnoanalytic procedures.

From my observation, I find nothing new about the available procedures in his or others' earlier works; the frequency and methodology utilizing dreams, free association, automatic writing, play therapy, dramatics, regression and revivification, crystal and mirror gazing, and the induction of experimental conflict are all a part of the armamentarium which he effectively describes. To illustrate the method, he includes a complete treatment record of a patient, with accompanying comments by another analyst who further clarifies what has been done.

Although there is no major addition with regard to theory or practice, the book is invaluable because of the clarity of detail. It represents the state of the art as of that date.

KLEMPERER AND THE EMERGENCES OF PAST EGO STATES

Edith Klemperer published an outstanding contribution to the field of hypnoanalysis in 1968. Of course, many theoreticians and clinicians with a wide variety of viewpoints had gone before and laid a groundwork, and she builds on this with her own research. The foundation stones for Klemperer's work are Erickson (1966), Gill and Brenman (1959), Gordon (1967), Kline (1963), Schneck (1965), and Wolberg (1948, 1964).

She makes a point which, I think, bears on the overall view of Gill and

Brenman (1959) and that is, hypnoanalysis does appear to be a different modality and that "the formulations from psychoanalysis…may not be universally applicable to hypnoanalysis." Whereas Gill and Brenman's basic thesis is that hypnosis is more of a handmaid to other therapies, and there is no place for a complete system known as "hypnoanalysis," Klemperer takes the position that there is conceivably a place for a separate system of hypnoanalysis, but that the time has not yet come for a basic theory and actual unification.

Earlier, Klemperer (1961) had promoted a fundamental difference in hypnoanalysis and psychoanalysis. Hypnoanalysis stresses visual associations whereas psychoanalysis is based on verbal associations. She asserts that:

Hypnoanalysis, pressing from image to image, takes him (the patient) constantly closer to the primary, archaic picture in which resides the probity of his problem. In psychoanalysis the therapy rolls from verbalization to verbalization rarely raising images. The difference between the visualizations of hypnoanalysis and the verbal associations that the patient offers the psychoanalyst may be compared to a direct line of communication which the former represents and a switchboard of connections for the latter (p. 64).

A fundamental assumption of her work (1968) is that hypnosis is a regressing modality and (p.5):

the archaic language of the unconscious is the image, the picture, which is plastic, flexible, changeable, two-or three-dimensional, and either sequential like a moving picture, or solitary like a photograph, or coexistent in space with other images like a kaleidoscope. By verbalizing his visualizations, the patient connects them to reality, to time and to place in the present, and in this way translates the primary process into the secondary one.

By contrast,

in psychoanalysis, interpretations of verbal and behavioral communications are made by the therapist according to his understanding of their hidden meanings and his evaluation of the patient's readiness to accept them.

Klemperer (1968, p. 1) cites E. Weiss (who is dependent on Federn):

It can be experimentally proven that ego states of earlier ages do not disappear but are only repressed. In hypnosis, a former ego state containing the corresponding emotional dispositions, memories, and urges can be reawakened in the individual. In Federn's opinion, the unconscious portion of the ego consists of the stratification of the repressed ego states.

The comparison is made to a tree trunk

where one ring forms around another, thereby repressing it. In analogous terms, psychologically one layer of ego state forms around another, repressing the earlier ego state into the unconsciousness.

As I understand the description, many different ego states may be represented in one symptom, which states are the series of visual images layered in the unconscious. Hypnoanalysis reviews these images, provoking abreaction, and then makes the connection with the consciousness so that a cause and effect relationship becomes understood.

Klemperer presents eight cases of various disorders to illustrate in detail the process of treatment. Essentially it follows the same psychoanalytic structure as we have seen in most of the preceding examples by psychoanalysts. The sessions are numerous (100 or more) and hypnosis is used as occasion demands. When it is used it is called "hypnoanalysis" and was recorded so as to be played back to the patient at the following session. When this was done, patient and doctor discussed the transactions; then interpretations were made as is usual in psychoanalysis.

Harold Stewart, in reviewing Klemperer's book (1970), rightly observes that in her system there is "no, or extremely limited, analysis of the transference relationship." And treatment is shorter than with psychoanalysis and more akin to analytic psychotherapy. The therapeutic results are reasonable, improvements are maintained, indicating dynamic changes.

THE CURRENT WORK OF DANIEL P. BROWN AND ERIKA FROMM

The most recent, and probably most thorough, contribution to the field in this vein of thought, is *Hypnotherapy and Hypnoanalysis*, (1986) by Brown and Fromm. Essentially this book is the continuation and updating of hypnotherapy as utilized by psychoanalysts. The book is excellent and, obviously, has the advantage of all who have gone before. Consequently, as one would expect, it covers the subject very well. Part I on "The Basics of Hypnosis" presents fundamental material subdivided as many authors have done before. However, modern research is taken into account and thus revisions of the subject matter are appropriately made. And herein is its great value.

Part II deals with "Clinical Hypnosis" with chapters on treatment planning, techniques, and finally two chapters on hypnoanalysis. Like Part I, this section is well organized, thorough, and up-to-date. Our concern is primarily with the chapters on hypnoanalysis.

In the chapter (7) on "Theory and Practice" a brief summary of modern psychoanalytic theory calls attention to the Libido Theory, Ego Psychology, Object Relations Theory, and Theory of the Self as important modern aspects that contribute to the total theory. Of course allusions are made to traditional Freudian aspects of psychoanalysis such as the part that primary and secondary process and the modes of ego functioning play in hypnoanalysis.

We have observed earlier in this chapter how that when the psychoanalyst imposes hypnotherapy on psychoanalysis (and calls it "hypnoanalysis"), the usual structure of free association, dream interpretation, dealing with resistances and transference continue to be the foundation of the therapeutic procedure. True, Brown and Fromm are scholarly in their treatment of these subjects. For example, many aspects of transference (and counter transference) are discussed, albeit in an abbreviated way, in a manner that is consistent and helpful for use with hypnosis.

In the chapter on therapeutic applications the authors' skills in hypnotherapy are made even more evident as the process of this form of hypnoanalysis is exemplified in the treatment of a series of neurotic and severely disturbed patients. Such issues as when to use hypnosis, and how to use a variety of hypnotic techniques, are clarified. I am impressed with the careful evaluation of the use of hypnosis with the psychotic patient. Concepts such as the hypnotizability and underlying dynamics of the severely disturbed patient are taken into consideration.

THE WORK OF WILLIAM J. BRYAN, JR.

In May, 1955, William J. Bryan, Jr., M.D., whose background was medicine and psychiatry rather than psychoanalysis and psychology, and several medical colleagues started the American Institute of Hypnosis in Los Angeles for the purpose of teaching "Medical Hypnotism" to physicians, dentists, psychologists, and nurses (Bryan, 1960). S. J. Van Pelt, Editor of the *British Journal of Medical Hypnotism*, as Bryan's mentor, was apparently a strong influence and probably was the source of the use of the name "Medical Hypnotism."

The institute started publishing a journal in 1960, (*Journal of the American Institute of Hypnosis*), and sponsored courses on hypnosis in the United States and abroad. Book lists in the early issues of the journal indicate a familiarity with most of the works listed on these preceding pages (*Journal*, July, October, 1961). Thus one may assume the work that Bryan and his colleagues were doing drew, at least in part, from predecessors in the field. Articles in their journal indicate that hypnosis was practiced and taught from the standpoint of an analytical psychotherapy. (Boswell, 1961; Bryan, 1961a, 1961b; Millikin, 1961; Paramour, 1961.) But as the successive volumes of this journal, and the course synopses, are examined, it becomes apparent that by 1970 an independent system of hypnoanalysis had evolved which was not implanted on a framework of psychoanalysis.

Strangely enough, according to Dr. Louis Boswell, dentists, like Drs. Garland Fross, Tom Wall, and Joshua Sloan, were a strong influence in promoting the analytical use of hypnosis. While physicians in medical treatment and surgery had assistants in case of emergency, most of the time dentists performed surgery in the office without access to as much assistance. The risks both to the patient and the dentist were great. Thus the dentists were influential in encouraging a system of brief hypnotic analysis of the patient with an emotional problem which could complicate dental treatment, especially dental surgery.

In an effort to keep the therapy brief it became a directed therapy rather than using free association. The procedure starts with taking a detailed case history after which a plan for therapy is outlined. It is expected that the therapist, after taking such a history, knows the diagnosis, the etiology, and has an approximate picture of the course of therapy, working toward a cure. Thus it is a medical model. In order to confirm the diagnosis and therapy plan, a word association test is given and a dream analyzed, both in hypnosis.

Therapy proceeds with each session utilizing hypnosis in a series of age regressions to the time and events which caused, or contributed to the cause, of the symptoms. The aim is not to psychoanalyze the patient's personality completely, rather it is to determine the cause of the presenting symptoms and thereby to eliminate them. Once this is done the analytical phase is over and a casette tape is made summarizing the analysis.

The next phase is reinforcement and readjustment, with reeducation having been a part of the therapy all along. The summary tape is listened to frequently, along with tapes pertaining to the patient's particular needs for ego strengthening. In this phase of therapy, principles of direct suggestion and/or behavior modification are utilized.

There are several interesting innovations brought in by Bryan's method. First, after the initial hypnotic session, the system utilizes tapes for inducing the hypnosis and for the education process. This saves the therapist's time and in addition produces the means for more effective education of the patient with well prepared scripts for tapes.

Second, the patient is placed in a treatment room after due preparation and orientation, with a sleep shade (mask) over his or her eyes, earphones over the ears, and left alone to be hypnotized by listening on the headphones. Music or desired sound effects may be utilized by this method. The room is equipped with a reclining, vibrating chair or couch and with a closed circuit television camera. The therapist has a console room with microphone and speaker in order to talk and listen to the patient, as well as a TV monitor to watch the patient while in therapy. Thus, the chance for the traditional transference relationship to develop is minimized. Note, both the key elements which add greatly to the length of traditional psychoanalysis, viz., free association and analysis of the transference, are eliminated from this procedure. The patient, as it were, is left alone with himself, yet not deserted. Such a procedure also eliminates too much dependency on the therapist. Yet personal contact at the beginning and end of the session is made.

The theory, although basically psychodynamic in nature, has also some notable revisions and innovations. For example, the nomenclature of the diagnoses is nontraditional. A description of the etiology (also after the medical model) is analogous to the development of an allergy with an Initial Sensitizing Event, a Symptom Producing Event, and usually one or more Symptom Intensifying Events (developed by Boswell, 1961).

The basic theory of the symptomatic expression of the disorder is that the patient unconsciously chooses the symptoms as a defense mechanism to protect himself from what he views as worse consequences without the symptom(s). This is based on a basic order of priority of various levels of survival and activity to the patient. Such a view enables the therapist to make a diagnosis in shorter time after first meeting the patient.

This method of hypnoanalysis may best be described as primarily a psychoanalytically oriented, short term therapy, directed, as in a medical model, utilizing hypnosis. In summary, an effort is made to eliminate the disadvantages of hypnosis using direct suggestion, while the basic advantages of hypnosis are retained. This holds true also regarding psychoanalysis viz., an effort is made to eliminate the disadvantages while the advantages are kept. It isn't surprising that the details are open to controversy. During the course of the therapy any of the traditional methods of assisting the patient to get in touch with the unconscious may be utilized. Furthermore, after the analytical phase is completed, positive suggestions, utilizing principles of behavior modification, are used to help remove the habit pattern which usually is so much a part of the system of symptoms.

CONCLUSION

In more recent years I have not observed any other changes in the trends set in the last 40 years. To be sure, we have more knowledge, and the results of ongoing research enable us to understand more of the use of hypnosis in a dynamic context, but the thrust of those practicing hypnoanalysis appears to be essentially in the two main streams as presented.

Allusions to treatment methods or procedures which indicate a dynamic use of hypnosis, of course, continue. For example Chertok (1982) describes Soviet approaches to the unconscious and hypnotic phenomena and follows this with some challenging ideas into some "still uncharted territories" involving hypnosis and the unconscious. He asserts that both the fields of hypnosis and unconscious are equally obscure but they are indeed closely linked. The thrust of this article is a positive and constructive point of view in behalf of hypnoanalysis.

Another example of recent contributions to the principle of hypnoanalysis in segments is found in the same issue of IJCEH as Chertok's article referred to above. Raikov (1982), a Russian, gives an interesting report on a study "designed to explore possible differences between actual hypnotic age regression and several role enactment controls," using neonatal reflexes.

Ericksonian psychotherapy represents an offshoot of its own. Milton H. Erickson's techniques at times were analytic and at times a kind of modified direct suggestion. The genius of this man was that he had such keen insight into his patients that he could draw from a vast reservoir of experience, skills and insights in order to apply just the right method to a given patient at just the right time. His students are many and they have contributed to the field of hypnotherapy voluminously and effectively. But it may be that one cannot learn "Ericksonian technique" completely because so much of what he did was integral to his own personality and individuality. At any rate, Ericksonian psychotherapy represents a branch of hypnotherapy different enough from hypnoanalysis as to be worthy of its own independent study. Obviously, techniques and procedures from this branch of hypnotherapy are effectively utilized in both hypnoanalysis and other modalities of psychotherapy.

Justification for a psychoanalytically oriented short term therapy, if such is needed, comes from the current popular interest in short term therapies. Wolberg (1980), in his usual forthright manner, states a case for the effectiveness of short-term psychotherapy with a psychodynamic orientation.

Both Wolberg (1980) and Flegenheimer (1982) give credit to their predecessors who advocated dynamic short-term psychotherapy: Alexander and French (1946), Davanloo (1980), Malan (1976), Mann (1973) and Sifneos (1978). One would need to check these references to evaluate the variety of systems recommended. But it is enough to say that sufficient changes have come about in our society, the types of patients and symptoms, and therapeutic procedures, to admit that the day of short term therapy has come. And, as has been true before, the effective use of hypnosis can make the therapy shorter. This is not to say that there is no longer a place for psychoanalysis or prolonged psychotherapy of an analytic orientation. There is, because there are still patients who cannot be cured by any other process.

In this chapter, I have summarized the history of hypnoanalysis from the sources available to me. I do not doubt that there have been oversights of those who have contributed much valuable information, and I regret this, but I believe the main ideas have been presented. As nearly as I can tell, as we are now in the nineties, there are two main streams of hypnoanalysis flowing parallel to each other. One is made up primarily of those who practice the essence of psychoanalysis, with hypnosis used as an adjunct at particular times during the therapy to accomplish an immediate goal. The other is the independent method of Bryan utilizing and combining many principles from the fields of hypnotherapy and dynamic psychology into an organized system, independent from others. Perhaps we have in this latter system the germinal existence of what Klemperer predicted, namely, that the day would come when hypnoanalysis would grow from an adjunctive role to a special and autonomous form of treatment.

"Hypno-analysis" was undoubtedly hyphenated at first due to the influence of the hyphenation of "psycho-analysis" in the early period. The hyphen began to be phased out in the latter term in articles appearing in *The International Journal of Psycho-Analysis* in 1950 at which time this journal was merged with the Bulletin of the International Psycho-analytical Association.

CHAPTER 2

THEORETICAL AND PHILOSOPHICAL BASIS

HYPNOSIS AS A TOOL

Since this book is not intended to be an elementary work on hypnosis, it is not within my province to examine or evaluate the many definitions of hypnosis and the issue of who can and who cannot be hypnotized. Nor is it within my scope to describe the many possible procedures for inducing hypnosis. There are many such books and articles available to serve as a starting point where that is the purpose of the reader. However, I will take a few pages to summarize, without detailed discussion, my own working view of the hypnotic trance since it is pertinent to much material I will cover.

The Left--Right Brain Issue

Modern research methods, rather than bringing us any closer to a solution to that age old question of "nature versus nurture," simply add more issues to the complexities of the enigma. In looking for solutions to psychological problems, how far can the psychotherapist go into an examination of biological origins? The quandary I refer to at this time is the issue of "right brain - left brain." There are those who swear by the brain lateralization theory (e.g., Gazzaniga, 1970; Jaynes, 1976;

Segalowitz, 1983), but others who would consider it a fad (Goleman, 1977). Segalowitz, in his recent work (1983), appears to be careful in his assertions and constantly reminds the reader that more questions have been raised by lateralization research than have been answered. Nonetheless, trends in that research coincide with some discoveries in hypnosis. One such issue pertains to defining hypnosis, and another probes an explanation as to why some people appear to be more hypnotizable than others. Information on brain activity is still too limited for a firm decision, but the hypotheses are intriguing.

Psychotherapists for years have been confronted by patients who consciously verbalize one desire and at the unconscious level feel something entirely different. This is the principle of the split-brain. There are other commonplace examples of this principle. This phenomenon is well illustrated in Hilgard's (1977) well known concept of the "hidden observer." Those psychotherapists who utilize hypnosis are well aware of the ability of the patient to suppress certain information or experiences as a result of hypnotic suggestion. Such dissociation has been a subject of investigation for some time. The concept of the split brain serves to explain much such phenomena.

The theory is that the left hemisphere of the brain, for the majority of people, is in charge of our waking activity most of the time, and processes information linearly. That is to say, this side is superior on linguistic and mathematical tasks, evidencing a propensity for problem solving and the like. The right brain is viewed as more adept at dealing with the abstract, emotional qualities such as intonation of music, dealing with art forms, visualization, fantasy, and is more proficient at identifying emotional stimuli such as interpreting facial expressions and tone of voice.

Naturally, with such theories erupting from studies of brain injuries as well as laboratory experiments, it was not to be long before such information would be applied to emotional disorders. Segalowitz (1983, p.215) states that:

It has now been reported quite often that depressed patients who have no brain damage, when given a battery of neurological tests, come out with a profile similar to that of patients with right-sided damage. The performance of the patients returns to normal as the depression lifts.

He goes on to point out that several types of research support a theory which links left-sided abnormalities to schizophrenia, because of its classification as a non-emotional thought disorder with related speech disturbance. This gives further credence to the hypothesis that it is the right side which is most closely linked with the emotions. Of course, the data are not all clear as yet.

Another interesting point which could be of interest to the hypnotherapist is Galin's (1974) assertion that the right hemisphere is the repository of the unconscious, whereas conscious thought emanates from the left hemisphere. The theory is that when thought originating in the unconscious mind (right side) makes contact with the left hemisphere it can be verbalized as conscious thought. Frustration (even hysterical paralysis) can take place when needs felt on the right side, because of some malfunction, cannot be expressed through the left side (Galin, Diamond & Branff, 1977; Ley,1980; Segalowitz, 1983).

Another note of interest is the speculation that when a person is dreaming, the right hemisphere is the more active of the two because of the visual images and emotional ideas that predominate. Indeed, Galin (1974), followed by Bakan (1978) and Segalowitz (1983), postulates that Freud's concept of the primary process should be localized in the right side because such thought processes have free reign during most dreaming.

Regarding hypnotic suseptibility, those traits which are viewed as correlating with hypnotizability such as the ability to concentrate, to be absorbed emotionally in a movie or novel, and other similar traits (Bowers, 1974; Hilgard, 1979) are traits which are most closely associated with the right hemisphere (Segalowitz, 1983). A related point is that during relaxation (hypnosis) there is a change in cerebral laterality with the right side becoming more dominant (Frumkin, Ripley & Cox, 1978). Thus the concept that the two hemispheres function for different purposes leads to the observation that, depending on the mental process at the time, the hemisphere appropriate to that type of activity is the one which is dominating. If this be true, then only one step is required to deduce that one hemisphere or the other can be activated by a person in accordance with the desired mental process. Or, by the same token, one can shift gears from one side to the other as desired.

I have taken the time to extrapolate the forgoing assertions because I wish to make some hypotheses concerning what hypnosis is and why it functions as it does clinically.

John A. Scott, Sr., Ph.D.

A Working Definition

There are many definitions and much more speculation as to how to define the "hypnotic state." I presume the reader has wandered through the maze of speculation on this subject - enough to want to avoid further summaries on it - and I will not repeat them here. But, based on the research on brain lateralization, I subscribe to the concept that when a person is hypnotized the right brain is dominant, enabling the therapist to be in communication with the patient's unconscious mind to a greater or lesser degree (Barnett, 1981). There are several reasons for this conclusion.

1. Greater hypnotizability has been associated with left-ward eye movements, and such movements indicate greater activity in the right hemisphere. Thus the highly hypnotizable subject is one who readily activates the right hemisphere, or one whose right hemisphere is the more dominant.

2. If it is true that the right brain is the repository of memory and that the hypnotized person has better access to materials stored in the memory (unconscious mind), then the hypnotized person is thinking predominantly with the right side.

3. If it is true that the right hemisphere is more proficient at identifying emotional stimuli, then we may presume that the hypnotized person, reliving certain trauma and producing appropriate affect, has the right hemisphere dominating at that time.

4. It is known that in dreaming the right side is prevailing. We know from experience that when a patient brings a dream for interpretation in therapy, that, when hypnotized, that patient can, on occasion, recall parts that were not written down upon awakening. Furthermore, the hypnotized patient can frequently assist in the interpretation where he or she could not in the waking state. Thus it is apparent that there is an association between hypnosis, dreaming, and the right brain.

5. When a person is relaxed, the right brain becomes more dominant. If the literature and verbal reports are accurate, we can conclude that most hypnotherapists induce hypnosis by relaxation procedures. Thus the hypnotized person is most likely stimulating the right side of the brain.

6. Imagination is a right brain activity and is well known to be directly related to hypnotizability.

Barnett (1981) has a lucid discussion with appropriate citations on the subject of whether there is a clearly definable state which can be recognized as the "hypnotic state." He concludes that there is no typical state. The many discussions by specialists on this subject support this contention. I agree. This is not to say that research done to ascertain a hypnotic induction profile is not beneficial to knowledge about the trance state. It is very helpful. However, from a pragmatic standpoint it is more valuable to the theoretician and teacher than it is to the clinician working with a patient. Barnett (1981, p.21), who does not subscribe to a check list of requirements to determine whether a person is hypnotized, succinctly ties a lot of loose ends together when he states:

However, if our definition of hypnosis is restricted to a specific set of responses to suggestion, we run the risk of assuming that a given subject is not hypnotizable if the set of responses does not occur when requested.

We shall return to Barnett presently, but first another concept should be taken into account.

Edmonston's work on *Hypnosis and Relaxation* (1981) has not received the recognition that I think it deserves. This researcher examines the physiological conditions inherent in hypnosis. A wide variety of physiological measurements and experimental studies are described and evaluated. He concludes confidently that relaxation is the foundation of the hypnotic state and predates all other theoretical explanations. Once the patient is relaxed, then the theoretical explanations - whether hypersuggestibility, circumventing of the ego mechanisms, regression in the service of the ego, emerging of primary process thinking etc. - all are free to be applied upon the matrix of the relaxed state. As far as I'm concerned, Edmonston proves his case. . . as far as he goes. But I feel he does not do justice to the concept of the so-called alert trance in his brief chapter on the subject.

The Alert Trance

There are those who feel that an "alert" trance is a contradiction to the hypnotic state (e.g. Edmonston, 1981) because some muscles or the entire body may not be relaxed.

The problem here is that, like many studies, experimental situations, laboratory conditions, and test groups may be different from clinical and reality situations and thus produce misleading expectations or conclusions regarding hypnosis. It was the physicist, Werner Heisenberg stating his "Uncertainty Principle," who said one can never perform the same experiment twice.

Clinical situations wherein there is an active trance would be exemplified by the patient who is reliving, in an age regression, a traumatic situation in which there is crying, shouting, cursing, perhaps accompanied by moving the hands to the head, twisting, or other signs of muscular activity - even tension. Yet, clearly, the patient is in a trance.

The Spontaneous Trance

Reality situations may be exemplified by what is sometimes called waking hypnosis. Such situations happen frequently with children wherein a particularly captivating or traumatic event takes place and makes a lasting impression on the memory system. For example, a child's face is pressed in feces by the parent and then made to look in the mirror (to teach bowel control), or a child witnesses a bloody physical fight by its parents, or is abused sexually, or other less dramatic experiences. On the other hand, positively, a child's first sexual curiosity, or a loving relationship with a grandparent, or playing with a pet, captivate the attention and leave a lasting impression on the mind. The child is entranced by the drama or shock of the experience, though certainly not relaxed. Such events are justifiably labeled as spontaneous hypnosis.

Other types of reality situations, alluded to by Hilgard (1977), are exemplified by certain emotional religious gatherings, tribal ceremonies, whirling dervishes, and the like. Such altered states of consciousness are generally labeled "waking" or "spontaneous" hypnosis.

If I understand Edmonston's position correctly, he would state that the reality and clinical situations described above would be different from "traditional" hypnosis (Edmonston, 1981, p.208). In other words, according to this researcher, relaxation is hypnosis and any state wherein the patient is not relaxed is not to be labeled accurately as "traditional hypnosis." This may well be. There is also the problem with semantics, and Edmonston may be right in claiming that such events as described above should not be recognized as traditional hypnosis. If this is true, then we lack an appropriate term to describe these other altered states of consciousness. (Many authorities in the field have bemoaned the use of "hypnosis" [Greek: "sleep"] anyway.) However, I do not subscribe to that narrow a view.

Concentration of the Mind

There is yet another element in defining hypnosis. And that is Van Pelt's phrase, "concentration of the mind" which he used in describing hypnosis at the Fourth Annual European Psychiatric Conference in Barcelona, Spain, in 1958 (Bryan, 1971a). Van Pelt presented a theory on how suggestion influences the mind and made application to the misunderstandings and misinterpretations people make during the course of life which influence later feelings and behavior.

Figure 1 illustrates this principle as presented by Bryan (1971a). The large circle represents the mind and the small circles within represent the units of mind power which register incoming data or suggestions from the five primary senses. A suggestion or impression streams through the mind, engaging a number of units of mind power. The degree of concentration or absorption increases the number of units receiving that impression. And the impression is what influences thinking and behavior. However, at the same time a primary subject is engaging the concentration, distractions from the environment are diluting that primary thought. This activity has been examined in Cognitive Psychology as questions of perception and examination of what the eye sees and what the brain records etc. These subliminal thoughts, although registering subconsciously, keep the mind from total concentration on the subject at hand. They are distractions. Unconscious perception or subliminal influences indirectly have a great deal to do with swaying decisions and controlling behavior (Dixon, 1971; Key, 1973).

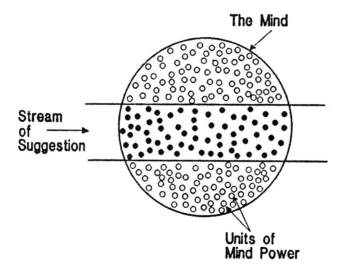

The Mind

Stream of Suggestion →

Units of Mind Power

Figure 1
THE WAKING STATE
**Diagram of the waking state, showing the mind, which is
represented by the large circle, and units of mind power,
which are represented by the smaller circles withing the
larger circle. Here shown, the power of the mind is not
concentrated, but scattered, therefore only a few units of
mind power are affected. Hence, effect of suggestion is
weak.**

For example, a wife can be telling her husband to pick up some items at the grocery. And, while the husband is listening and making a mental list, movement elsewhere in the room plus some degree of physical discomfort can, subliminally, dilute the concentration. In fact subliminal influences are a strong factor in our thinking, a principle well known to advertising agencies (Key, 1973, 1976). When husband goes to the grocery something may be forgotten from the list as he wonders whether or not his small child was able to get a shoe on. The point here is, that in most circumstances, the mind, being capable of many thoughts at once, can register many ideas simultaneously. It is rare that the attention is completely captivated.

The principle of concentration is illustrated in Figure 2. Here a suggestion or experience is so captivating that all of the units of mind power are focused on that one thought. There is little, if any, distraction. Such an experience makes a deep impression. The more the mind is focused on a particular thought, the deeper the impression of that thought and the more likely that thought is to influence further thinking and behavior. The depth of the impression depends on the strength of the impact of the experience or suggestion. This may be said to be the hypnotic state.

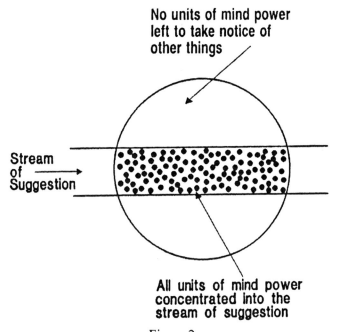

**No units of mind power
left to take notice of
other things**

**Stream
of
Suggestion**

**All units of mind power
concentrated into the
stream of suggestion**

Figure 2
THE HYPNOTIC OR CONCENTRATED STATE
When the mind is sufficiently concentrated, all the units of mind power are within the stream of suggestion. Later, in the waking state when all the units of mind power are again dispersed, each will carry a dose of the suggestion, forming within the individual a compulsion to act in a particular fashion.

A traumatic experience is such a condition. The experience, the side effects, and the interpretation of these effects, may remain in both the conscious and unconscious mind or may be repressed and remain only unconsciously. The trauma may be pleasant and constructive, or unpleasant and destructive, to the psyche. Furthermore, it may be an actual event or it may be a movie, a dream, hallucination, an imagination or be the construction of a planned hypnotic experience. The after-effects may be the same in any case. Such a forceful experience may be called hypnotic because the behavior is a consequence of the experience (or "suggestion").

Another analogy to illustrate the principle of concentration is the working of Ohm's Law, the formula of which is "I" equals "E" over "R". It simply means that the amount of current ("I") which passes through a given channel or wire ("R", resistance) depends directly on the amount of power ("E", voltage) behind that current (Bryan, 1971a). The same principle is seen in the amount of water flowing through a pipe; the amount depends on the force behind that flow and the size of the pipe.

It is obvious to all students of human behavior that in assessing the seriousness of an emotional disorder there are three primary variables, viz. 1) the force of the trauma including the intensity of emotion (or series of conditioners), 2) the resistance of the individual (ego strength with or without supporters), 3) resulting impact on the psyche (serious or non-serious). This principle may be translated into human behavior by the formula of Ohm's Law thus: The consequences of a given experience equal the power of that experience divided by the resistance of the psyche.

Consequences = Power of experience
Resistance

Other formulations of the equation are these:

Resistance = Power of experience
Consequences

Power of experience = Consequences X Resistance

Consider this example. It is well known that one of the most severe traumas the human can suffer is the loss of the mother in infancy (Bowen, 1978; Kaplan, 1978; Mahler, Pine & Bergman, 1975). Let "power of trauma = 100," minimal "resistance" of the newborn = 1. Work the equation.

Consequences (X) = 100
1
Answer: Consequences equal 100.

If we look for an emotional disorder as "consequence" equal to 100%, how about post traumatic stress disorder or childhood sexual abuse?

This mathematical equation of Ohm's Law illustrates elements which combine to form the basis for a diagnosis. I am illustrating the way in which the waking state (mind not fully concentrated) is to be contrasted to the hypnotic state wherein the mind is fully concentrated. The point is this: The degree of the concentration of the mind determines the consequences in human thought and behavior. Truly casual incidents have little consequences. But incidents that have an impact, provoke appropriate consequences. However, a series of casual incidents repeated over and over can build up and by their accumulation or familiarity provoke appropriate consequential behavior.

For example, Pavlov's principle of the "conditioned reflex" applies here. A dog is offered food simultaneously with the ringing of a bell say, forty times. Consequently, the ringing of the bell will provoke salivation by the dog. Theoretically, if the circumstances were such that the dog could be offered the food one time with 40 times greater intensity, the after-effects would be the same. The first case would be a "conditioning" training. The second would be "hypnotic" training.

This area of research on "intensity" is called motivation. It refers to the physiology of "intensity" wherein the "need state of the organism" is taken into consideration.

In summary, the behavior of an individual, whether good or bad, depends on the units of mind power, i.e. the pressure or voltage behind that behavior pushing it into certain channels (Bryan, 1971 a). This can be achieved in one or both of the following two ways:

1. The suggestion or impetus is repeated so frequently that the "pressure" to behave in a certain way provokes that behavior.
2. Concentrate the units of mind power into the stream of suggestion in such a manner as to build sufficient pressure at one time to evoke a resultant behavior.

Number 2 above would be the hypnotic state wherein the mind is so concentrated that all or most all of the units of mind power carry a dose of the hypnotic suggestion. If the trance is deep enough and the suggestion is compatible with the person's mindset, then the compulsion to behave in accordance with the suggestion remains an influential force. The person may have been accidentally or spontaneously hypnotized, or may have been almost instantly hypnotized by Ericksonian technique, or hypnotized by a traditional ritual. Any of these methods would result in the concentration of the mind. The person may or may not be relaxed. But, the mind is concentrated.

This concept would be related to the split brain material in that activity

John A. Scott, Sr., Ph.D.

perceived by the left brain, is presented to the right brain in the presence of a strong emotional desire to pay attention. This causes a recording to be made in the memory system.

Summary

The definition of hypnosis which I prefer rests upon the preceding descriptions regarding brain lateralization, relaxation, and concentration in this way: The state of hypnosis is that condition wherein the right brain is dominating the thought processes, the mind is concentrated, the critical factor is minimal and by some unknown neurological correlates, there is an emotional sensitivity which goes beyond just right brain functioning. It is likely that the limbic-hypothalamic system is on ready so as to intensify the bodily responses that would be consistent, and in harmony, with the kind of stimuli which is received. Rossi's new study (1986) gives a clearer picture of the physiological mechanics of this state than any research I am acquainted with and will be referred to in more detail in another context.

The state of hypnosis is thus differentiated from the content and activity which transpires while the person is in this hypnotized state. The person may be alone or in the presence of others. This state may have come about spontaneously or by suggestion (direct or indirect) from persons or conditions of the environment. Such a state implies concentration or fixation of the mind on a given subject or situation without distraction and would be accompanied by appropriate affect to the thought. Such a state implies contact with the subconsciousness.

Such a state of mind can come about in a variety of ways. One way is spontaneously, in that a certain condition or set of circumstances can be traumatic, surprising, or sufficiently exciting so that the mind is immediately focused, the critical factor is inhibited and an impression is made deeply on the memory system. The primary process is dominating, hence the events and their accompanying interpretation are on an emotional level and therefore may or may not be accurate to the actual facts. For example, a child who witnesses the death of a parent and concludes that it is because of something he or she did and thus assumes unrealistic guilt. Or an adult has an accident and for a few seconds faces immediate death and remains thereafter emotionally scarred.

Another way in which the trance state of mind may be induced is by conditions of a crowd of people with the accompanying excitement generated by a political event, a religious gathering, sporting activities and such like (inciting such epithets as "mob psychology" or "mob violence"). In such conditions the individual performer or masses from the audience would be "hypnotized." The degree of intensity must be such that the concentration of the mind is extreme, but this happens.

One would find in the above examples phenomena characteristically descriptive of traditional hypnosis with regard to being suggestible and having after-effects that could be described as the result of posthypnotic suggestion, yet relaxation probably would be lacking in all of those examples.

Of course, the trance state is induced by the hypnotherapist on individuals for clinical or experimental purposes by plan (as differentiated from the above spontaneous circumstances). Access is gained usually by the relaxation process. It seems to me this is the category that Edmonston is referring to and he proves his point effectively. However, the Ericksonian school of thought would protest that relaxation would not be the only way to purposefully induce a trance state on an individual. Erickson's indirect method might not be as deep as the relaxation procedure unless the person was a particularly good subject. However, he could entrance his patients spontaneously and, as we all know, achieve desired results.

Conclusion

Thus the common denominator to all of the above entranced states is some, as yet poorly defined, state called the concentration of the mind. I assume that a person is in hypnotic trance when the right hemisphere is dominating the thinking and that a person may be induced into this state: (1) purposefully by suggestions of relaxation, or (2) accidently by sudden captivating circumstances. This implies that when the therapist or hypnotist is communicating with such a person one is communicating with the subconscious mind.

It seems to me this takes into account the circumstances of the bilateral brain, spontaneous or waking hypnosis, relaxation as the primary means of induction for clinical purposes, and communication with (and exposure of) the subconscious mind. Later I will rely on this definition of hypnosis when describing an innovative procedure of induction. But for now we continue with further theoretical and philosophical concepts.

John A. Scott, Sr., Ph.D.

THE PRINCIPLE OF PSYCHOSEXUAL DEVELOPMENT

It is clear to anyone who studies in any depth the development of human personality, that humans grow in stages. One school of thought may describe the growth and development of the child with an emphasis on observing the physical stages of development, while another authority may observe the same child with emphasis on the stages of cognitive ability and another based primarily on the stages of relationship with the primary others. This is not surprising since development is so complicated in its many aspects such as drive development, ego functions, and object and self relations. Furthermore, development can be interrupted at any point by a wide variety of means.

Pine (1985) in his work on the subject rightly states, that we don't have to be committed to any one particular theory. And he does a masterful job of what might be called reconciliation of a variety of views in his work on "Developmental Theory and Clinical Process." He stresses that the child grows in a series of "moments" or brief experiences each day and these separate moments may be placed in any number of classifications according to drive, ego, object, and self, as the case may be. There are different points of emphasis in each moment and in the combination of moments that make up the days to such an extent that by two years old there is such a complexity of intrapsychic experiences that it is impossible to separate single threads of development that belong to one classification or another.

I present below a summary of the traditional psychoanalytical classifications. I have found it easy to teach to students and it serves as a good foundation upon which to build further theories on development.

English and Pearson (1963) present the analytical stages of psychosexual growth and development of the human personality. These stages are outlined as follows:

I. The Oral Phase from birth to about one year. II. The Anal Period from approximately one year to three years. III. The Genital Period from approximately three (or three and one-half) to six years. IV. The Latent Period from approximately five or six years to eleven or twelve years. V. The Adolescent Period from approximately eleven or twelve years to twenty-one. This may be subdivided into pre-puberty, ten and a half to twelve years, puberty, thirteen to sixteen, and post-puberty, seventeen to twenty-one. VI. Maturity.

As the child grows and develops, there are basic needs which must be met for the child to proceed to the next stage in its growth. If some of those needs are not met, or if trauma comes to the child, it will not be prepared to go to the next stage of growth and development, and may regress to an earlier stage of development. Consequently, a crippling or arresting of the maturing factors takes place (English, 1963; Finch and Cain, 1968; Strupp, 1968; Winnicott, 1965). Thus, if such debilitating events take place in the Oral Period of development, the child is ill prepared to proceed to the next period, and consequently, will not be well prepared to enter any of the succeeding phases of growth and development. The after effects of the initial crippling processes are like a permanent injury which the child continues to bear the rest of his/her life.

Winnicott (1965), refers to the "facilitating environment" in which the particular needs of each individual infant will be met in a way which provides an impetus to growth. For the infant to grow in a wholesome way, appropriate amounts of frustration and gratification in proportions suitable for the individual child need to be provided. Thus, the wholesome maturation of the child may be adversely influenced by the intrusion of trauma and/or the deprivation of basic needs and/or over-frustration and/or excessive gratification for that particular child (Greenson, 1975, p. 83). Or there simply may be a lack of environmental cues to provide or enrich understanding. For example if speech is not well learned by 7 to 12 years old, little ability to do so will persist. Some authorities also question this same principle regarding reading. The advanced student of psychology is familiar with these patterns and conditions.

SOME PRINCIPLES OF PSYCHOANALYTICAL THEORY

The term "psychotherapy" literally means "treatment of the psyche," but there are many conceptions as to how this process should be carried out. It is not my intention in this section to describe in detail the psychoanalytic process. Obviously, that would be too involved. But, I do wish to call to the reader's attention a few fundamental concepts of the psychoanalytic methods which are utilized in hypnoanalysis. Essentially, it is the verbal method of treatment of the psyche (Munroe, 1955, pp. 34-68; Wolberg, 1967).

The patient is a person who is sufficiently disturbed by his mental processes or emotions or actions that he becomes convinced that he needs assistance in coping with these problems. The goal of the entire undertaking is to assist the patient in improving his thoughts, feelings and/or actions to such an extent that they become more acceptable to him, or follow a more comfortable or desirable pattern with his associates. This involves a self-awareness, not only of what the problem is, with its ramifications, but how the patient came to acquire the problem and what is necessary in order to alleviate the problem.

These are components which are common to the psychotherapeutic process (Harper, 1959, p. 9):

1. The patient is one who is aware of having a personal problem, or a mishandled life situation.
2. Though he has feet of clay, the therapist is a person who has had therapy and is relatively free of such disturbances, and who is capable of understanding the person in distress to such an extent that he can be of assistance to her/him in resolving the problem.
3. There should be a positive feeling toward the therapist by the patient.
4. There should be a positive and empathetic feeling of understanding by the therapist for the patient.
5. The patient understands that the therapist has this concern and ability to assist him with his problem.
6. The therapist has available to him certain methods or procedures which he utilizes in the course of such assistance.
7. The patient is able to express emotional catharsis to the therapist.
8. Between the therapy sessions there are prescribed a series of actions whereby the patient begins to readjust or realign his views or behavior concerning his environment and associates.
9. A gradual process persists wherein the patient is weaned away from the therapist to become independent and functioning in his environment.

Classical psychoanalysis, of course, draws distinctions between analysis and psychotherapy. Whereas in the above paragraph the therapy concepts are common to most all psychotherapy, the following are principles of the psychoanalytic method of psychotherapy. If treatment is to be deemed psychoanalytic, a couch is to be used and no fewer than four sessions per week are held in order to develop and treat the transference and transference neurosis. Two fundamental hypotheses which Freud held throughout his career were these: First, the concept of psychic determinism, or causality, which means that each psychic event is determined by the ones which preceded it; that is, each event in the present and each decision or course of action at the present time is determined or caused by certain events or influences which precede it (Breger, 1968; Brill, 1938; Harper, 1959).

The second main hypothesis of Freudian psychoanalysis was that unconscious mental processes (rather than conscious processes) were the real bases of human behavior and are usually the ultimate causes of our actions (Brill, 1938; Jones, 1961; Wolberg, 1967). This implies, therefore, that the emotional problems currently faced by the patient are in part caused by events or influences buried in the unconscious mind. Freud and Breuer called attention to the theory of Hysteria being caused, not so much by the trauma itself, but the memory trace, which "resembles a foreign body that continues to irritate the mind" (Jones, 1961, p. 178). The concept holds that as a child one is too weak or inexperienced to solve his problems or to deal with traumatic events. Consequently, these events become repressed and/or forgotten, but not without their influence upon the feelings and/or behavior of the adult. Thus, the emotional experience of recalling unresolved childhood problems and facing them is an essential part of the psychoanalytic process (Brill, 1938).

A further basic point of Freudian psychoanalysis is the consideration of two basic kinds of mental processes called the primary and the secondary processes (Brill, 1938; Munroe, 1955). The primary process is the predominant method of thinking engaged in by the young child, but it persists also at the unconscious level in the adult life, and it insists upon manifesting itself by dreams, pathology, humor, bodily movements, dress, slips of the tongue, and the like.

The secondary process of thinking is the procedure of conscious reasoning usually attributed to the normal adult. It is primarily verbal in its expression, and is essentially reasonable and logical (Brill, 1938; Munroe, 1955).

The concept of mental illness (or emotional disorder) is an expression of unresolved intrapsychic conflicts. That is, the roots of psychic illness are to be found in infancy or childhood.

During the course of therapy, it is assumed the patient will gain insight and understanding into the cause and effect relationship of his problem. Much of the unconscious material, as well as vaguely remembered incidents and impressions, will become conscious. Also, maturational progress will be made. In this respect hypnoanalysis is related to modern psychoanalysis (Gill & Brenman, 1959, p. 332). Furthermore, the analyst encourages the patient to give up his unhealthy defenses in favor of more healthy ones. During the course of therapy defenses must be resolved, regressions overcome, and symptoms and conflicts understood in a cause and effect relationship.

A major difference in hypnoanalysis and psychoanalysis, is that whereas in psychoanalysis all decisions and behavior are analyzed, consuming years of time for therapist and patient, in hypnoanalysis (at least theoretically) only those events are analyzed which contributed directly to the persons problem. Such events are the ones which had the most voltage or emotional impact on the person and thus produced alterations in feelings and subsequent behavior. This is not unlike Freud's and Breuer's theory on the source of hysterical symptoms, alluded to earlier, as being caused by the "memory trace," which is like an infiltration into the memory system, necessitating an effective abreaction in treatment (Jones, 1961, p. 178).

SOME PRINCIPLES OF BEHAVIOR MODIFICATION

Behavior modification has had its adherents for several decades, but the great momentum of the behavior modification school got under way in the early 1960's (Harper, 1975, p. 109). It has since become a major trend in the field of psychotherapy and has dominated the schools of psychology in most of the universities. The basic proposition behind the behavior modification theory is that there is no underlying or unconscious reason for the "sick behavior," but rather the outward symptoms are the illness (Harper, 1975, p. 110). Thus the therapy procedure is to induce a modification of the so-called sick behavior in order to effect a "cure" (Bandura, 1969, pp. 2-9, 49). Obviously, this is counter to the basic principle of psychoanalytic therapy which states that the outward behavior is due to underlying feelings and motivations which are maladjusted.

In my opinion, it depends upon what the sick symptoms are as to what the underlying cause there may be. This is the problem of aligning oneself with a particular school of thought. One is sometimes coerced into being on one side or the other. But there are varying degrees of one outward symptom in the same way that there is variety of kinds of symptoms. For example, one person who smokes may simply be addicted to the tobacco habit, and desire to quit that habit. There may be no underlying compulsion for that person to smoke. Thus, the smoking habit is itself the illness and may be broken by basic behavior modification methods or by hypnotherapy (Bandura, 1969, pp. 48-52; Kroger, 1977, pp. 170, 172, 3 14-416; Stein, 1964, p. 230; Wagner and Bragg, 1970, p. 258).

Another person who smokes has the same appearance in his symptomatology as the first, namely, the act of smoking. The second person, however, has an underlying unconscious compulsion to smoke. It may be a compulsion to have something in the mouth as a kind of pacifier for an underlying need in assuaging what would be called a "nervous condition" (English and Pearson, 1963, p. 23; Bonelli, 1980), or the compulsion may be "proof of life," for companionship, or for acceptance and the like. The background and conditioning are entirely different from that of the first person. It is quite likely that behavior modification methods will not be successful in helping this latter person to quit smoking. In my opinion this accounts for the failures in most "stop smoking programs." However, if behavior modification did succeed in helping the person to quit, there would probably be a continuation of some sort of oral activity (frequently eating) as a symptom substitution for the smoker's underlying need for a pacifier (Bryan, 1964a). As evidence for this principle one has only to attend any meeting of Alcoholics Anonymous where smoking is almost universal as a symptom substitute for alcohol. The smoker from infancy may have had a dependency upon oral pacification, or else he would develop intense "nervousness." What I am saying is that behavior modification is not the best modality of treatment in every case of emotional disorder (Wolberg, 1971, II). Neither is psychoanalytic psychotherapy the cure-all in every case.

There are some behavior modification principles which may be utilized on occasion in hypnoanalysis. Three major procedures have emerged from the various behavior modification schools of thought. These are as follows (Harper, 1975, pp. 110-113):

Systematic desensitization (Kroger and Fezler, 1976; Wolberg, 1971, 1973.) The nature of hypnoanalysis is such that the principles of systematic desensitization may be effectively used in some cases of emotional disorder, particularly in those cases involving fear and anxiety. If it is determined that is an unconscious compulsion for certain phobic behaviors or certain anxiety producing situations, the underlying unconscious factors must be understood and removed as a first stage. The second stage would be to utilize the principles of systematic desensitization. If a person becomes extremely anxious under certain conditions, as, say eating in a crowded restaurant, there is obviously some event or events from the past which have caused that person to develop such anxiety. The therapy will be most effective if the event or events which provoked such a response can be understood, brought to light, and then rationalized out of the person's memory as the provoking cause (Bieber, 1980).

The next step in the therapy would be to help the person go back into the crowded restaurant mentally to eat with a feeling of accompanying peace and tranquillity. By repeating the process under favorable conditions a number of times, the person gradually is desensitized to the anxiety producing conditions of eating in a crowded restaurant. Whereas he was hypersensitive to eating in a crowded restaurant, he now becomes desensitized to those conditions and is able to eat in a crowded restaurant, and enjoy his meal as other people do. Systematic desensitization is very much like the physical desensitization of allergies; that is, the person who is allergic, say to the grasses, receives injection of grass in increasing amounts over a period of time until his immunity is gradually built up (Bandura, 1969; Wolpe, 1973).

Aversion therapy. When a person is engaged in some type of behavior which is undesirable for one reason or another, he is discouraged from engaging in such actions by associating the behavior with certain unpleasant consequences. The aversive stimulus coincides with the unwanted emotional response (Kroger and Fezler, 1976; Wolpe, 1973). If a child throws his food on the floor, and in association with this act receives a spank on the hand, this is aversion therapy. Many forms of sexuality judged to be immoral, or various forms of self-indulgence, such as drug addiction, alcoholism, etc., as well as sociopathic and criminal behavior are types of behavior which may be helped in the latter stages of the cure by aversive therapy. As we shall see, these principles are utilized in hypnoanalysis. The aversive stimulus does not necessarily have to take place by using physical means of discomfort. *The aversion may be created in the mind.* In one sense of the word aversive therapy is the opposite of desensitization in that one is endeavoring to create a painful climate in association with the undesirable behavior in order to discourage the continuation of such behavior.

Operant conditioning (Bandura, 1969; Kroger and Fezler, 1976; Wolpe, 1973). Basically, this is a method of encouraging desirable kinds of behavior. In essence it helps the person to be motivated to do the right t by some kind of "reward" called a "reinforcer." When an individual needs to be able to engage in a desirable or healthy activity, a reinforcer stimulates to repeat the behavior pattern. On the child level, the child is given a cookie after doing chores. "Operant behavior 'operates' on the environment and produces some change in it" (Harper, 1975, p. 113). This is the essence of operant conditioning. Among adults, as we shall see (Wolpe, 1973), the encouragement may take place at the emotional level. The principles involved in the preceding paragraphs are utilized in hypnoanalysis, but the methods of applying them are different from those used in the practice of typical behavior modification. Examples of such utilization will be presented later.

THE MEDICAL MODEL

"Behavioral medicine" is a subject of widening interest and concerns the interdisciplinary characteristics of physiology, medicine and the psychological component. Thus the line of demarcation between the influences of the physician and the influence of psychology gets thinner as such concepts as these are brought out. It is known that ideas can effect the physiological activities of the cells in the body (Barber, 1984). In fact the most important system of health is the brain itself. It is these areas of the healing arts that we have in mind when we refer to "Medical" in Medical Hypnoanalysis.

Examination and Diagnosis

The basic process that a physician follows in the treatment of a physical illness is this: First, there is a description of the symptoms and an examination of the patient to verify such symptoms. Then a tentative diagnosis is made. In some cases, it then is advisable to verify the tentative diagnosis by making certain laboratory tests or further particularized examinations. As a result of the tests and examinations, a definite diagnosis is concluded. Knowing the diagnosis, there is a specific procedure that is known to be best for that disease or injury. The doctor proceeds with the prescription of medicines and/or therapy procedures which have been found to be most effective in the curative process. Usually the patient makes the desired progress and the illness is arrested or cured.

The principle is the same with Medical Hypnoanalysis. When the client comes in, he expresses his symptoms. The therapist immediately is looking for the diagnosis of the patient's problem. Consequently, the initial interviews need to be directed into investigating all of the areas of the patient's life, detecting the sources of pathology in order to make a tentative diagnosis. The aim is to do this within the first two hours.

The therapist next will utilize a projective test known as the "Bryan Hypnotic Word Association Test" and perhaps dream analysis as methods of verifying the tentative diagnosis.

Directed Therapy

As early as 1920, Ferenczi (1950), sometimes called one of Freud's most able followers, was advocating that the therapist take a more active part in the treatment of patients. His point was that active love and less passivity would come nearer effecting a cure. Winnicott (1958) felt that when dealing with patients whose analyses were related to the early stages of development, they should be "managed" and not "analyzed." Many others have argued in behalf of psychotherapy's following more of a medical model by seizing the initiative in the therapeutic relationship. Stuart made this point most impressively. With reference to traditional non-directive therapy, he said it was tantamount to "putting the sickest person in the room in charge of the restorative process" (Stuart, 1980, p.xii). In Medical Hypnoanalysis the therapist is in charge of the therapy throughout the process (cf. Wolberg, 1971, Vol. II, 38). This form of hypnoanalysis is directive and follows a basic medical model.

Once the diagnosis is verified, the therapist continues to direct the therapy procedures in such a way as to help the patient understand at the subconscious level the underlying ultimate causes of the problem and alleviate the symptoms.

Therapy Progresses According to Plan

Mowrer (1961, 1964), Szasz (1960), Volgyesi (1967), and many others see one of the problems with psychoanalysis to be that the therapy takes too long for many people to receive benefit from it. While it is true that the communication that comes out of free association is all pertinent to the patient and his personality (Greenson, 1975, p. 64), nonetheless, the detail of the analytical process prolongs the therapy to the extent of being discouraging to some patients. Admittedly, there are some patients who need to go through this procedure and psychoanalysis is the most desirable therapy for them. However, it also must be admitted that the majority of people have neither the time nor the money to afford psychoanalysis for their emotional disorders. The patient in psychoanalysis is often repetitive and conversant in areas which do not apply to his problem directly (Bieber, 1980). Hence, this pattern of the medical model is utilized in Medical Hypnoanalysis and certainly facilitates the curative process. The average psychoanalyst may treat approximately 100 patients in a lifetime, whereas the hypnoanalyst can see more than that each year for analysis.

The Triple Allergenic Theory

There is another aspect of the medical model which is utilized. That is the principle of allergies (Boswell, 1961; Van Pelt, 1962). An allergy develops in this way: When an individual is first exposed to a substance which is detrimental to the body, there is no "allergic reaction" that is obvious to the patient. But in the blood stream the foreign substance, called the antigen, stimulates the production of antibodies. After the antigen has been absorbed and eliminated from the blood stream, the antibodies continue "floating" in the stream, acting as guards against the intrusion of that particular antigen the next time it occurs. Thus, when the person has a second exposure to the antigen, (the same foreign substance), the antibodies are activated immediately to neutralize the effect of the antigen, and in so doing, the body has the "allergic reaction" (Boswell, 1961). Thus, one is said to be allergic to that substance thereafter.

The first exposure to the antigen by which the body is sensitized, is called the **Initial Sensitizing Event**, (ISE). At this time there are no outward symptoms. The next exposure to the antigen is called the **Symptom Producing Event**, (SPE), wherein one is very much aware of the allergic reaction as one comes in contact with the foreign substance. Each successive contact with the substance is now called the **Symptom Intensifying Event**, (SIE), that is, the symptoms are reproduced each time one comes in contact with the substance, and indeed, the symptoms may become worse over a period of time and may even generalize to connect other related substances.

This principle is applied in hypnoanalysis in this way. The patient in infancy or childhood may have a certain trauma to take place in its life, which would be called an Initial Sensitizing Event. Or there may be deprivations over a period of time early in life which would be viewed as an

Initial Sensitizing Period. The psyche of that person receives certain blows like the intrusion of a foreign substance which makes the person sensitive or weakened thereafter.

There may be only one such event, such as the death of one's mother within the first six months of life. Or there may be more than one Initial Sensitizing Event, such as are found in the "battered child syndrome," or the continual deprivation of love and attention so that early in life the child is "set up" for an event which comes later and causes the undesirable symptom(s) to appear. The latter event would be called the Symptom Producing Event. This is sometimes called in the literature the "precipitating cause" or, in the vernacular, the "straw that breaks the camel's back."

Usually, the Symptom Producing Event is remembered by the patient and a direct association is made between the symptom and the event as, "Yes, I remember when it happened, I've had this problem ever since my accident." But sometimes the patient does not associate the Symptom Producing Event with her particular problem, and it will be up to the therapist to make the connection.

Generally, the Initial Sensitizing Event, or events, are lost in the unconscious mind and it is highly desirable that they be brought to consciousness and understood as a process of therapy. This comprehension of the allergic process is not only helpful to the understanding of the therapist in his progress in therapy, but likewise it is helpful to the patient when carefully explained.

Figure 3 depicts major traumatic events in a person's life beginning at birth. Birth is pictured at the left end of the continuum and a number of events which may be viewed as spontaneous hypnotic trauma are depicted along the course of life. The degree of impact on the psyche depends on the "voltage" of each event. Obviously, those with the most voltage make the deepest impression and stimulate after-effects such as fear or anxiety. In this case the underlying common denominator with several such events has been the threat of death.

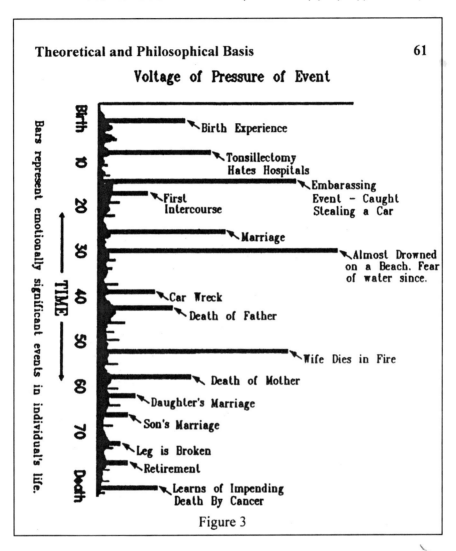

Theoretical and Philosophical Basis   **61**

Voltage of Pressure of Event

Figure 3

There is another minor point in which Medical Hypnoanalysis follows a medical model, and that is the use of several treatment rooms. Discussion of this will follow in a later chapter.

Criticism of the Medical Model

Before leaving this subject it is only fair to refer to Korchin's (1976) critique of the Medical Model. His comments are succinct and appropriate. He has picked out extreme conditions and has rightly brought them to the attention of the therapeutic community. Although his criticisms are appropriate to much of the literature, they cannot be universally accepted as valid.

In the preceding model, we have seen that "medical" implies a certain philosophical point of view, as well as subscribing to a circumscribed procedure. At the same time, out of duty to the patient, physiological evaluations are necessary in many psychological conditions. The concept of this theoretical base is that humankind is tripartite: soma, psyche, and pneuma, i.e. body, mind (emotions), and spirit. The interrelationship of these elements must be recognized by physicians, psychologists, and clergymen. Any concept of client-centered therapy must acknowledge this tripartite composition and treat the total person.

Another factor is the degree that the patient participates in the therapeutic procedure. A concept that the hypnotherapist must contend with constantly is that much of the population believes that a person who is being hypnotized is a passive recipient of treatment which works magic. The belief is that the patient is like an anesthetized patient receiving surgery and that no participation is necessary. This is certainly a false view regarding hypnoanalysis.

Eniatric healing, i.e. healing within the self, is a principle that is recognized by physicians in the less critical cases. The physician serves as a facilitator or director and helps the body speed the process of healing. So, emotionally, the mind seeks to heal or protect itself, the therapist must recognize himself as facilitator and partner in the overall curative procedure.

The patient participates to the extent that the investment of emotion and participation is at times painful. In fact a caution for the hypnoanalyst is, in pursuing rapid analysis, not to go too fast for that particular patient.

It is true, that in the medical model the concept is that the doctor knows best. But the knowledge of the doctor (in addition to her/his scholastic training) is dependent on the information presented by the patient - verbally and non-verbally. And based on an accurate input of data, the doctor is supposed to know what to do, and do it. Again, the patient must be a participant and share in the work of therapy.

One of Korchin's (1976) strongest points is that he charges that there is an over-emphasis on diagnosis, labeling, and stigmatizing the patient to the point that it prevents fostering change. Across the board in the psychotherapeutic community, I expect this criticism is valid. It does not apply in Medical Hypnoanalysis. But more will be said on this further in this chapter.

Korchin's last point is that emphasis on pathological themes in life fosters neglect of sources of confidence and strength. This approach focuses on weaknesses of the patient rather than strengths. I have been guilty of this at times. Any of us working with the suffering of humanity may at times get caught up in the challenge of curing the sick by our skills and fail to capitalize on the ability of the patient to utilize his own resources for the curative process. To that extent, we hinder therapeutic progress. I suspect this is not just because of working within the framework of the medical model. Whatever the procedural method, the therapist should recognize, and capitalize on, what strengths and assets the patient has. In fact, early in each therapy session I play a tape to the hypnotized patient emphasizing a positive mental attitude.

THE RANK ORDER OF LIFE'S PRIORITIES

Surviving is what life is all about. Because of the struggle to survive, the unconscious mind chooses the symptom or emotional disorder as a defense against a threat from which it suffers. That is, anxiety precedes (and hence signals) defense (Pine, 1985). There are many factors which enter into such a choice. For example, a little girl who grows up in a home where mother is "always nervous" will likely suffer from the same kind of symptoms if she identifies with her mother. Some children fix their symptoms on obesity because one or both of the parents or another close family member has been obese. Of course, the example of another family member is not the only source or influence on the unconscious mind in its choice of emotional symptoms.

The unconscious mind is, of course, effected by many and varied sources such as reading, friends, environment, movies, and even frequently by negative suggestions from physicians or psychotherapists such as: "You may suffer from pain all of your life from this," or, "You have schizophrenia and it frequently takes many years to get over this, if ever."

Whatever the source of influence, if there is one, it is still up to the unconscious mind to select the particular symptom that expresses the inner pain, or serves as a defense against a condition perceived subconsciously as a worse threat. Recognizing the order of importance of various factors which are necessary to survive will help one to understand more about the symptom and the underlying cause of that symptom.

The unconscious mind has a way of picking the lesser of the evils as the outward expression (i.e., the symptom), of the inner threat or conflict which originates at a more basic priority level of life. The impulse of the unconscious mind is to "reason" in something like the following manner. "I am faced with a terrible threat, but I want to survive. Maybe if I give up something less important I can keep something more important, that is, survive." For example, if a sexual symptom is presented, then there is a quest for its cause. If it isn't simply due to lack of education, it may be due to unconscious factors. The defensive process reasons that it is better to have a sex problem than to lose one's soul or to cause death. (Bryan, 1971b; Note 1). The sexual symptom of impotency may be the outward manifestation of an inner fear of losing one's soul for improper sexual conduct. Consequently, it is better to have a sexual problem than to miss out on eternal life. If one is impotent he cannot commit the sin of adultery. Thus impotency becomes a means of protection against what is perceived as a more serious threat. Another possible explanation for impotency rests at the second priority level, a threat of causing a pregnancy that might result in a loss of life, or has already resulted in a loss of life. Thus, it is better to be impotent than to cause a loss of life (Bryan, Note 2).

In order to understand this rationale more clearly, consider the following rank order of survival factors. These are the intuitive priorities of life.

The First Order: Spiritual Survival

The need that is most important and therefore considered to be the highest priority of all of man's needs is the need for spiritual survival-the need for the survival of the soul after death, or a relationship with the Deity, which may be expressed through love. Anthropologists have found that among the elements that are common to all peoples the world over is the innate instinctual need for some kind of an acceptable relationship with a higher power (Bryan, 1971b, Note 2; Strong, 1947; Thiessen, 1949).

For want of a better term, C.S. Lewis (1944a) refers to the "experience of the Numinous" by which he means that awareness that humans have for the Ultimate Power or Presence in the universe, which in our Judeo-Christian culture we recognize as God. Lewis observes that it is probable "that numinous awe is as old as humanity itself" (Lewis, 1944a, p.7).

Lewis points out that there is a second basic factor common to all human experience and that is an innate sense of "I ought" or "I ought not," i.e., the concept of right and wrong behavior. Another way of putting it is that somehow, built into our systems, is a "sense of fair play...a real law which none of us made, but which we find pressing on us" (Lewis, 1944b, p.17).

This lays the foundation for the universal concept that when this fundamental law is violated one becomes conscious of guilt. In the development of religion, for primitive man, a third factor becomes apparent and that was the "Numinous Power to which people felt awe is made the guardian of the morality to which they feel obligation" (Lewis, 1944a,p.10). It was Barth (1957) who referred to the conscience as speaking "of an existence higher than joy and deeper than pain," nonetheless a fundamental human trait.

Since God is looked upon as the Author of the ultimate standards of our behavior, this point of view will come out in the concept of adherence to the basic moral/ethical standards of one's culture. This takes in the many ramifications of the guilt complex. This basic concept appears instinctual to all human-kind. As therapists we must reckon with this.

For too long psychotherapy, generally, has endeavored to treat disordered lives while ignoring the existence of the spiritual needs and kindred concepts of the patient. I am convinced that this contributes to the number of failures in therapy. Pascal (1655/1958) makes the point that man is in misery without God. Throughout my life I have observed this to be true. In thirty-seven years of dealing with the foibles of human behavior I have never seen an atheist get well or say he found fulfillment. There probably are some exceptions, I just haven't seen them. And Oates (1973, p.22) bluntly states that, "both personality and religion are seen as the highest value of mankind."

The point has been emphasized by many psychologists as well as pastoral counselors for years that for the most part humans find their fulfillment and victory over the vicissitudes of life by and through their relationship to God (e.g.Clinebell,1966; Ligon, 1938; Link, 1939; Oates, 1973; Pruyser, 1968; Tournier, 1965, and a multitude of others). Of course, there are sick expressions of formalized religion and sick people who express religious views, but there also can be a healthy relationship with God which is a stabilizing force in daily life and adds a stabilizing sense of values to existence very much like a support group of relatives and/or friends. At any rate, all who deal with the disordered lives of hurting fellow humans need to be aware of the first need in an ordered life, and that is to be at peace with God. . . whatever that means to the patient.

Viktor Frankl has been vocal in stressing some aspects of this principle while utilizing another terminology (1963, 1969). While his term, "noogenic neurosis" has not caught on, it applies in this context. Frankl contends that the spiritual dimension is a "specifically human dimension" with which psychotherapists must reckon.

A person may be very much alive physically, but if there is no freedom of will (our second order), and no will to meaning (our first order), there is no meaning to life. Frankl (1969, p.50) quotes Albert Einstein: "the man who regards his life as meaningless is not merely unhappy but hardly fit for life." In essence this is what I'm talking about here.

Frankl (1969) goes on to associate a value system of some sort with the will to meaning. First, he states clearly that it is not the purpose of Logotherapy to supply the meaning for persons, rather it is the person's possession of values which alleviates the search for meaning. He comments tersely, (op.cit.p.57) "Man is pushed by drives. But he is pulled by values." Because universal values are on the wane, people are caught in a feeling of aimlessness and emptiness or, as I am used to calling it, an "existential vacuum" (op.cit.p. 64). He elaborates further that attitudinal values include meaningful attitudes toward pain, guilt, and death.

Love as an Expression of God's Presence

In our culture our expression of a relationship to God may come out in a number of ways. Since "God is love. Whoever lives in love lives in God, and God in him" (Bible, I John 4:16). We thus express our relationship to God by expressing love to our fellows. The ability to give and receive love is not only an evidence of maturity, but the expression of God in us. Fromm (1956), Glasser (1965), Rogers (1977), and other psychotherapists stress the value and importance of "loving" relationships. Classical statements by Buber (1937, 1955), Niebuhr (1963), Tillich (1952), and others emphasize the place of love in the interpersonal relationships of humans to their fellows in society as basic to survival. One obvious evidence that love (or acts of love) is the most fundamental of mankind's instinctual drives is that there are occasions when a person will give up physical life in order to save another loved person. For example, a mother will risk or give up her life in order to save a child. A person will risk or give up one's life in order to save a friend. Such acts are prompted by love.

Gabriel Marcel (1950) makes a strong statement when he contends that our relationship with other persons is basic to the whole of our experience, and this is a clue to the nature of reality. And, of course, the ultimate reality is God. The essence of Tillich's sermon to the medical profession is (1957, p.71):

> *The medical faculty needs a doctrine of man in order to fulfill its theoretical task; and it cannot have a doctrine of man without the permanent cooperation of all those faculties whose central object is man.*

A statement which I regard as a kind of response to such a sermon comes from Bernard S. Siegel, M.D., Clinical Professor of Surgery, Yale University School of Medicine. He boldly asserts: "...true healing occurs only when psyche, soma, and spirit are integrated." This is the core of the Holistic Health concept and the foundation of Medical Hypnoanalysis.

The more direct expression of the need for spiritual survival is the need for preserving the soul after death. For some people the artificialities of our modern society have caused the repression or denial of this instinctual need and it remains in the unconscious only to come out by expressions of prayer in times of physical threat. However, in most cases people are consciously aware of this need, particularly as they grow older. After sexual libido has subsided, after physical health has deteriorated, after gratifying the ego by fulfilling life's ambitions, still there remains the desire to live on after death. When nothing else matters any longer, the one urge that lasts longest, and is therefore most basic, is the yearning for the after life.

In other cases the need to live after death can be shown to be present in the unconscious mind, and concern for preserving the soul by doing what is "right" is of more concern than any other factor of survival.

Hence, this relationship to the Deity is the most fundamental instinctual need humans have (Bryan, 1971b, Note 2). It is not to be limited to a mundane view of church or synagogue membership. Rather, the ramifications of one's spiritual needs extend to the meaning of life, the sense of true reality (Joyce, 1985). An excellent recent work on this subject is E.M. Stern, Editor, Psychotherapy and the Religiously Committed Patient (1985). Regardless of his or her personal belief, or disbelief, psychotherapists need to face this issue honestly and forthrightly and deal with the patient in terms of the broad human perspective, religiously. Thus, mankind's first priority is **spiritual survival**.

John A. Scott, Sr., Ph.D.

The Second Order: Ego Survival

Second in rank order of a persons priorities is ego survival. This need is closely related to spiritual survival. The relationship of the self to reality has to do with purpose of life; one's identity and individuality are understood and defined. One's ability to answer the questions, "Who am I?" "Why am I here?" "Where am I going?" with some degree of certainty is a key element here. One's individuality of thinking, of tastes, choice of friends, companions, career, family relationships, religious views, philosophy of life - all are related to the personhood, or ego, or the self.

The ego or personal identity may be threatened, or even devastated, in infancy or childhood by any one or a combination of mistreatments and deprivations. It may happen by rejection at birth, by lack of proper care in infancy, confusion of one's gender, by oppressive or inconsistent parents, by denial of loving relationships, deprivation of encouragements, disinheritance from one's traditional or family roots, rejection by friends, unsuccessful school experiences and the like. Under such conditions the "will to meaning" and having a purpose in life may become practically non-existent. When the psyche is bombarded by such experiences, defenses and symptomotology appear, but at a level that is not as fundamental as ego survival or spiritual survival. That is, symptoms will be either in the nature of self destructive tendencies, psychosomatic disturbances, confusion in relationships, sexual malfunctioning, phobias, anxieties or such like. But take note: all such symptoms are of lesser importance than ego survival or spiritual survival.

Third Order: Physical Survival

Third in rank order of a person's priorities is physical survival. In order to survive physically one must have air, water and food. When the ready availability of any of these three elements is perceived to be threatened, anxiety is produced and one searches for some means of coping with the threat. This may or may not be successful. If one does not cope successfully, panic results. Much symptomotology is due to this pattern, yet not recognized by many therapists because such symptoms are disguised or far removed from the real provoking cause.

For example, one can only survive a few minutes when deprived of air, therefore, when this threat to physical survival is perceived, defenses are mustered. In many cases the defense is to prove to the subconscious mind that one is still breathing. This is evidenced by either hearing oneself breathe (asthma) or seeing one's breath (smoking). Thus, the symptom breath (asthma or smoking in some cases) becomes the defense against facing the threat of loss of life.

Under some circumstances the subconscious mind accepts the idea of death or "dies a little." After a person has been through a death threatening accident or surgery, in order to convince the subconscious mind that one is still alive, the defense may be frantic activity or compulsive acts for reassurance of survival. On the other hand, another person may express the symptom of depression, i.e. grief over one's own death. More will be said on this view of symptomotology later.

The Fourth Order: Socio-Economic Survival

The fourth most important order of importance is Socio-Economic Survival. For this item we have to separate males from females. For males this can be stated as the "territorial imperative." In both the fowl and the animal realms, there are those species wherein the male demonstrates his leadership and control by staking out his territory. Some birds do this by the bird song whistled at certain boundary points. Some animals define their boundaries by urinating at certain points. At any rate, when the territory is defined, mating takes place within those boundaries. Other males are prohibited from entering the private domain of the "owner" (Bryan, Note 2). If the male does not control territory, he will not have females with which to mate.

In the human realm, there are indications of a similar kind of need. Of course, our artificial society has altered the manner in which this is expressed. In humans the male has the need to work and provide for the female and children or make the nest for the family.

The female equivalent is the "maternal instinct", which is the impulse to bear offspring and thus "fill" the nest. Once again, our artificial society distracts from this fulfillment, but the urge is there, nevertheless. Of course with many women this urge is sublimated and her creativity is fulfilled by other means. It is often postponed for a variety of reasons, but the maternal instinct coincides with the male need to provide the territory and wherewithal for mating.

Lois Davitz (1984) investigated "baby hunger" systematically and interviewed 200 women regarding maternal feelings. Many women, some of whom did not plan to have children, became dramatically aware of the need to have a baby. This was manifested by some in a change of attitude, by health and bodily changes, by behavior that was totally out of character, expression of physical symptoms before pregnancy, menstrual dysfunction, and by dreams. Single women, career women, and women in marriage without children, at a specific point in time became aware of this deep seated urge. This drive to have a baby took on a higher priority than job, career, dating relationships, or even the commitment to remain single.

An example of how this is a natural priority more basic than the sex drive is that, usually when a male has his job threatened, or his financial condition is collapsing, the sex urge is diminished, inhibited, or he may become impotent until the threat is past (Kaplan, 1974). Females may have sexual dysfunction (level five) because of conflicts or worries at the maternal level of life, which has a more fundamental priority in rank order. For example, when a woman is worried about her children, or the children are awake in an adjoining room, or a similar situation, she may be unresponsive sexually or asexual. Of course such a sexual symptom may be the result of a threat at a more fundamental level of priority also, such as fear of death, destruction of her reputation (ego), or threat to her soul. Consequently, we consider the fourth priority for the female to be the maternal instinct.

Thus, species survival requires the male to prepare and provide the nest and the female fills the nest in this joint venture for the survival of the species.

The Fifth Order: Species Survival (Sex Instinct)

The next most important factor in total survival is the sex libido (Bryan, Note 3). This is in the Number Five position of priorities. One way that this order of importance of things can be tested and evaluated is to recognize the various sources of activities or beliefs which interfere with a wholesome sexual relationship.

If a person has a symptom of sexual malfunction (not due to physiological or ignorance factors), the therapist should look at one of the more fundamental priorities (orders 1 through 4) as the ultimate source of the disturbance. The subconscious mind has selected a symptom which is not as important to him or her as the real source of the problem.

The Sixth Order: Miscellaneous Behavior

This sixth order is more or less a "catch all" for behavior problems not as basic as those which are higher on the priority list. Symptoms may be evidenced because of personal anxiety about getting along with others, personal feelings, health (when not life threatening), and some psychosomatic problems. Some obesity, smoking, or drinking problems would be placed in this category, but the ultimate roots of the problem may well be in a lower order more fundamental to survival. For example, separation anxiety (a form of depression) starting at the time of divorce, could be the waking diagnosis. The underlying diagnosis could be found in any one of the first five orders, depending on the previous experiences and relationships of the patient. It has been my experience that most of those with separation anxiety have the underlying diagnosis as the Identity Problem (second order) or Loss of Love (first order) and the ISE with the birth experience.

Admittedly, this order of importance of the various factors in survival is not the same as the traditional Freudian order. But understanding this order is most helpful in understanding the etiology of one's emotional symptoms. The unconscious mind, as has already been recognized, has a way of selecting a symptom or a set of symptoms for an expression of its inner anxiety which constitute a defense mechanism to prevent a more devastating personality disorder.

This order of priority may be graphically illustrated as follows by listing the most fundamental as number one at the bottom and coming up with number two as the next most important, etc.

6. MISCELLANEOUS (Behavior due to drives, desires, and impulses related to culture and conditioning.)

5. SPECIES SURVIVAL (sex instinct).

4. SOCIO-ECONOMIC SURVIVAL (Male: Territorial Imperative. Female: Maternal instinct).

3. PHYSICAL SURVIVAL (Requirements: air, food, water).

2. EGO SURVIVAL (Individual personhood).

1. SPIRITUAL SURVIVAL (Relationship with God, guilt, love relationships, desire for life after death).

John A. Scott, Sr., Ph.D. ① Caddie

Application

Suppose a patient presents a symptom of anxiety. This may be looked upon as a symptom above (or of lesser importance than) the list of the first five. The dynamic source of that anxiety should be sought in a conflict or trauma related to Number Five or Four or Three or Two or One. That is, the subconscious mind selected anxiety as an outward expression of an underlying unresolved conflict. Such anxiety could be due ultimately to sexual frustration (No. 5), or it could be due to concern over one's job (No. 4), or due to unresolved death threats (No. 3) or poor self image (No. 2), or due to unresolved guilt (No. 1). Its ultimate source could be found in any one or more of those lower than Number Six. Suppose a person presents a sexual symptom. Look for the dynamic source of the symptom in the area of Number Four or Number Three or Number Two or Number One. The reader can pick his or her own examples from experience.

If a patient evidences a symptom of suicidal action, found in order Number Three, (slow as with smoking, or fast as with a drug over-dose), examine him or her in the areas of order Number Two or One for the unconscious unresolved conflict. The person would have the Waking Diagnosis of suicidal but the Unconscious or Underlying Diagnosis might be an Identity Problem feeling worthless, having no purpose in life etc. Or, the Underlying Diagnosis might be the Guilt Complex and the person is needing to punish himself because of guilt feelings.

If a patient presents the symptom of existential anxiety concerning a meaningless life, despair, depression related to the personhood or ego, the ultimate source of the problem will be found in some aspect of order Number One. Frequently it is due to guilt and/or loss of love.

Thus the unconscious mind in all of these cases, and many others like them, has a way of picking the area of the symptomatic expression at a higher level of priority than the level of the real underlying problem. This is because it is too painful to face up to the subject which is the actual source of conflict so an area of lesser intensity is selected for the symptomatic expression. In most cases that concerns some form of survival. Coping with, or admitting, the real issue would be too devastating. Hence, in an effort at self preservation, the unconscious mind selects a symptom which it can more easily tolerate than dealing with the real issues. Many have tested this theory in the clinical setting for years and have found it to be reliable.

78

If one views the symptoms as an outer or visible expression of an underlying or inner conflict or trauma hangover, it facilitates the history taking and therapeutic procedures. Efforts to treat symptoms can be frustrating to the therapist and can mislead the patient because in so many cases symptom removal is not a "cure" of the real problem at all. Repressed material comes to the surface in the guise of symptoms (Cf. Freud in Brill, 1938, pp. 129-140, 172). Thus, as far as the therapist is concerned, one knows that ultimately the analytical solution will come from one of the lower, more basic levels of priority.

This whole concept is compatible with the "Systems Theory" (Skynner, 1976) in that the inter-relationship of one individual in a family circle with another is effected by the underlying root problem of the identified patient. For example, the presenting patient may be acting out and through such actions of phobia, anxiety or other symptoms of a disorder, be controlling the whole household. The therapist may instigate therapy by making an effort to alter and adjust the household in group therapy. This may meet with some success, but it isn't likely to cure the ultimate problem. Understanding the unconscious cause of the patient's problem and curing at that level will make family group therapy effective.

The patient's problem may be determined by the hypnoanalyst to be at the spiritual level. Understanding the influence of a religious system (for example Calvinism repressing love and sexuality) on the family system of the patient in childhood will help the therapist understand the ultimate dynamics of the patient's problem. Furthermore, it will help the patient understand why he is acting out such behavior as the presenting symptom.

It is helpful, in making an explanation to the patient, to use a metaphor like this. One may have a weed in the middle of a lawn. As one goes over it with a lawn mower the weed is continually cut down, but continues to crop up again. Only when the weed is pulled out by the roots will it stop growing in the lawn.

A whole family or office or business may be suffering the effects of one person's emotional disorder and that disorder be due to one, or more, Underlying Diagnoses. Cure the diagnosed disorder and the consequences will have a domino effect on all others who are relating to that patient.

The foregoing is the theoretical explanation for the etiology of neurotic problems and serves as a foundation for the diagnostic principles which follow.

John A. Scott, Sr., Ph.D.

DIAGNOSTIC PRINCIPLES

Strupp (1973) points up what other researchers have found, and that is diagnosis in the psychotherapy field is imprecise to say the least. In a research study sponsored by the National Institute of Mental Health, Strupp presented 237 psychotherapists (including psychiatrists, psychologists, psychoanalysts) with a filmed psychiatric interview and recorded responses from the observers. Regarding the diagnostic evaluation there were "multiple diagnoses" with almost 40% of the respondents diagnosing the patient as having "Anxiety," "Hysteria," and "Paranoia." These three "were chosen with almost equal frequency, followed by 'Obsessive,' 'Character Disorder,' 'Psychopathic,' and some minor ones" (Strupp, 1973, p.218).

Wolberg (1980) gives an example that could be typical of many patients. A patient was presented with symptoms so broad that he could be typed as "Somatoform Disorder," "Anxiety Disorder," "Psychoneurotic," or "Reactive Depression," "Obsessive Disorder," "Phobic Disorder," and "Personality Disorder." The nomenclature would depend on which aspect of the symptomatic formation was being emphasized at the time. This confusion concerning diagnosis is not surprising, though it is disappointing that it has to be this way. But the fact is that there are many who suffer from a "mixed psychoneurotic disorder" with a long list of other elements mixed in such as anxiety, depression, somatic elements, phobic characteristics and others.

We have to face it: Psychiatric diagnoses are not as easily delineated as are physiological diagnoses. The very nature of emotional disorders makes many patients subject to interpretative nuances which are highly subjective, and tests have not solved the problem with precision. Costello (1970) gives a report on the usefulness of the Wittenborn Scale, used for identifying the dimensions of mental illness. Twenty-one different factors were used in the diagnostic process and applied the Scale to 3000 patients. No one factor has been repeated in each of the studies. One might conclude that we diagnosticians are at times as confused as the patient.

Costello states that both therapist and patient have preconceived ideas about the emotional problem and tend to fix these ideas on the diagnostic process. Further, patients in a hospital setting tend to act in accordance with hospital influence. Costello (1967) indicts the patient to this degree that the aspect of the symptomotology which is most annoying to the patient is what is emphasized to the therapist. But this is not necessarily what is wrong with the patient. In fact, Wolberg emphasizes the situation by stating diagnosis is in a hopeless state of disorder.

In all fairness, it must be recognized that some of this criticism was in the day of DSM II. Although DSM III is obviously improved, much of the criticism of the earlier period could apply to DSM III as well. Now we have DSM III-R in a further effort to find our way in the maze of appellations which are so confusing to patient and therapist alike. It is debatable whether we are much better off or not. Korchin (1976) in his list of criticisms of the "medical model" stresses that there is an over emphasis on diagnosis and this prevents fostering change. The patient may also feel stigmatized by these labels, with accompanying social inferiority. Such traditional diagnostic terms emphasize pathological themes in life and the sources of strength and confidence are neglected, i.e. weaknesses are emphasized rather than strengths.

North (1985) honestly and frankly recognizes that the use of the "dreaded vocabulary" of psychiatric jargon, even subtly, influences the therapist to be pessimistic and helpless. There is little doubt that the average psychotherapist is severely restrained by the textbook examples of emotional disorders. By this I mean that traditionally we have come to expect certain disorders to be incurable or barely treatable and others to take a very long time in therapy. We have been hesitant even to use the word "cure" because we expect a relapse. And so we see a patient, make a diagnosis, and then settle down for a prolonged process of intervention methods which we hope in due time will make some change or else help the patient to live a little more comfortably with the disorder.

This condition is no better with the marital therapists. In fact the problem is compounded because instead of dealing with an individual patient, the marital therapist is dealing with a plurality of persons and the unwritten expectation is that with the serious case of marriage dysfunction the only solution is divorce. The relationship disintegrates before two or more people can get their act together and live together in harmony.

As a whole we have surrounded ourselves with such fixed parameters and self-limiting boundaries that we do our patients a severe disservice. Under such circumstances, the average patient is going to respond in accordance with the prescribed system and the subconscious expectations of the therapist.

The hypnoanalyst must free himself or herself from traditional strictures concerning who can be treated and how fast they can be cured. Real progress in any field usually comes from those who are not afraid to free themselves from the shackles of blind tradition and usually those pioneers come from the fringes of the profession or from the outside. New, fresh thinking is necessary. The patient can be more effectively treated and sooner get well if there is an expectant attitude of optimism. This expectation must come from the therapist who believes in what he or she is doing. The hypnoanalyst is out on the cutting edge of an exciting new therapy and is therefore free to be innovative and progressive in a brave new world of psychotherapy. If such an enterprising therapist utilizes a revised or new set of diagnostic terms, believing there is a cure for each of these conditions, he has already gone a long way in the cure of his patient.

Today patients have read enough in the popular press concerning emotional disorders to fear traditional diagnostic terms and when labeled with one may erroneously conclude that the disorder will last much too long if it is curable at all. Other patients may conclude that they will be on medication indefinitely or even permanently and thus suffer side-effects, addiction etc. Such fears may complicate the situation and send the patient into another more serious disorder (and diagnosis) as a result of indiscreet revelation by the doctor (Bowen, 1978; Menninger, 1985; Szasz, 1965).

There are reasons, presumably justified, for fitting a patient into a diagnostic scheme for institutional regulations and insurance requirements if not for others. As Wolberg (1980) points out, there is a temptation to "coordinate diagnosis" with acceptable categories for which insurance will reimburse the patient. This leads to another problem of inflexibility. Furthermore, in many cases, clinical diagnosis does not bear directly on preferred techniques in some syndromes.

In spite of the draw-backs, diagnosing is here to stay - certainly with the time, effort and expense that has gone into DSM III, and III-R, it is clearly a part of the system. Efforts have been made to improve on the DSM III system. A good example of which is Gear, Liendo, and Scott (1983). In their stimulating and challenging book, these clinicians refine the typology by which a patient is evaluated by including five independent variables: "the defensive qualification, reality testing, affect organization, centeredness, and attitude toward organizations." As helpful as this refinement is, it does not prevent the confusion which has already been exemplified.

Probably the only way to make a radical improvement is to break with the old system and play with a different set of rules. Here the hypnoanalyst has the freedom and perhaps even the responsibility to instigate a new, or at least, a revised system of diagnosing to go along with the new system of therapy. Is it possible that there could be another way of diagnosing?

Perhaps Medical Hypnoanalysis provides a solution or at least will stimulate the consideration of another system.

THE DOUBLE DIAGNOSIS

I have no intention of using double talk or of being inconsistent with the preceding paragraphs, but suggest the following as an intermediate step in a revised concept of diagnosing emotional disorders of the non-psychotic type. A "double diagnosis" would utilize current nomenclature as a "waking diagnosis" (WD). Such terms as anxiety, depression, obsession, phobia, somatoform etc. describe the patient's condition. As Costello states (1970), these terms tell us what's going on, that's all. The waking diagnosis (WD) could be any descriptive term in addition to those listed in DSM III and III-R that the patient might use in describing the symptoms.

The underlying or hypnotic diagnosis (UD) is the root cause of the symptom, usually at the unconscious level. The underlying diagnoses are related to the relative importance of factors in surviving as discussed in the preceding pages of this chapter. The task of the therapist is to determine as soon as possible, in taking the history, what the underlying or dynamic diagnosis is (UD). In most cases the patient will not recognize the unconscious factors in producing the symptoms, consequently it is up to the therapist to determine this. This is where a knowledge of the possibilities of the underlying diagnosis is so helpful.

We have already seen the levels of life's priorities in an ascending order of importance. The theory has been advanced that a symptom is an expression of a threat to an aspect of existence at a more basic level of life than the level of the symptom. This may also be viewed as an unresolved conflict as a result of a loss.

Kearns (1985) calls our attention to the fact that life is made up of a series of losses and one must adjust to loss at every stage of life. There is "loss of the womb at birth, the breast at time of weaning, the mother as one goes off to school, the home and family as one starts a career, our children as they leave home" and of course, in aging, the threat of loss of life. Such a loss or separation may take place under adverse circumstances to the extent that it produces a threat to survival.

That threat, or unresolved conflict, requires some means of identification and that is the underlying diagnosis. The following is a partial list with terminology which can be used with the patient at the proper time for clarification of the cause and effect pattern in the emotional disorder. The list proceeds from the most fundamental priority level upward to those levels of lesser importance.

UNDERLYING DIAGNOSTIC TERMINOLOGY

Diagnoses at the First Order: Spiritual Survival

There are several possible diagnoses here. The three main ones are: Guilt Complex, Separation Anxiety (from a loved one) and Existential Meaninglessness (or Existential Vacuum).

The Guilt Complex has been described in so many ways and from so many points of view that there is no point in trying to summarize or even cite the literature pertaining to it. Feeling guilty with the accompanying need to punish oneself is so popular that it is manifested as an element on a high percentage of all emotional and psychosomatic disorders. Naturally, one will distinguish between real guilt and neurotic guilt.

The waking diagnoses may cover a wide range of terms such as Obsessive-Compulsive, Depression, Anxiety, low self esteem, somatic symptoms, hopelessness, alienation from God and others. The underlying diagnosis could be the Guilt Complex.

The Persephone Complex (Bryan, 1961b). Persephone, of the Greek myth, spent three months above ground each year, hence the name, Persephone Complex. Situations involving this complex in which the patient is alive only part of the time, are unusual. The symptomatic expression of this complex may be that the patient feels depressed only at certain times or seasons of the year with some regularity regardless of the kind of activity that is going on around them. Bryan cites an example of a woman who outwardly had neurotic depression. She was withdrawn, could hardly talk to others, had a shell around her, just existing, not alive. She had the appearance of having the Walking Zombie Syndrome. She had previously been diagnosed as having a postpartum psychosis. She was actually in and out of depression, giving the impression of being Manic Depressive. She was depressed nine months of the year and well three months. The symptom producing event had been the birth of her first child.

When this woman had her baby and realized what a beautiful child it was, she was overwhelmed with guilt because she had aborted an earlier pregnancy. Now she saw what a beautiful baby she might have had if she had not had the abortion. Repressed guilt and remorse produced a repetition of the nine month pregnancy cycle with attendant depression.

The woman's understanding of the unconscious pattern was the key to her cure. If depression starts with a birth, it is advisable to check and determine if there has been an earlier abortion. With the increase in frequency of abortions and the attendant public conflict over the issue, similar situations to the above may become more prevalent.

Separation Anxiety or loss of love, is the result of some form of separation, from a loved one by death, emotional separation, or physical separation by being removed by distance. Because of being insecure, many people diagnosed as "depressed," are living under the ongoing threat of separation even though such has not actually taken place.

Meaninglessness is a broad term. Frankl (1969) refers to an "existential vacuum" by which he means the same thing. Frankl makes the point that we make a decision and choose our value system. This has to do with what in the church we call faith. And Frankl asserts, "And what our patients need is unconditional faith in unconditional meaning" (1969, p.156). When those people, discussing suicide, refer to ending it all because life has no meaning, they are stating in so many words that they do not know who they are and have no ego strength to continue (priority number 2) or that there is no longer any purpose to life for one reason or another (priority number 1). Some therapists have referred to problems at this level as the Walking Zombie Syndrome (Spiritual)) but this is too easily confused with the Walking Zombie Syndrome. Frankl's terms, "Meaninglessness" or "Existential Vacuum" or "Existential Meaninglessness" are quite sufficient.

Diagnoses at the Second Order: Ego Survival

Identity Problem (ID). This is reflected by allusions in the Word Association Test or in other contexts to, "Who am I?" "What am I doing here?" Or it may be manifested by some form of Gender Confusion. There is a consciousness of a lack of personal worth, no self assurance, a sense of helplessness. Ritzman (1982, 1984) points out that this problem usually starts at birth or with the mother in the prenatal period. Rejection in infancy is a most frequent cause. However, lack of identification with a parent figure in childhood may also be a strong contributing factor. Or, identification is made with a parent figure who is weak, inconsistent or illusive.

Cinderella Complex. In the last few years there have been a number of symptoms of a wide variety becoming more and more prominent with women. Many of these cases are due to an underlying conflict of gender and role issues which these women have not resolved. There is the struggle between dependence and independence with its attendant frustrations. The details of this complex are given behaviorally by Dowling (1981), who aptly named the complex, and by Hafner (1986) who presents a brilliant historical and analytical description.

Mistaken Identification is a specific form of an Identity Problem. An actual case example will best describe this diagnosis. An 18 year old male was diagnosed as having neurotic depression. He had been depressed like his mother had been since he was 12 years old when his father, who was an airline pilot, was killed in a crash. He had been told all his life that he would be just like his father. To the child this meant dying in a crash like his father, therefore he changed identification and became like his mother, who was depressed all the time. In this way he was able to avoid pilot training and prove that he was not like his father. In therapy he learned he did not have to be like either his father or mother. He could become himself.

Diagnoses at the Third Order: Physical Survival

The Walking Zombie Syndrome (WZS) or **Life-Death Syndrome** or **Death Complex** is the diagnostic title given to those having inner conflicts or perceived threats concerning physical life (Bryan, 1961b, 1962). Medical Hypnoanalysts have used this title (WZS) for several years and have become so used to it that it does not have an ominous air about it. However, many patients are frightened as much by this term as they are by "schizophrenia." Although "Zombie" aptly applies to many, "Death Complex" or Life-Death Syndrome is preferable to many other patients in this category. Suicides and suicide threats, as are many forms of depression and anxiety, are indications of WZS. This is an allusion to the fact that the individual has suffered a death-like or near death experience, physically or emotionally. In short, the unconscious mind has accepted the idea or the shock of death and, to some extent, has died a little. In other cases the threat of death has brought on an intense struggle to survive at the unconscious level; and this may manifest itself in a kind of compulsive or frantic activity. Many people with "Type A" behavior (as a waking diagnosis) are actually those with the death complex engaged in a life and death struggle (Scott, 1988). In some cases this is brought on by closely identifying with a loved one who has died.

Any form of perceived threat to the life may bring on the series of events leading to this syndrome. The ISE may be birth itself and this may be followed by such trauma as choking or drowning experiences, hemorrhaging, accidents, being locked in a closet, being lost (rural outdoors or in the city), hunger, surgery, being anesthetized, overhearing an authority figure refer to possible death, being "scared to death" etc. The experience may be realistic or perceived in fantasy or even come from the impact of a nightmare. But whatever is perceived in this manner has the potential of functioning in the series of events that lead to the Life-Death Syndrome and leaves an emotional scar in the memory system which must be reckoned with sooner or later if the patient is to get well.

This syndrome is evidenced in some patients by some degree of acceptance of the idea of death and is seen with some anorexics and passive, inactive and severely depressed people (who are mourning their own death or the death of another).

A slightly different aspect of this same system is seen in those patients who are putting forth a brave struggle to survive. As proof of life they may be frantically active at work or other ways, compulsive eaters, loud, or boisterous.

A third manifestation of this complex is exemplified by those who vacillate between being alive (and lively) or partly dead. These patients alternate in their behavior and sometimes are difficult to diagnose. The waking diagnosis may be manic depressive, but the underlying, dynamic diagnosis could well be the Walking Zombie Syndrome (Life-Death Syndrome).

Usually, at the unconscious level, there is a struggle going on with a part of the mind which is striving for survival, as if to say, "You really are alive and I will do something to prove it to you." Those patients who manifest this syndrome with a general demeanor of having accepted death already, betray this by their somber dress, lack of energy, speech, depression etc. This diagnosis may be evidenced by symptoms such as smoking and wheezing of asthma as unconscious proof of breathing (i.e. "alive"), obesity as proof of being healthy (i.e. "alive"), pain, (and other somatic symptoms) as evidence that one is still alive.

This is another way of recognizing the Freudian concept of the death instinct and the life instinct and how both instincts are present within the individual (Jones, 1961). When some aspect of the death instinct is prevailing it is recognized as the Life-Death Syndrome. The fear of dying - natural to the "normal" person - is not the same as the belief, subconsciously, that one has died. (For a discussion of Voodooism and walking zombies see Zuckerman, 1985.)

The Ponce de Leon Syndrome (PDL) (Bryan, 1964b; Fried, 1980). This is a more acceptable way, to the patient, of understanding and discussing immaturity. Ponce de Leon looked for the fountain of youth believing that if he could drink from it he would remain perpetually youthful. Figuratively, many individuals have drunk from the fountain of youth. The emotions therefore have failed to keep pace with the chronological age. This may be caused by certain trauma which have arrested the emotional progress of the child, or it may be caused by the deprivation of experiences and/or teaching which contribute to the emotional growth and progress of the child. At any rate there is an arrest of the emotional maturation process.

The symptoms of immaturity are manifested in many ways. Generally the processes of separation and individuation have not taken place sufficiently for the person to feel, talk, and act maturely.

Diagnoses at the Fourth Order: Socio-Economic Survival

At the fourth level diagnoses will apply to male/female relationships in the family unit. Marital diagnostic categories fall into this location. There are three diagnoses in this order: **Marital Maladjustment, Marital Neurosis, Neurotic Spouses**. Greater detail about these will be presented in Part Two of this book. **Marital Maladjustment** refers to conflicting behavior between spouses, usually due to misunderstanding and ignorance. The subjects of such conflicts are usually easily identifiable, consequently also easily treatable. Husband and wife are usually reasonably well adjusted psychologically and reasonably mature.

Marital Neurosis refers to those couples who have basically healthy personalities, but the interaction of the two together cause personality conflicts which disrupt the marriage. It is the relationship, rather than the individuals, which becomes neurotic. Unconscious factors are the ultimate source of the conflict and for the most successful treatment, such factors should be identified and adjusted.

Neurotic Spouses refers to the fact that one or both of the spouses were neurotic when they got married and the relationship simply aggravates the pathology in the personalities. These, too, need to be treated at the unconscious level in order to effect a successful relationship. Keep in mind that the neurotic spouses will be identified and diagnosed by any of the diagnoses at a lower level of priority. For example, a couple may be in the throes of separation or divorce and when underlying diagnoses are made one may have the Walking Zombie Syndrome and the other have the Ponce de Leon Syndrome. The first stage of treatment would involve curing these respective syndromes and the second stage be readjustment to each other as mature and stable personalities.

Diagnoses at the Fifth Order: Species Survival

The fifth order in life's priorities is species survival or sexual libido. Symptoms expressed at this level may simply be due to "maladjustment" and/or ignorance, and no dynamic factor is involved. Obviously, information and practice are all that's needed in treatment, and there are many sources for such guidance. In other situations, sexual problems are symptomatic of subconscious factors at one of the lower levels of life's priorities.

The first diagnostic category of this order is **Sexual Arrest**, (Bryan, 1971b; Note 4). This is an aspect of the **Ponce de Leon Syndrome** (PDL). When some traumatic event or maturational deprivation takes place during childhood of sufficient strength to effect the emotional (or sexual) growth of the child, she or he becomes arrested prematurely, i.e., emotional growth is slowed down or even frozen at that age level. The person's thinking and/ or actions become locked in at that level to such an extent that years later during adulthood, the thinking patterns and actions which accompany them, are characteristic of the child. Bryan (Note 4) has demonstrated that the "flasher," the man or woman who receives gratification by exposing himself, or herself, is really the child of 4 to 8 years old who is in effect saying, "you show me yours and I'll show you mine." The so-called "peeping tom" is in the same category.

Many cases of dyspareunia, vaginismus, orgasmic dysfunction, ejaculatory incompetence, secondary impotence (to use categories of the waking diagnosis) are actually due to PDL with Sexual Arrest (underlying diagnosis). With other persons, the UD will be found to be some phase of the relationship disorder, or the Walking Zombie Syndrome or an Identity Problem or Guilt Complex or Existential Vacuum.

When the dynamics are explored and treatment followed for the underlying or hypnotic diagnosis, a cure is generally effected.

The preceding are the primary underlying or hypnotic diagnoses. Usually any one of the diagnoses taken from DSM III or IIIR and viewed as a waking diagnosis will have an underlying hypnotic (dynamic) diagnosis in one of the above categories. To recognize the disorder in this way clarifies and simplifies the treatment process, and increases the cure rate.

The therapist should keep such possibilities in mind and take a careful case history, then, based on this, make a tentative diagnosis. Later the diagnosis can be checked by the word association test and dream analysis for verification or alteration of the diagnosis. As in the physician's treatment for physical ills, the laboratory testing is done to confirm or alter the diagnosis, so also with this procedure.

APPLYING THE PRINCIPLE OF THE DOUBLE DIAGNOSIS

A person may appear with a statement such as "I am depressed" and continues to describe the various aspects of depression in the many ways that they may be manifested. The waking diagnosis therefore would be "depression." The case history would point this up very clearly. The therapist recognizes that the symptom is above the fifth order, in the miscellaneous behavior level and would be on the alert from then on in the history taking for signs of disturbance at a more basic priority level.

The underlying cause of the person's depression may be due to severe guilt feelings for real or imagined sins (first order). Consequently, the pathology (and treatment) would be related to some aspect of the guilt complex.

Another example: The symptom might be "pre-orgasmic dysfunction" (the waking diagnosis). This, in turn, adds to the problem--the problem of "marital disharmony." Consequently, there is a compound waking diagnosis (WD). Previous therapy or experience has demonstrated that it is not due to ignorance on her part or the part of her partner. After taking the case history and examining the word association test along with the dream analysis, it is ascertained that the underlying diagnosis is the Walking Zombie Syndrome (WZS). The woman suffers from flattened affect in that she is unable to have deep emotional feelings about anything because at some time or another her unconscious mind accepted the idea of death, or she suffered death-like experiences (Bryan, 1961a). She, therefore, is locked in a life and death struggle at the unconscious level and is incapable of functioning and feeling sexually.

Just as there may be more than one waking diagnosis, there may also be more than one underlying (or hypnotic) diagnosis. If this is true, it must be recognized and therapy must be directed toward the resolution of the underlying and ultimate causes of the symptoms.

An example: A patient may be suffering from neurotic depression with suicidal impulses as the waking or symptomatic diagnosis. The underlying hypnotic diagnosis may reveal the Walking Zombie Syndrome, Ponce de Leon Syndrome and the Guilt Complex. The therapy required here would be to treat all three of these underlying causes, then the symptoms should disappear.

A more complex example of this is found in a case in which a woman suffered from neurotic depression as the waking diagnosis. The underlying diagnosis was Sexual Arrest. The woman was 45 years old and had difficulty "going out" (Agoraphobia). She would start for a destination and before arriving would turn around and return. She stated she would "like to go out more . . . and do what other women do" (unconscious reference to sex) but could not. Her sexual relations with her husband were unsatisfactory. Therapy revealed she was rejected by her mother and her father was alcoholic. She was seeking a father figure she never had. Intercourse with her husband was symbolic of intercourse with her father. This unsatisfactory, frustrating relationship with her husband drove her to extramarital relationships which brought on conflicting guilt feelings. The woman, in some respects, had an emotional level of the 8 year old (which was her age when her father died) and the physical need of a woman. She was relating in some ways to her husband as if he were her father. Analysis of these issues brought about a cure.

One other example will exemplify several principles discussed on the previous pages. A wife presented herself for therapy for depression. She had been deserted by her husband who later came in and participated in joint therapy. It was apparent immediately that she had the Ponce de Leon Syndrome, but the etiology to this was not immediately clear. Then when reference was made to having hemorrhaged seriously at the birth of her first baby to the extent that she almost died, it was obvious that the Walking Zombie Syndrome was involved. Due to the long standing nature of her flattened affect I suspected that there had to be at least one previous death experience, if not more. But nothing of that nature was mentioned when taking the case history. Then in a hypnotic session two previous threats of bodily harm and/or death became evident. One was at 9 years old (ISE) and one at 11 years old (SPE), thus the hemorrhage at the birth of her baby was a SIE. Having the Walking Zombie Syndrome at such an early age produced the Ponce de Leon Syndrome. Both factors contributed to her inability to express affection, companionship, and sexual responsiveness to her husband. An essential, critical factor in the analysis would have been missed had I not looked for an early ISE to the WZS. It was the WZS which contributed greatly to the PDL syndrome and both of these combined to form the compound underlying diagnosis, with a waking diagnosis of depression due to marital conflict. Incidentally, the husband was suffering severely due to the PDL syndrome.

SIMPLIFICATION OF TERMINOLOGY

Attention has already been called to the fact that many emotional illnesses are aggravated by well-meaning psychotherapists who use terminology in expressing the diagnosis which is frightening to the patient (Stuart, 1980) and frequently inhibits or even prevents a cure (Fried, 1980). Thus, unwittingly, the therapist may contribute to the patient's problem. Yet it must be recognized in our society that the patient is accustomed to having a label for his problem, and frequently asks the question, "What's wrong with me?". Consequently, some sort of explanation is called for. North (1985) suggests answering that question by simply using terms the patient uses. Consequently, the use of terms which can be accepted by the patient and explained to the patient will be helpful for both the therapist and the patient.

The terms Identity Problem, Separation Anxiety, Ponce de Leon Syndrome, Life-Death Syndrome are not frightening or discouraging to the patient. They aren't used until the evidence for their use is already so apparent to the patient that he/she will usually agree that the term fits. And then the assurance that they are completely curable is encouraging, even stimulating. When people have previously been told they would have to learn to live with a psychiatric condition, I have seen their eyes light up when informed they had one of the above and that it was curable.

CHILDHOOD HYPNOTIC EXPERIENCES AS THE SOURCE OF THE UNDERLYING DIAGNOSES

Frequently the cause of the patient's problem is due to a "negative suggestion" given to a child while in a spontaneous hypnotic trance. This means that when a person is in a hypnotic state, remarks made to that person, whether positive and constructive or negative and destructive, will have a strong influence later in life.

We have seen in the preceding pages that hypnosis is the focusing of all the concentration power on one subject with no distractions. Anytime the

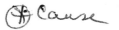

mind is in this high state of concentration, one is said to be in a hypnotic trance, which may be very deep or light, depending on the degree of concentration. Thus, any event which captures the attention puts a person in a hypnotic state.

The concentration powers of small children would indicate that by this definition of hypnosis, children are in a hypnotic state much of the time. This explains how they are able to learn so much in the first six years of life. The "repetition compulsion" applies here in that a part of the childhood learning process is the repetition of ideas, skills etc. This enables the child to learn. Furthermore, people who are being prepared for surgery, being treated by physicians, lectured to by parents, arguing with a spouse, making love, even watching TV are, to some extent or another, in a hypnotic trance.

Rebukes made at times like these, or imaginings of the mind made at times like these, make a deep impression on the memory system. It is for this reason that many neurotic problems originated while the individual was in a hypnotic state and while in it heard something that produced a lasting effect. A commonplace example can be seen when a mother repeats to a child such a phrase as, "You'll never be a good reader." Or the parent who says to a child: "You were an accident; we had already decided not to have any more children before you were born."

Such "negative hypnotic suggestions" do not have to be repeated to have a lasting effect on a child. In fact they are repeated frequently in the mind of the child, at times with accompanying misunderstandings, and thus chart the course for later emotional disorders. A threat that is only perceived can be just as traumatic as a genuine threat. The will to survive is in conflict with the threat coming from the environment and, depending on the level of priority where the threat is perceived, a defense system of some sort is set up in order to cope. The defense, in an effort to cope, in due time becomes the symptomotology. But the real battle is going on at a deeper level of the mind and this is where the cure has to take place.

SUMMARY OF HYPNOANALYSIS: THE SEVEN "R's"

Introduction

Previously, many who practice Medical Hypnoanalysis summarized the process by "The Five R's." They were: Relaxation, Realization, Re-

① Primary goal of Medical Hypnoanalysis

education, Rehabilitation and Reinforcement. I, personally, found it easier to explain to my patients that the hypnoanalytic process could be summarized by a two phase process: The Analytic Phase (which included the first three "R's"), and The Rehabilitation Phase (which included the last two "R's"). Although this was inadequate for clarity and completeness, it was functional. Balog (1985) proposed summarizing the hypnoanalytic process more completely by "Seven 'R's'." They fit into the two phase system, offering a more complete perspective, and are presented here in the two-phase framework.

The Analytic Phase

Rapport is obviously the first "R." It means "connection" or "relation" especially "harmonious or sympathetic relation." There are several different kinds of rapport, and the kind a given therapist uses depends upon his or her theoretical background. One point of view of some therapists who use paradoxical therapy, is the attitude of, "I'm not here to be your friend, I'm here to cure you."

Basically, the type of relationship the psychoanalyst has with the patient is that nondescript passive relationship which permits transference to take place as a therapeutic modality.

Neurolinguistic programming encourages an acute analysis of eye motions, face movements, and a meticulous response by the therapist to get in step with the patient. Although this system has a great deal to offer, some therapists feel this maneuvering is too mechanical or even hypocritical and are uncomfortable with it. Apparently some patients are also uncomfortable with this "mocking."

Client Centered Therapy and Reality Therapy emphasize the person centered therapist who can establish close relationships in order to conduct therapy.

All of these have their place, and for those therapists and patients who are compatible with these procedures they appear to be effective. In Medical Hypnoanalysis there is a slightly different approach to the relationship between clinician and patient.

A primary goal of Medical Hypnoanalysis is to assist the patient in identifying the original experiences and/or relationships which caused the problem in the beginning. When the patient can get in touch with the origin of the neurosis and through catharsis release pent up and unresolved emotion, a release takes place which starts the curative process.

A relationship with the patient, therefore, which is conducive to this identification of the original problem and its accompanying catharsis is the kind of rapport that is desirable.

Araoz (1985) calls attention to the fact that some kinds of rapport actually discourage this effective recognition of the inner awareness and true experience of what is happening inside of the patient. That when the interaction of the patient and therapist focuses verbally on the subject, it distracts from actually experiencing the problem. In fact, such verbalizing may increase resistance.

Those forms of therapy which focus on words and facts - that is the left brain processes - distract from impressions, interpretations and feelings which are right brain processes, and the real root of the problem. Consequently, rapport between the Medical Hypnoanalyst and the patient should be of the type which enables the analyst to lead the patient to a sensitive awareness of the inner self and past experiences which were crucial to the developing personality. Such a therapist should be kind and convey an attitude of non-judgmental receptivity to the revelation of the most sensitive subjects and deeds of anyone's life. This kind of openness can be felt by the patient if it is present in the personality of the therapist. Furthermore, the therapist should describe to the patient enough about the process in the beginning for the patient to have an idea of what age regressions are all about.

In order to accomplish treatment, the patient will have to make some journeys back to the past. For some patients this can be scary because it leads to the realm of death, threats, abuse, neglect, abandonment, and pain. He or she needs a loving and supportive companion with whom to make this journey. This, then, is the role of the therapist: a traveling companion on a difficult journey. This type of patient has a weak ego and, in some cases, may be near the brink of a psychotic break. Consequently the need for the "traveling companion" as a therapist.

Other patients who are not so delicate will progress with a slightly different type of rapport. They need a leader, in whom they have confidence, who will point out to them a course, which, though rough at times, leads them along the path to wellness. They will travel that path alone, facing the perils of the journey mostly on their own. In both types of cases the therapist is a "leader" who directs the patient to find the answers which have remained lost in the unconscious for a long time. Traits which are typical of a person-centered leader or facilitator are those traits which the patient must see in the analyst. He or she must be capable, knowledgeable, caring, concerned, compassionate, and directive. Some types of patients need a "permissive" type of direction, while others need more of an "active" type of direction. Whatever it takes to establish this kind of relationship early in the process between those personalities, is what is required.

Relaxation is the second "R." Generally we take this to imply hypnosis. We have seen earlier in this chapter that hypnosis traditionally has been induced by relaxation procedures. Indeed Edmonston (1981) equates hypnosis with relaxation. And, although this is generally true, we have already seen that there are exceptions.

Edmonston (1981) uses a variety of indicators such as EEG functioning, alpha and theta production, body temperature and other factors to demonstrate the validity of his claim, viz., that hypnosis is relaxation. Furthermore, we have seen earlier in the chapter that there is a relationship between the hypnotic state and right brain dominance. The relaxed or hypnotic state enables the patient to concentrate the mind which is so essential for the analysis to take place. The relaxed, concentrated mind also is the precursor to change.

Recognize the problem is the third "R." An anecdotal exhortation of Sir William Osler was "Listen to the patient. He is telling you the problem." The hypnoanalyst should be skillful enough to detect the diagnosis after hearing the patient's first three sentences. Obviously, the verbal and non-verbal communication of the patient is vitally important.

The therapist will observe first the clothing, walk, stance and seating position and manner of the patient. It is possible that before the patient says one word that such body language will betray the underlying diagnosis. Such non verbal communication may be manifestly childish or zombie like and speak as loudly as words the condition of the personality. Body language must be considered significant not only in the diagnosis, but in every phase of communication with the patient (Morris, 1977; Steere, 1982).

Of course, verbal communication is obviously the key to the conscious intentions of the patient's self revelations. First there is the manifest content, i.e. the obvious verbal message which consciously serves as the framework for the communication. Then there is what Langs (1978) calls the Type One derivatives, wherein the therapist listens for key words which bridge from the manifest to the latent content of the patient's communication.

Careful and meticulous listening is the key to recognizing the true problem. If the therapist listens only to the manifest content, ignoring dress, body language, latent content, and the bridges between manifest and latent content, he/she will be misled in most cases. Thus, by whatever means, it is essential that the clinician "recognize" the underlying diagnosis as soon as possible.

Remove faulty ideas is the fourth "R." The guts of any therapeutic process is to change. In the clinical environment, the person with the problem seeks a therapist in order to change something. And the first step in change is to remove the unwanted or undesirable behavior or feelings (symptoms). And the second step is to replace the undesirable with that which is more desirable . . . change!

This is the battle ground of the therapeutic armies. Attack and counter attack takes place in this no man's land and after repeated encounters each side claims "victory." The various schools of thought are want to define what change is and to what extent it is achieved by their own peculiar method of therapy. Are all patients to be grouped together and we clinicians define that they all need the same type of change? Does each patient need total personality restructure? or merely modification of one tidbit of behavior? or realignment of one relationship? or re-education on a subject? Are all changes to be made only at the conscious level? only at the unconscious level? or both? Can change of one behavior take place without effecting the total person to some extent? When a therapist sees progress made at one level when the symptom(s) is cured and yet knows that treatment is needed in other areas, what is he/she to do?

We therapists should do less in-fighting among ourselves and spend more energy on becoming better stocked with an armamentarium of diversified procedures which effectively achieve the goal of the individual patient as soon as possible. Of course there are a number of variables. These need to be client centered. We therapists must be at least as flexible as we ask our patients to be.

If the person's problems have roots at the unconscious level, then they must be traced there, identified, and removed. If they don't go that deep, then there is no need to spend time roaming around in a vast store house of memories searching for something that does not exist.

A fundamental principle of Medical Hypnoanalysis is that the patient's identified problem (symptom) is what is to be cured, and that is all. If, in the process of treatment, other problems or other goals appear and the patient wishes to add them to the list to be cured or achieved, well and good. Let this be clearly defined and the goal of therapy be restructured.

In achieving the first stage of change of a symptom which is not merely a bad habit or superficial behavior manifestation, identification of the

John A. Scott, Sr., Ph.D.

roots of the problem is necessary. This involves surveying the periods of infancy and childhood for relationships, trauma, deprivations, frustrations, and other sources of personality malformation. Investigating the various stages of growth (by whatever theoretical outline suits one) makes such an evaluation simpler.

Fried (1980 p.45) stresses that we deal with "impact insights." These "focus on the leftover, still active, still festering wounds that were made" in the person's earlier experiences. In order to save time, we do not need to deal with all of the past, but rather just those past experiences which relate to the identified problem. It is as if there is a thread connecting the presenting symptom to the remote source of that symptom, usually in childhood or infancy, and recognizing that connection at the emotional level is the key to change.

Two questions are immediately manifested in this pattern, viz., "How can those specific experiences (relationships) be easily and quickly identified?" and "Once the source is identified, what then?"

The answer to the first question is to take a careful case history followed by a word association test and perhaps analysis of one or more dreams. This prevents spending time ambling all over a lifetime searching at random for key experiences. A great deal of time is saved by this procedure.

The second question implies that more than insight is necessary to effect change. The emotion and the personal interpretation of the original event(s) on the part of the patient is necessary. This is why just a conscious, non-feeling recitation of a cause will not effect a cure. Many times patients will say in effect, "I know what the cause of this is, but that doesn't help." In rare instances they are right and do know the cause, and the reason they still have the symptom is that the cause and effect have not been rehearsed at the subconscious, feeling, right brain level. And that the misinterpretation or wrong judgment of the child at the time of the original event(s) has not been understood and reckoned with. Araoz (1985) refers to the "patient's own internal personality processes" and means the same thing.

Thus, to remove faulty ideas, the source must be identified at the emotional level. Since emotions are anchored in both body and mind, and effect each, they serve as a bridge from present mind-body symptoms back to the impact of the experience which started the symptom. When there is an original source, it must be reckoned with. Just as the only way to do away with a weed is to pluck it up by the roots, not just cut off the top.

The source experience must be adequately reckoned with. The several ways to do this will be dealt with in more detail later in explaining "process".

Essentially, the patient must reinterpret the causal experience so that there is a different explanation than the one that registered originally. Wrong thinking, or as Ellis (1962) says, "irrational ideas" are the foundation of neuroses. Some kind of procedure must correct the wrong ideas carried in the memory system from childhood.

Replace faulty ideas with accurate ideas is the fifth "R". Once those faulty ideas have been identified and corrected or removed, correct ideas or interpretations must be replaced. Insight now turns to the present. There is a place for working in the past, but the time comes to reckon with the present and the future. Patients can come to understand that they have been victims of circumstances and, through no fault of their own, they have suffered. But now that they understand, they can take charge of their lives and change the future. It is at this point where some principles of behavior modification may prove helpful. Wickramasekera (1976) describes how hypnosis may be used to manipulate cognition. Furthermore, it is at this juncture in therapy where operant conditioning, aversion therapy or systematic desensitization may be utilized with hypnosis. All kinds of situations can be visualized and rehearsed in hypnosis.

If clients are immature, they are helped to grow. If they have an Identity Problem, they acquire a sense of selfhood and dignity. If they have been walking zombies, they come alive with all which that implies. If they have lived in an existential vacuum, they develop a concept of meaning and values. The ability to share in more mature interpersonal relationships will replace dependent, inadequate relationships.

One change will bring about other changes in a kind of ripple effect. One becomes a more "fully functioning person" (Rogers, 1977) by being decisive, feeling capable and confident, perhaps making adjustments in the environment with circumstances and persons. Drug use by prescription or recreation may be eliminated. There is an improvement in self-esteem. Greater maturity will be evidenced by self-discipline, concern for others, consistency in one's ethical/moral behavior etc. Freedom from anxiety, depression, hatred, frustration will be more manifest.

Such change is sometimes slow due to habit and resistance, but the hypnoanalytic process can facilitate change more rapidly than many expect.

The Rehabilitation Phase

The analytical process comes to a point where the experiences that caused the problem have been identified emotionally and factually in a cause and

∆ benefits

effect relationship. This is clear to the patient and to the therapist. The therapist then records a summary approximately ten or fifteen minutes long called the personal tape. This includes a summation of the patient's problem, word association test, dream analysis, and the primary causal events or relationships and the reinterpretation of such. The tape concludes with a positive outlook for future growth and change, readjustments etc. Rehabilitation, as the Second Phase of hypnoanalysis, now begins.

Rehearsal of change is the sixth "R". Hypnosis continues to be the primary tool as one looks ahead to the future instead of to the past. During the earlier stages of therapy positive and constructive elements of the patient's personality and experiences were recognized and identified. If not, it should be done by this stage in process. Always, or nearly always, when the patient fixes on the painful symptom(s) there is a way to call attention to the opposite good or healthful feeling and identify that. Therapist and patient need to spend some time calling up good feelings in the imagination if not from actual experience.

During the period of rehabilitation, visualization of desirable feelings and actions takes place. Rehearsing experiences in the environment and with the persons that are part of the patient's life amounts to a "dress rehearsal" of what will actually be taking place in the near future. In addition, positive suggestions on expected feelings and attitudes are given; education on needed subjects presented and readjustment with significant others is encouraged.

Reinforce by regular practice is the seventh "R." Rehearsal leads to practice. Many patients, like a child learning to walk, will stumble some at first. Others learn to walk almost immediately. Some patients, however, continue to have resistance, are fearful, hesitant, unsure of themselves. Rehearsal may require relying on the help and encouragement of significant others in the relationship. It depends on the ego strength of the patient. Positive suggestions for strengthening the ego must be repeated.

Most therapists agree that when wrong behavior and feelings have been prevalent for years, reinforcement by regular practice is essential to maintain good emotional health. For a time the old feelings and attitudes have a way of persisting in the patient, like an enemy lurking at the door, and must be constantly repulsed for a long time. To reinforce is to strengthen. Some patients have a flight into wellness and drop therapy too soon. One should guard against this. Thus, careful evaluation by the therapist will be necessary in order to prevent premature cessation of the relationship. Tapering off is necessary and a request by the therapist for the patient to return "no matter how good you feel" for further strengthening is highly desirable.

SUMMARY AND CONCLUSION

A great deal of material is brought up in this chapter, all of which could be further expanded. In fact for a person to practice hypnoanalysis successfully it must be expanded. This presentation should be looked upon as an outline, and as such many details from various theoretical perspectives could be added for greater clarity. It is becoming apparent to the reader by now that Medical Hypnoanalysis is composed of theoretical and philosophical concepts held in common by several theoretical perspectives. In one sense of the word, many of the concepts have been utilized to a degree in other therapeutic modalities at one time or another. However, there will be in future chapters, as there have been in this chapter, some ideas and practices which are unique to Medical Hypnoanalysis. This will become obvious in due time.

First, in this chapter, "hypnosis" as a tool was discussed. As such it was described on a foundation of activity which involves trances at three levels: the relaxed trance, the alert trance, the spontaneous trance. The common denominator to all three types is the concentration of the mind. When the mind is concentrated it permits all suggestions to have a higher voltage or impact on the memory system, thus producing longer lasting and/or more serious consequences.

Secondly, a few principles of psychoanalytical theory were presented. Historically, hypnoanalysis has been closely related to psychoanalysis and thus shares some concepts in common with that therapeutic procedure. These common roots are recognized even though Medical Hypnoanalysis is clearly an offshoot and now includes other therapeutic concepts and practices.

In spite of the traditional tension between the psychoanalytical and the behavioral schools of thought, Medical Hypnoanalysis provides a ground for some degree of combination of procedures. Granted, the marriage is not a close one and there are many instances where there can be no union. However, methods which have had as much support and success as these two diverse procedures, must have something to offer to a sick public. Hypnosis provides that common ground.

Medical Hypnoanalysis utilizes the so-called "medical model." The principles of this inherent concept have been around a long time in the curative process and continue to be propagated in the medical and dental schools of the world. Since many from these disciplines later utilize hypnosis, it stands to reason that they will adapt readily to the psychological concept of the medical model as well. No wonder, then, that physicians and dentists, as well as psychologists, find a basic compatibility with this framework of treatment for neurotic disorders. Thus, the basics of this methodology have been outlined in the foregoing pages.

The preceding discussion of the rank order of life's priorities and how this conception facilitates a grasp of emotional disorders is not found elsewhere. The psychological atmosphere historically has been resistive to this kind of arrangement of priorities but I am persuaded that there is more of a compatible mood abroad in the land today. But whether it is among therapists is not so important as whether therapists recognize these instinctual priorities to be present in the people they treat.

Another innovative factor in this chapter has been the suggestion of the alteration of diagnostic principles. Most authorities agree that the traditional nomenclature has a number of disadvantages, but little has been done about it. The idea of the double diagnosis with its waking diagnosis and the underlying diagnosis is new to the psychiatric world, but has been around long enough in Medical Hypnoanalysis to be found very useful. Along with it a new list of simplified diagnostic terms brings hope for greater clarity to the patient, if not to the clinician. In addition a few remarks have been made concerning the relationship of childhood experiences to these underlying diagnostic categories.

Finally, in this chapter, an outline of the complete course of Medical Hypnoanalysis has been presented with the title, "The Seven 'R's' of Medical Hypnoanalysis." Naturally, much could be added, but as I said, the whole chapter is a mere outline of the theory of an entire treatment system. However, as in the principle of projective tests, every therapist who reads this and the following chapters will both project and reflect on the subject matter and, with some synthesizing, surely come out with many concepts useful for helping a sick person get well.

Enough on theory. Let's go to practice.

CHAPTER 3

CONSULTATION AND CASE HISTORY

φ Waking & underlying diagnosis

It is vitally important for the quick and effective treatment of any emotional disorder to have specific goals in mind during the treatment. In this respect, hypnoanalysis continues to follow the medical model as pointed out in the preceding chapter. That is, the therapist determines what the specific diagnosis is and then follows prescribed treatment procedures in order to cure that specific disorder. Consequently, it is necessary, as soon as possible in the encounter with the client, to determine not only the waking diagnosis but the underlying diagnosis as well.

The problem with many psychotherapeutic procedures is that the client or patient is allowed in every session to discuss at random any subject describing the various pressures or discomforts he experiences from day to day. This takes up much time, inhibits the poor from getting therapy, and permits the patient to reinforce his defenses to cover over the real underlying or subconscious problem (if there is one), and thus simply prolongs the treatment (Mowrer, 1961, Harris, 1969). Furthermore, the average person, knowing very little of the psychodynamics of emotional disorders, is apt to overlook much pertinent data about his history and personality. Therefore, in order to get to the heart of the problem quickly and to move toward the desired goal, it is necessary for the therapist to take charge of the interview as soon as possible. Of course, catharsis and ventilation are vitally important. There is a place for these, but they should not be overdone to the neglect of the real underlying problem.

The skilled therapist will consider it important to learn immediately as much about the patient as possible, even to the extent of training the office receptionist to make careful notes of her first phone conversation with the patient if something other than a routine appointment is discussed. The receptionist's conversation should be short and questions are to be referred to the therapist at the time of the initial appointment. In one sense of the word, therapy starts when the patient calls on the phone. Furthermore, a kind of therapy is taking place when the patient walks into the office and talks to the receptionist or assistant by giving initial, routine information pertaining to address, age, marital status, next of kin, etc.

The receptionist is urged to write down observations made while the patient is in the waiting room such as conversation that takes place, chance off-hand remarks, mannerisms, punctuality of arrival, who accompanied the patient and the like. In response the receptionist should give positive, constructive suggestions to the client by way of reassure that there are things that can be done to solve the problem, that there procedures that will be helpful, and that assistance is in the offing.

The Initial Contact in the Office

The highly skilled therapist will be a stickler for detailed meticulous observation of body language, off-hand remarks, jests, turned phrases, metaphors, "Freudian slips," hesitations, and even sighs and coughs. These are all means by which the therapist may know patient's subconscious mind which is the seat of the problem. It is for this reason that the office personnel should be trained in the basics of observation and note taking.

To aid in securing pertinent data from the patient a complete case history form was composed for this type of therapy (a copy is attached as Appendix A). When the patient arrives at the office for the first appointment, the receptionist secures basic information and records it at the top of page one. She/he secures the age, address, birthdate, birthplace, marital status, next of kin, employer, phone, etc.

As the receptionist fills in such vital statistics, anything unusual should be noted with a red pen in the margin or at the bottom of the sheet. For example, frequently the client will ask, "What do you mean by the next of kin?" The receptionist should reply, "Whomever you consider to be the next of kin."

If a man or woman, married and having a home, puts down the next of kin as mother or father this may indicate an unusually close attachment to parents. This note will, of course, be evaluated along with other data by the therapist. Similar care for details should continue.

After the basic data are secured by the assistant, the emotional state of the patient, if unusual at all, should be noted. It should also be noted on the form who comes with the patient, and whether any unusual comments were made by the patient or observers, whether there is consistency in the stated age and the date of birth, etc. For example, if a husband is named as the identified patient and his wife takes over in answering questions on basic data, this is significant.

The use of colored pens in note-taking by the therapist is unusual, but most helpful. A uniform system is not only helpful in the therapist's own review of his notes, but is also helpful in case of referral or consultation with colleagues. The words of the patient are put down with a blue pen. What the assistant or the therapist thinks in evaluating the client, but does not tell him/her, is put down in red at the time those thoughts occur. What some other member of the family says about the client should be put down in black. Green is used for remarks made by the therapist to the patient. In this way, anyone, having to refer to the notes after they have grown cold, is aware of what was said or thought and by whom. This routine soon becomes automatic for the therapist and pays dividends in efficiency with review and analysis in the long run.

It is also vitally important in the initial conversations which the client has with the assistant and with the therapist, that the exact words of that person be recorded. The first consultation is such that it is as if the patient has been having an emotional build-up for some time, like waters accumulating behind a dam. Now this visit to the office of someone who will give help affords the patient an opportunity to let the stored up material burst forth, and the words selected to reveal his/her inner feelings. Information thus obtained is vitally important in establishing an underlying diagnosis. When the assistant gives the history form to the therapist, a verbal and written report of observations should be given.

A glance at the history form in the Appendix will demonstrate that the various sub-sections of the case history form are numbered and lettered for easy cross-reference.

Case History

Section I. Present Illness. In keeping with most patients' propensity for more than usual self-revelation at the first session, the therapist, before anything is said, should make observations concerning the general appearance and demeanor of the client. Here a knowledge of body

Make diagnosis from appearance + body language

language is essential. Observations and evaluations of the client's dress, appearance, posture, nervousness or lack of it, position in the chair, voice and such like should be made and noted in red on the form. Frequently a tentative diagnosis can be made before a word is said because the patient has betrayed by dress, posture, mannerisms etc. what the underlying problem really is.

After this has been noted on the form, the first question is with regard to medicines or drugs that have been taken that day. If there is any doubt about the purpose of the medication, the therapist should ask why it has been prescribed and notes made. The purpose of this question is to have an understanding of the client's condition before discussing the problem and the background details. One might have reason to be skeptical about the body language and answers given by a person who is under the influence of drugs or alcohol. As stated before, this observation must be considered and evaluated in light of other data.

The best way to get the patient started with the history is to ask, "What is your problem?". Then, as the patient begins to talk, it is essential to write down the exact words used, and if necessary, ask the patient to pause, so that every word may be recorded. Furthermore, a notation should be made of body language, shifts, sighs, clearing of the throat, nervous coughs, and such like with the red pen. The therapist should become so skilled that in most cases he can diagnose the patient's underlying problem by carefully observing the body language and writing down the exact words of the first three sentences the patient utters. Careful observation and note taking at this time can save the therapist hours of analysis time in the future.

This is the client's opportunity for ventilation and catharsis. And, as a usual thing, the client, after a few minutes' time, will become repetitious. Some patients stop too quickly and it is necessary for the therapist to ask a few probing questions in order to clarify the problem. Here is where a statement of the symptoms and the waking diagnoses may be determined. At the same time, by careful observation and by intuitive thinking, the therapist may be able to determine the underlying diagnosis. Usually, the basic information as to the problem and the clarification of the problem can be made on page 1 of the history form within five to fifteen minutes. However, when the problem is long and complicated or the patient is particularly verbose, more of the history can be taken on page 12 which is the back page of the form. At any rate, when the patient has expressed the situation sufficiently, the therapist then goes to page 2.

It should be stressed that the intent of a detailed form for taking a case history is used in order to gain, in two hours time (more or less), a broad over-all general view of who the patient is, along with enough background information to gain a sense of the direction that the therapy will possibly take. It should be stressed that much of the material (perhaps even most of it) will not be used in the hypnotic sessions which will follow, but those areas indicating emotional trauma will be the subjects of hypnotic age regressions for evaluation. English and Pearson (1963) state that history-taking is a rapid means of studying and knowing the particular individual, his needs, how he has met them, and his resulting conflicts.

In order to ascertain the present condition of the patient now ("N") in comparison to the condition when worst ("W") and feeling best ("B"), there are three circles at the bottom of page 1. On a rating scale "0" equals feeling best and "10" equals feeling worst, insert the numbers the patient suggests and put the date beside the respective circle. This is helpful to therapist and patient for comparison and clarification both now and later.

At this point the therapist states he/she has questions about every area of the patient's life and asks "Is there any area that you would rather not be questioned about?".

The purpose is to prepare the patient for a wide variety of questions, some of which are intensely personal. The patient may hesitate and sometimes state that he or she will say so if there is some doubt about answering some questions, or replies, "I'll let you know." There are some patients who do not want to be questioned about certain subjects. This is a real clue at the beginning of the interview as to where the area of resistance lies, or even the ultimate root of the problem. The therapist does not need to argue the issue at this point; he will note to himself that sooner or later the subject will have to be approached, but will exercise care in bringing up a sensitive subject. However, deductions may be made about the strength of the person's ego, areas of resistance, and other factors concerning the problem by asking this question early in the history.

Under I,c. in the history form, "Duration of Illness," one should ask for the date when the problem started. This is vitally important. When a specific date or period can be given (at least the year) then obviously sooner or later the therapist seeks to determine what else happened on, or immediately before, that date that precipitated the onset of the problem. The point of this question is to secure the Symptom Producing Event if at all possible and as soon as possible. Of course the therapist has to evaluate carefully what the patient says about the origin of the problem, because many patients have repeated to themselves and others that a specific event

*obesity - the
lie*

brought on the symptom(s). Sometimes they are accurate, and other times they are repeating a set of defenses which will have to be altered in time.

Some patients cannot give definite answers and so the reply is that it has been coming on gradually for a long time. Then the therapist inquires when the problem first started or when the client became aware of having a problem. The second date is then secured: "When did the problem get noticeably worse?" This is particularly useful in cases of alcoholism, drug use, obesity, marital problems and the like. There are other situations where the client replies that the problem has been present all of his life - frequently a clue to birth trauma being the Initial Sensitizing Event. Of course, in some cases the client makes the situation much easier by stating that the problem has been present ever since such and such a year when such and such an event took place. That event will be the Symptom Producing Event in most cases.

Questions on the case history form continue:

d. "Conditions Causing Variations." If it can be known what conditions make the problem worse, or, on the other hand, what conditions make the problem better, it will help in determining the cause and cure.

e. "What would you do if cured that you cannot do now?" Information at this point is helpful in determining whether or not there is possible secondary gain from the continuation of the symptoms. The therapist should be on the alert. For example, if the patient says, "Well, if I were cured I could go back to work," it might indicate that the illness continues because the client does not want to return to work. Another case indicating secondary gain would be that a woman might say, "If I could get over this situation, I could get pregnant and have a baby." Outwardly she may talk about the desirability of having a baby, but subconsciously there may be fears of childbirth or reluctance to having children, and thus, secondary gain encourages the continuation of the problem. Of course, this is taking place at the unconscious level, but the therapist must be alert to this kind of condition for future reference.

g. "Present occupation," etc. This section is intended to determine whether a person is satisfied with his/her occupation. Frustration or anxiety concerning one's work is often a contributing factor to the continuation of the problem. Questions in the manner listed here are helpful in evaluating this issue.

Section II. Past History. The next subject in the printed history form is the medical history. One of the purposes of taking the past medical history is to determine, by asking specific questions about a variety of childhood and adult illnesses, if the client has had any negative experiences concerning the illness. The most serious such experience would be a brush with death (real or perceived).

It should be determined if the client has had high enough fever to be delirious, if there has been choking, coughing, drowning or strangling experiences of any sort, if there has been the threat of death, either in the patient's mind or in the mind of the parents or relatives who watched over him/her. Frequently, in childhood, trauma and/or fright become Initial Sensitizing Event(s) which set the child up for future problems.

It is not so much the fact of the event as the impression or interpretation of that event to the mind of the child which makes it traumatic enough to have after effects severe enough to contribute to the present symptoms. Information in this paragraph may indicate the presence of the Walking Zombie Syndrome very early because there has been a "death-like experience" which has left an emotional scar on the mind.

In other cases, a series of illnesses may encourage a relationship between mother and child which promotes and encourages the Ponce de Leon Syndrome. Many a sickly child has been discouraged from maturing by the need for continual nursing and attention by the mother or mother substitute. Also, in this paragraph, one will find a number of illnesses such as colitis, ulcers, hypertension, and the like, which can indicate earlier anxiety states. It is important therefore, when going down this list to determine to what extent one had the disease, serious or not, complications or not, when the illness occurred, and how it was handled by parents or physician.

The same principle applies also to surgery and/or hospitalizations. One would be surprised how frequently patients who are middle age or older, have had Initial Sensitizing Events through circumcision or tonsillectomies, where an ether mask was used in anesthesia. Early excretory problems in children may indicate problems of adjustment in the relationship with ones mother, etc. Inasmuch as the "child is father to the man" impressions, trauma, relationships, deprivation of needs, early conditioning, reactions to frustration, and such like, need to be recognized by the therapist - and the sooner the better in the therapy. Details in this area may be reviewed in such works as Bowen (1978), Mahler, Pine and Bergman (1975), English and Pearson (1963), Saul (1980).

Medical history is vitally important because of the integration of body, mind, and soul. This case history form, therefore, takes into account this complex integration of the human personality, and, by doing so, enables the careful therapist to investigate the various facets of the foundations of the personality as soon as possible.

C. "Mental States Exam" at the bottom of page 2 is for the personal use of the therapist in making his/her own psychiatric observation of the patient. Likewise, the questions for "Type A" personality are for the therapist to use where applicable.

Section III. Family History. The purpose of asking the patient at this point if there were other family members who had critical illnesses which are listed here is to determine whether the presence of these other illnesses in the family, when he or she was at an early age, was an adverse influence. The patient's unconscious mind, in most cases, selects the symptoms which he has and frequently these same symptoms were seen in other family members at an early age. Furthermore, inquiring about diseases that could be either crippling or fatal will bring out traumatic influence. Such diseases would be cancer, tuberculosis, heart disease, and the like. Other relatives, such as grandparents, who might be crippled in the home with arthritis, tuberculosis, or diabetes, may call for the child's giving way to invalid relatives, by loss of love and attention from parents, giving up a room, or by being forced into a relationship that is repressing or threatening. While one child may take such upsetting conditions in stride, another may be traumatized. The same principle applies to the presence of an alcoholic in the household.

An example of how asking specific and detailed questions, such as these, can influence the case, is that of a youth who, as a child of seven, set fire to a large field and his father died in his arms of a heart attack while trying to put it out. This traumatic event would not have come out, at least not very early in the therapy, had he not been asked specific questions about childhood experiences and accompanying dates or ages.

The next significant question on the case history form is whether the childhood was happy or unhappy, and where it was spent. In answer to where it was spent, information will be helpful, particularly in marriage cases, to know something of the socioeconomic background. The one answer, happy or unhappy childhood, generally speaking, is a very important indication of the length of time the overall therapy will take. Clearly, an unhappy childhood will indicate a longer period in treatment than with the person who was happy and content in childhood. The therapist should keep in mind while taking the history that, at the conclusion, he or she will need to formulate a concept of approximately how long the therapy will take so as to set a flat fee where this is desirable.

Getting the father's name, age, health status and occupation all reveal something of significance about the man of the house when the child was growing up. The socioeconomic level is important in cases of marriage counseling, even if not in individual therapy. Age and health can tell something about the kind of relationship the father had with the child. In securing information on what sort of person the father was in relationship to the client, it is important to get the information pertaining to whether the father was affectionate or not, whether he was present and gave much companionship or not, the kind of discipline administered, and whether he was the dominant parent and provided leadership, or whether the mother was the more dominant figure in the family. Other general feelings and impressions pertaining to the father will give leads on what the male pattern of conduct was in the family. The same kind of information should be secured next on the mother. It is helpful to ask the patient to take herself or himself back to childhood and describe the parents from that perspective. I say something like this, "Put yourself back in childhood for a moment and tell me, from the standpoint of the child, what you saw your father to be like. . . how did you interact?"

It should be mentioned here that in taking an outline of the case history in this way, one is interested in getting only the high points or allusions to the significant incidents at this time. A brief notation made elsewhere on the case history form or on an additional sheet of paper should list those incidents in the patient's life which should be investigated later in detail when the patient is hypnotized. It may be necessary to tell the patient "I do not need the details of that incident at this point. We will get them later," and then move on to the next subject.

Some hypnoanalysts do not "direct" the therapy by citing the relationships and/or the experiences which are suspected of contributing to the symptomatology. They prefer to let the patient lead the therapy to those underlying events which started the problem by means of the so-called "affect bridge." This is a satisfactory method sometimes, but should not be used exclusively to the neglect of checking out those events which, in the mind of the therapist, are likely to have contributed to the symptoms. The patient usually does not know the chain reaction of contributing factors and in most situations does not even remember the Initial Sensitizing Event. In many cases, where the therapy outcome is a failure, it is due to leaving too much of the dynamics up to the patient.

To illustrate this principle, we may consider that a female patient has almost casually referred to the fact that her parents divorced when she was

John A. Scott, Sr., Ph.D.

5 years old. There is no show of emotion. She has probably told this many times. But the therapist realizes there could be a great deal of repression of emotion regarding such an incident, consequently the incident, date, and patient's age are noted on a list which will be used as a basis for age regressions later in hypnosis. The therapist then continues with the case history, noting other "suspicious" events on the same list. Then, later, during the ensuing therapy sessions the patient "re-lives" these "suspicious" events while hypnotized, enabling the repressed feelings to be given up and the trauma, for what it really was, to be made evident. In this way a true catharsis can take place. We shall see in a subsequent chapter the value of securing the appropriate emotions which accompanied the traumatic event(s).

In continuing with the history, the next information in the family history is the kind of relationship that existed between mother and father. Obviously, strife, separation, and divorce will make an impression and have a possible influence over the child's personality development. Discipline, whether too strict, too lenient, or inconsistent will be a determining factor in such disorders as guilt, compulsiveness, and anger. Likewise, how the child is loved or not loved strongly controls that child's adult responsiveness. Furthermore, the kind and manner of communication and problem solving techniques influences the child's ability regarding these important aspects. If there has been a separation or divorce, the same type of information should be secured about step-parents.

Next in order, the therapist secures information concerning siblings. Obviously it is significant if the client is an only child, but it is equally important to secure information as to the patient's place in rank order with other siblings. The ordinal position, whether oldest, middle, or youngest, is significant as one of the determining factors in the personality of the patient as is the type of relationship the client had with those siblings (Dempster, 1964; Forer, 1976; Hoopes & Harper, 1987; Kemper, 1966; Schachter, 1959).

Hoopes and Harper (1987), in an impressive publication, stress that the sibling relationship in the family is a system within a system and must be evaluated as such. Some psychotherapists err in seeking primarily a series of traumatic experiences as the sole pattern of conditioning in most or all emotional disorders. One or a series of belittling experiences in sibling interaction may set the foundation for adult disturbances. Evaluation of birth order roles and sibling patterns is essential in individual and marital therapy.

Age and sex differences are equally important. It should be stressed that the kind of transference the patient has with the spouse as well as with the therapist is, in part, dependent on the relationship with siblings and parents as a child.

The final question in this section of the history relates to knowledge concerning the mother's pregnancy and birth. Inasmuch as the birth trauma is frequently the Initial Sensitizing Event in the analysis, it is advantageous to learn as soon as possible if there is cause to suspect this. Many patients have been told about birth problems and at least are consciously aware that there were problems. Such knowledge justifies including an age regression back to birth to check out the significance to the patient. Subconscious clues to the significance of the birth trauma may come in the form of the use of words such as "stuck" "choke", "coming out", "cave", "tunnel", "all my life", "ever since the beginning" etc. Since the uterine and birth experiences are so important, an entire chapter (7) is devoted to the technique of age regressions to birth.

Section IV. Sexual History. Since people become so intently emotional on this subject, and since it plays such a significant background in impressions, trauma, guilt, marital relationships, and such like, it is vitally important that the therapist inquire about every aspect of the person's sexual behavior and experiences.

Several aspects of sexual history taking have also been emphasized by Masters and Johnson (1970). Some are:

1) Recognize that sexual malfunction may be the symptom of psychological pathology or the malfunction itself may be all there is to the problem.
2) History taking should involve specific details of unsuccessful sexual relationships and trauma, while, at the same time, revealing what is the pattern of typical sexual behavior.
3) History taking must be detailed and specific.
4) In history taking, information gleaned from sexually oriented questions must be correlated with other aspects of the person's experience and should be viewed as a part of total human existence.
5) When sexual behavior is altered, the person's social and moral value system must correspond with the change in behavior if it is to be successful therapy in the long run.

The first area of inquiry should be the early sexual incidents. Questions are asked about the time when the child, between the ages of four or five and eight or nine, has a natural curiosity about his own body and the body of the opposite sex. Efforts to satisfy such natural curiosity expressed in childhood play frequently lead to harsh lectures or punishment from adults which influence the child concerning sexuality the rest of his life. Sometimes the actual incident is a very natural childhood expression of curiosity, but what the parent makes of the incident may be quite significant in the child's personality. Furthermore, there are more traumatic sexual incidents between children and adults than the average person is aware of, and unless the therapist makes specific inquiries about these, they could be delayed in being exposed during the therapy sessions, if they ever are. Specific questions should be asked. It is also important as one progresses with the history to get ages and dates of specific events.

Another question concerns puberty--what age it was reached, and sources of sexual information which the child secured about this period. It is well known that sexual information, secured in frank and open conversations with the parents, is stabilizing (Harper, 1971). It is also important to secure information about the patient's feeling, concerning masturbation, practices of it, guilt feelings, and such like. In my opinion, the adolescent period is second only to birth as the most critical juncture in a person's life. It is the second birth and all data pertaining to this period should be treated as significant and properly evaluated.

Next, information concerning premarital sexual relationships, impressions, feelings, guilt, pregnancies (either had or caused), and such like, will come out by asking questions in this area. Getting "all of the gory details" may not be necessary. One need not be voyeuristic in gathering this information. However, finding traumatic events, embarrassing moments or other life changing events is relevant. These areas are taboo and many patients will be thankful for the opportunity to discuss them.

In cases of marital friction it is important to check on practices which the couple engage in sexually, how they feel about them, whether they are frustrated about such practices, antagonized by them, or in conflict with each other over them. This includes positions and practices in intercourse, oral sex, etc. It is not so much what is practiced that is important, as it is how the couple feels about it, and whether it is a source of sexual frustration, conflict, or guilt. This same principle holds true by inquiring concerning experiences outside of what most consider normal (Johnson, Note 34).

An inquiry should be made to ascertain if the male has had intercourse with a prostitute, or if the female feels that she has been, to some degree, at any time, rewarded or paid for sexual relationships. There is a surprisingly high incidence of wives who feel that their husbands make prostitutes out of them by rewarding them for sex. On other occasions, some women use sex in this way in order to manipulate their husbands.

It is likewise important to find out if either male or female has problems relating to having an orgasm, whether it requires an unusually long time or special manipulation in order to secure this, the conditions under which it is secured, lack of sexual arousal, and frequency of sexual relationships. Not only will these specific questions about the details of their relationship bring out information which contributes to the relationship that the husband and wife maintain in general, but incidents and feelings which lie buried and unexpressed, yet which cause resentment, may be exposed by this line of questioning. Attention should be called to the fact that there is a proneness on the part of the patient to hide or cover up incidents of guilt or severe embarrassment. Consequently, such incidents may not be revealed to the therapist unless the therapist specifically asks the questions (Johnson, Note 24).

Experience or feelings about extra-marital sexual intercourse obviously have a great deal to do with guilt feelings and with the marital relationship. Experiences in premarital or extra-marital encounters influence the kind of response that one will make to one's marriage partner. Here resentments and regrets may be very significant in understanding the total relationship. It should be kept in mind that in history taking, it is not essential to get a complete record of the details of sexual trauma, but it is significant at this point to secure allusions to the specific events. The patient can be assured that he does not need to go into the details at this time, but that they will be secured later. By this procedure the patient is prepared to reveal the details some time later but does not feel pushed to do so presently, thereby gradually the patient comes to realize that anything of significance may be freely discussed. Such a procedure enables the patient to feel more comfortable in answering when further inquiry is made concerning traumatic incidents, periods of impotence, non-orgasmic response, or nymphomania. In the event that some sexual information is being withheld, it should be asked if there has been any other significant sexual event that has not been revealed so far in the interview.

The sex history is concluded by inquiring about the number of pregnancies that the male has caused. Premarital pregnancies, had or caused, may be quite significant in the patient's personality. Males frequently put unwelcome pressure on a woman to have an abortion. Here information is secured concerning miscarriages, abortions, births, and unwanted pregnancies. It should be noted whether pregnancies were planned or accidental, when the birth took place, sex of the child, feelings about the pregnancy and the birth, as well as any significant physical or emotional problems in conjunction with the birth. Note the date of marriage and the date of birth. This gives a means of cross checking as to whether the person or persons got married because the woman was already pregnant (See Appendix A, case history form p. 4).

Section V. Psychological History. The first element here is to ask if the patient, before starting to school, had incidents of sleep-walking, nightmares, or repeated fears. Obviously, the intent of this question is to determine the amount of disturbance, as nearly as possible, that the child underwent in the first five or six years of ifs life. The patient may not remember much from this consciously, but there may be clues that should be listed for further investigation when the patient is relaxed and open minded. The patient might say something like this: "I don't remember it, but my parents did say that I walked in my sleep a lot when I was a small child." This may give a clue as to the amount of anxiety during this period of time (Rubottom, Note 5).

The next question in this section concerns the age of starting to school and whether the child was happy or not in school. Certainly a favorable response is that the child was happy and enjoyed school. If not, there may be leads as to the degree of anxiety suffered either at school or at home during these years (Rubottom, Note 5).

Specific questions may be asked at this point concerning how the patient got along with teachers, fellow students, principal, and others during the school age period. Were there failures, disciplinary problems, and other events related to the school experiences which would be vital in determining the personality development? Here is a good place to find out if the person had friends as a child, and particularly if one had a close friend who served as a confidant. This helps to ascertain the probabilities of a successful marital relationship as well as give an indication as to whether the therapy may be short or long term (Sifneos, 1987).

A catch-all kind of question comes at this point with inquiry into accidents, deaths, illnesses, high fevers, operations, embarrassing moments, emotional incidents, sex habits, or any other possible traumatic incidents during the school age period. Such incidents may have happened directly to the patient or they may have happened to other members of the family but would have effected the patient in one way or another. The therapist must watch for unconscious clues in inflection, body movement, and non-verbal language, in order to evaluate what the patient might list at this point. Likewise, the therapist should be aware that the patient may tend to minimize some embarrassing incident simply because of hesitancy to "reveal all" at this time. Or the patient may have suppressed painful experiences from childhood. Many children are able to practice repression to a very strong degree. Consequently, what is revealed at this point may appear to be of only minor importance by the way the patient words or describes the incident, but it could very well be like the tip of the iceberg, wherein one sees a very small amount at the surface but deep underneath there exists a severely traumatic event (Bryan and Rubottom, Note 5).

Section VI. Habits. The first has to do with addictions of any sort--alcohol, tobacco, drugs, coffee, any other beverage that a person is "hooked" on to such an extent that it may indicate symptoms of an oral character, dependence, insomnia, "nerves", etc. Questions on the presence and regularity of sleep, bowel movements, meals (balanced or not), and exercise give further clues as to whether the patient's life is well-ordered or infused with anxiety. Another question which may appear to be innocuous, but which is often very revealing, is to ask if there are abnormalities. Frequently the patient will say, "What do you mean?" The therapist may reply, "Anything that you consider abnormal." Nervous habits should be investigated. These would include nail biting, thumb sucking, stuttering, hives, nervous tic, twitches, sniffles, and any other. This question gives the patient the opportunity to express a personal view of the body image which could play a large role in the total psychological pathology. Some replies include: "My nose has always been too big." "My breasts are too small." "I've always been shorter than my peers," etc. (Appendix A, p. 5; Rubottom, Note 5).

Section VII. Social History. This section of the history starts on page 5 of the Case History. Obviously its purpose is to ascertain the interpersonal relationships the patient has in the immediate environment. As with the other divisions of the history, the answers here may only point in the direction of a sensitive area of the patient's life which must be investigated in detail later by means of hypnotic age regressions. As has already been pointed out, no one question or answer is going to be definitive, but the alert therapist, through experience will learn how to take leads from the patient which are significant. Of course, some questions are going to be more indicative of pathology than others, such an example is the first one in this section: "What do you think people say about you behind your back that you don't like?" One type of answer may indicate paranoid tendencies; another, on the other hand, may indicate a feeling of security, self assurance, or a lack of self-confidence.

Another question in this section: "If you could change one thing in your life, or in your circumstances, what would it be?" This one question may be quite revealing. One would expect the patient to answer that he wants the problem or complaint initially described in the history resolved. If it is answered quickly, and with determination, consistent with the original symptoms, one can see how determined the patient is to deal with his problems.

On the other hand, the patient may answer in such a way as to cast doubt on whether he really wants the symptoms changed. The answer here is sometimes quite different from the stated symptoms and may give valuable leads to the therapist. For example, a man might describe his "problem" as "impotence with my wife," and proceed to focus his complaints on inability to sustain an erection, etc. An hour later or a week later when asked, "If you could change one thing in your life or your circumstances in life, what would it be?" he might say he would divorce his wife. This is a pretty clear indication that the impotence is directly related to his wife. Thus the etiology may be reasonably well established with the answer to this question.

A different type situation would be exemplified by the person whose chief complaint is "depression" with its various ramifications described during the first few minutes of the first session. Then, later, when the question is asked concerning what one thing he desires changed in his life, the reply is, "Oh, I would lose all this extra weight, doctor." There is a disparity here which the therapist must take into account during therapy.

However this question is answered, it affords an opportunity to clarify the goals of therapy. The therapist might well ask specifically at this point, "If this is alleviated, eliminated or cured, would you consider your problem or symptom solved?" This helps patient and therapist to establish clearly specific goals for therapy (Bryan, Note 6). As has already been stressed, this method of hypnoanalysis, instead of being a free floating relationship, is designed to deal with specific problems in a specific way and to reach a specific goal. Having a definite goal, or contract, also enables the patient and the therapist to establish a time when the therapy relationship should begin to come to an end, i.e., when a specific problem has been dealt with. It could be necessary for the therapist to say at some time, "We accomplished the goal you came in for; now, if we continue the therapy for some other problems, it should be clearly stated what the problem is, and treated as a new problem." Or, it should be defined as a part of the over-all problem and treated as such.

Another question in this category should be, "On what do you spend your money, and what would you like to spend it on?" This enables an individual or a couple to expose their feeling about money and whether or not it is a contributing factor to their problems.

A similar question, and one that is optional, is, "How do you spend your time versus how you would like to spend your time?" It is clear that such a question could reveal frustration and anxiety, compulsion or confusion.

One should ask the question as to whether the person is single (this would be revealed at the very beginning if inquiry is made as to the marital status of the patient) and why. Another question in like manner is about one's general attitude toward the opposite sex.

A "cross check" question calculated to expose sexual frustration and attitudes is this: "Have you ever considered it desirable to eliminate your sex drive, even temporarily?" A person with a high degree of sexual frustration may answer "Yes." Another person may say he has no sex drive, another one might have a desire to eliminate the spouse's sex drive. Sometimes this comes out in this question. It also serves as a cross check on sexual information sought in the previous section.

The question should be asked concerning the social life of the individual or couple, relationship with friends, hobbies, and outside interests. It will reveal whether they have any recreation, and if so, if this is a bone of contention, or a source of strife, between them. The kind of friends, hobbies, and outside interests they have will be a help in revealing the type of personality that is being dealt with. A similar question to this would be to inquire about the occupations of their relatives and friends. The socioeconomic level in which they circulate will, to some extent, reveal information about their personality and behavior.

"Have you ever thought about suicide?" "Have you attempted suicide?" "Describe and list." The therapist should inquire about suicidal thoughts in the first session, perhaps indirectly. If his/her practice is to take this section of the case history in a second hour, then more details may now be secured. It is a rare person that has not at some time or another had the thought of suicide cross his mind. However, it is another thing to give some serious consideration to it. Since an individual who commits suicide nearly always gives some thought to it before the actual act, it is helpful to know if the patient has given serious thought to it prior to this occasion, and certainly it is more revealing if an actual attempt has been made. An evaluation of that attempt could be made at this time. This is the reason for asking the patient to describe and list such conditions, and also gives the therapist an opportunity to evaluate the potential suicide tendencies at this time. If an attempt has been made, the therapist asks how one attempted or planned to take one's life. This can be quite revealing about the personality as well as how serious the person was in making the attempt. For example, Bryan cites a man who took a hose, cut off the end to put in his mouth and connected the other end to the car's exhaust. The hose appeared to be a phallic symbol (circumcised). Enough detail on the patient was known to conclude that homosexuality was connected with death.

A source of trauma in the lives of many has been time spent in military service. Here one should be particularly concerned about whether service was done in a foreign country or war zone, or in the United States, and any experiences which would cause guilt or trauma or anxiety should be determined.

A similar question, which is not important in most cases, concerns whether the patient has ever been arrested. However, if the patient has been arrested, it should be known and some particulars about the arrest should be exposed--how many times, what the charges were, what they were reduced from, if there were any sentences and/or convictions and what the dates were. Many a patient would pass over an experience like this, and yet, it is important to inquire, because if an arrest has taken place, certainly the therapist should know about it.

Inquiry should be made about how and where the person is living. What are the living conditions--house, apartment, renting, buying--what are the particulars with regard to this situation? Who shares the house or apartment? Are they too crowded? Are there invalid relatives or dependent people serving as a source of anxiety? If there are pets in the household--are they a source of conflict? What kind of a neighborhood are they in? Is it a source of pressure or anxiety?

Point blank questions should be asked by now as to whether the person has ever had serious marital problems. If so, one must be prepared to take the details which will come later in the section on marital history. The therapist may be treating the person for an outward symptom of alcoholism

when possibly a marital situation could be ultimately an aggravation to that problem. Many psychological symptoms and behavior problems are indirectly aggravated by a marital dysfunction which should be known.

The final question in the social history is "What is the most disturbing emotional experience in your life?" The therapist should watch for a long pause at this point, or a quick definite answer. This question, by itself, could very well give the therapist, the Symptom Producing Event. There could be several given in this answer, or there may be none given. By asking this question in this way, the patient may relate an event that had not previously been revealed in the case history. This is unusual, however. Usually the patient has already referred to this incident and the answer to this question simply gives a point of emphasis or a means of cross-checking.

Section VIII. Religion. There are some therapists who take a "hands off" policy on the subject of religion under the mistaken concept that because the subject is a matter of one's faith it is too personal or sacred to touch. Furthermore, many therapists feel uncomfortable about the subject of religion and have their own problems and biases in this area, and are thus not prepared emotionally to deal with this very critical area of the patient's life. This subject is so vital to so many patients that it would serve the therapist well to have several courses in religion and/or theology so as to be of greater help to the patient. The single most helpful course would be one on current American denominations or current religious thought.

The first question in this category is with regard to one's general religious beliefs--what were the childhood religious practices or faith, whether the patient attended a religious body consistently, was it considered strict, what were the beliefs peculiar to that body, and particularly, what is God considered to be like? The answer to this latter question may reveal subconscious feelings and attitudes toward the patient's father or other authority figures.

Another question in the same category is whether the patient has lived in accord with childhood teachings, or is living in accord with the present religious doctrine, or personal religious beliefs. Each of these questions elicits a different area of belief and actions and can help to analyze whether there is an issue involving the guilt complex or not. This could be summarized with a specific question: "Is there anything you feel guilty about?" This, of course, reveals whether there are guilt feelings on the surface. The previous questions will help the therapist to determine whether there are unconscious feelings of guilt, or underlying conflicts which may be creating guilt of which the patient is not aware.

Section IX. Marital History. Since all previous questions on this history form pertain to the personality of the individual involved, that information will be useful to the marital therapist in evaluating the person in the context of marriage as well.

The experienced marriage counselor is fully aware of the fact that individual marriage partners may be interviewed or tested separately and not betray psychological pathology and yet have a marriage so dysfunctional that it is on the verge of divorce. In such cases the kind of personality that one has just does not adapt to the kind of personality of the partner. Thus marital therapy must consider the kind of relationship the two personalities form in order to be the most effective (Johnson, 1961; Krich, 1967; Leslie, 1964; Stone, 1953). This is the principle of synergism.

It is precisely at this area that I modify Medical Hypnoanalysis and apply it to marital therapy, which is described in Part II of this study. With this in mind I have added the following questions on the marital relationship to the case history form. I have chosen to discuss them here rather than in Part II because it is in this section that we are considering the case history. It should be noted however, that when the therapist knows in advance that the person (or couple) have come specifically for a marital problem, that the entire previous history should be slanted to take into account the "couple relationship."

Obviously, where there are present or potential marital problems, information in this category is vitally important. This section of the history may be taken much earlier in sequence, should the therapist feel it would be advantageous. The first area of the history should be to inquire about how the couple met--where, under what circumstances, and pertinent facts about the courtship, especially was the courtship smooth or rough? Were there breakups, conflicts? If so, what about? Was the engagement ever broken?

There follows a category concerning the marriage, and if there was more than one, then basic data on all of the marriages. The first marriage should be listed first in sequence. Determine the age, the date of marriage (does the person recall the date?), spouse's age, spouse's name, separation date, cause of separation, divorce date, and the cause. I have had patients who not only could not recall significant dates and ages pertaining to an earlier marriage, but in a few instances, could not recall one (or both) of the names of the spouse. Were there children in the first marriage? What are their ages? What are the relationships now between parents and children?

If there was another marriage (or more than one), then determine the same information about it.

It is very helpful to know what appealed to this person about the spouse at the approximate time of engagement. In the case of multiple marriages a pattern may emerge which should be recognized in order to prevent making the same mistake again.

The following questions about the current marital relationship will give leads on present or potential problems (Morris, 1965):

1. "For what reason did you get married? Was it forced, without love?" Frequently, information given in response to this question will lay the foundation for the problems that they now encounter in marriage (or in personal anxiety). If the person or couple went into the marriage with inadequate reasons, like marrying in order to leave home, or for financial security, or because friends were getting married, or to give an unborn baby a name, then the marriage most likely got off to an inadequate start. The therapist should also ask what the previous living conditions were. This will help to determine if there was pressure to leave an unhappy situation by getting married.

2. "What is there of lasting value on which your marriage rests?" Obviously this helps to determine if there is currently any foundation for continuing the relationship. This should be evaluated. It should be kept in mind that when one is in the midst of a crisis, one is less prone to feel, or to recognize, that there is something of lasting value in the marriage at the present time.

3. "When did marital difficulties of a serious nature start?" The answer to this may give the therapist a Symptom Producing Event for the marital problem. It is significant that the answer to this question all too frequently is "from the time we got married." Obviously, this indicates that the marriage should never have taken place. Other answers will indicate that a traumatic event (or perhaps several) effected the relationship adversely. There are other situations in which the rift came on gradually.

4. "How would separation or divorce affect the family?" This is calculated to reveal the kind of encouragement or discouragement that the person may find from relatives on his or her side of the family. For example, one of the parties may be staying in the marriage only because of strong pressure from other members of

the family. In this kind of conflict, the person is usually developing an acute anxiety situation.

5. "Whom do you know in your family or close acquaintance that is unhappy like yourself?" Here we have an indication of influence from other members of the family on the marriage. This kind of influence can be subtle and indirect, even at the unconscious level. There are some families which have negative suggestions given to them to the extent that "Well divorce seems to run in our family." This party, then, is simply living up to the family reputation. The single life of a friend can be influential. On the other hand, this particular party could be the first one in the family seriously to consider divorce, and this in itself becomes traumatic.

6. "How do you communicate with your spouse?" An evaluation of the communication level is critical for therapy. The answer to this question may indicate that information on good clear open communication should be given in the initial stages of marital therapy (C. Ard, 1969; Satir, 1969).

7. "What subjects do you fight about most?" The most fought about subjects in the American home are finances, sex, religion, in-laws, choice of friends, choice of recreation activities, and child rearing (Morris, 1965). These subjects have already appeared in the case history in one form or another, but a specific answer to this question will help to determine the sources of conflict for this particular family. Of course, sometimes the answer to this question is "We fight about everything," which is an indication that there is a basic personality conflict, and this cannot be adequately evaluated on the basis of just one subject.

8. "What do you think your spouse would like for you to change?" It is surprising how many husbands and wives accurately reflect the feelings of the spouse in this regard. By taking the same case history of both husband and wife, a comparison may be made on the answers to these questions. Of course, there are many couples whose communication is so poor that neither one is aware of what the spouse desires to be changed.

9. "What would you like your spouse to change?" Encouragement to verbalize a specific answer here discourages further generalized complaining which some are prone to do. It may also give a basis for opening communication with the spouse.

10. "Do you want to make your marriage a success?" When both

husband and wife give an answer of "Yes" to this, it will be helpful in determining the course of therapy and the goal of therapy. On the other hand, if both answer "No," it is going to be a very difficult procedure to bring them around to re-evaluation so that both agree to try to preserve the marriage. However, this may happen. Sometimes the case history is taken at a time when there is a severe emotional crisis and neither is in the mood to do anything about sustaining the marriage at that point. A note should be made about this negative feeling and appropriate evaluation made with this in mind. When one spouse wants to preserve the marriage and the other does not, I suggest that the therapy proceed anyway in order to better understand the unconscious roots of the problem and then make a further evaluation of the relationship and determine what the purpose of the next stage of therapy will be.

11. "Have you thought of separation or divorce?" There are couples who have come this far in describing their marital problems and in giving their symptoms and yet have not given thought to separation or divorce. It is important that the therapist be aware of this; or one has thought about it and the other has not. This should be determined by a comparison of both of the case histories.

12. "How do you get along with your in-laws?" Since this is the fourth most frequent source of marital discord, it is important to evaluate the answer to this question. It may be a revealing clue to the presence of the PDL syndrome.

By the time these searching questions have been asked and the patient has probed his mind for answers, aspects of the problem have likely been brought to mind for the first time in such a way as to cause a more honest re-evaluation. Frequently a patient will return a few days after having been asked these questions with a remark something like this: "I've been thinking about those questions you asked, and I realize there are some aspects of this marriage that I hadn't thought about before. This has caused some real provocative thinking and some more meaningful communication between us." This demonstrates that a thorough case history, taken carefully, can have a great cathartic and therapeutic value (Bryan, Note 7).

When taking the same case history with the marital partner, references may be made to each other. Of course, these references should be recorded on the appropriate form and written with a different color pen, say, black, so that the remarks are easy to find and immediately understood as being the observation of one concerning the other. As would be expected, observations on each other can give significant leads as to the type personality and the type relationship that they have. This in turn can help to sharpen the therapy and to shorten the total time involved. The therapist should keep in mind that in treating the marital relationship, the "relationship" is treated as the patient. The husband and the wife are looked upon as being an alter ego to each other so that information is gained from each one which is taken into account when evaluations are made and insights provoked.

Inasmuch as hypnoanalysis proposes to reveal the psychodynamics of the personality in individual therapy, so the use of this means of therapy in the marital relationship proposes to reveal the subconscious factors involved in marriage partners. Since the emotional reactions of marital partners are intensified through the intimate interrelationships of married life, the most helpful solution to the seriously disturbed marriage is an analytical one. Marriage does not solve emotional problems, rather, in most cases, it intensifies them. Of course, there are neurotic individuals who can have happy marriages, but they are in the minority.

By the same token, many healthy personalities have made the wrong choice in a mate and have unhealthy relationships. But the chances of healthy personalities having happy marriages are much higher than not. Whether the personalities are healthy or neurotic, an analytical approach to their discordant marital unions is the most effective way to a lasting, harmonious relationship. For this reason the questions in this history form are calculated to help the therapist make an early decision on the subconscious factors in the relationship.

In concluding the case history, there is one last general question: "Is there anything you haven't told me that you think I ought to know?" Sometimes the previous questions have provoked thought or memories in the patient which have not been revealed thus far. Asking this question occasionally brings out pertinent and helpful information which previously had been overlooked.

EVALUATING THE CASE HISTORY

If the therapist has made notations of his own thoughts and "gut reactions" in red as he progressed in filling out the case history, he will be able to determine to a great extent the kind of personality he is dealing with and/or the degree of dysfunction in the marital relationship. If he does not have an opinion by this time, reading over the case history or histories will help him to assess the degree of dysfunction and at least have a tentative idea of the diagnosis of the person (or persons) involved in the interview. The diagnosis at this point is only tentative. The word association test and dream analysis which will follow will help to verify the tentative diagnosis or else give a new lead and indicate where a more accurate diagnosis will lie.

It is important that the diagnosis be made as soon as possible. Always, in taking the history, ask more questions when the urge hits; probe and probe, seeking the diagnosis quickly.

There are three goals in taking the history. viz.: 1. Investigatory: A careful, thorough investigation at the beginning is to the advantage of both patient and therapist. A diagnosis (at least tentatively) should be made and the plan for therapy should be laid out at the conclusion.

The history form requires that the therapist secure the year of each major event and the patient's age at that time. Then a comparison be made to ascertain the patient's consistency. For example, if the male patient's father died at 59 of a heart attack and the patient is now 59 and having chest pains, one must consider the strong possibility of close identification with--and indirect suggestion from--the father's influencing the patient.

The therapist should note carefully the events from the patient's life that appear to have had a great deal of emotion involved at the time of occurrence. These situations may be compared to Ohm's Law by which the amount of voltage (or pressure) behind an event determines the degree of trauma associated with that event. If repression has taken place, then an abreaction in hypnosis will be vital in achieving relief of the patient's anxiety.

2. The active hypnoanalyst should implant suggestions of insight and understanding from the beginning to the patient. The effective therapist should always be treating, treating, analyzing, curing; start the patient thinking immediately.

3. "Close the sale." One assumes that the patient will benefit from the suggested therapy. This philosophy here may be viewed as somewhat evangelistic in that the therapist must be committed to his work: He must treat the patient with dedication, and set the fee without guilt. Again, Sir William Osler is quoted as saying, "Collect the fee at the height of the fever" (Bryan, Note 8). Many hypnoanalysts set a flat fee and treat the person till he or she is well. The therapist may not make as much money as in open-ended, on-going, long term therapy, but this type of fee arrangement is better for both patient and doctor. The patient knows what

the therapy will cost and the doctor is motivated to proceed with therapy as rapidly as possible. This is an innovative procedure, but it can be done. If the patient prefers to pay on a per session basis, this should be permitted.

INTRODUCTORY HYPNOTIC PROCEDURE

One of the unique features of hypnoanalytic procedure, which probably results from the physician's experience, is that use is made of several therapy rooms which enables the hypnoanalyst to treat as many as four patients at once. Of course, the patients would have to be at different stages of therapy, but by the use of electronic equipment and tapes the therapeutic procedures could be hastened.

The suite of offices for such procedure requires a consultation office, several (perhaps four) smaller treatment rooms and a console room which serves as a base for the electronic equipment. Each treatment room has a tilt-back vibrating chair for the patient to recline in or a couch, and a closed circuit TV camera focused on it. The TV screen which monitors the patient is in the console room. Also in the treatment room there is a black sleep shade mask which the patient wears with a tissue between the mask and the patient's eyes for sanitary purposes. In addition there is a microphone which leads to the speaker in the console room, and a set of headphones which the patient wears so that he or she can hear the therapist's voice or tapes from the console room (Boswell, 1966; Bryan, 1965a; Ferrara, 1981; Fross, 1969; Hartman, 1968).

After the patient has completed the history and the therapist has an outline of the therapy procedure in mind, and the fee arrangements have been settled, the patient is given the initial hypnotic induction.

If the patient has not been hypnotized before, some preparatory information is given as to what to expect. This is easily done by verbal description or by showing the patient a video tape of the hypnotic procedure with appropriate explanations. Next the patient is taken to the therapy room and is seated in the chair, which is tilted back, or is asked to lay prone on a couch. The therapist induces hypnosis and then puts the eye mask over the patient's eyes and places the earphones on the patient's ears. Of course, this may also be done by the doctor's assistant. The therapist then leaves the room, shutting the door.

In the initial induction a series of tapes is now played from the console room through the patient's earphones which further conditions the patient to the routine procedure. A hypnotic induction tape, made by the therapist from an Academy script, is played which may start like this: "As you continue to relax more deeply, I am going to place you in a soothing, pleasing, hypnotic SLEEP." At the word "sleep" the vibrator is turned on in the chair by remote control from the console room. Each time the patient returns and hears the word "sleep" on the induction tape, the vibrator is turned on which facilitates the hypnotic trance. Theoretically, the vibration on the back assists in placing the conscious mind in a dormant state, and in turn leaves the subconscious open to suggestion.

After the patient is sufficiently deep into the hypnotic state, a tape is played giving "initial protective suggestions" (see Appendix C) to the effect that the patient will not be hypnotized while operating machinery which would be dangerous to himself or others; that in the event of an emergency the patient would be wide awake and alert to protect himself or herself; that he will never be hypnotized against his will or by anyone other than a professional person for his benefit; that he will become hypnotized at the word "sleep" and will awaken at the count of "three" feeling good in every way. During this initial session an explanation is given that the tape system will be utilized on occasion for giving routine suggestions and for educative purposes in order to save the patient money and in other ways to facilitate treatment. Also, an explanation as to how hypnosis works is presented on tape, together with positive expectations of successful therapy.

During this session the therapist observes the patient closely and determines the kind of hypnotic subject he or she is. This observing is done first before the therapist leaves the room where the patient is. Later, it is done by watching a TV monitor screen in the console room. After the session is over, the therapist checks with the patient as to feelings and may give a "self-test" for hypnotizability. There are various degrees or levels of hypnosis and the patient finds his own level. Positive expectancy is a decided favorable advantage.

The electronic innovations have a number of advantages over face to face therapy. In principle the system is utilizing the Freudian procedure of having the patient lie prone on a couch with the doctor out of sight. With the black sleep shade over the patient's eyes, all outside distraction is removed. Earphones remove outside audio distractions and bring the therapist's words in close to the ears where a deeper impression is made. By using tapes one knows the exact words used at all sessions, except, of course, when the therapist is talking with the patient directly, at which time notes are kept. A microphone is attached to the patient's collar or is near enough to pick up the voice and even breathing patterns, which are heard by the therapist in the console room through a speaker. The patient, as it were, is lost within herself or himself, which condition is most helpful in therapy, and enhances age regressions tremendously.

In many patients (alcoholics and drug addicts for example) the constant repetition of suggestions may be vital to therapy, as in brain rinsing; having a tape to play over and over increases the effectiveness (Ferrera, 1981).

Using the tapes in routine procedure is as follows: Upon entering, the patient is taken by the assistant into a therapy room and placed in the chair or on a couch and prepared as referred to above. At each session, after the first one, an "induction" tape is played in order to hypnotize the person. In so doing many varieties of visual and audio imagery may be used as an adjunct. For example, sound effects of the sea shore, or flowing water, or music may be used to deepen the hypnotic trance. With modern electronic equipment impressions can be made on the mind in a way that never would have been possible before. If the person is a "difficult" subject, such tapes can be played for as long as needed to achieve complete relaxation. While this is going on, the therapist can be treating another patient who has already been adequately prepared. When the patient and therapist are ready, the direct communication between them begins. This may last for thirty minutes or so. Then the therapist moves onto another who has been in a state of preparation. Educational or explanatory tapes may be played further for the earlier patient, according to need.

Such tapes may be encouragement to relieve depression, or instruction in marriage, or repetitious, positive suggestions for eliminating a habit pattern, etc. There is no end to the possibilities for furthering the treatment by this method. Of course, it requires a stock of hundreds of tapes from five to thirty minutes in length. It also requires thousands of dollars worth of electronic equipment, including automatic tape players which mechanically transfer from one tape to another without having to be individually handled. The patient may be in for any length of time, depending on physical comfort. Usually two one-hour sessions is sufficient for one time. If the situation is such that a long period of therapy is required, (due to a crisis or the patient is in from some distance away) it is best to let the patient up after an hour or so for a brief intermission before returning to the chair. The session is closed with a final "wake-up" tape.

SUMMARY AND CONCLUSION

The preceding pages describe the method of taking the patient's case history. Detailed questions are asked about every area of the person's past experiences in order to elicit those episodes which were traumatic enough to contribute to the development of the patient's symptoms. While so doing the therapist is encouraged to observe carefully the exact wording and body language which the patient uses while answering the questions so that both the conscious and unconscious implications may be ascertained.

Medical Hypnoanalysis may or may not be concerned with altering the total personality or even with dealing with other facets of the personality which the therapist may consider as "problematical." Rather, the therapist stipulates that when the patient requests that certain symptoms be removed or resolved, that these be clearly identified and an understanding be made between therapist and patient as to what the aim of therapy is. However, this method of hypnoanalysis should not be confused with the practice of hypnotherapy which is concerned with direct symptom removal. Hypnoanalysis involves the patient's gaining insight as to the ultimate causes of the symptoms and working through dynamically so that the symptoms are resolved or alleviated. When this goal is reached, and the change is reinforced, then therapy should cease.

Of course, if by relieving repression, other problems suddenly appear, then by mutual agreement these may be treated. Or the total personality may need analysis. When this is mutually agreed upon, then, by all means, therapy should proceed. The hypnoanalyst generally does not believe in an ongoing, ill-defined and ambiguous kind of therapy. The careful taking of a detailed case history clarifies the goals and defines the course of therapy as well as lays the foundation for the Bryan Word Association Test, a discussion of which follows.

CHAPTER 4

THE BRYAN WORD ASSOCIATION TEST

INTRODUCTION

By the time the therapist has taken a thorough case history he should have a reasonably good idea as to what the diagnosis of the patient should be. He now prepares to give the word association test, while the patient is hypnotized, in order to verify or redirect this diagnosis. This test is a projective technique designed originally to reveal more of the patient's subconscious thinking. Before describing the procedure, it will be advantageous to set forth some principles of projective testing. This will be followed by examples of analysis of some patients' word association tests, and finally a critique of the value of such a test.

Definition of Projective Tests

A distinction is made between "projective" and "objective" tests. The basic purpose of objective tests is to measure differences "between individuals or between the reactions of the same individual on different occasions" (Anastasi, 1968, p. 3; Cronbach, 1949). Generally speaking, these tests ask specific and direct questions to the subject with the expectation of receiving a specific reply upon which the scoring is based. "In projective techniques the assessor confronts the subject with ambiguous stimuli and asks ambiguous questions. For example, he asks, 'What might this be?' 'Tell me what you see here' (while showing an inkblot), or he says, 'Create the most imaginative story that you can (showing a picture), including what the people are thinking and feeling . . ." (Mischel, 1971, p. 162). Thus projective tests are distinguished by the assignment of a relatively unstructured task to the subject (Anastasi, 1968). This gives an opportunity for unlimited variety in the responses.

Basically, objective tests are intended to measure differences between individuals, as well as compare a "before and after situation" in the same person, whereas in projective techniques (generally speaking) the purpose of the test is to know more about subconscious elements in the person and not necessarily compare him to anyone (Anastasi, 1968; Mischel, 1971). When a clinician evaluates a patient he/she may put him in a broad category of his fellows, but basically, that individual has to be evaluated within himself. We are justified at this point in seeing this as a broad difference in the two kinds of tests: Objective tests deal principally with the ego and the conscious mind; projective tests deal with the subconscious. More will be said on this later.

Characteristics of Projective Tests

This test is a disguised testing procedure in that the subject usually is unaware of the type of psychological interpretation that is taking place.

Projectives are a global approach to the appraisal of the personality in that they are concerned with the emotional, motivational, interpersonal and intellectual aspects. Projectives have demonstrated effectiveness in revealing covert, latent, or unconscious aspects of the personality (Anastasi, 1968, p. 494).

Procedures and Techniques

Anastasi (1968) further describes procedures which are used to ascertain such unconscious aspects from the subject. They are:

1. Word association tests in which a word is seen or heard as a stimulus and the subject responds with another word (or thought) which immediately comes to mind as a result of this prompting.
2. Sentence completion tests are similar to the above in that a partially constructed sentence is seen or heard by the subject and then completed by him as rapidly as possible.

3. Ambiguous "blots" are shown to the subject who is then expected to describe what is seen.
4. A series of pictures is shown to the subject with the expectation that he will then tell a brief story about the pictures, describing what is seen and what the accompanying feelings are.

Mischel (1971, p. 164) lists six bases for classifying projective techniques.

1. Mode of response: the subject is required to associate (e.g., words), to construct (e.g., a toy world with dolls), to complete (e.g., sentences), to order (e.g., pictures), or to express himself (e.g., finger painting).
2. Stimulus attributes of the test material: that is, differences in the stimulus materials with respect to degree of structure or sense modality involved.
3. Manner of test interpretation: for example, interpretive emphasis on the content as opposed to the style of test responses.
4. Purpose of the test: for example, tests purporting to reveal specific attributes, to make a diagnostic classification, or to provide an overall, general personality assessment.
5. Method of administration: individual or group administration, administration by self or by examiner.
6. Method of test construction: for example, a theoretical versus an empirical strategy of test construction.

I have gone into this much detail on the definition because, as we shall see, when dealing with the criticisms and objections to projective techniques, a clear understanding of what is meant, and what one is trying to do, will have a great deal to do with the final evaluation.

HISTORY AND PHILOSOPHY

A Brief History of Projective Testing

Galton, who used a word association test in 1879, seems to be one of the first, if not the first, to use the procedure. Later Kraepelin adapted it "for use in a study on the nature of abnormal behavior, and began a line of investigation that is still active" (Anastasi, 1968, p. 279). In

1895 Binet and Henri first used ink blots on a group of subjects at Harvard (Mischel, 1971). Wundt introduced the word association test into experimental psychology and was followed by Jung, who in 1909 lectured on it at Clark University (Assagioli, 1965; Hall & Lindzey, 1970). Indirectly, Freud's research influenced the further development of projective techniques, as one would expect (Mischel, 1971). Jung, in giving such a test, was careful to record the time of the subject's pause before replying to the stimulus. He felt that a prolongation of time or hesitation to reply indicated the sign of a complex (Assagioli, 1965). Felix Deutsch is credited with utilizing key words from the patient's own usage in an association test and concluded that the technique of therapy should focus on symptoms and conflicts which the association test, so constructed, revealed (Harper, 1959).

Herman Rorschach, a Swiss psychiatrist, constructed the inkblot series in 1921, while H. A. Murray at the Harvard Psychological Clinic developed the first set of pictures which came to be named the "Thematic Apperception Test" (TAT) (Anastasi, 1968, p. 499). These tests have, since their origination, had further study, experimentation, and revision.

Since World War II tests of every type have become more popular.

Philosophy of Projective Testing

Freud's method of "free association" has opened more doors than just that of the unconscious and one of them has been that of projective testing, which is just another way of revealing the unconscious free of inhibitions. Personality psychologists became intrigued with the psychodynamic theory and sought to use tests as a shorter method to understand the dynamics of personality (Mischel, 1971).

Of course, almost any test can be adapted to be used more or less projectively so long as the test materials serve as a "screen" on which the respondent "projects" his characteristic thought processes, needs, anxieties, and conflicts (Anastasi, 1968).

Rotter (1951) calls attention to the fact that persons taking a projective test are free to respond to the stimuli as they wish, knowing that the answers are not evaluated as "right" and "wrong" and consequently not "scored" as passing or failing.

THE BRYAN WORD ASSOCIATION TEST

The material for this test is available on the case history forms. The following references and allusions to the test are specifically directed to this form, a copy of which is in the Appendix D. Observe that there are 195 words, or partially finished sentences, which the patient is to complete, although the therapist actually is the one who writes in the responses. The patient is placed in a reclining chair or on a couch and hypnotized in preparation for receiving test instructions.

Each word, or partially finished sentence, is numbered to provide a means of cross references, not only within the text itself, but also to refer to notes that are made later during therapy. In addition, there are 26 numbered blank lines. This enables the therapist to supply 26 words, or partially finished sentences, that are peculiar to the patient. Further detailed references will be made to these in the following paragraph.

It will also be noted in a cursory overview that there is a section blocked off in bold lines having to do with sexual responses. Terms here are vernacular and are most helpful when properly understood in evaluating the patient's sexual feelings. It is generally best to take the test at two different sessions. For one reason, it is too long to try to complete at one sitting. For another reason, the person may be more responsive at one time than another. The depth of the hypnosis varies according to the circumstances of the patient's life. The time the test is taken should be noted in the appropriate corner, and the time and date of the second session, and the time noted when it is concluded. Most patients require approximately 30 minutes for taking each half of the test (though some need more) in addition to the time it takes to become hypnotized and hear the directions, which the requirement to respond to the words and phrases on impulse rather than thinking or planning the answers.

Occasionally, when a particularly provocative word or sentence is called out to the patient, the patient will abreact. The clinician should immediately let the patient take the lead and encourage catharsis to take place. For example, on number 148, "Scream," a patient who had been in a mental hospital produced a violent reaction when stimulated by this word. The sounds of screaming patients in the night came back to him immediately, and he relived the pain and the horror of the period of time spent in the mental institution. Although it was exhausting, it was good for him to let this pressure out, after which the test was concluded for that occasion.

John A. Scott, Sr., Ph.D.

One time I spent approximately nine sessions on the test with a woman patient who abreacted every few responses. By the time we finished the word association test we had finished the bulk of her analysis. We had the ISE, the SPE and several SIE's so put together that she understood the entire problem. This is a rare exception, however.

Preparation for the Test

It is important to continue to scrutinize closely the patient's body language when using the word association test, and to facilitate this procedure a code of abbreviations is listed for the therapist to rely on. In referring to the test (see Appendix D) it will be noted that the abbreviation list, appearing as a prologue, provides for the operator to use letters to indicate various body movements made by the patient from the stimulus of words and phrases given by the operator. Such notations may be entered on the line where the stimulus appears or in one of the blank boxes preceding the stimulating word or phrase. The columns for these boxes are lettered at the top by "x", "y", and "z". These boxes may also be used by check mark or an asterisk to indicate particular emphasis on that response.

The test has 195 entries, in its original form (many of our members use a shortened form now) some of which are single words, some are incomplete sentences and, in addition, there are 26 blanks. Before starting the test with the patient, the therapist should fill in most of those blank lines with materials taken from the record of the case history. The guidelines for this procedure are as follows: "What do I want to know about this patient?" With this in mind the therapist then reviews the history and selects ideas or words that apply specifically to that patient. These selections should be made by skipping around in the history so as not to fill in the blanks in the same order that the history was taken. Patients can be sensitive to the same order as used previously and consequently anticipate what the operator might ask next. Words peculiar to that patient which were used in describing the symptoms, conditions, relationships with other people, words of description about himself or herself, peculiar phraseology, etc., are to be looked for. The operator may cross check on the patient's self-image by taking sections of his own sentences and inserting them in the test. This will enable the therapist to see if the person's feelings, while in this hypnotic state, are the same as they are in the waking state (Hartman, 1966).

Some principles of polygraph procedure are utilized. For example, the test includes a scattering of "null" words throughout. Such words usually have no significance, except by mere chance, but do lull the patient somewhat between the "hot" words. Whenever possible, however, "null" words have been selected that have several possible meanings or applications, and thus the response by some patients will be of significance to the clinician. Effort was made to avoid a pattern of "null" and "hot" words in sequence so as to prevent the patient's discovery of such a pattern, which could have an influence on responses.

There are some routine words and phrases which the operator should select from the history and insert in the test. These are:

On #1 insert the first name of the patient; #3, the last name. On #5 insert the first name of the father and on #7 the first name of the mother. The following blank lines could have the first names of the most significant others in the patient's experience. Other peculiar phrases and key words which the patient used should be supplied in the following blanks. For example, an alcoholic will frequently use the word "bottle" which should be inserted. "Bottle" may have a double meaning for that person. It may refer to a baby bottle, or it may be used in reference to a liquor bottle. In blank #51 a sentence should be included by saying, "My father, George. . ." (supply first name of patient's father) and in #55 use the patient's mother's name as "My mother, Sue . . . ." The same principle is applied with #59 by supplying the name of the patient's spouse, as, "My husband, Bill...."

Some of the incomplete sentences which were filled in by a woman who had an inferiority complex were these: "My home life," "I could relax if," "I lose weight when," "If I could have gone to college," "When I get in a car," "I could gain weight if," "I feel dumb when," "I'll be somebody when," and the like. In the case of a woman who was pre-orgasmic, some of the sentences supplied from her case history were these: "I get jealous when," "My affairs," "I could have a climax if," "My religious beliefs," "The way I used to feel. . ."

A man who is serving in the Navy would have terms and phrases filled-in in the blanks which are peculiar to his circumstances, etc.

Note that it is best not to fill in all of the blanks before starting the test. As the test proceeds, the clinician will think of other terms or partially finished sentences which should be added. Most of the evaluation of the patient is done as the test proceeds. By using a red pen, the operator follows the principles of the old geometry axiom, "Quantities equal to the same quantity or to equal quantities are equal to each other." This simply means that a series of words or thoughts may be aligned in the patient's mind in such a way that there is an underlying common denominator. For example, if the patient on #58 HORRIBLE, answers "Hospital." on #70 ABORTION, answers "Hospital," #72 BABY, answers "Abortion," on #73 GUILT, answers "Abortion," on #75 PUNISHMENT, answers "Guilt," #160 FRIGID, answers "Punishment," one will immediately see that all of these could be related by drawing a line in red from each answer to the other. It is obvious that the patient had a horrible experience in a hospital where an abortion took place; there is a feeling of guilt and the person is punishing herself by sexual repression. These events and feelings are related in the patient's subconscious mind, but the relationship may not be one of which the patient is consciously aware. By drawing lines from one related word to another, as the clinician evaluates the test, it becomes apparent to the therapist what the correlation is, and in due time he will assist the patient in recognizing the pattern.

It is true that at this point the clinician is following intuition, which is subjective, but in the later therapy sessions, these insights and interpretations can be checked out with the patient, and in most cases they are verified. A black pen is used to supply the words and partially finished sentences in the blanks; a red pen is used for the therapist's own intuitive responses by drawing lines or writing notes based on observations and feelings at the time the response is given. Also notes should be made in red of the patient's responses in a non-verbal way. Any movement, long pauses, hesitations, coughs, laughs, repeats, sighs, etc., are significant and indicate what is going on beneath the surface in the patient's mind.

With regard to the section of sexual terms (numbers 119 - 137), this is blocked out by heavy lines so that if the therapist desires for any reason to skip the section, it is clear where it begins and ends. Frank, racy, vernacular terms are included in the form, because, with many people, these terms elicit feelings which may be positive, negative, or passive. Since there are many strong emotions connected or related to sex, a few terms like this may elicit responses which the therapist might not otherwise get. In other cases, the use of these terms may verify information which has already been secured in the case history and thus reveal nothing that is not already known (Bryan, 1966b, 1967b, 1969c, 1969d).

Observe that all but two of the sex terms have possible multiple meanings, enabling the patient to avoid reference to sex on most responses. This is revealing. Depending on the answers, it may indicate purposeful avoidance of sexuality or it may indicate immature, undeveloped or arrested sexuality. Angry, aggressive responses may indicate hostility toward sex.

Angry responses to terms relating to the opposite sex, but passive, accepting responses to terms referring to one's own sex, indicates antagonism toward the opposite sex. One may reveal a highly sensuous nature by reveling in the terms or accentuating responses with words or sentences that are highly sexually provocative. Such a person may be obsessed with sex or possibly addicted. On the other hand, the patient may reveal a concept that all sex is dirty or sinful and act as if trying to wash his/her hands of the filth and stay clean from such contamination. If the patient is severely inhibited or immature most of the responses will be non-sexual. Persons in between the extreme of totally sexually oriented on the one hand and sexually inhibited on the other hand will usually give a non-sexual reply on the first three terms, then when number 123 is called out, they will reply to that and to others with words of sexual connotation. The kind of emotion that is expressed with the responses will also be an indication of the attitude of the patient regarding his or her sexuality.

There are some females who reveal a subconscious prejudice toward males or masculine sexuality by responding to the terms applicable to females by such words as, "slang," or "woman" or "female body." But with regard to the terms that exclusively apply to males may give a reply such as "vulgar," "ugly," or "bad," or a similar derogatory response. This, of course, reveals a coldness toward male sexuality (Bryan, 1969c).

Obviously, the therapist should evaluate the patient sufficiently during the case history to determine if, for some reason, it would be inadvisable or injudicious to include the section on sex in the word association test. This may apply particularly to the very young or the very old. If the therapist is convinced that the patient is severely inhibited sexually there is no point in using the sex term section because it could cause severe resistance to the rest of the test or even to the entire therapy.

When a male therapist is giving the test to a female patient, and her responses indicate antagonism toward males and passivity to herself, he should be wary. She may be prone to sue or to make charges of "advances." The operator should have an assistant near by at all times under such circumstances.

An Example of the Bryan Word Association Test

A copy of the Bryan Word Association Test, found in the Appendix, illustrates the method of procedure wherein words, taken from the case history, have been interjected into the test. Such words have been inserted in the blanks at numbers 1,3,5,7, 14, 18, 21, 25, 31, 33, 41, 51, 55, 59, 63, 80, 86, 91, 107, 109, 142, 154, 159, 167. These words or phrases were taken from the case history and have to do with the patient's specific problem.

In the accompanying word association test the patient's name is called Mrs. John Jones (maiden name Gertrude Smith, daughter of George and Alice Smith). Although these names are fictional, the test is actual.

Analysis

This female patient was referred by a physician. The presenting symptoms were overweight and depression. The history reveals she was nervous and unhappy in her marriage. Furthermore, she was having an extramarital affair. Her marital history revealed enough information to conclude that she had an unhappy marriage and a husband who apparently did not love her or appreciate her, which furnished the underlying motivation for her extramarital relationship. Information gained from the religious history, as well as observing her in a depression, prompted the therapist to diagnose her tentatively as having a Guilt Complex (also referred to by some therapists as the Walking Zombie Syndrome {Spiritual}), and that the underlying problem of guilt and punishment probably caused the overweight condition. These speculations on her diagnosis were made at the conclusion of the case history, and furnished the basis for the words and sentences inserted on the Word Association Test.

Upon giving her the test, the tentative diagnosis appeared to be sustained. Response #17 being linked to #88 suggests the Death Complex element in her analysis. As far as her personal feelings about herself are concerned, note the responses referring to herself: #21, 23, 24, 54, 58, 98, 160. This makes it clear that she has self-hatred and a very low self image. Furthermore, she is depressed and feeling guilty. Feeling guilty is causing her to bring punishment upon herself, a part of which is the overweight condition. Note #65, 73, 75, 95, 63, 178, 189, 161.

She has a poor image of men also. Consider #87. Men are to her dirty. She has an unhappy marriage, obviously, clearly stated in #80, 96, 114, 59, 168, in reference to her husband. At the same time, she considers sex dirty (#169) and all responses on the sex words indicated the same feeling. She considers herself in an adulterous state (#73, 143.1, 151) and that she should be punished (#156, 107), but her boy friend gives her the emotional support she needs. For example, #44, 74, 140, 143, 145, 154, 155, 183, 186. As long as she's overweight, she's unhappy (#91), which is another way of saying she's punishing herself for her adulterous, extramarital relationship (#151). She also thought she was being punished when a younger brother was seriously ill (#107, 156).

By reading other responses in this test, further observations regarding this person's personality will be noted. This particular case was chosen as an example because it illustrates how much insight the therapist may gain about a patient within the first four or five sessions. Here the analysis is well on the way, as far as the therapist's knowledge and insights are concerned. The unconscious mind of the patient has revealed itself in a most impressive way.

As the therapy progressed in this example, the accuracy of the preceding statements and observations about them, was demonstrated. One should be cautioned not to draw conclusions too hastily from just one statement or bodily response, but to consider the overall impression based on all observations.

The following deductions are based on the test alluded to in the preceding pages. Since the printed test has 26 blanks for the therapist to fill in words or phrases that are peculiar to the patient, reference will be made first to some of those blanks and how they are best used.

1. JONES: "John." Instead of responding with the usual "me" or "Gertrude," she responds with husband's first name, which may indicate that she does not think of herself closely related with this name. To put it bluntly, she's not emotionally married to her husband.

3. SMITH: the last name of her parents, that is, her maiden name. When this name was called out, she replied "Mother" (M), which indicates that her mother is the dominant figure to her.

5. GEORGE: father's first name.

7. ALICE: mother's first name.

14. GERTRUDE: the patient.

18. JOHN: husband's first name.

25. BILL: the name of the boy friend in the extramarital relationship.

33. JEAN: the second child.

37. UNCLE WILLIE: uncle.

The therapist's personal observations in the actual test, written with a red pen, appear here in the accompanying sample in parentheses.

It is important for the therapist to write notes to himself throughout the test because his observations and feelings at that time are apt to be more accurate than later; furthermore, such impressions are easily forgotten. By using a different color pen (red), it facilitates distinguishing his thoughts from the patient's responses when he reviews the test later. For these same reasons lines are drawn from one answer to other related questions and answers while they are fresh on his mind. Admittedly, this process is unorthodox and produces a rather "messy" page, but the procedure is most helpful. The value of the test is in the fact that while the person is hypnotized, the unconscious mind is open and responsive, and thus true inner feelings are most apt to be revealed. If, after the test is taken, the therapist is aware that no observations have been made and no connecting lines showing the relationship of one thought to another have been drawn, it may be that the patient is not reflecting inner problems. Or it may indicate that the person is not sufficiently relaxed to be revealing the inner mind. It might be necessary to do the test over. It should be done over, if it is confused and does not fit together, if the patient is not relaxed enough, if there is a long span between the first half of the test and the second half, or if there is a long span between the time the test is taken and the time therapy actually begins. One other thought: no significant or meaningful responses may indicate little or no pathology.

Sometimes the first half of the test will yield nothing of significance. The therapist will observe that he has very few cross references and no notes; that is, it is a very routine set of responses. Then on the second half of the test, the responses take on a new depth, displaying abreaction, catharsis, cathexis, etc., indicating a revelation of the unconscious. The responses from the patient will vary in the hypnotized state from those in the nonhypnotized state. Thus it may be necessary occasionally to postpone giving the test till another occasion when the patient will be more receptive to hypnotism (Hartman, 1966).

Recognize that the WAT gives a clue to the patient's inner thinking processes, like a window into the unconscious mind, and the stimulating words or phrases are bait for triggering the patient to respond according to his unconscious thinking patterns and his inner personality. This test can save hours of typical and traditional psychotherapy if it is correctly done.

Other Examples

The following are random responses on more than one word association test and are given to illustrate the type of answers that one may expect on some of the stimulating words and how these answers relate to other answers. Furthermore, these examples show the kind of deductions that may legitimately be made to the patient responses

10. MOTHER - "Life"

13. LIFE - "Mother"

Here, because of the similarity of the responses, a line is drawn from 10 to 13 because the word "mother" is the common denominator. The operator notes: "may need to check the birth experience. Equates life with mother and reemphasizes mother." It could indicate a struggle for life, or it simply could be an obvious equation of mother and life, but it needs to be checked.

The following responses come from the same patient.

11. PROBLEM - "Me" (Shows realization that the problem is within himself).

15. ANXIETY - "Frustration" (usually refers to sexual frustration).

18. MY LIFE WOULD BE FULFILLED IF - "I could get married."

32. SEX - "Woman"

40. EXCITING - "Sex"

59. MY GREATEST DESIRE IS - "satisfaction" (Meaning sexual satisfaction).

79. MOST OF ALL I WANT - "Sex."

In the above series of responses from a male patient, all are actually linked. It is clear that the patient has a strong sexual desire and considers himself frustrated at the present time. Furthermore, he desires satisfaction of the frustration and desires this in marriage, so a key part of his problem is sexual frustration due to waiting to get married in order to have sex. More from the same patient:

66. HOW - "Can I get married?"

A line is drawn from #66 to #18; there is an obvious connection. Other aspects of this particular case come out as follows:

45. I FEEL GUILTY WHEN - "I masturbate."

48. THE ONE THING I NEED MOST IS - "Someone to love me."

67. MY GREATEST FEAR IS - "Not being loved."

20. IF ONLY - "I were more attractive."

Obviously the therapy should include assisting the patient in building greater self-confidence.

23. DESIRE - "Want."

28. WHY CAN'T I - "Meet girls?"

Observe what is falling into place at this point in the analysis. This particular person is sexually frustrated, has an inferiority feeling, and is not dating girls. He is in conflict over masturbation and feels guilt because of his inner desires. After #28 the patient moved his right hand, which would indicate some nervousness in his feelings about why he cannot meet girls.

42. PENIS - "Envy" (The patient moves again.)

All of the above gives an idea of what the problem is. Now as we analyze other aspects of this particular test, we can find out more about why he has this problem. Note the following:

3. FATHER - "Name" (He simply repeated the name.) (Note: "Father is just a name.")

37. I WAS DOMINATED - "By my father."

51. GOD - "Father."

A line is drawn from #51 to 37, equating the two. He's dominated by his father, and God is father. The feeling of being dominated by the two and at the same time having a sense of guilt indicates a picture of the complex. His image of God comes originally from his father who dominated him. He sees God, therefore, as a dominating father, ready to criticize if he steps out of line.

73. I FEEL INADEQUATE WHEN - "I am around girls."

89. I REALLY DESIRE - "Companionship." (Draw a line from "companionship" to "around girls.")

90. WOMEN ARE TO ME - "Above me." (Noted that he feels inferior, is in conflict because he desires companionship of girls, but is inadequate when around them.) Note the following:

98. I RESENT - "My mother." The source of his feeling of inferiority, then, comes from his relationship to both father and mother. This spills over into his fear of being around girls, and consequently no prospects of marriage.

68. I BECAME - "Afraid."

101. I WAS JEALOUS WHEN - "My brother was born." (Note: the time when he was left out.)

121. PRIDE - "None."

126. STEAL - "Toys." (When? Guilt?)

129. CHILDREN - "Mine." (When? Where? Guilt? Draw line between two "guilts.")

134. BLACK - "Woman." (Did he have ic.? Guilt?)

136. WHERE - "Did I go wrong?" (Several responses indicate the strong possibility of guilt. It helps to look at the test at a glance, see the areas which have to be checked out. Some of these responses obviously are

not clear, thus, they need to be brought up later in the analysis to see what is behind them.)

172. IF I KNEW I'D NEVER BE PUNISHED - "I'd rape someone."

169. DIRTY - "Sex." (Guilt.)

178. WHEN I'M NUDE - "I am ashamed." (Draw a line back to "penis," #42.)

174. MY DEEPEST THOUGHTS TELL ME - "I am inadequate." (Compare with #121, PRIDE - "none.")

184. AT THE VERY BOTTOM OF IT ALL - "I hate myself." Compare #121 and 174.)

185. I'M JUST TIRED OF - "living," should be compared with #96, MY BIGGEST FAILURE - "is in being."

97. I WAS NEAR DEATH - "When I was born."

186. I FEEL BEST WHEN - "I go to church."

Note the relationship now between birth, life, mother, and a feeling of being near death. He feels best when going to church because here is the source of spiritual life, also the source of resolution for his guilt, but it presumably offers only temporary relief. On #98, he said, THE GREATEST OBSTACLE TO MY HAPPINESS IS - "my soul." It turned out that this man had been in the army, and had engaged in sexual promiscuity with prostitutes. His sister had gotten all of the attention, according to his feelings, and he got the idea because of the way his sister was treated that it was better to be a girl than to be a boy, so he began to deny his masculinity, which shows conflict over his naked body and his penis. His case ended up with the following summary:

ISE #1 - four years old. His father belittled him and whipped him with a venetian blind slat unjustly. By this time he already felt that his little sister was the favorite in the family; she didn't get whippings and he was whipped.

ISE #2 - source of guilt. When he was seven years old he visited his grandmother's house. A cousin, who was twelve years old, was visiting and, quite child-like, they decided to take off their clothes to play with their penises. This boy did not want to, but he did. He expected to be found out and consequently punished, but when this did not happen he started a pattern of punishing himself for his sexual thoughts and inclinations. Based upon this, a complex developed. It was composed of fear, shame, lack of understanding about sexual drives, guilt, pleasurable feelings about sex--a mixture of strong emotions developed in his mind. He sought an outlet for these powerful inner drives but was torn within himself for not knowing which way to go. He received repeated warnings about sex and noticed that his sister did not have a penis. It felt good to have a penis; but his sister, who did not have one, was treated better. He was the one that received the threats and punishment, then guilt began to build up. This boy could have become homosexual, but this did not develop. His strong inner conflicts caused very neurotic responses until after his analysis. He responded well to therapy and became readjusted and started dating. He had both the Ponce De Leon Syndrome and a Guilt Complex.

Miscellaneous Considerations

In the above examples, it becomes clearer as to how the word association test, within two sessions, can give the therapist much valuable information on the type patient he is treating. Some of the responses can be relied upon as definite leads, with dependable information of what is going on at the unconscious or preconscious level. Other responses will be more vague and merely give hints as to unconscious patterns. These will have to be examined further during the course of therapy.

Of course, much of the material on the word association test will reveal nothing of value in the analysis. It takes a broad base of material in order to have some which will apply to every case. But what does apply in any one case is most helpful and is worth going down the list of 195 stimuli in order to get the information that is gained from even so few a number as a dozen significant responses. A few nonsignificant responses are given frequently, such as PLEASE - "Don't Eat the Daisies" and BELIEVE ME IF - "All Those Endearing Young Charms."

A number of colors are listed and may be viewed as "null" words, but occasionally will be quite revealing, such as, BLACK which may stimulate a response indicating strong racial feelings or morbidity. WHITE or GREEN may stimulate a vivid hospital or doctor experience.

The clinician can expect to get a few opposites such as LIFE - "death," BLACK - "white," SWEET - "sour," etc. If the operator desires to add more words than there are designated spaces, they may be added at the top of the columns.

Furthermore, the operator should be cautious to exercise great care not to insert himself into the test in any manner. For example, if, in childhood, the clinician's father beat him and he has a patient whose father beat him, then the clinician may be tempted to insert too much of himself into the questions or interpretations. Be aware that the therapist's conscious mind is relating to the patient's conscious and subconscious mind and, likewise, the therapist's subconscious mind is relating to the patient's conscious and subconscious mind. This is an inter-reacting relationship. A part of the therapist's mind is going into the analysis and by the same token a portion of the patient's problem is going to be borne by the therapist.

The test should be given under conditions wherein the client is deeply hypnotized, reclining, and in an atmosphere which is free of distraction and interruption. The test is calculated to stimulate the feelings of the unconscious mind. Thus, the atmosphere and situation must be conducive to complete freedom on the part of the patient to reply. During the test it may be necessary for the clinician to pause at times and to encourage the patient to further and deeper relaxation.

Incidentally, a number of years ago, after discovering that many patients were developing blocks and anxiety because of taking a "psychological TEST" I quit referring to this as a "test" and to the patient referred to it as the "word association exercise". Furthermore, I stress in the tape telling about the procedure, that there are no "right and wrong answers, only responses."

PROBLEMS WITH THE WORD ASSOCIATION TEST

Not everyone responds to the word association test in the same manner. Obviously, this is partly due to a variation in the personalities of the people who take the test. It may be due, however, to other problems. Those problems are primarily due to some form of blocking, which is evidenced by responses of repetition of the stimulating word(s), or by defining it.

After the clinician calls out the word or phrase, there are some patients who have long pauses before they respond. One of the reasons for these long pauses may be that the client is blocking the answer; that is, the stimulus word or phrase has significance to him and the unconscious mind has the urge to respond, probably with an answer of significance, but the ego, or the super-ego, is acting as a censor and consequently prevents the urged response from coming forth (Note 70). In this case, the therapist should pause in giving out the stimulus word and give some suggestions calculated to put the patient into a deeper state of hypnosis and follow this with a reminder of the testing procedure such as: "Each time I call out a word or phrase a thought will immediately come to your mind. Immediately you will think of a person or a scene or a memory or a feeling that is related to this word or phrase. You will call out that word or phrase to me immediately. It is okay to say anything that comes to your mind. In fact, you will say anything that comes to your mind immediately as it pops into your mind after I give you the word or phrase. (Repeat.) We will now continue with the word association exercise." (Pick up where the words were blocked and continue with the test.)

There are some situations where the therapist feels persistence like that referred to above is not appropriate to that patient. In spite of the fact that it prolongs the test it could be advisable to find out why the patient is blocking there. Stop and talk about it.

There are some patients who become so deeply hypnotized that it appears to be too much effort for them to make an immediate response to the stimulus. They are so lethargic that speech does not come readily. Usually if the therapist will encourage them to speak up promptly they will respond.

Occasionally a patient will get in the pattern of repeating the same word or phrase without any further response. A similar type of response is made by the patient who simply repeats a synonym or defines the word. In a few other cases, there are those whose predominant response is to give the opposite of the word that is called out by the clinician. In any of these instances the clinician should pause, repeat phrases calculated to deepen the hypnosis and give the patient instructions over again. Specific instructions can be given to take care of the problem. For example, the therapist may say, "I do not want definitions of the words. Tell me what you associate with that word or what that word reminds you of."

Usually these methods will take care of the resistive patient and will enable the therapist to continue with the test more successfully. If, however, the therapist feels that the patient continues to block by any of the above mentioned methods, it may be necessary to tell the patient that another time will have to be set for taking the exercise and that he or she will feel good about coming back the next time and will respond freely and openly according to the instructions. Then when the patient does return to continue with the test, sufficient time should be given for complete hypnosis, after which, the instructions should be repeated so clearly and forcefully that the patient knows exactly what is expected.

GENERAL OBSERVATIONS

There are many more deductions that may be made from the word association test than listed here, but some of the more outstanding implications are given in the following pages. It should be kept in mind that one answer does not reveal the entire psyche, but one answer may show a trend or it may give a lead for further investigation. It will take a combination of factors to draw hard and fast conclusions. Some of the answers will give a basis for further detailed questioning as the therapy progresses. The following paragraphs give some broad indications of the manner in which responses from the test reveal the type of personality of the subject (Bryan, 1969c).

The general patient orientation will be revealed by the responses on a combination of the following key words: Concerning himself he may reveal himself to be oral, vaginal, phallic, or anal character. Responses in regard to parents will indicate an orientation toward parents, toward self, or others. This in turn will give an indication of the maturity level of the patient. For example, the patient who is egocentric is generally immature.

If the patient uses "always" and/or "never" for such stimuli as, ANXIETY, DESIRE, EXCITING, HOSTILITY, GUILT, CHEAT, AFFECTION, etc. this may reveal something of his lack of sophistication or obsessive-compulsive personality type. The same principle holds true of responses such as "good" and "bad." There are patients also who use the word "Me," frequently throughout the test. This may indicate a large ego, or other form of egocentricity with its appropriate problems.

Concerning life and death responses, the clinician should be on the alert for terms of a morbid nature. These can crop up anywhere in the test and could indicate the presence of the Walking Zombie Syndrome or perhaps a tendency toward being suicidal.

Fear Responses: Fear of therapy may be indicated by THERE MUST BE: "another way than this." Or HYPNOSIS: "fear" or "no."

The CAUGHT and PUNISHMENT duality (#172, 173). Responses here will show the strength of the superego. If after the word CAUGHT, the patient says "I'll do it," it might indicate the need to be caught and be punished. If, on the other hand, a person says CAUGHT: I'll do it," and for PUNISH: "I wouldn't do it," it may indicate the thought is "Catch me all you want to, but just don't punish me." If on both of these questions the response is something like "I still wouldn't do it," there is a strong super-ego and the person does not need to be restrained by law or force.

There are several "desire" questions (#82, 92, 93, 103, 106). The intensity of the subject's desire or need, hence a reflection of something missing in the life, may be indicated by replies to this series. For example, MY GREATEST DESIRE IS: "love;" MY GREATEST NEED IS: "love;" I REALLY DESIRE: "love," etc.

On the other hand, replies to these questions may all be different, indicating there is no desire or ambition which has become an obsession.

Another series which enables the therapist to cross check the patient's thinking is the series relating to guilt (73, 75, 84, 88, 89, 96, 169, 180). The same principle applies; namely, if there is a recurring theme in all of these, the person is obsessed with guilt with regard to certain acts or thoughts. For example: GUILT: "abortion," PUNISHMENT: "abortion," MY GREATEST FEAR IS: "punishment." Of course there are other terms which more directly stimulate feelings of guilt such as LIE, STEAL, DIVORCE, SEX, etc. (Bryan, 1 969d).

The questions on nudity will reveal the person's feelings about his/her own body. Self-abnegation may be appearing in several places and obviously indicates lack of pride or self-confidence, self-consciousness, and the like.

The question TESTS LIKE THIS (#179, 48, 49), give the patient an opportunity to express hostility to the clinician or process, or favorable and optimistic expectations.

WHEN FIRE BREAKS OUT (#182). As Nadelson (1978) points out, it is helpful at the beginning of therapy to know something of the patient's problem solving philosophy and procedures, and this stimulus gives some indication of this aspect of the patient's personality. In the waking state a reply like "Call the fire department" would be typical. But in the hypnotic state there are a variety of impulsive replies indicative of the type of personality of the subject. A reply like "Call the fire department" would indicate an attitude of calling an expert to handle the problems properly. A reply like "Put it out" might indicate a self-made person who feels confident to take care of things on his own and indicates a patient who will likely cooperate in therapy, doing his own part. A reply like "Run like the dickens," is not too desirable. That person is not likely to take responsibility in problem solving. A response like "Hot" usually accompanies a rather passive, nondescript individual. A response like "It excites me" is a person that should be watched carefully (Bryan, 1 969e).

There are other questions having to do with confidence or a lack of it, such as #161, 171 (which is a double entendre--it may be sexual, it may be regarding competence) and 189 and 191.

The question AT THE END OF THE ROAD has many possible answers, but it usually indicates what the patient expects in the way of therapy for himself, an optimistic or a pessimistic future. Another one of a similar nature is IF I EVER REALLY LET GO. A possible reply is "I'd be okay." This would indicate that the person at the present time is inhibited and the inhibitions need to be removed. On the other hand, the patient may warn that he cannot let the inhibitions go without self-harm.

There are times when the therapist can, and should, make comments. A question may be asked to clarify a response. Reassurance may be given. Confidence may be instilled. For example, on the word PERSONALITY an obese, female patient responded with, "I'd like a better personality." I said, "I can help. You have a good personality underneath. Its buried under layers of anxiety and depression and even under the layers of fat. But it will emerge during the process of therapy."

An obsessive male responded to the word SUFFOCATE with "death." Thinking of a death threat, I asked, "Have you ever felt you were suffocating?" The patient replied after a pause, "No, but it seems like I've had a time when I couldn't breathe." I questioned when this might have taken place, to which he made this provocative reply, "I don't know. If I'm real relaxed or sleeping the thought comes to me." Obviously, the patient has been in a hypnotic state and in that condition was spontaneously on the verge of an age regression. It later proved to be a faint allusion to the birth experience which was the Initial Sensitizing Event.

In conclusion, there are enough stimulating words and phrases in the test to give the therapist an indication of the overall, general personality type of the subject. General impressions of the degree of depression, anxiety, sexual orientation, confidence or lack of it, maturity level, attitudes toward significant others in one's life, and expectations of the future will be indicated on this test. For the two hours time spent in taking it, it is productive of much insight. If there are sufficient ambiguities in the mind of the clinician after the test is given, these can be checked out in direct conversation with the patient in hypnosis (Bryan, 1971d, 1971e; Lasin, 1964).

John A. Scott, Sr., Ph.D.

DIAGNOSING

Reference has already been made to the "medical model" and the explanation of the "double diagnosis." The Waking Diagnosis (WD) is usually a summary of the patient's presenting symptoms, such as "depression," "orgasmic dysfunction," "migraine," etc. The Underlying (or Hypnotic) Diagnosis (UD) is a recognition of the unconscious conditions ultimately causing the symptomatic expression. The WD characteristically is readily apparent. The UD is not as obvious at the outset, but should be recognized by the clinician as soon as possible, and hopefully can be done (at least tentatively) in the first interview or by the conclusion of the case history. Once the UD is made tentatively, the therapist seeks to verify it as soon as possible and center the analysis around the events causing or contributing to the problematical situation. This is where the word association test may be most helpful, i.e., it may verify the tentative UD or it may point to another possibility. Therefore, as the test is given, the following list of varying conditions and responses should be observed.

Responses which would indicate the Walking Zombie Syndrome (Death Complex) are related to what could be called general morbidity. The subjects of death, dying, or kindred ideas, are on the patient's subconscious mind and may be reflected in the vocabulary, figures of speech or even in dress, posture, and facial expressions. The other side of the coin would be statements reflecting the desire to live such as, "If I could only be more alive," and other indications of the inability to function, the inability to have deep feelings, or lack of zest for life. Most any words, phrases, or thoughts which might be used to indicate depression or flattened affect will be signals of underlying morbidity (Bryan, 1962).

Indications of the Ponce de Leon Syndrome are childlike and generally immature responses. Answers to the provoking words and phrases of the word association test which indicate the theme, "I want what I want when I want it" indicate the presence of this syndrome.

Responses will be "I" centered and reflect an unwillingness to share in a "give or take" relationship, to share with others, or assume responsibility. Other indications of this syndrome are use of terms implying a continued tie to "mother or daddy," grasping selfishness, inconsideration for others, child-like answers on sex terms, career responsibilities, inter-personal relationships and such like (Bryan, 1964b). For example, #98 MY BIGGEST FAILURE - "is not being able to succeed in my job." #101 IT'S SO EASY TO - "wait till tomorrow." #104 I ASK MYSELF - "why

154

I'm not better at organizing." #105 THE ONE THING I NEED MOST - "is to be more sure of myself." An experienced therapist will pick up on those manifestations of general immaturity.

The diagnosis of Sexual Arrest would be manifested by any indication of sexual behavior which is generally characteristic of the pre-adult personality. This will be implied by answers given to sex terms, inter-personal relationships, and feelings about one's own masculine or feminine development, as well as attitudes and relationships with the opposite sex.

The presence of the Guilt Complex is indicated by feelings of guilt, alienation from God, fear of (or need for) punishment, accident proneness, concern about hell, a view of God's being judge, self-depreciation and similar thoughts. Manifestations of this syndrome are occasionally similar to those of the Walking Zombie Syndrome (Bryan, 1969a; Gottschall, 1969).

The presence of the Identity Problem (ID) will be indicated on the word association exercise by reflections on one's selfhood, self-abnegation, confusion or doubt concerning one's sexual orientation, perplexity about how one fits into relationships with others, and any other indication of uncertainty about the self or one's future. The general theme is implied by "Who am I?" types of statements.

Separation Anxiety is a frequent underlying diagnosis found with people who are broken hearted over a love or marriage disintegration. Intense loneliness, despair, despondency in feeling the loss of love is often the repetition of separation at an early age from a parent. The unresolved emotion of the first separation (even at birth) now is accumulated with the present loss and the pain is not just the pain of the current separation, but a replay of all previous separations with the accompanying emotional and physical symptoms. Responses on the word association test will betray these feelings when the appropriate stimulus words or sentences are used.

In those cases where the marital relationship figures prominently in the symptoms, the therapist will be alert for expressions of belligerent feelings regarding the spouse, sexual frustration, dislike for habits or practices of the spouse, feelings of being restricted or persecuted by the spouse, desire to be free of marital responsibilities, treatment (or view) of spouse like a parent or child, etc. Keep in mind that a waking diagnosis of marital problems of some sort may have an underlying diagnosis of any one, or combination, of the hypnotic diagnoses previously mentioned.

As in the practice of medicine, based on a statement of the symptoms, the doctor makes a tentative diagnosis; then he follows up with the appropriate tests which either verify the diagnosis or indicate changing it to another one. For the psychotherapist, the principle is the same and, after the case history, the word association test and dream analysis are the primary means by which the therapist determines the underlying diagnosis. Once the underlying diagnosis is made, therapy should continue to demonstrate the cause and effect relationship of the events which caused the condition to the patient. This takes place in the therapy which follows the word association test and the dream analysis.

CRITIQUE

In the following pages a brief survey will be presented of the primary objections that have been made to projective tests without evaluation at this point. Some of the objections are valid, some only partially valid, and some are not valid at all. It may be that the value of projective tests, like beauty, is in the eyes of the beholder. A brief evaluation of these objections will be made in the next section of this chapter.

Objections

A. *It is extremely difficult to establish what is measured* (Blatt. 1975, p. 333f; Mischel, 1971, p.l65)

Those who make this charge are concerned about the lack of objectivity of these measures. They are concerned that the report may be just a series of descriptive statements; furthermore, that the content can vary from day to day.

B. *Scores depend on the clinician's judgments* (Blatt, 1975, p. 327; Macfarlane & Tuddenham, 1951, pp. 36, 46.)

The substance of this charge is that the clinician's judgments are subjective and based in large part on "intuition." The interpreter projects himself too much into the test situation. Furthermore, there are methodological problems in that many interpretive steps in such tests provide opportunity for a wide range of disagreement by the testers. Another facet of this charge is that the test is not standardized (Schafer, 1967, p. 17), that is, these tests are not constructed in such a manner that the procedure, apparatus, and scoring have been fixed so precisely that the same test can be given at different times and places (and this is assumed to be a requisite for any successful, scientific test).

An additional element in this objection is that the projective tests are not susceptible to statistical treatment in the way that objective tests are (Macfarlane & Tuddenham, 1951, p. 36). And along with this charge is the one which states that such tests, currently used, do not yield an adequate sample of scored variables to relate to adequate validation criteria (Blatt, 1975, p.331; Macfarlane & Tuddenham, 1951, pp.46, 51). This is another way of saying that the measurement of personality is so complex and the theories of personality (and personality disorder) so varied, that a test with its limited number of questions and subjective replies cannot measure exactly what the problem is, or its scope, as compared with others in the population. Mr. A. who takes the Rorschach or a word association test, will give a different set of answers from Mr. B. and all others who take the tests. Of course, some of the answers might be similar or even the same, but there are not large blocks of the population who have taken the same test and given similar replies to the extent that precise categories and classifications can be determined.

C. *Skills of the administrator are not uniform and open to doubt in many cases* (Blatt, 1975, pp. 329, 330; Draguns, Haley, & Phillips, 1968, pp. 26, 27, 32.)

Any test to be effective must be used with clinical sophistication. Many tests have a standard procedure wherein the administrator has the same training and preparation as other administrators of said tests. Often this is not true with administrators of projective tests.

Projective tests are more susceptible to influence from the clinician who may have empathy or antipathy with the subject.

D. *Projective tests cannot predict behavior* (Blatt, 1975, p. 331; Macfarlane & Tuddenham, 1951, pp. 46, 51, 52.)

The ideal in testing is to be able to predict recidivism of a parolee or schizophrenic, success in college or psychotherapy, or aggressive or suicidal behavior. Projective tests are not capable of doing this.

E. *Projective tests do not make a contribution to the treatment process* (Blatt, 1975, p. 336.)

Blatt cites this objection stating further that projectives are merely ancillary to direct therapeutic treatment so that they do not achieve what people claim they achieve.

Other objections (Rotter, 1951, p. 293.)

1. *Projective tests are limited in that they give insufficient material for a description of the whole personality.*

2. *The tests may provide evidence of emotional disturbance, but without indicating the precise nature of disturbance.*

3. Under usual testing situations, these tests create tension which may result in a barrier to good rapport between the subject and clinician.

Summary: Objections which have been cited opposing or challenging the effective use of projective techniques fall into one of three categories, viz., concern about the administrator, doubt about the nature of the test, and status and conclusions with regard to the subject. Patently some of these objections have greater validity than others. A brief evaluation will now be made.

Evaluation

In the following paragraphs a brief evaluation will be made of the preceding objections in the light of the Bryan Word Association Test, the projective instrument which has been described in the preceding pages.

A. It is extremely difficult to establish what is measured.

First, I believe those who rely on this objection are establishing aims for projective tests which may be used for other types of tests. A projective test should not be considered as an instrument to do everything, and no such generalized ambition has been claimed for the Bryan test. Assagioli (1965, p. 94) points out that generally tests are expected to do too much: diagnose, predict, establish psychological types, etc. And Blatt (1975, p. 333), evaluating the above objection, states that in testing we have come to expect "conjunctive statements in our evaluation which integrate a number of observations across a number of different inferential lines."

It is not the aim of the word association test to put the patient in a specific category that is extremely limited, as in an IQ pocket, for instance. The purpose of the test is to aid in making a diagnosis and, in my opinion, this general statement can be made by most clinicians who use some form of projective instrument. This test is used by hypnoanalysts immediately after completing a case history, at which time, hopefully, a diagnosis is at least tentative. In a relatively short time, the therapist may obtain a great deal of information about the inner feelings of the patient on many different subjects such as guilt, sexuality, relationship to parents and other family members, needs, goals, frustrations, fears, hostilities, childhood trauma and expectations for the future, to mention a few. Some tests reveal more about the patient than others, naturally. Of course, some patients respond better than others, but always more is learned in two hours time by this means than could be learned in a much longer period of time by conventional therapeutic methods.

What is measured? In a way, nothing! This test is given in order to gain access to the patient's unconscious mind in a relatively brief period of time on a number of sensitive subjects.

B. Scores depend on the clinician's judgment. C. Skills of the administrator are not uniform and open to doubt in many cases.

I have chosen to discuss these two objections together because they deal with the administrator of the test.

First, there are no scores as such in the Bryan Word Association Test. It is more accurate to refer to an "evaluation" than a score. Secondly, it is certainly true that the skills of the administrator are a vital element in testing and in any form of clinical procedure. Skills cannot be expected to be exactly uniform in any therapy, but hopefully they are sufficiently uniform in clinical work to achieve success with the patient. If administrators may be uniformly trained in administering objective tests, so may they be trained to administer projective tests.

Suppose a clinician does not use the projective test. Does the above stated objection apply any less to his other therapeutic procedures? Not at all. Competency in all phases of the clinical setting is certainly desired, but there is no justification in challenging the competency of a clinician because he uses a projective test.

Any test administrator should be trained to be competent in the use of tests or any other procedures he/she will use in treating the public. Those who give projective tests can be trained and should be trained, just as anyone else should be. Any therapist who has been trained in psychotherapeutic procedures, in the functioning of the unconscious mind, and in drawing inferences from the subtleties of a patient's verbal and non-verbal revelations, can be trained to make valid deductions from projective tests.

A therapist dealing with emotional illness is in a somewhat different position from the physician who is dealing with the physical body. In the latter case the doctor or lab technician can, by actual count, determine that the red blood corpuscles are too low, or that there is albumin in the urine to such an extent that proper treatment is necessary. Treatment is often given in measured doses and fixed quantities, as we all know. We also know that with emotional disorders we cannot be as concrete in judgements and evaluations, and cannot expect to be. Furthermore, varying methods of treatment are used in psychotherapy. Then we must apply this knowledge consistently.

No clinician should rely solely on a projective test for an evaluation or diagnosis without using his/her better judgment based on other criteria as well. A physician prescribes certain laboratory tests because she/he already has ideas about what needs to be checked. The lab work either verifies his/her suspicions about the patient or gives him/her a new lead to check out further. Thus, the ultimate conclusion concerning the patient's illness comes about as a result of a series of checks and balances, hypotheses and verifications. So it is with the psychotherapist. He operates on the same principle, but he relies on data of a different kind.

Macfarlane and Tuddenham (1951, pp. 48, 50) list general requirements for the administrator of a projective test. The clinician should have a wide sampling experience, long experience in sifting evidence, and in making and revising clinical hypotheses, and long thorough-time contacts with the same patients to check their judgments.

D. Projective tests do not make a contribution to the treatment process.

This objection is very little more than a quibble. Projective tests do make a contribution to the treatment process. A more legitimate question is, just how much contribution does the test make? It will vary with the test, the administrator and especially with the patient. The very nature of a patient's illness may make him/her less communicative at the unconscious level than others. Herein is the primary reason that standardization and controlled variables will never be a part of projective tests. The very meaning of the word projective carries with it an inherent variability and subjectivity and these elements will always be a part of these tests.

Macfarlane and Tuddenham (1951, p. 50) state that in essence the nature of a projective test is such that validation is not feasible. They observe that it would take 4,860 cases to establish reference norms to make projective tests reliable and dependable. They arrive at that figure by establishing a series of pigeon holes or categories that would be minimum subgroups (or types) for people to fit into in order to be compared to others in socie ty. Such categories are: "two classifications with respect to sex, three with respect to age, three with respect to maturity level for age, three with respect to class level, and three with respect to intelligence." This makes 2x3x3x3x3, or 162 sub-groups. "If 30 cases are chosen as the minimum sample size for each sub-group, we require 4,860 cases drawn from a limited age range and classified crudely with respect to only a few of the relevant variables" (Macfarlane & Tuddenham, 1951, p. 50).

The above classifications are minimal. To be precise in validating subjects, surely the subject's biological heritage would have to be taken into account along with his rearing, influences, family and social contacts, etc. Therefore, when the psychotherapist seeks to know more about the unconscious mind of his patient with regard to his anxieties, pressures, fears, tensions, and the sources of these, and how the patient has been dealing with them, he has to use judgment of a different sort than an IQ test or other objective, test. Every psychotherapist knows that when a patient is finally "diagnosed" as a particular kind of neurotic or psychotic, that this, indeed, is general and another opinion may be slightly (or even greatly) different from the first one. There are variations within each person because each person is different from every other person. The projective test should be viewed, consequently, as a window into that unique individual's own peculiarities. The word association test, as other projective tests, therefore, is an aid in treatment in that it reveals information about the patient that the therapist is unlikely to get by any other means, or at least quicker than he would by any other means if he were to get it at all.

E. Under usual testing situations, these tests create tension which may result in a barrier to good rapport between the subject and clinician.

Admittedly this is a possibility. It has been dealt with in several ways in the clinical setting. Some clinicians have another person give the test for this or other reasons. Some therapists give the test themselves but have taken this objection into account. By assurances to the patient that there are no "right and wrong" answers and no "pass or fail" scores, they have allayed the fears and tensions of the patient. Hypnoanalysts, in giving the Word Association Test give these assurances and have the patient hypnotized at the time the test is given. There is no need for a projective test such as this to be a barrier to good rapport.

I will offer one additional reason for using the Bryan Word Association test in therapy. Regardless of the benefit to therapy for the clinician we have found it is of great benefit to the patient. For one, it allows an additional hypnosis session (or two) for the patient to become accustomed to the hypnosis process. For another it allows the patient to hear herself saying the answers to these stimulus words and to observe her abreactions (if they occur). This is sometimes a powerful statement to the patient about the potential for success of the therapy. A positive expectation aids rapport.

John A. Scott, Sr., Ph.D.

CONCLUSION

A number of the more prominent objections to the projective test have been listed. Each therapist, utilizing a projective method, should take into consideration these objections and profit by them. But such tests have their place and are a valuable adjunct in the therapeutic process.

CHAPTER 5

THE PRINCIPLES OF DREAM ANALYSIS

Iamblichus is quoted as saying, "The nighttime of the body is the daytime of the soul" (Gilman, 1958, P. 232). This quaint observation tersely describes a commonplace mystery--that of dreams--which has challenged mankind since ancient times. Consequently wisemen, soothsayers and prophets have used dreams as a means of giving explanations of events or foretelling the future (Bible, Genesis 31:11; 37:5 etc.; Murray, 1957; Olmstead, 1923).

In modern times, psychotherapists have endeavored to be "more scientific" in their explanation of dreams, but it has always been an inexact "science" (Gilman, 1958; Woods & Greenhouse, 1974). Much of the older material that has been written on the subject of dream interpretation is unreliable. Dream books, for example, which state that dreaming about a specific subject always means a specific thing, no matter who dreams the dream, are unreliable (Gilman, 1958).

There are general principles of interpretation which may be applied to individuals but it is misleading to go down a list in a book and say, "This means that," to everyone who dreams about the subject (for example see Becker, 1974).

THE NATURE OF DREAMS

A graduate student named Eugene Aserinsky, working in the laboratory of Nathaniel Kleitman at the University of Chicago in 1953, accidently discovered the phenomenon of eye movements beneath the closed lids of sleeping infants (Kleitman, 1963). Further laboratory work with volunteers using eye and brain recordings enabled researchers to record and measure the presence, frequency, duration and rhythms of dreams. Furthermore, associations with many variables were recognized and identified (Roche, 1966). Physical conditions that accompany dreaming are great relaxation of muscles (motor muscles are almost without tonus) and specific brain wave patterns usually accompanied by rapid eye movements (REMs), though not always (Green, Ullman & Tauber, 1968; Roche, 1966). For most people there are four or five dream periods during the night coming in cycles spaced about 90 minutes apart (Foulkes, 1966; Roche, 1966), but there are individual variations.

Dement (1960) and Fisher (1960) have done extensive research on the effects of dream deprivation and have observed that subjects so deprived have shown anxiety, irritability and difficulty in concentrating. In fact, there are indications that if a person were deprived of dreaming long enough, it would result in a serious disruption of the personality. Others agree.

Tufts University sleep researcher Ernest Hartmann tells us that during dream sleep the brain restores a chemical, depleted during the day, which we need to focus our attention and think logically (Goleman, 1976). Gilman (1958, p. 43) pointedly states, "We must dream in order to live."

Thus we need our dreams, and to insure that we have them during periods of sleep, there is, in the brain, a subtle chemical mechanism that "acts as a dam to prevent our waking hours from being flooded with the distraction of dreams" (Goleman, 1976). Jacobs (1976) working with Dement at the Stanford Medical School, theorizes that high levels of serotonin in the synaptic gaps at the axon terminals of raphe neurons, act as the "dam" to prevent dreams. Then when the serotonin level drops, the chemical blockade is opened and the signs of dreams begin (Jacobs, 1976).

Psychological literature over the years has accumulated a variety of explanations as to the purpose of dreams: we balance our emotional accounts by acting out our repressed desires, mostly in symbolic form (Freud, in Woods & Greenhouse, 1974); we reveal our conflicts to ourselves (Stekel, 1974); we continue the lifestyle of our waking life (Adler, in Woods & Greenhouse, 1974); or we strive to return to wholeness by tapping the unconscious sources of knowledge available to all dreamers (Jung, in Woods & Greenhouse, 1974). Modern research indicates there is some truth in all of these views. Since it is not within the province of this research to summarize and analyze the various dream hypotheses, the reader is directed to Breger et. al. (1971, pp. 7-10, 18-21), Green, et. al. (1968, pp. 146-179) or Woods & Greenhouse (1974, pp. xvii-xix, 177-228) or others for authorities and literature.

THE CONTENT OF DREAMS

Freud's early theory that dreams are the royal road to the unconscious is borne out by modern research (Breger et al., 1971; Foulkes, 1966; Woods & Greenhouse, 1974). Dreams are meaningful and reveal our inner selves, our feelings, motives, frustrations, and conflicts. Although our knowledge concerning the process of dreaming has made great strides in the last two decades, it is still viewed as complicated and somewhat theoretical.

The memory system, consisting of stored input from external experiences ever since birth, gives rise, in the dream, to reality-like experiences (images, thoughts, fantasies, expressions of conflicts, and the like) in the relative absence of external input during the sleeping stage (Breger et al. 1971). In doing so the dreamer unconsciously selects residues or "props" from daily experiences and adapts them to the ongoing unresolved unconscious conflicts, problems, or themes (Breger et al., 1971; Foulkes, 1966; Gilman, 1958), such themes coming from the interpersonal involvements of daily life. The props, selected often from daily activities including places, things or people, are adapted to the primary theme which is primitive (Gilman, 1958). Poetzl (1960) announced that he found that the details of daily life that go unnoticed by the conscious mind serve as a source of dream material. Although Poetzl's conclusions have been challenged (Pulver & Epps, 1963) because of inadequate experimental procedure, Foulkes (1966) has seen evidence to demonstrate that, at least in some dreams, the Poetzl phenomenon applies.

Gilman (1958) points out that primitive language is used because in the process of sleep the higher centers of the brain such as the cerebral cortex and frontal lobes are practically dormant, thus leaving the lower centers more or less in control. This is reminiscent of Freud's theory that without the censorship of the preconscious the primary process takes over in dreams (Breger et al., 1971). The dream situation, then, deals with interpersonal relationships and feelings in a primitive manner (Gilman, 1958).

The foregoing survey applies to the average person having typical night-to-night dreams. For those under stress, or having emotional problems, dreams take on peculiar characteristics (Gilman, 1958; Woods

& Greenhouse, 1974). For example, in the study made by Breger et al. on the effects of stress on dreams, they included experimental subjects involved in "group therapy" and persons who were due to have surgery, and demonstrated that persons under stress have their dreams effected by stress (Breger et al., 1971). This research revealed that day-to-day concerns of an emotional nature, which are not resolved, tend to be subject matter for dreams (Breger et al., 1971). But such themes are, of course, expressed symbolically. Because the conflicts behind the dream have not been resolved, the same themes will recur, using different props and characters, much as the theme of a symphony may recur in a different key or in different time later in the composition (Gilman, 1958). These dreams or internal images, based on the memory system, utilize data accumulated from every source on working out solutions to life's problems (Breger et. al., 1971), but such solutions involve impulses from the primary process as well as solutions fed in from external experiences (Bregeret. al., 1971; Gilman, 1956).

DREAM INTERPRETATION IN HYPNOANALYSIS

Gilman (1958, PP. 69-94) presents, very effectively, some general principles which are necessary to understanding the meaning of dreams in psychotherapy. They are summarized as follows:

1. The patient (or dreamer) is always personally involved in the dream either as a participant or an observer to the action or circumstance of the dream image (op.cit., p. 75).
2. Some degree of emotional catharsis is taking place in the dream. The basic instinctual drives produce energy which seeks to be expressed. That which is not expressed in the conscious waking state finds an outlet in the dreaming state (op.cit., p. 75).
3. Conflicts between the libidinal drives, on the one hand, and the controls of the superego, on the other hand, are not always satisfactorily resolved in the conscious state, consequently, periods of sleep are useful for the expression and outlet of these unresolved conflicts (op.cit., p.77).
4. When these conflicts are expressed in the dream they are always expressed symbolically (Gilman, 1958, p. 79).
5. When these conflicts are expressed in the dream the unconscious mind utilizes the dream imagery in an effort to solve the conflicts

or problems. Sometimes this is successful, sometimes not. When not successful, the problem or conflict continues to seek a solution in the dreams by repeating the general theme in varying images as if continuing its search for solutions. If the libidinal energy continues to build up a higher charge than can be reckoned with in the dream process, physical or emotional symptoms frequently become pronounced. The principle of self-preservation of the emotional health may be said to apply here: the mind seeks to cope with one's problems, utilizing all past experiences, in order to prevent an over burden to the conscious mind (op.cit., pp. 78-80).

6. The surface meaning of the dream usually conceals the real issues, and is never to be taken literally.

As a means of preventing an over-load on the conscious mind there is a censor which serves to block off the real issues of the dream when the dreamer awakens. This must be one of the reasons we do not remember most of our dreams and those that are remembered arc remembered only in the coded form of symbols and apparent meaninglessness (op.cit., pp. 81, 82).

7. The subject matter of dreams is valuable in psychotherapy for the following reasons (Gilman, 1958, pp. 83, 84):
   a. It is relevant in that it frankly expresses the conflict;
   b. It is timely in that it deals with current issues;
   c. It is personal in that the subject matter pertains to the dreamer;
   d. It is intimate in that the dream pertains to the inner thoughts.

8. Dreaming has continuity in several respects. In some cases it is obvious when the same type of dream recurs over a prolonged period of time. In other situations the same theme recurs, but with varying symbolism from time to time. In still other cases the symbolism of setting remains essentially the same but there is a variation in the details of the action. Nonetheless, the dream will be repeated in its essence until the conflicts depicted by it are resolved (op.cit., p. 84).

9. It requires a second party to assist in interpreting the dream. The very nature and purpose of the dream is such that it is rarely obvious to the dreamer. Since the dream is an image in the unconscious mind and one cannot adequately comprehend his own unconsciousness, it requires the objectivity of another person

to assist the dreamer, at least at the beginning of psychotherapy. (Some patients learn the principles of dream interpretation and enough about themselves to interpret their own dreams after a period of practice with a therapist.) The helping person must know the personality, background and life situation of the dreamer in order to be able to assist (op.cit., pp.88, 89).

10. The interpretation process is started by the therapist's reflecting "back to the person what has seemed to him to be the significant statements, and then sees if it provokes any thought in the mind of the patient" (Sullivan, 1953, p. 337). Then both dreamer and the therapist work together in exploring the possibilities of the dream imagery until the interpretation "feels right" to the dreamer. They can know it is correct when it is consistent with the person's total life situation (Gilman, 1958, p. 89; Wolberg, 1948,11, p.319).

THE HYPNOTIC SUGGESTION TO DREAM

Whereas the psychoanalyst throughout the course of therapy interprets the dreams of the patient in the continuing pursuit of revelation of the unconscious, the process of Medical Hypnoanalysis may abbreviate the length of therapy by dealing with one dream one time. Of course there are exceptions to this, particularly in those instances where the hypnoanalysis met with blocks and resistances which prolonged therapy. To be effective with such abbreviated procedure the following principles may be utilized.

1. Since the underlying theme of the patient's dreams continues to be basically the same until the conflict is resolved (Gilman, 1958), the chances are good that a sample dream is a fair representation of conflicts of the unconscious mind.

2. While in hypnosis a patient may be given a suggestion to dream on a given subject and respond accordingly. Freud (1938) maintained that a person could have some degree of control over his dreams and cites an example of the Marquis Hervey who could "gain such power over his dreams as to accelerate their course at will, and turn them in any direction." Stoyva (1974, pp. 392-395), verifying earlier works of Schrotter, Roffenstein, and Nachmansohn (cited ad. loc. without reference), concluded that a subject under hypnosis can be told what to dream about and he will likely respond. Sacerdote (1974), in a study dealing with obesity, supports the same concept. Others agree that a subject in dreaming will generally

follow suggestions given when hypnotized (Brenman, 1949; Hartman, 1967; Wolberg, 1948, II).

The hypnoanalyst gives the suggestion, while the patient is still in hypnosis (immediately at the conclusion of the word association test), to have a dream relating to the problem which underlies the presenting symptoms. About 50% of the patients will respond positively at the first suggestion. Among the group who do not respond positively, the suggestion may be given a second time and after the second suggestion about 50% of the remaining group will respond positively. Along with the suggestion to dream about the problem at hand, the patient is also told that upon dreaming, to awaken and write the dream down immediately and bring it to the next therapy session. To cover the contingency that the patient may not awaken and write the dream down, the suggestion is also given that the patient may have a sudden thought to arise quite unexpectedly; this should be written down immediately and brought to therapy. It is known that the longer a report of the dream is delayed after the REM period of sleep the poorer the recall and the greater the possibility of contamination with consciousness (Breger et al., 1971; Foulkes, 1966). Hartman (1967) maintains that the first product after the hypnotic dream suggestion, "often contains an important aspect of the patient's problem." Bryan's hypnotic suggestion to dream is abbreviated as follows (Note 13):

You have just completed the word association test. Now as you sink deeper and deeper relaxed, you sleep, and all other thoughts fade away into the distance and you pay attention only to the sound of my voice, letting yourself sink further and further down, deeper and deeper relaxed... You're going to have a dream. It's going to be a very vivid dream. A dream so vivid that it's going to wake you up; you are going to take a pencil or pen and paper, which you have placed by the side of your bed before going to sleep, and you're going to write down every detail, writing on one side of the page only. Maybe it will be one page, maybe half a page, maybe even two. When you have finished completely writing it down, then you'll roll over and go back to sleep and sleep soundly the rest of the night... then you will bring that piece of paper with the dream on it into me the next time you come... this dream is going to be d from other dreams, because this dream is going to have something to do with the very basic cause of your problem... The dream may be crystal clear to you or you may understand very little of it, but regardless of what you think of the dream, how insignificant you may think it to be or how you interpret it, you'll nevertheless bring it in exactly as you recall it. . . no dream is too large. No dream is too small. . . Between now and the time you return to this office in addition to the dream or in place of the dream you may have a sudden thought. . . it may come to you suddenly when you least expect it. . . it may come like a bolt out of the blue. . . you will immediately recognize it as being in some way sign to your problem. . . you will write that thought down immediately and bring it in with you the next time you return to my office...

A total of ten minutes is taken to give the suggestion. It is repeated, elaborated upon, and three minutes of silence is included in order to let the suggestion sink in and take effect.

RAPID DREAM INTERPRETATION

Bryan (Note 13) stresses that since it is the patient who had the dream it is the patient who must actively cooperate with the therapist in interpreting the dream. However, the therapist should be skeptical when the patient on rare occasions arrives saying, "I know the meaning of this dream." It is likely that he does not, and, too often by himself, can go off on a tangent in self-interpreting, reinforcing defenses. At the first therapy session following the dream suggestion, the patient is asked, upon arrival, if he (or she) has had a dream. If so, and if it is written down, the assistant takes it to the therapist, who reads it while the patient is escorted to the therapy room preparatory to the hypnotic induction. The patient is hypnotized by the use of tapes while the therapist is going over the dream, making observations and notes as to possibilities to discuss with the patient. After being hypnotized the patient may be given a tape with some basic principles of the meaning of dreams before interpretation starts with the therapist. The interpreting process is less complicated when the patient is hypnotized because of being in closer contact with the unconscious mind than in the waking state. Wolberg (1948, II, p. 319) had previously emphasized this, stating that such a dream should be interpreted in hypnosis, since the symbolism would be "more apparent in hypnosis than in waking life" (Hartman, 1967).

Bryan's twelve principles of rapid dream interpretation are as follows (Note 13):

1. The therapist may start with an overall view of the dream as a whole or select segments either in or out of sequence to discuss with the patient. A principle object, figure or scene may be selected and an inquiry is made of the patient: "What is the _____ in your life?" What is the hill? What is the lake? What is the automobile?

Occasionally the patient will have an immediate insight as to the significance of the symbol chosen. On other occasions by interacting with the therapist an association is made which leads to meaning.

Using the same method, the therapist may insert a person in place of an object or locale, and may ask, "Who is the big stranger?" "Who is playing the role of the person driving the car? Take the mask off. Who is behind the mask?" After having taken a thorough case history and after having given the word association test, the therapist should have a good idea of who the significant people in the patient's life are and therefore who to look for in the dream. In a dream people play roles as in a Shakespearean play, where masks are worn, sex is changed, color of hair is changed, costumes are deceiving, therefore it is necessary at times to take the costume off, take off the mask or the wig in order to ascertain who is really playing that role.

2. Inasmuch as dreams are regarding subjects that one cannot discuss at ease in the waking hours and regarding feelings that cannot readily be expressed, one is not surprised that there is a great deal of sexual material disguised or obvious in many dreams. However, as Gilman (1958) states emphatically, there is not as much sexual material in dreams as Freud would have us believe. Nonetheless, phallic symbols do appear and must be recognized for what they are: the symbol may be any elongated or pointed object.

3. By the same token, vaginal symbols should be recognized. Such symbols include holes, boxes, any kind of receptacle, even a large one, such as a house, may be used.

4. Bryan (Note 13) maintains, as does Gilman (1958) and Wolberg (1948, II), that the interpretation which the therapist feels, is accurate. The message of the dream may be consistent with other material which the patient resists also. Consequently, to get the patient to try the dream for size, Bryan (Note 13) will ask, "Who dreamed the dream? You did didn't you? This is what the dream is saying." In many cases, the dreamer later will come to realize the accuracy of the interpretation and other thoughts commensurate with the interpretation will fall into place and have significance. However, there are occasions when the patient does not accept the meaning and other possibilities must be explored.

5. Body symbols should be recognized. It is general knowledge that

genital symbols are used in dreams, but symbols representing the body are also used. The body is usually looked upon as a container and usually as a large one, like a house, and there may be sections of the house which are of significance also, such as the attic being equal to the mind.

6. The principle of denial. Frequently, the subject will make a statement about what he dreamed, but then at the conclusion, starting with the word "but", he will give a type of contradiction which helps in understanding the dream, that it is not really what it appears to be at first on the surface. For example, someone says, "I dreamed I fell in a lake, but I didn't drown. I felt great." His overall concluding feeling of "feeling great" actually denies the reality of a life threatening experience. The feeling of the patient in the situation has a great deal to do with the reality of the situation, and may betray a disguised set of circumstances. In the above example, the apodosis following the conjunction "but" is more reliable or factual than the imagery of the protasis which comes before. Falling in the lake represented a pleasurable experience.

Another example: "I dreamed I was in an army barracks (protasis), but everyone was dressed in white" (apodosis). The army barracks was an outward symbol or representation of another set of circumstances. When a person is in a large area and people are dressed in white, it typically indicates a hospital. The phrase "but everyone was dressed in white," is similar to reading the body language of a person who says one thing with his mouth, but the body language (the message from the unconscious mind) indicates just the opposite as being true. So the after-thought (apodosis) or the concluding and apparently contradicting phrase, will be more indicative of what the real situation is than the outward appearance of the scene or setting. The setting or the situation, or even the persons in the dream, are often disguising the real situation.

Another example: A woman said, "I dreamed of my brother, but he was blond." It wasn't really her brother whom she was dreaming about; it was her husband disguised as her brother. Her husband was the blond person in her life and he was in the dream because she treated her husband like a brother. As in the waking state the therapist looks for the off-handed, incidental or casual sounding remarks as a revelation of the real truth of the situation (Bryan, Note 13).

7. Together the patient and therapist interpret the scene, the people,

and the actions of the dream. People most likely to be in the dream, albeit disguised much of the time, are close relations--parents, spouse, children, therapist, and of course the patient. The action involved in the dream in most cases involves escape or fleeing, violence or a struggle of some sort, eating (which may symbolize survival), and sexual activity. It is important that the patient share as much as possible in the interpretation of the dream(s).

8. Principle of the broad sweep. Occasionally a patient will bring in several dreams from one night (in some cases a large number of dreams collected from several nights sleep). On some occasions the patient who does this is defending himself by diversive action. We have already seen that a series of dreams usually has one underlying pattern or theme, thus, such a theme should be sought out in a situation like this. The patient should recognize what the common denominator is and how, even though disguised, there is a recurring theme. This may be referred to as the "broad sweep" which may be recognized in a series of dreams without going into a great deal of detail with each dream and thus consume much time needlessly.

In the event the patient has only a little material in a brief dream, it may be necessary to deal with more details in order to arrive at an interpretation.

9. The composed dream. On rare occasions the patient will compose a dream and write it down in place of writing one from a sleeping state, confessing to such action before (or even after) an interpretation. One should not be disturbed. The composed dream may be as helpful in revealing the unconscious mind as a sleeping experience. As a matter of fact, if the person does not dream, or to be more accurate, does not remember to write down a dream and bring it for interpretation, the therapist may suggest that the person make up his own dream. This may be as revealing as if the person had had a dream at night. An alternative to this is to suggest, while in hypnosis, that the person will have a dream at that time and will express it to the therapist as it unfolds (Epstein, 1981; Sacerdote, 1974; Wolberg, 1948, I, II).

10. The therapist should be on the alert for a dream that suggests danger, particularly if there is more than one dream indicating harm coming to the patient. Such may indicate the imminence

of suicide. The patient should gain insight into such unconscious provocations and their source in order to stave off possible harm. In the event the patient is blind to what appears obvious in the dream, the therapist should take the precaution of giving strong and repeated positive suggestions, in hypnosis, that the patient will remain alive, well, healthy and strong and that together patient and therapist will solve the problem in due time.

11. The authority symbol. Usually in every family there is an authority symbol or "magic wielder" who has had great influence (positively or negatively) over the patient. This is one to whom power and influence are attributed directly or indirectly as one who can do anything, or fix anything, or one who has all of the answers. Messages, like tape recordings, may continue to come from that person by way of the memory system and be a controlling influence up to the present. While suggestions or influence from that person may have been beneficial at one time in childhood, such influence may be counter productive at the present. Or such influence may have been painful or harmful in childhood and continues to the present time to have the same kind of influence, even though the patient consciously denies such. Recognizing such an authority in the dream may be an effective avenue of comprehending the patient's ongoing unhealthy subjugation to the past.

12. The therapist in the dream. Frequently the therapist will appear in the dream as an authority figure disguised as a policeman, fireman, judge, teacher or similar personage. While such a role may depict the therapist as a benevolent savior or healer, it is also possible that the role may be that of a protagonist. Obviously, in either case it will be helpful to both therapist and patient to interpret the dream forthrightly and discuss the patient-therapist relationship.

EXAMPLES

Mrs. C. , 25 years old, with a type of Phagophobia. She had difficulty eating her evening meal in that she would start to choke on her food unless it was really soft. She could eat breakfast and lunch with relative ease. It was the evening meal that presented problems. She became scared before she started to swallow.

Her dream was as follows:

I dreamed that I was at home and I was cooking. I was making tuna salad and I needed something to go in it that I didn't have. My grandmother was visiting me so she went outside maybe to the garden or somewhere to get that ingredient that I needed for the salad. She didn't come back in a reasonable amount of time so I got worried and went after her. I think it was raining and I know it was dark. She was nowhere to be found and I was really worried about her. I called for her but she never came. As the dream was over, I was walking back to our house and just before I got to the door, I thought something was about to get me. I also thought that this was what got my grandmother.

It was apparent that there were several key elements in this dream, namely, food, grandmother (who went out and did not return), darkness, and fear that the same thing that got grandmother would get her.

Interpreting the dream led, in an age regression, to a relationship with her father which turned out to be the symptom producing event of her Phagophobia. Her father drank considerably and in the evenings when he would return, he frequently would be drunk and abuse the family. Her mother worried, frequently stating that he might not come back because he could have an accident and die. Consequently, she associated fear, darkness and death with mealtime in the evening.

In addition to this, the father, sometimes upon his return, would lie down upon the couch and take a nap. Frequently he would wake up gasping for air. As a little girl, she (the patient) was upset because she thought he would choke to death. A Symptom Intensifying Event was the relationship with the grandmother with whom she was very close. When her grandmother was on her death bed in the hospital, she could not eat well while lying in the bed. The patient would help her to eat; all she could eat would be pureed meat and vegetables and she went in at night time to help her. Once the grandmother gagged and the patient became afraid, thinking she might die, because she was feeding her. Sometimes the grandmother would even choke drinking juice out of a straw, which also scared the patient. The grandmother died and the patient identified closely with her death, feeling that "I felt I lost a part of me." The identification with the grandmother was that the grandmother died, (that is, she didn't come back) and the thing that got her grandmother was what she feared would get her.

In short, she had the Walking Zombie Syndrome and was identifying with both father and grandmother which proved to be the contributing factors in her phobia.

Example B

Mrs. H. female. Mid forties. Presenting symptom: overweight with suicidal tendencies.

Patient's dream:

"I woke up dreaming that my husband had cried out in pain in his sleep. I had tried, or someone had tried, to remove a mask he was wearing on his face. It couldn't be removed because it was bonded to his skin. I was very upset and asked him repeatedly how much pain he was having. He woke up enough to convince me I was dreaming the whole thing. Then I remembered I was supposed to write down a dream."

In analyzing the dream with the patient, the patient added that she saw her husband in pain. The mask looked like her husband, it was transparent and translucent:

He hides behind it. Husband doesn't have any emotion. The mask separates us. It is like he has a shell and I am afraid to break the shell. I am afraid he is not as tough as he acts. I don't want to hurt him. I am afraid I might break something in him if I push and try to change him. I am afraid he can't bend. At times he uses my emotions as an excuse to let his emotions out.

The following therapy revealed that the overweight condition was part of a very complicated psychopathology, a part of which was that it was a means of slow and socially acceptable suicide. It was an evidence of the futility she had in her relationship with her husband who, though he vowed his love, faithfulness and loyalty to her, in fact was not capable of expressing his affection and emotion. At a later time, when his wife was scheduled to have surgery (due to tumors which she wished on herself), he scheduled to be out of town up until the very morning of the surgery. And, as always, was unable to give her the emotional support she was crying out for with this and many other symptoms.

Example C

Mrs. W. Married. Female in mid-forties. Symptoms: smoking and depression, along with "increasing nervousness." Her dream:

I was in my kitchen preparing for a party. I think someone was getting married but I don't know who it was. A lot of people were outside. My memory is not too vivid but it seemed my mother was giving the party. My mother brought two ladies in to meet me and introduced us. I had never seen them before. The next thing I remember is a group of people being lined up for a photographer. It looked like a bridal party but there was an empty space in the center of the people who were posing. There was no bride nor groom. The only face I recognized in my dream was my mother. While I was watching the pictures being taken of the wedding attendants, I remembered that I was going to wake up and have to write it down for you. I was afraid I wouldn't remember it. I looked again at the people being photographed. They were dressed in street clothes and there were no flowers, but just a plain wall behind them. I was looking at all the people there for a face I could recognize but they were all strangers. I was trying to count the number of people photographed when I woke up and I didn't finish counting them.

It became apparent to the patient as we shared in the interpretation that the party was being given for her. She was not in the picture. The wedding was really her wedding but she came to realize "I am not really married - it is now clear." The reason for the strangers was that it was an act, a farce. It came out that she did not feel married to her husband, that it was all a sham for people to see on the outside. She and her husband frequently attended prominent social gatherings and appeared to people to be closely married, when in fact they had separate bedrooms and no sexual relationship.

At first the patient vowed she would not separate from her husband, later, when she did separate, she vowed there would be no divorce, later she came to realize that the only solution for her was to get a divorce. With each stage in the separation procedure she had greater peace of mind, symptoms disappeared, and a new zest for living came into being. There were other complexities in this particular case, involving the Walking Zombie Syndrome.

SENOI DREAM INTERPRETATION

Herod (1982) in a remarkably clear article describes the method of dream interpretation that the Senoi Indians of the Malay Peninsula use. Their principles of interpretation are shown to be adaptable to hypnoanalysis.

The Senoi use dreams to turn negative aspects of fear, threat, conflict into positive and constructive traits or events. This adjustment is made every morning for both adults and children. For example, if a child encounters a monster, he is encouraged to fight it and overcome it. If, in a dream, one injures another member of the tribe, that one is to present the "injured" member with a gift. For all of the negative aspects of the dream a positive course of action is suggested which will overcome the negative.

Another feature of the Senoi method is, after identifying the other significant person in the dream, to present that person with a gift symbolizing the dreamer's power over that person. Likewise, the other person in the dream is to present the dreamer with an object which symbolized its/his/her power over the dreamer. These acts are, of course, done in the imagination. But note, the dreamer is in control.

Herod (1982) cites Corriere and Hart (1977) as adapting the Senoi principles of dream management and coming up with six recommendations which are readily adaptable for use in hypnoanalysis. These principles are listed as follows:

1. Ask the patient to embellish the dream. Ask him to tell it with feeling as if he were reliving the dream.
2. Next, ask the patient to rethink the dream as if it were a movie. The movie is going to stop on one significant picture, one frame that is the most significant of the whole dream. Once he has identified that picture, ask, "how do you feel in this scene?"
3. Ask the patient to contrast this significant picture with an event or scene which contains the opposite feeling or a feeling he would like to have. Embellish this scene and identify the feeling.
4. Ask him then to go back to the single frame picture and feeling which he had in the original dream. Proceed with, "Remember when you felt this way in real life? See what you saw; hear what you heard; and feel what you felt as if you are experiencing this event all over again."
5. Next ask the patient what is left out or what he could do or say that would make the real event turn out the way he wanted it to be.
6. The patient is encouraged to look at the original dream picture and determine what could be done in the dream that would make it turn out the way the dreamer wanted it to be, i.e., make it turn out so that he feels the way he did in the contrast picture (Corriere & Hart, 1977, p.161).

These excellent recommendations are readily adaptable to dream interpretation in hypnoanalysis. The individual peculiarities of patient together with the nature of the dream and the symptoms would determine which principles would be most effectively used in any particular case.

CONCLUSION

The overall philosophy of hypnoanalysis - in that it is a brief therapy, directed almost exclusively toward the immediate alleviation of specific symptoms with their underlying causes in the unconscious mind - applies to the interpretation of dreams, to wit, the patient is asked to dream about the problem and its roots. Typically the dream resulting from that request is the only one interpreted, and the interpretation is done in hypnosis.

In the event that a fitting interpretation eludes both therapist and patient, the hypnotic suggestion to dream is given the patient again. At the same time the therapist would do well to go back over the case history and the word association test with that dream in mind seeking a clue to the thrust of the dream. Should the apparent interpretation of the dream be different from the general thrust of the history and word association test, another session on interpretation may be called for, or the possibility that the dream is revealing another facet of the personality not previously recognized, must be considered.

When over half of the dream appears clear to therapist and patient it should be considered successful. One should not endeavor to interpret everything; getting caught up in too many details should be avoided. There is always filler material to give the dream continuity, to try to interpret such could be misleading. Furthermore after-thoughts such as postscripts or addendums should not be overlooked. Little thoughts that come in secondarily as the patient is ready to leave the session may be quite significant for the thrust of the dream material.

The therapist should keep notes on the dream so that when the summary of the analysis is made the message of the dream may be effectively utilized along with other analytical material. It is altogether possible that during the process of therapy new understandings will become apparent to such an extent that some elements of the dream will be clarified or modified. Such new insight would, of course, be applied to the therapy later on.

CHAPTER 6

CLINICAL PROCEDURE

ELECTRONIC EQUIPMENT AND THERAPY ROOMS

Many physicians, dentists and psychotherapists appreciate the value of hypnosis but feel because of the time it takes to hypnotize the patient, it is not practical to use in therapy except in unusual situations (Boswell, 1966). This disadvantage has been successfully overcome by the development of an electronic system of using tapes and TV monitors in the therapeutic process, previously described in Chapter 3 (Boswell, 1966; Bryan, 1965a; Fross, 1969; Hartman, 1968).

Advantages of this electronic system, in addition to those listed earlier, are as follows: The use of electronic equipment enables the therapist to see more patients by enabling him to spend less time performing repetitive functions in hypnotizing the patient and in giving routine suggestions.

The process enables the therapist to be physically removed from the patient during the periods of deepest hypnosis, thus eliminating the risk of accusation of personal affronts. The transference relationship is less complicated by this procedure since the patient is more or less left alone to face him or herself in a kind of confrontation with self-history and self-honesty. The issue of transference and of whether analyzing it is a necessary part of hypnoanalysis is dealt with elsewhere. Frequently, the patient, left alone during the hypnotic period, will uncover material which likely would not be obtained by any other process. Furthermore, the process has the effect of lowering resistance, thus curtailing the total treatment time.

When the analysis of the patient is completed, it is summarized and recorded on a cassette tape. Then it may be played back over and over to the patient until he or she is thoroughly familiar with every facet of the analysis.

Finally, there is a distinct advantage to the therapist. He can remain in a more relaxed state himself while treating more patients than he could without such a process.

To review the hypnoanalytic process: The first time the patient is to be hypnotized, the therapist works with him or her in person and gives the suggestions for hypnosis; following which, protective suggestions are given by tape and the general process to be followed is outlined. In succeeding sessions the patient is taken to the treatment room by therapist or by an assistant and placed in a reclining chair or on a couch with a blindfold over the eyes, and earphones with a microphone placed on the head. In this prone, quiet condition an "induction tape" and other tapes that facilitate total relaxation are played. This may take anywhere from fifteen to thirty or forty minutes, depending on the individual needs of that patient. Then the therapist, in the master control room, takes his own microphone and talks to the patient who hears through the headphones. In a typical case of hypnoanalysis, therapy proceeds generally in the following order:

First hypnotic session: introduction, protective suggestions, description of procedure to follow.

Second and third hypnotic sessions: the Bryan Word Association Test is given.

Fourth session: dream analysis.

Fifth and succeeding sessions: age regressions until those events or periods of time in earlier life which contributed to the symptoms are uncovered and worked through.

Next session: a summary of those events presented in chronological order and explained on the basis of the principles of the psycho-allergenic occurrence of symptoms (Chap. 3).

Next, a series of sessions for re-educating the patient in inducing change and reinforcing such changes or modification in feelings and behavior. This would include proper corrective procedures for patients having any of the diagnoses previously described.

This process of Medical Hypnoanalysis will be described in the following pages under these headings:

Age Regression Procedure.

Application of the Principle of the Seven R's.

Case Management.
Case Progress and Resolution.

AGE REGRESSION PROCEDURE

The hypnoanalyst, after having given the initial induction, after reviewing the case history, and after giving the word association test and dream analysis, is now ready to proceed with a series of age regressions in order to determine the ultimate cause(s) or roots of the symptoms. If a list of the traumatic or main events of the patient's life has not been made, it should be made at this time in a brief summary way. These experiences may be referred to as "high voltage events" (see Chap. 3). They need to be investigated in some detail so as to evaluate their effect upon the patient's life. A process called age regression, enables the hypnotized person to bring to the fore latent or previously hidden materials. It is best to make a list of such events as the history is being taken, at which time the therapist's initial response as to the significance of previous trauma is likely to be most reliable. The standard of judgment is to ascertain those experiences which he suspects have had a profound negative influence on the personality and behavior of the patient.

For example, if the patient, as a child, had a tonsillectomy where an ether mask was used, an age regression would be needed. The fright or panic resulting from a threat of suffocation should be noted along with the age and date of the happening. This event, or any death-like or frightening experience the child had in the earlier years, including the birth experience, would require an age regression (Bryan, 1961b, 1964b, Note 14; Shepard, 1967, 1971).

Certainly the child's relationship with significant others must also be taken into consideration. If there were negative influences from the family background or parent-sibling relationships, even though not obviously traumatic in nature, such a conditioning process is not to be considered negligible in evaluating sources of psychological pathology.

Once a list of such events or periods, along with the age of the child when they took place, is delineated, one is ready to proceed with the age regressions. There may be anywhere from three to twelve events which need to be evaluated in order to determine the ISE, the SPE, the SIE and other relevant aspects of the entire case.

The disorientation which may be created by being hypnotized offers a wide range of therapeutic possibilities including personality changes,

time distortion, emotional changes, and psychosomatic phenomena (Wolberg, 1945). Such alteration in consciousness makes age regressions possible. Kroger and Fezler (1976) and Kroger (1977) like Bryan (Note 15), distinguish between revivification (actions which are characteristic of a reliving of past experience) and age regression (a pseudo-revivification of past events in a framework of present time), and varying degrees of each level. However, Gill (1948, 1954) believes that total revivification is not possible. While some hypnotic behavior can be simulated by non-hypnotized subjects, some other reactions of hypnotized persons are real and cannot be simulated (Sheehan & Perry, 1976, p.201).

It depends on the depth of the hypnotic trance as to how far back into the patient's past the therapist should go on the first age regression experience. If the person is a "good subject" of hypnosis then going back to a pre-school age experience could be profitable. On the other hand, if the patient is not a particularly good subject of hypnosis, the first age regression is best held to the level of more recent years (Rubottom, Note 1). The reason for this is that an unsuccessful first age regression will be a discouragement to the succeeding regressions, the patient having received a negative suggestion by the first failure. The poor or average hypnotic subject can be conditioned to go into a deeper trance by practice (Bryan, Note 16). Thus, if the first age regression goes back only a relatively short time, it will likely be easier to recall--even re-live--the event and consequently give the patient greater confidence in the procedure.

After some experience with the process of age regression and what is expected, the patient will regress more readily to the more remote periods of life or to occasions which have repressed material, and at the same time come nearer to a revivification of the more crucial and influential events. As has previously been mentioned, the Initial Sensitizing Events are nearly always "forgotten" (Bryan, Note 17) because they generally happen within the first five years of life.

It is at this point in the procedure that the advantages of this method of hypnoanalysis become more apparent, in that only the events in the patient's life which have contributed to the current problem are analyzed. Of course, in picking out those specific causes the therapist may have to check out other events and by the process of elimination separate those which have had a profound effect on the personality from those which did not. It is rare that the therapist can select from the case history at the beginning those events which were exclusively the underlying causes of the symptoms. Even so, the therapist is more apt to be able to evaluate the

traumatic events in the life than the patient, once he knows the patient's history well. This differs from traditional psychoanalysis and client-centered therapy as well as most other therapies. Instead of giving the patient freedom to continue to wander around aimlessly with the story of his life and the re-telling of events which frequently are of no particular significance (or even reinforce the problem), along with endless repetition of the same patterns in his history, the therapist takes the lead and directs the course of the analysis toward a fixed goal.

Based on his experience, the therapist understands the cause and effect relationship of early influential factors on the formation of the patient's personality. He also knows that specific types of behavior as, for example, the phobias, are caused by specific types of earlier influences. The patient does not know all this, therefore the therapist should take the lead in directing the course of the therapy. The purpose of the age regressions is to enable the therapist jointly with the patient to make this kind of investigation into the past experiences of the patient, and how such experiences effected the course of his life.

When the therapist is ready to start the age regressions, he/she may have a prepared list of events, as an agenda, somewhat like the following: T and A (tonsillectomy), age 3, 1933, ether mask, fear.

Parents divorced, age 6, 1936.

Moved to farm with grandparents and aunt--changed school, age 7, 1937.

Mother remarried, new home, 1939.

Stepfather mean, 1939-1941 (9-11 years old).

Returned to farm, 1941. Death of grandfather.

Trouble in school, failed and expelled, eighth grade, 1942.

Motorcycle wreck, unconscious, almost died, 1946.

Attempted suicide, 1948.

It is clear that such a list of traumas would need to be investigated for their total effect on the unconscious mind. A lot will depend upon the kind of relationship this person had with the grandparents and how the stepfather effected him. In assessing the effect on the present personality problem, age regressions might reveal that while these relationships sound traumatic, in point of fact they did not have a serious adverse effect upon the patient. The patient has the Walking Zombie Syndrome (Death Complex) and the key events in the case were the tonsillectomy as an Initial Sensitizing Event and the motorcycle wreck as the Symptom Producing Event, while the suicide attempt would be a Symptom Intensifying Event.

Age regressions will enable the therapist to evaluate the degree of trauma and the after-effects upon the patient (Shephard, 1970, 1971).

The age regression enables the client to relive the experience in such a way as to determine the kinds of feelings that were experienced at that crucial time and whether repression took place. It also enables the patient to experience abreaction and catharsis of the particular event. The therapist therefore should be intent on evaluating the kinds of feelings the patient had by observing closely the age regressions.

It would be readily apparent that the patient who has profound emotion in reliving the experience had profound emotion either felt or repressed at the time the event originally took place. If the age regression is vivid and yet the patient has passive emotions about it, it is likely (but not certain) that that particular event was not a determining factor in the patient's current problem. Both Kroger and Fezler (1976) and Wolberg (1948, II) refer to the value of revivification, the latter especially stresses the fact that such an experience increases the hypermnesic effect of hypnosis, opening up pathways to "forgotten memories and experiences which would not be available to the individual at an adult level." A deep trance is a big advantage to revivification, even though not always to achieve. A verbatim procedure will be given shortly.

While a number of methods of age regressions may be used, the following procedure utilized the auditory, visual and kinesthetic senses so as to heighten, for various types of individuals, the vividness of the experience. Furthermore, an outmoded method of transportation (the train) is utilized in the visualization process, giving the episode more of a historic flavor. A couple of minutes time is taken in order to give the patient an opportunity to make a mental journey into the past. Finally, being transported to a specific time or period, and being discharged from the train at that point, adds a touch of realism. This is done most effectively if a tape, about three minutes long, with the sounds of a train pulling out of a station and proceeding on a journey, eventually coming to a stop, is played in the background to the therapist's descriptive words. This is an added advantage to the use of electronic equipment.

The following description is used with the sound effects of a train in the background (Holzman, no date).

Now then, let's take a little trip. If you will, picture yourself going to an old-fashioned railroad station. As you go to this old-fashioned railroad station, there's a train there. It's a very short train--it has only one car. Picture yourself getting on that train. Sit down by the window. As you look out the window, you see a large wall calendar on the station wall and it says February 6th, 1985. That's today's date. I want you to notice also that above your head is a cord. Pull that cord and that starts the train in motion backwards.

First it starts with a jump and a lurch and then it moves very slowly. Trains are ways of transportation out of the past. And so this train will take you back into the past. It begins to move very slowly and this date of February 6 disappears toward the front of the train. Another calendar date comes into view from behind you saying February 5th. That's yesterday. And that date disappears toward the front of the train as the train moves backwards, and as it goes backwards another sign comes into view saying February 4th. You become aware of the fact that this train is rather strange--it's taking you into the past. It picks up momentum now and goes a little faster.

Another sign comes into view saying 3rd, 2nd, 1st. The train moves faster now. It moves backwards, back into the last month, the month of January. And then into December and November, 1984. And as the train continues to move you can feel it. You can feel the motion and vibration of the train and you can hear the train as it moves backwards into the past. As it goes into the past you realize that it has gone back into 1984. October, September, August, July, June, May, April, March, February, January. Then into 1983, and you get the picture of the train going through the night. As you travel into the past--clickety-clack, farther back, clickety-clack, farther back, clickety-clack, farther back (monotone, rhythmic voice). As you ride the train, you get the feel of the motion and the rhythm, as you go back further into the past: 1983, '82, '81, '80, 1979, '78, '77, '76. It's taking you into the past. It continues now to go into the past. From the age of 14, you're going back into the past to the age of 13 and 11, 10, 9, 8, 7, 6, 5, 4. Get the feeling now--get the feeling. You're back now to the time when you were three years old. The train comes to a halt. The train comes to a halt at the time when you had that tonsillectomy. Get the feeling that you're there. You see yourself as a little boy of three

You hear what you heard then. You see other members of the family as they appeared then. You see your house, your room, other surroundings. You are going to relate to me what took place as if you were living through the events of that day. So you tell me what happens, first, and then second, and third. You can start anywhere you want to... anywhere that comes to your mind regarding the events of your tonsillectomy. . . You are right there. . . Now tell me how old are you and where are you and what's happening.

Typically, at this point, the story unfolds, with realism varying in degree from one patient to another. The deeper the trance, the more vivid the events portrayed. In a "good regression" the patient will generally have

John A. Scott, Sr., Ph.D.

a number of details such as the kind or color of clothes that are worn, the room decor, the size and appearance of the principle parties involved, etc. What is most important, however, is the way the patient interprets the event(s) and the affect it has. Traumatic events which have had a long-time influence on the person usually have a great deal of emotion either repressed or expressed, and during the regression this should be recognized.

 It should be stressed that the joint participation of the therapist with the patient is important in order to encourage abreaction. The therapist should pick up on the emotion that first appears with the patient and encourage its free flow. This may be done by a show of excitement in the voice, by repeating the words the patient used with more intense emotion accompanying them, or by acting the role of an adversary or an accomplice in the situation so as to be a sounding board for the patient's reaction. Pent-up emotions are thus released and a new or more realistic evaluation of the particular circumstances under investigation may be made. Releasing inhibited emotions paves the way for a more realistic integration of personality (Kroger & Fezler, 1976). It is Watkins (1949) who observes that the abreaction experience serves to complete what has been an ongoing neurotic expression of unresolved emotional trauma.

Resolving the Trauma — ∤m R⁷.

The hypnotic abreaction experience may be resolved in one of several different ways, or a combination of them.

(1) By rationalizing the experience into meaningless oblivion. The underlying theme is: "That once may have been a good idea, but it has outlived its usefulness." For example, the clinician states:

Your mother's suggestion that you should not have intercourse because you might catch a disease or get pregnant may have been okay for you as a thirteen year old girl. Your mother meant well and for your age that may have been the best she could do under those circumstances. But that idea has outlived its usefulness. As an adult woman you can see that it no longer should prohibit you from enjoying intercourse with your husband, etc.

(2) Reinterpret the experience. The underlying theme is: "Long ago and under those circumstances you misinterpreted what was said (or what happened)." An example:

You can see that when you were a child four years old and had a tonsillectomy, the ether mask over your face produced a fear of death. As a child' you couldn't understand clearly what was being done to you--you just knew

188

that you felt your breath was being taken away, that you were suffocating. This left an emotional scar which we are going to remove. You understand now that that was not a death-like event. You lived through it fully and completely, you are fully alive, and therefore there is no longer a need for a life/death struggle to continue to take place at the unconscious level in your mind.

(3) Outright denial. The underlying theme is: "You really did not do what, at that time, you thought you did." For example,: "As a small child you thought you were responsible for your father's death because you wished him dead, but you really were not. You know that now," etc.

(4) Acceptance. The underlying theme is: "Yes, what happened to you was true, but you can live it down, or you have changed (or are changing) now. It will not ever be true (to effect you that way) any more, etc." An example:

Now that you have re-lived the painful event wherein your daddy left home, you can see what a severe blow that was to you as a little girl. He left you at a time that was crucial in your life, a time when you needed him, a time when you expected his love and presence, but you did not get it any more, and you can see that that was a severe blow to you at that time. Of course, you understand, however, that your mother and father were acting on their own; you can understand also that you had nothing to do with their separation. There were circumstances beyond your control in their separating. As you look back upon that you can understand it now, and the emotional blow that you suffered at that time does not need to continue to influence your feelings now in regard to your relationship with men. You were the victim of circumstances at that time, now it is over; it's past; it's done. We therefore set aside that event as being a continued negative influence on your feelings. You are going to overcome those feelings and look beyond those events. Your parents did not intend to harm you. They, too, were the victims of circumstances, perhaps over which they had no control, etc.

I am continually impressed with the patient's need to have a rationale for those events, experiences and relationships which are recognized as contributing causes to the neurosis.

The foregoing procedure, simple though it sounds, is amazingly effective and in principle has some similarities to the Rational Therapy of Harper (1960) and Ellis and Harper (1961). A major difference, however, is that the rationalizing or readjusting of the thinking patterns of the patient, through hypnosis, is at the unconscious level, and here is the ultimate "scene of the crime." It should be continually emphasized that when conversing with the hypnotized patient one is conversing with the subconscious. Therefore, when giving an explanation to the patient, in an effort to nullify the after-effects of the emotional trauma, the clinician repeats the rationale several times to the hypnotized patient, which results in a change of thinking and attitude, hence accompanying change in actions or symptomology. This, of course presupposes that the events which were elucidated in the age regression were indeed the causes of the symptoms or are accepted by the patient as the causes.

Although Frankl (1965) does not refer specifically to a therapeutic procedure like this, his underlying philosophy certainly recognizes the desirability of a kind of compensating rationale when a person is under duress. In referring to his experiences in prison camps, Frankl observed that when people were under trauma or stress, if they were able to develop some meaning from the crisis, or to turn it into learning experience, or to extract some redeeming features, no matter how tragic the circumstances, their sanity could be preserved and the will to live strengthened. If the individual can seize on such a glimmer of hope and reject negative and defeating thoughts, the ego can be fortified and it can make the difference in defeat and survival. Of course Frankl was referring to a reality situation, whereas the erasing process in hypnoanalysis intends that in age regression the patient reconstructs the situation and only then extracts constructive meaning from the historic trauma, but the mental-emotional process is the same.

The preceding description of the age regression process presupposes that the therapist knows to what past age or date he wishes to return the patient in order to examine certain episodes suspected of being Initial Sensitizing or Symptom Producing Events. These dates or periods or events are known from the case history and thus the investigation by age regression may be specific. There are occasions, however, where one cannot be specific. The therapist cannot be certain about what particular time he is aiming for as a key event in producing symptomology. He may be trying to ascertain when the patient first had this kind of feeling or symptom as for example, the fear of crowds, and how it got started. While hypnotized, the patient is asked to re-live a recent experience where there was a pronounced awareness of the fear of crowds. He is urged to get in touch with his feelings at that time, and using the same basic procedure for bringing out his feelings, the therapist assists him in a full abreaction.

Once the feeling is clearly there in this current reaction, then the patient is urged to go back in a kind of free floating age regression to a previous experience where he had the same fears. The patient at once may go to the original scene of such a response, which is what is being sought after all. On the other hand, the patient may go back simply to an earlier experience of a similar nature and then back to yet another one previous to that one and so on until in a series of regressions the ISE is brought to the fore (Boswell, 1961).

This process could take several hypnotic sessions if the Initial Sensitizing Event is deeply repressed. Once the patient can relive the original incident and come to a clear understanding of the circumstances which first induced this kind of fear and a complete catharsis can take place, the present neurotic response will be alleviated. It is as if the bomb is now defused. The person is no longer influenced by forces from the unconscious mind which are not understood. Here the rationale is simply that the patient should understand that the symptoms are an acquired characteristic, and an acquired characteristic can be removed the same as it can be acquired.

The process of following an emotion backwards in a patient's history has been known for a long time. It works. But we have not known until recently how and why it works. Rossi (1986) explains that in state-dependent learning at the time of a trauma the bio-chemical state of the body is at a peculiar balance. In order to have the best recall of that event, that same bio-chemical balance must be reproduced. When this is done in hypnotic abreaction, the chances of accurate recall are much enhanced.

Another thought pertaining to the above procedure of age regression is repeated over and over by Rossi (op.cit.) and that is that with every access (to significant events in the patient's life) reframing takes place. That is, the patient will tend to make a reevaluation of the event and even perhaps reduce the impact on the psyche.

Observations on Age Regression

1. The therapist should repeat what the patient tells, as it is told, and make the situation as vivid as possible. The more vivid the experience the more cathartic benefit to the patient. This is often achieved by the therapist's asking feeling questions and for details. Furthermore, the therapist should show the appropriate emotion in his or her voice and by the vocabulary that is used so as to further encourage a replay of the emotion of the patient's event. Excitement begets excitement.

2. The clinician can further assist by speaking in the present tense

and encouraging the patient to do so, as, "You are there, see yourself, what is happening now?" etc.

3. Death-like experiences are particularly significant events and displays of emotion in relation to such situations during age regressions must be evaluated.

4. If the therapist has dates and events in front of him as he regresses the patient, they will help trigger details, which, in a chain reaction may evoke further significant data. Such data may not have been forthcoming in the waking state.

5. Attention should be paid to the first day of school, first sexual experience, first surgery, first job, the adolescent period etc. The reason for this is that "first impressions are lasting impressions" in that such events (and/or periods) as these often captivate the attention to such an extent that there is a natural state of hypnosis. Thus indelible impressions are made.

6. Frequently childhood trauma is misunderstood or misinterpreted by the child, resulting in the core of the neurosis which continues to manifest itself in that peculiar symptomatology. Toward the conclusion of the age regression the clinician can minimize the after-effects of the traumatic event or give the patient a different rationale for what happened originally. A different interpretation, whether coming from the therapist or from the observing ego of the patient, serves to correct irrational or grotesque conclusions which were made at the original time. In this manner the pent-up emotional charge is decathected.

7. The therapist finally stresses to the patient that the event is now over and in the past, and there need not be any further adverse effects. The patient should then agree and make a commitment to release, or be freed of, the symptomatic expressions. It is as if therapist and patient are uniting to change an old memory "tape" in the mind. The old negative suggestion, or destructive experience, is now being replaced with positive, constructive suggestions such as, "You can see things differently now...you can understand why this would happen in this way. . . you have new feelings, a new life ahead . . .," etc. A review of the event in the waking state at least once will help the patient integrate the event into the current life situation so that it no longer operates as an unconscious conflict or trauma. The unconscious has now been made conscious.

8. In situations where the parents have been so harsh or overbearing

that the patient only has adverse memories of them, there may
be an advantage in minimizing those harsh traumatic scenes of
mistreatment and seizing on one scene of kindness and expanding
that in this "erasing" and reframing procedure. The desire to
have some loving association with the parents is innate in the
unconsciousness and frequently when the therapist finds the
slightest hint of love and kindness by an otherwise harsh, cruel,
or vindictive parent--or even creates the possibility of love or
kindness--the patient will capitalize on this and respond favorably.
The therapist may go so far as to suggest, "Visualize the kind of
relationship you would have liked with your parents. . ." and this
can be beneficial to the patient.

Whatever it takes to decathect the old trauma and stabilize the patient
with more wholesome and constructive affect will be worthwhile. I stress
off and on throughout treatment that, "We are not here to place blame on
anyone or find fault or to judge others. We are here to understand more
about yourself and your view of your past. You and your parents have been
subjected to forces beyond your control, etc."

The preceding observations are based on the assumption that the
age regression is to an event which has been repressed or "forgotten"
and needs to be brought to the consciousness with its attendant
emotion and interpretation. Or it may be more accurate to describe it as
"misinterpretation," as a possible contributing source of the symptoms.
Of course, there are other age regressions to events which are remembered
in the conscious mind (perhaps vaguely, perhaps not). That is well and
good. However, there are some events which have such a strong emotion
associated with them that they are too much for the patient to deal with
at one time.

The therapist must be on the alert to such situations. Occasionally the
patient will reveal to the therapist the reluctance to talk about that event
any more. Or, when the therapist mentions going back to that event, the
patient refuses to do so or blocks returning to it. It is safest not to coerce
the patient into reliving that situation under those circumstances. The
therapist can say something like this, "That's OK, we can return there
another time." Then in the waking state an explanation can be given as
to why going back to that event or relationship is important and a more
prolonged preparation can be made.

If the event is not specific in the patient's mind, but there is a generalized fear attached to the circumstances or general period which the therapist wishes to regress to, a hypnotic suggestion can be made to the effect that, "We can explore that situation another time when you will be ready. Perhaps you'll want to think about that between now and the time you return and will be curious to know more about your inner thought on that subject. In fact, you may desire to know more about another side of yourself under those circumstances. . etc."

When the therapist determines that the time is ripe for the difficult age regression, a method may be used which softens the impact of the feared event. The therapist may say, "I will be your traveling companion as we return to so and so . . ." Or the patient may be encouraged to see a similar event on the television screen or on the theater stage and thereby observe the event from a greater distance at first (Wolberg, 1948), then later regress to the event more realistically. Obviously, such a fearful situation must be cathected sooner or later. The patient may be told something like this. "When a physician examines a person who complains of a stomach ache he or she will poke around on the lower abdomen until the patient flinches. At that spot the doctor will say, 'Oh you have appendicitis.' The site of the pain identifies the source of the problem. So with emotional pain. The painful event will usually be a contributing factor to the symptom." Patients understand this and usually are cooperative in agreeing to the regression.

The point here is that it is important for the therapist to pay attention to the patient's defenses and respect them. It is easy enough from the objective view of the therapist to belittle or ignore the pain the patient might have from some presumably innocuous event of the past, but in the mind of the patient that event was an emotional catastrophe, and must be treated gently and with consideration.

When the analysis is complete, a brief allusion to the rationale used in the more pertinent age regressions should be used when the summary is made and recorded. A description of the summary tape will be given shortly.

It should be kept in mind, as has previously been said, that these original conditioning traumas, in most cases, have taken place far enough back in the patient's experience that very little, if any, memory remains in the conscious mind. This would be the Initial Sensitizing Event. There may only be one, but occasionally there are more. Of course, the Symptom Producing Event, which is usually consciously remembered, is treated in the same manner. But the general aim of the therapist is to demonstrate that the

Initial Sensitizing Event(s) laid the groundwork, or the pre-conditioning of the patient, to such an extent that the one precipitating event (SPE) was able to be effective and create the symptoms only because the person had been weakened by the previous event. As the therapist sees this, and helps the patient see this, he sees the cause and effect relationship and in turn explains this to the patient. The pattern of what happened should be repeated until the patient understands it and becomes so familiar with it that it is no longer such a "touchy subject." The principle that "familiarity breeds contempt" may be understood here. An experience that may have been painful to the patient earlier, becomes less painful each time the person goes over it in hypnosis until it becomes almost commonplace.

Rossi (1986) stresses over and over that each time we gain access to these "state-dependent" situations some degree of reframing takes place. It is as if there is a kind of leveling effect which reduces the impact on the psyche. Understanding and repetition are a necessary part of the age regression procedure. Thus, the painful material is transferred from the vague, shadowy, misunderstood realm of the unconscious to the enlightened and more logical world of the consciousness of the patient. He or she is now helped to cope with it under present circumstances.

Occasionally the patient will give the therapist a hint from within himself of the rationale for softening the blow of the traumatizing event. This may be seized upon and expanded. For example, a woman who had been neglected by her mother during childhood to such an extent that she never received attention, affection, love and support, in an off-hand way in trance referred to the fact that her mother was old when she, the patient, was born, and did not have a husband at home to help her, and also had a number of other children to care for.

Although the patient had suffered much pain by this neglect, yet there was a part of her mind (the observing ego) that could see an explanation for the mother's behavior. However, previous to the hypnotic session, she had borne a grudge against her mother without respite. I capitalized on the hint of this redeeming rationale and expanded further as if to reinforce the patient's grasping for an explanation and it in turn softened the impact of the deprivation. But it must be stressed that the reasoning used in the age regressions, whether it originates with the clinician or with the patient, must eventually be acceptable to the patient and be in harmony with the patient's general thinking patterns.

John A. Scott, Sr., Ph.D.

THERAPEUTIC GOALS

First, it is necessary in most cases to find and eliminate the root cause(s) of the symptoms. Most assuredly the patient originally comes for help because of suffering from the discomfort of certain symptoms and is concerned about the removal of those symptoms if at all possible. And, although an analysis which has been thoroughly done will have secondary advantages to the patient (such as growth, adjustment with one's fellows, better feelings physically, etc.), the patient will not be content unless the symptoms are removed, or at least alleviated. And, in some cases, the best one can do is to help the patient learn to cope with the symptoms. In any case, when pathology is removed from the subconscious, the person will be helped and there will be added advantages in the way of increased comfort and likely an improved ability to relate to others. But if the analysis goes as it should, the clinician should find and eliminate the root cause of the problem and assist in rehabilitating the patient to a symptom free existence (Bryan, Note 18).

Second, in most cases it is necessary to break a powerful habit pattern in addition to working through the analytical procedure. The patient has been adjusting to the painful conditions (or symptoms) likely for some time, even though there is a great deal of discomfort connected with the undesirable habit pattern. Nonetheless, these patterns must be altered.

Third, it is necessary to understand the patient's secondary gain (if there is any indication of its presence) and to eliminate that as a part of successful therapy.

Fourth, the patient is helped in maturation. In most situations there has been a certain degree of growth arrest along the way with its attendant confusion in coping with problems, hesitancy in decision making, and disorder in interpersonal relationships. Ego strengthening and personal development must follow close on the heels of the analysis summary.

APPLICATION OF THE SEVEN "R's"

The beginning hypnoanalyst will find this schedule helpful as a kind of check list. Then, after experience is built up, the procedure will become automatic. But the following subdivision of therapeutic procedures will serve as a useful guide in treatment (Balog, 1985).

The Analytical Phase

Rapport must be established to some degree with the patient within the first session or the patient will not return. A warm, accepting attitude on the part of the therapist is essential. And the groundwork for this is laid in the first three hundred seconds. The first five minutes of the first hour sets the tone in the mind of the patient for all that is to follow. A good sales person knows this. A successful public speaker plans the opening sentences more carefully than any part of the body of the address. Certainly the hypnoanalyst should give diligent attention to establishing a milieu in which a troubled person can freely pour out the guts and expose the naked soul. I believe a warm smile is a most effective communication to the patient.

Let's face it. A therapist may have all of the technical information and experience necessary to cure a given patient, but if he/she does not have enough charisma and style in the first few minutes to launch therapy, the treatment will never get off the ground.

The therapist can put his best foot forward in those first crucial minutes in a number of ways. King (1987) stresses the following. First, the decor should be of such a nature that it does not detract from the kind of image the therapist wishes to convey. In fact, the office environment should reflect the personality of the hypnoanalyst, by so doing he/she will be comfortable and thus present a comfortable impression to the patient

Second, the same thing may be said about the analyst's dress. One's dress makes a statement about the personality. The style (not necessarily what's most fashionable) reflects the inner person and should be decided on with care. Obviously, grooming should be clean and neat.

Third, the voice should be a moderate tone with low modulation. This will be conducive to the kind of communication that will be so important in the following sessions. The first sentences coming from the therapist will also be vital to setting the tone which is to follow. It may be a simple greeting or a few words about nondescript subjects such as the weather, state of the country, a news story or the like. I frequently ask the patient if they found our address with ease, were the directions given satisfactorily over the phone, or were the parking facilities convenient. I am interested in their comfort and well-being. I then will make a statement about my note-taking and trying to keep up, which is calculated to elicit a smile. Fry and Salameh (1987) make a strong case for the use of humor in psychotherapy and support a feeling I have had for a long time that emotional disorders are so grim that it behooves the therapist to elicit a change of pace by breaking up some of the morbidity that patients bring into the office. The opening statements are a good place to start.

Fourth, the patient consciously and/or unconsciously expects from the therapist the following traits to some degree or another: authority, confidence, certainty, consideration, credibility, empathy, inspiration, integrity, intimacy, luster, presence, resolution, self-assurance, understanding, vigor, vivacity (King, 1987). Any way the hypnoanalyst conveys these traits quickly is going to be conducive to more effective therapy than if such were ignored.

Fifth, it goes without saying that the analyst's personal problems have already been dealt with in therapy so that they do not intrude into the relationship with the patient. Such could block the patient's communication from the beginning.

Sixth, obviously, communication with the patient is an absolute necessity. Presumably a part of the therapist's training has emphasized this all important aspect of the therapeutic relationship.

All of this is to say that the patient is made to feel important enough and central enough to have the courage to speak and tell to a stranger the most personal, intimate and sensitive thoughts of a troubled experience.

Relaxation. This is the hypnotic induction. There are many good books which give a variety of induction techniques suitable for most any patient. The experienced hypnotist already has his or her preferred procedure and, as has already been stated, this book is not intended for the beginner. It is appropriate to observe that Ericksonians have a technique that differs from the traditional one; and, the authoritative traditional procedure has been modified to a more permissive procedure. This latter, permissive technique, is to be preferred in modern treatment.

It is also important for the hypnoanalyst to know the patient well enough, by the time induction is done, that any peculiarities which the patient may have are taken into account in the type of induction used and the wording incorporated in it. For example, a person who fears water should not have water scenes included in the induction.

Recognize the problem. By carefully going over the case history the analyst should be able to put together a treatment plan and know the sources of the problem. If this is inadequate for some reason, perhaps the Bryan Word Association Test will shed more light on the underlying dynamics of this particular person's problem. Further, the dream analysis may clarify or add information to the unconscious conflict. At any rate, the therapist will, by this stage in the therapy, have a list of situations and or relationships which the patient has revealed as possible sources of the symptoms.

A series of age regressions aiming directly at identifying the underlying trauma or conditioning should put together the ISE, the SPE, and the SIE's and the their attendant affect. Once this takes place the patient, as well as the therapist, will recognize the cause and effect and the underlying pathology will be understood.

Remove faulty ideas. As the events and relationships are relived in the age regressions, irrational conclusions, faulty thinking, negative hypnotic suggestions, and false impressions need to be removed or modified. It is usually best to deal with these corrections as the events are relived in the therapy period. Sometimes there is not time enough, for whatever reason, to make the adjustments or corrections during that treatment session. Sometimes coming over a traumatic event and making the correction one time is not enough. In these situations it is necessary to repeat the regression at subsequent sessions. Sometimes the therapist may be wrong in making the identification of an event with a problem or symptom and the patient will absolutely not accept the therapist's interpretation. At other times the therapist may be positive in the interpretation and the patient may resist it. In either case eventually there needs to be a meeting of minds for the case to go smoothly.

Replace faulty ideas with accurate ideas. As the faulty ideas are removed they must be replaced with accurate ideas. Healthy thinking replaces unhealthy thinking and change begins to take place. When catharsis takes place the mind is receptive to change and alteration. Sometimes the mere suggestion by the analyst that "this is the proper point of view" on this subject, is all that is necessary for the patient to make a major change in concept. At other times it takes repetition and exploration both from within the therapist and the patient to overcome deep seated errors in thinking.

The Rehabilitation Phase

Rehearsal of change. When the faulty ideas have been replaced with accurate and healthy ideas and this is understood by the patient, a personal tape is made with the case summary on it (the "P" tape). This process has already been outlined. This tape is to be replayed till the patient is quite familiar with it. And, as it is played, further positive suggestions are

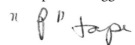

given for change. Here is where behavior modification techniques and visualization procedures are invaluable. Such changes in thinking and in acting are rehearsed in therapy. This type of "dress rehearsal" makes change in actual life possible.

Reinforce by regular practice. There have been times when I have actually accompanied a patient on a ride or to the dentist in order to assist in reinforcing change. This is rare. In the majority of cases a dress rehearsal by visualization in the therapy hour is enough to produce the change in due time. Here is where a good hypnotic subject will produce change more rapidly than the poor subject. Continued support and guidance by the hypnoanalyst will be necessary until the patient is secure in a new and improved way of life.

CASE MANAGEMENT

In the course of therapy, there are several situations which may be frustrating to both therapist and patient. One is the tense patient who refuses to relax and be hypnotized. Two, the patient who resists age regressions (and there are several variations in this category). Three, the person who keeps bringing up current problems and diverting the therapy from analysis to a discussion of current problems. Four, the person who keeps canceling or postponing appointments. Five, the patient who does not get well. We will consider these in order.

1. The tense patient. There are people whose anxieties are so severe or their "nervousness" is so intense that they are unable to relax sufficiently to get into a trance state. They keep shifting and moving, or their voice reflects tension so that is clear to the therapist that they are not relaxed sufficiently to do age regressions. People like this can be told that their state of nervousness is a hindrance to the therapeutic process. Therefore, they need to follow instructions very carefully when they come to their sessions and concentrate on the mental imagery by which they relax. In addition to this, such patients may be asked to practice the same process of relaxation several times each day between sessions and thus condition themselves. They need not spend longer than three to five minutes at a time. This may be done even in the morning before getting out of bed, a time or two through the day, and in the evening when they go to bed.

1) Progressive relaxation by starting with the muscles through the scalp and continuing through each body section and limb down through the toes should help them to condition themselves to become more relaxed. Relaxing with the therapist at the office is imperative, and it may be learned by practice. If the patient refuses to practice and refuses to cooperate in relaxing at the office, a frank talk should be held as to why he or she is refusing to cooperate.

2) An alternative to the above procedure is to use an Ericksonian method of indirect hypnosis. During a talk in the office the therapist may indirectly lull the patient into relaxation or by such verbal steerage captivate the patient's attention so as to give guidance and direction for the more formalized stage of relaxation as a prelude to hypnosis. Rossi (1986) describes ultradian rhythms as natural cycles which the body goes through every 90 minutes throughout the day. Left and right brain hemispheric dominance alternates in this cycle. If the hypnotist watches the patient carefully and picks a time when a natural relaxation or drowsiness takes place, the hypnotic induction may be done more effectively.

3) Another means is to use a brain wave synchronizer or some other mechanical means of lulling the patient's attention into lethargy. In a home where I had no such means with a resistive patient I used a candle. Because of the picture of Freud and his swinging watch there are patients who expect some mechanical means of fixating their attention.

2. The patient who resists age regressions. These patients fall into two categories. One is the category of those who have had such painful experiences in the past that they do not want to go through them and endure the pain again. If the patient has a weak ego and the therapist considers the pain so severe that re-living the experience could possibly cause a psychotic break, then the age regression should take on the aspect of seeing the experience on a TV screen, or viewing the experience like a play on the stage. In this way the patient recapitulates the experience on a more remote level as a spectator to someone else who is having an experience like the original trauma in which he was involved personally. The patient could then be encouraged to express his views and feelings about the circumstances enabling him or her to decathect the supercharged emotions.

3. Another type of person who resists age regression, there being too much pain involved, is the patient who has the PDL syndrome.

Such an individual is simply so immature that he or she does not like to have to face discomfort in any form. By asking leading questions, the therapist may lead the patient into the age regression before he is fully aware of it. Most of the time he will go along and cooperate, especially when he understands that it is a necessary part of successful therapy. This patient may be helped to understand that the principle of "familiarity breeds contempt" will help him to get over the hangover of pain which has resulted from the original situation--like surgery, it is a painful, but necessary, experience, and after it is over the patient feels better (Rubottom, Note 1).

It may be necessary to go through especially traumatic events several times in order to drain out the emotion as well as get all of the pertinent facts of the trauma. The therapist needs the information and the pattern of responses to the crisis. The patient needs the relief of tension due to repressed feelings, and both need to cooperate in making the connection between the vague, unclear and hidden circumstances which create anxiety, as well as a full rational knowledge of such events at the conscious level (Rubottom, Note 1).

4. There is another type of resistance to age regression, and that is that the event is so early in life, or so deeply repressed, that the person cannot adequately "relive" the experience. And yet there is good evidence from the case history, the word association test, or the clinician's therapeutic experience to believe that the source of the problem lies in such an event. For example, a patient had a phobia about venturing far from home in a car alone, this in turn, was related to a phobia about a hole in the ground, particularly about the possibility of finding a well or a construction ditch that was not properly covered. One would most likely expect a childhood experience having to do with falling in a well or a ditch as the Initial Sensitizing Event. Every conceivable such situation was explored during therapy and no such event could be found. The therapist suspected the birth experience as the original cause and had reason to believe this was possible from such statements as "I've had this problem all of my life," and an allusion to having heard that her mother had a difficult delivery when she (the patient) was born. The birth experience proved to be the Initial Sensitizing Event (Rubottom, Note 1). Freud (1949), LeBoyer (1975) and many modern clinicians maintain that the first trauma of life

is the birth experience itself. While a few patients can regress to birth readily, others must have help to go this far back, and still others apparently are unable to relive this experience; perhaps the reason in some cases of those who cannot go back to birth is that the experience for them was not traumatic. thought Sheom

The therapist may offer the most assistance by observing the hypnotic sessions carefully enough to recognize when the patient is most deeply hypnotized and then graphically taking the person back to the time of birth. By vividly describing the prenatal conditions, such as floating in the warm fluid, having all of one's needs met, etc., a familiar feeling may be triggered which in turn will bring on the birth sequence by a chain reaction of events.

The patient may need to be cautioned that there is no need to try to remember the details like other events of the past, but rather to get in touch with an impression of the circumstances no matter how vague. Pauses may assist the patient. Furthermore, imagination may be helpful in starting the sequence of events which lead to a revivification of birth, such as describing the feeling that the fluid has suddenly been drained and that it is like a tent that has collapsed around him, etc. Very often, when the event is so described, the patient makes contact with such feelings and proceeds to reveal his own individual experiences, such as a reluctance to be born, a fear of being mashed, strangling, etc. After being born there may be expressions of fear of being dropped, being cold, being alone, the lights painfully bright or being in pain. Rough treatment is possible as the reflexes are checked immediately after birth.

It is no wonder that more and more women are resisting going into hospital delivery rooms to have their babies these days. The experiences of not a few mothers who have been mistreated by delivery room nurses without the presence of the attending physician, or even by the physician himself, has soured some women on traditional hospital procedures. This is not to mention the circumstances of the separation of mother and baby in some hospitals for unrealistic periods of time. Instead of being a warm, emotional experience between mother, father and infant, it has become too frequently a cold, sterile, mechanized, traumatic procedure which takes its toll on personality formation by becoming the first trauma and the Initial Sensitizing Event to much subsequent emotional damage (Bryan, 1961a, 1964b; Scott, 1975; Sheppard, 1967, 1971).

5. Another difficult situation in case management is the patient who keeps bringing up current problems in the therapy sessions before the therapist can do age regressions and continue with the direct progress of the analysis. This is most frequently done by people who have had previous therapy and are used to talking over the current day to day problems with the therapist. It should be kept in mind that these day to day problems are simply offshoots of the main root problem, and they will continue to be present until the root problem is analyzed and properly dealt with. These day to day counseling problems can prolong the therapy indefinitely, provided the therapist permits the client to go off on these tangents (Bryan, Note 17).

Of course, there are situations that arise in the patient's life which do need attention from time to time and these should be dealt with at the time. Every therapist knows that in the life of the emotionally disturbed person, many crises are apt to arise. One cannot (and should not) avoid dealing with critical junctures in the life of the patient at the time they arise, but the main course of the therapy must not be permitted to come to a halt while patient and therapist divert time and energy into unproductive bypaths. Such divergences may be the patient's way of resisting therapy.

It might be well at this point to bring out that the patient should be told early in the therapy not to make major decisions which will alter his life processes during the course of therapy. Of course, there may be times when such a major decision is unavoidable, but the patient should be aware that the analysis may alter to some degree his patterns of thinking, his opinions, his desires, or needs. Therefore, major decisions that cannot be easily undone should be avoided or postponed until therapy is concluded.

6. The next problem in case management is the patient who is not present at the appointed time. There are some patients who frequently postpone their appointments, cancel at the last minute, or simply do not show up. Their so-called reasons are made to sound very legitimate but the therapist must confront the patient openly and honestly as to why such is taking place. A frank talk will often help him to face up to the issue that he is indeed avoiding therapy, and it might be helpful to talk with him about why he is avoiding it. If the patient pays his fees in advance, such willful negligence usually does not take place.

7. The patient who does not get well. This can be a most disappointing

The Clean Sweep

and frustrating relationship. The patient has kept appointments, been cooperative, and struggled with the therapist in what might have been a long and even difficult analysis. It may look like the case has been put together in a cause and effect relationship to perfection, yet the patient does not get well. A procedure called the clean sweep may provide the solution to this type of dilemma.

The clean sweep is a technique whereby the patient is encouraged to take an age regression from the present time backwards in life in five year increments with the purpose in mind of reliving any events which contributed to the problem but which have not been analyzed as yet. The patient is told that the unconscious mind is aware of what is being sought and thus can be depended on to produce the significant event. The therapist might use a suggestion similar to this:

> Inasmuch as we have not found the most significant event in your life which has contributed to your problem, and since your unconscious mind knows what this event is, we are going to depend on that part of your mind to produce such an experience as we go back in your life searching for it. As you travel backward in time from 1985 to 1980, is there any significant event which we have not analyzed that contributed to your problem? As we journey backwards from 1980 to 1975 is there such an event? etc.

This may bring out a trauma which has somehow been missed up until now, and it will prove to be the missing link in the explanation for the disorder. Such a regression may take one or several sessions to cover events from the present back even as far as birth. An event which, for the average person, may appear to be commonplace, such as a circumcision, may for this particular person be an ISE.

The visualization for such a procedure may be with the patient standing on the observation platform of a train moving backwards through life and from this vantage point he or she can see 180 degrees from extreme right to extreme left in a clean sweep as the journey is made (Rubottom, Note 1).

The clean sweep usually will give productive material from the patient's experience which provides the answer to the blocked analysis. There is another procedure for use when the therapist and patient are convinced that the analysis is complete and there is no missing traumatic experience. The clinician should review the seven "R's" with the patient, demonstrating how the patient's own analytical experience fits into this scheme of procedure. If the patient is convinced he is through the analytic phase of treatment, then the next step is to get well. This kind of re may be all that is necessary for the patient to proceed with reduction of symptomotology.

Still another procedure which may be useful in these circumstances is the "affect bridge." The patient is asked to relive one of the events which serves as an example of the symptom. The patient is told to get in touch with the feeling of that moment and to amplify it and identify it carefully. Once this is done he is told to follow that same feeling back to earlier times and examples where that same feeling was evident. The feeling can be traced (like crossing a bridge) back to the original event where that emotion first occurred. Rossi (1986) describes how such is possible in terms of "state dependent learning." When the emotion of that original event is recreated in the body, the setting is conducive to repeat other experiences which took place while the body was in that same state.

8. The hysterical patient. On rare occasions, due to an age regression, or due to the intense anxiety of day to day stress, the patient may be in a state of hysterics during a session with the clinician. It is imperative that the therapist remain calm, remembering that a calm voice and demeanor is contagious, and that soothing words, a touch of the hand, and peaceful word pictures filled with confidence for the future, will help to allay the fears of the most excited patient. One may have to spend an unusually long time with such a patient, but the hysterical antics will nearly always run their course as fatigue sets in, if not sooner. A word picture may be drawn, giving the patient a feeling of being somewhere else under circumstances of peace and ease. A previous knowledge of what scenes the patient responds to most readily will be a decided advantage under these emergency circumstances. Of course, where the therapist feels there is a patient too distraught to continue to respond to the practice of self-hypnosis at home and hypnosis in the office, it will be necessary to prescribe appropriate medication and/or hospitalization (Rubottom, 19).

CASE PROGRESS AND RESOLUTION

The preceding pages have described the clinical procedure which is more or less peculiar to this form of therapy. Obviously, the therapist will take into account attitudes, relationships, and the psychological understandings and insights coming from many other sources of previous study and experience. One will function more efficiently in this field who has had a background in traditional psychoanalysis, and its relatives: ego psychology, and psychology of the self. For a single example, compare Chessick (1985). In addition, the current rash of books on short term dynamic therapy furnishes stimulation in this area (e.g. Fleigenheimer, 1982; Malan, 1976; Phillips & Wiener, 1966; Sifneos, 1987; Wolberg, 1980). And one should have at least, an acquaintance with behavior modification.

As far as case progress is concerned, the patient needs to expect to get well and to have confidence in the therapist and therapeutic procedures (Kroger, 1977; Bryan, Note 19). Whatever is necessary to give the patient confidence is going to be helpful to the ultimate resolution of the problem. Yet the therapist cannot afford to give a promise that an individual is going to be completely well at a given time, but he may be assured that many people with similar type problems have been successfully treated and are now doing well. Furthermore, the patient should be assured that a great deal of progress will depend upon his or her desire to get well, and complete cooperation to that end is essential. It should further be emphasized that the ultimate cause and solution to the problem will come from within the patient's mind and that the therapist serves as a catalyst to assist in putting together the cause and effect relationship of the problems. And this, of course, is followed by replacing the unwholesome or unhappy feelings and responses with positive, constructive, and healthy feelings and responses.

Occasionally, at the beginning of therapy, an eager patient will ask how long it will be till he or she is feeling better. A simple illustration is helpful to the non-initiated lay person. The patient may be told that the total procedure is very much like putting a jigsaw puzzle together. There is at one side a pile of pieces that appear meaningless. In starting to put the puzzle together, one may look for corner pieces to start with and find one which will go in the lower left-hand corner and maybe the upper right-hand corner, and a few pieces along a straight edge, and by trial and error, one begins to put the puzzle together. As a piece is added here and there, the puzzle slowly begins to take shape, but it is not until the very last pieces are put into the proper places that the picture is complete. So it is with the therapeutic process. During the early process of therapy facts are gathered and scenes reenacted which at first may not appear to be connected or related to the symptoms, but as this process continues, the total picture emerges and becomes meaningful in reaching ultimate solutions.

Analysis progress

This illustration may be recorded on tape and played for every patient because there are some who expect after two or three sessions to be feeling better, and indeed some do, because there is a relaxation of tensions and a developing confidence in the therapeutic process. But for other people, many sessions go by before they begin to feel any better at all. This is not unusual and it does not mean that the process is unproductive. It simply means that in many situations it takes a whole series of therapeutic sessions before things start falling into place. The patient needs to be helped to see this to keep his confidence up. At the same time, in this type of therapy there is opportunity for the therapist to give some immediate temporary relief of symptoms by positive hypnotic suggestions in many cases.

The symptoms may be temporarily removed or supportive encouragement may bolster a depressive mood. Such procedures may give the patient some relief from the immediate pain while the analytical process continues. Progress is made in the analysis as a series of age regressions are made with the patient. The basis of these regressions is the outline or list of traumas or deprivations that were noted in the taking of the case history. The therapist may have a list that is longer than necessary by including on it some suspected traumas which do not prove to be traumatic to the patient after all. On the other hand, the therapist may overlook some significant event in the patient's life in the case history, but the patient may bring it out some time during the course of therapy. The word association test may cause the therapist to add a period or another significant event from the patient's life to the list of age regressions.

The patient may react to this series of therapy sessions in any one of a number of ways. First, usually during the first six or eight sessions, the patient's condition will remain static for the most part. He may be wondering what's going on, or how all this will fit together. All the same, as he continues to come, he will have faith that the therapist is going in a specific direction, knows what he is doing and will bring about the cure. The patient needs to be reassured of this periodically by the therapist.

As the case progresses the patient will likely begin to feel better for the above-mentioned reasons. If, however, he does not, there is another possibility and that is that with some patients, as the events from the past are brought back to the conscious mind, some of the accompanying emotions, grief, anxiety, hatred, and the like are brought back to the surface. Thus, this draining of negative feelings and emotions causes the patient temporarily to regress and even feel worse than when the therapy started. The patient may be told that this is analogous to the person who

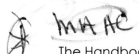

has mild feelings of discomfort because of a tumor, but surgery is necessary and the pain connected with the surgery is much more severe than the tumor itself. But the surgery is necessary in order to remove the tumor and the consequent ill effects which would result if the tumor were not removed. In one sense of the word, an analysis is emotional surgery. The diseased organs, or the tumor-like growths which do not belong in the emotions, have to be removed. Sometimes the removal is painful, but in the end there should be a sense of relief if the therapy is properly carried out.

The therapist at the conclusion of his age regressions is now able to see from the response of the patient that the significant events which have contributed to the problem have been understood and resolved. Usually the patient will have a feeling within himself that the particular age regressions are indeed the source of his problem.

If both the therapist and the patient are in doubt about the cause and effect relationship of the events from the patient's life that have been checked by age regression, further work is necessary.

A connection must be made between the anxiety feelings of the patient at the present conscious level with the event from the past which provoked the anxiety feelings, so that the patient can see a cause and effect relationship between stimulating events from the past and the resultant emotional anxiety of the present.

As has been said previously, when an age regression takes place, and there is obviously a release of repressed emotion, the patient needs to see that repression has taken place in the past and that the emotion needs to be drained in order to release the inner pressure. After this takes place, then the patient should receive a rationale from the therapist explaining how that particular event could have happened in the past but does not need to affect the patient any longer. This is the procedure for "setting aside" the traumatic event.

After helping the patient to understand more thoroughly what happened, and giving the patient a rationale to "explain away" the kind of reasoning she or he has concluded from such an event, it then is necessary for the therapist to give counter-suggestions which are positive and constructive. For example, if a person has had the Walking Zombie Syndrome, the therapist can state positively and definitely to the patient that he is alive, he has lived, he is healthy, he no longer needs to wheeze in order to have proof that he is alive and breathing (or whatever his symptom is, is no longer going to be present). Permission is granted or a suggestion is given to give up the symptoms. Further strengthening suggestions are given such as, "You are going to feel stronger and healthier each day; your lungs are going to be stronger with each passing week," etc.

In the case of a woman who has had the Ponce De Leon Syndrome, the hypnoanalyst should determine approximately where the age arrest took place and then through age progressions help her to relive those missed periods up to the present chronological age. This is done by adding the traits and characteristics of each developmental stage which she was deficient in from the childhood age where the maturation slowed down to the present calendar age. For example, if it is determined that she is emotionally and developmentally arrested at five years old, then while in trances she is given by description and visualization the traits and characteristics of each stage of growth in the psycho-sexual development up to her present age. It is as if she missed receiving those maturing experiences and learning those lessons from life when she first lived through these periods. Now she relives these periods vicariously and makes up for lost time. The therapist may conclude and repeat something like this:

> From this day forward you are going to have confidence in yourself as a woman. You are going to have confidence in your ability to relate to a man, if this is your desire. You will feel secure in your work or profession. You will be capable and confident in your decision making and in handling money. You will take your place as a woman with other women in the world, and take great pleasure in this, etc.

Thus, each time an age regression takes place and the significant event is analyzed, two things must be accomplished: an explanation of the event which takes away the production of anxiety must be given. Secondly, the anxiety event and irrational beliefs (or belief systems) with their unwholesome interpretation must be replaced with positive, healthy, constructive thoughts which will put good health into the mind of the patient, rather than pathological impressions that the patient previously had.

PREPARING THE PATIENT'S PERSONAL ANALYTICAL SUMMARY

When the above procedures are finally finished, the therapist looks back over his notes and picks out the traumatic event or events which served as the Initial Sensitizing Event(s) with a brief summary of what the event(s) were. Then he lines up in his notes what the Symptom Producing Event was and the Symptom Intensifying Events. Thus the analyst knows the complete case in his own mind before giving the summary to the patient.

When the above procedures are finally finished, the therapist looks over his notes and prepares to make a personal tape (PT) or summary of the highlights of the analysis, following this outline (Bryan, Note 20): 1. Introduction 2. Statement of symptoms 3. Diagnosis 4. Summary of pertinent points of the WAT 5. What the patient's dream revealed 6. Initial Sensitizing Event or Events of the DX 7. Symptom Producing Event 8. Symptom Intensifying Event or Events 9. Summary of positive suggestions

The introduction includes a kind of disclaimer to the effect that the analysis has not intended to place blame on anyone or to find fault or judgment against anyone. Rather it has been to understand what has happened in the patient's life to bring on the symptoms. Furthermore, although in this summary we are dealing with much negative or painful material, there really are many positive experiences from the patient's life which we have not dealt with because they were not the subject of our investigation.

Second, regarding the statement of symptoms, the therapist should simply read selected statements from the patient's own original words describing the disease or problem. This establishes a goal of therapy in the beginning.

Third, the diagnosis is simply stated. Presumably it has already been described clearly to the patient.

Fourth, summarize the information gleaned from the dream and WAT. Usually this will be in keeping with the therapist's early suppositions concerning the ultimate cause of the problem.

Fifth, the Initial Sensitizing Event is linked up in sequential order so that the patient can understand how the ground work for the symptoms was laid prior to the Symptom Producing Event.

Sixth, the Symptom Producing Event is described, showing the patient how such an event brought on the symptoms.

Seventh, if there are further intensifying events, these are pointed out, showing how they fit the entire scheme of things, so that there is a chain of events now described to the patient from the beginning of the problem up until the time that the patient came in for therapy. It will also be advisable to show a verification from the Word Association Test and the dream(s) as to how these events or feelings were significant in the patient's life.

Personal tape as desensitizing

John A. Scott, Sr., Ph.D.

At the conclusion of the personal tape, a list of positive suggestions dealing with alterations in thinking and behavior patterns should be given. The tape thus ends on a positive note. The clinician should be cautious to conclude on a strong, positive, encouraging theme. If the summary contains too much negative material and the patient has a delicate or weak ego, it may be overwhelming and defeating instead of encouraging. It is good to remind the patient that there are many good points and positive traits and characteristics present. These should be maximized in the summary while at the same time giving counter-acting positive suggestions to replace the negative feelings and symptoms that the patient brought in at the outset of therapy. For some patients, life has been so miserable and so filled with trauma, that even a summary account of that trauma is defeating. The summary tape should be of such a nature that the patient can listen to it a number of times until the analysis is thoroughly understood. Patients who question the reason for this procedure may be told the principle of desensitization, wherein, listening to the summary on tape over and over brings on a kind of familiarity of the destructive pattern which relieves internal tensions.

In subsequent visits to the office the patient hears the P tape along with further positive suggestions relating to gaining strength, confidence, security and other individual needs. As the person's life improves the sessions taper off and eventually cease.

Even after the patient understands the cause of the problem, and some of the emotional pressure has been decathected, symptoms may occasionally reappear. But reassurance to the effect that the symptoms will become weaker and weaker and soon disappear will have a constructive effect on the patient. If, after the disappearance of the symptoms altogether, they suddenly reappear, the patient should be reminded, by hearing the P tape and a series of positive suggestions again, of the progress that has been made and in most cases the symptoms will immediately disappear.

The latter period of therapy, as has been mentioned before, is called the period of reinforcement. During this period the principles of behavior modification may be effectively used in hypnotherapy. The patient is urged to visualize himself acting in the manner he desires (Kroger & Fezler, 1976). He is encouraged to picture himself conquering the situation which previously has been difficult, or succeeding at the tasks that he found previously produced anxiety. Whatever his symptoms were, or whatever his goals are, he is encouraged, while hypnotized, to picture himself succeeding

212

and overcoming the problem, whatever it may be. As he pictures himself doing this while deeply relaxed and comfortable, he will thus prepare himself for going through the event in actuality without anxiety. Strong, positive, and reassuring suggestions must be given to some patients over and over. As confidence grows and expectations for success increase, the changes will be locked in the patient's life. Proof of the success of the analysis is measured by the successful changes that are brought about (Bryan, Note 21).

One other thought must be added. Just as it is possible to quit the analysis too quickly and thus fail to "cure the patient," it is also possible to over-analyze the patient (Bryan, Note 22). When the specific events which caused the problem have been brought up, when they are understood, then the therapist should move on to the conclusion rapidly, cure the patient of his presenting problem, but not do more. The therapist should get to the heart of the problem, but not tack on other events or situations which are not a part of the patient's problem. Such confuses the patient and prolongs the analysis. The therapist should recall that a question was asked from Section VII, 6 of the case history: "If you could change one thing about yourself, what would that be?" This should be related to the presenting symptoms brought by the patient in the beginning, and the therapist should have asked at the beginning something to this effect: "If you are cured of this problem, or if this symptom is removed from your life, will you consider the therapy to be a success?" Thus the commitment is made by the patient then that he or she has a specific goal in mind for therapy. When that goal is reached, the therapy is over.

Most of the time there will be additional side effects which are constructive and helpful to the patient, because in curing the presenting symptoms, the underlying emotional pathology must be properly resolved. When that is resolved, there are additional side effects and advantages which usually result there from. But this is looked upon as an unexpected blessing. Theoretically, when the main goal is reached, the analysis is over. If the patient finds some other symptom arising, then that may be considered to be additional treatment or even a separate analysis for that specific problem. From a practical viewpoint such separation of symptoms or delineating of the analysis is not always advisable or even practical. It depends on the nature of the problem and the ego of the patient as to which course is preferable to be pursued.

CONCLUSION

The therapist must be realistic in his goals and expectations and always be honest and open with the patient. Enough procedures should be revealed to be effective, but not so much analysis that the patient becomes overwhelmed or confused, which can happen with some unsophisticated or poorly educated people.

The patient should be encouraged to return no matter how good he or she feels at intervals of three months, six months and a year, so as to receive reinforcement and continue the relationship with the therapist. This further reassures the patient of the clinician's interest and concern. A satisfied patient makes for a satisfied therapist. Bryan (Note 23) stresses that the patient should be shown how the therapy is a success, then stop the investigation and leave something to God. The patient cannot be made perfect.

An example of an age regression to birth will follow.

CHAPTER 7

AGE REGRESSION TO BIRTH

It is important that all hypnoanalysts have, as a part of their armamentarium, the ability to take the patient back to the birth experience. The reason is that many disorders, particularly drug/alcohol addiction, have this crucial experience as the Initial Sensitizing Event. Failure to recognize the significance of the uterine environmental experience, birth, or immediate post-birth conditions, as an ultimate cause for many emotional disorders explains why they do not respond well to therapy. Barnett (1980) has expressed impressively a type of experience most of us have had more times than we like to admit. That is the patient is analyzed and improves, (we hope cured), then regresses; the symptoms reappear, although perhaps not as severely as in their first appearance. Then these patients are reinvestigated by a hypnoanalyst, with particular reference to the birth experience in which there was extreme emotional distress. Once these negative feelings are relieved the patient returns to a symptom free condition. At last the Initial Sensitizing Event is dealt with and the results are successful.

Barnett (1980) also reports that in a series of 737 patients whom he checked for having negative or positive birth experiences, 215 (29%) had a negative birth experience.

Even though Freud stressed the importance of the birth trauma, psychotherapists since that time have, as a group, paid very little attention to the importance of this early period of time in their therapeutic procedures. Perhaps this neglect is not due only to skepticism; it may be due to lack of training or experience in analyzing the prenatal and birth process.

There are brighter prospects on the horizon. In recent years there has

215

been an increase of interest in both the clinical and experimental, physical and emotional, aspects of this most important period. Medical research has produced a plethora of reports on the many ways the developing fetus can be adversely influenced by intrauterine asphyxia, anoxia, drugs administered during the prenatal period, alcohol (even prior to pregnancy), abnormal parturition, difficult labor, premature birth, prenatal stress on the mother, maternal smoking, neurotic depressive mothers, analgesic medications during labor and delivery etc. The following references serve as the briefest of examples of such research: Brown, Grodin & Manning, 1972; Burstein, Kinch, & Stern, 1974; Erskine & Baum, 1982; McDonald, 1968; Shaywitz, Cohen, & Shaywitz, 1980; Standley, Soule, & Copans, 1979; Stott, 1973; Windle, 1967; Yang, Zweig, Douthitt & Federman, 1976.

Since the time of Freud there have been therapists who speculated on the emotional consequences of the birth trauma, but how to deal with it from a therapeutic standpoint has been a matter of speculation. Primal Scream Therapy has been put forward as one solution. But it may be that this modality has emphasized the birth trauma to the neglect of other influences which have also been factors that must be taken into consideration in making the patient whole again. Nonetheless, with as many sources of possible prenatal and perinatal trauma, the modern psychotherapist should have as a part of his or her armamentarium a method of abreacting such uterine and post-uterine trauma. Hypnosis is a means of succeeding at this. However, while the emotional abreaction serves to release pent-up tension, this alone may not be sufficient to cure the patient. This event should be put in the proper perspective with other subsequent trauma which have a common denominator, that is, with the SPE and any other SIE's. This procedure refers, of course, to Medical Hypnoanalysis (Bryan, 1961; Sheppard, 1967, 1971; Barnett, 1980; Lewter 1981; Ritzman, 1982a, 1982b, 1983). It is my purpose in this chapter, first, to review studies and research indicating that the fetus or neonate has a nervous system sufficiently developed to be sensitive to hapless conditions or trauma, and that such stimulation, in many cases, adversely effects the developing personality. This material falls into two areas. One is that the developing nervous system is physically capable of receiving and registering such stimuli, and the second has to do with a theoretical concept known as "early mechanical memory." A second purpose is to present a practical procedure for regressing the patient back to the birth or prenatal experience.

Sensitivity of the Fetus and Neonate

Frequently trauma related to the prenatal and/or perinatal environment must be re-lived with the appropriate emotional abreaction in order for the patient to get well. Some of our medical colleagues are skeptical of this possibility because they believe certain physiological prerequisites have not developed far enough in the first few months of life for the impressions to be so made that they can be recalled in the typical memory function later in life. In other words, some neurologists have said that one cannot recall an event as early as the birth experience because it is not physically possible. The nervous system is not developed sufficiently. Of course, a large number of the general public is likewise skeptical just because they don't understand how it can be done.

Recent research has changed the thinking of many on this important subject. Just in the last decade more work has been done in the area of cognition of the neonate than ever before. In fact, Richard Held, Head, Department of Psychology, Massachusetts Institute of Technology, maintains that such studies have tripled, changing our view of what infants can see, hear, understand, and remember (Held, 1979a, 1979b).

As a result of hearing of the research of Jacques Mehler, the French Cognitive psychologist, Robin Fox, anthropologist of Rutgers University, called a conference of neurologists and psychologists to share their research. The conference, sponsored by the Harry Frank Guggenheim Foundation, was held in New York in November of 1981, and was entitled, "Neonate and Infant Cognition" (reported in Pines, 1982).

Although it is not my purpose to review in detail the proceedings of that conference, or of all the research that is presently in progress, I do wish to summarize some of the main issues. At the present time new questions are being asked concerning newborns that neurologists and psychologists did not dare ask even as late as twenty-five years ago because it was thought that it would be extremely difficult, if not impossible, to develop research methods in order to answer these revolutionary questions. Some of them are: "When do the cognitive experiences of the human being actually begin?" "Can they start before birth?" "What abilities does the baby bring into the world?" "May the infant 'hear' in the uterus - if so, how clearly?" "What are possible consequences of what is heard?"

"Can babies really see at the time of birth - if so, what?" "How soon can infants recognize their own names?" "What other responses do infants give to indicate recognition both by vision, by touch, by sound?"

John A. Scott, Sr., Ph.D.

It is now possible to study the prenatal environment more closely and to answer such provocative questions - at least to some degree.

Physiological Foundations

In the second week of gestation of the human embryo, head folds develop, limbs bud, and the germinal foundation for all organs has been differentiated (Arey, 1974). It is only in the last months of gestation that rudimentary mental processes begin. Prior to that time each of the sensory organs start with a minute beginning and go through stages of development in preparation for mature function. By the fifth or sixth week twelve pairs of cranial nerves have appeared (Arey, 1974). The brain exists very early as a tube-like mass, and, as it continues to grow, it results in a series of bends and folds which later differentiate into the various regions of the brain which are established in broad outlines by the sixth month. By the eighth month there is a great increase in the area and volume of the cortex. On the surface the convolutions and fissures are obvious, while inside, the nerve cells and their parts are continuing to multiply and mature.

In the meantime the various organ systems which supply sensory stimuli to the brain are gradually developing. Nerves which are differentiated for vision, hearing, smell, taste, and touch are growing and the various stages in progress can be traced from the earliest specification of cells through stages of folds, or grooves, or pits, until there is the ability to hear, to smell, to taste and to respond reflexively to touch by the last weeks of gestation. Some senses are more mature than others by the seventh month. Delgado (1969) states that "as the fetus grows many organs perform something like a dress rehearsal before their function." Although theoretically the fetus and neonate show very little response to pain for several hours or days after birth.

At least two research projects have attempted to ascertain whether learning can take place prenatally (Sontag & Newberry, 1940; Spelt, 1948), but these studies have been criticized for too broad conclusions from limited data (Annis, 1979). Clinical experience in hypnoanalysis has indicated that by the last weeks of gestation, impressions - however vague - may be made in some instances on the fetus by way of physical or emotional shock to the mother or the birth experience itself (Davids, DeVoult & Talmadge, 1961; Freud, 1949; Leboyer, 1975; McNeil & Weigerink, 1971; Stott, 1973; Verny, 1981).

It, therefore, becomes clear that by the last two, or even three, months of gestation there are elements of the sensory system mature enough to receive stimuli which will register in the brain sufficiently to say that the mind is now beginning to develop. But this is a gradual process and one should not be dogmatic about the exact time the mind begins to function, nor the degree to which it can function when it begins.

The Uterine Environment

Regarding the auditory sense of the fetus in utero, it was reported at the neonate conference that a French obstetrician had inserted a hydrophone into a pregnant woman's uterus before delivery and made a recording of what it picked up. A conversation between the mother and a male doctor was audible with a clear distinction between the male and female voices. Furthermore the music of Beethoven's Fifth Symphony, which the mother had heard, was quite clear (Pines, 1982). Infants who were conditioned prior to birth by hearing the music repeated, responded positively after birth to the same music. They recognized it as familiar. Infants who had not heard it prior to birth did not respond positively. All of this is significant when one considers that the familiarity of the mother's voice, heard so frequently prior to birth, must play a part in the bonding with that mother (cf. Mehier, Bertoncini, & Barriere,1978).

There are other procedures whereby the fetal responses may be evaluated. Sensitive electrodes can now be used to record the babies' heartbeats, and thus register changes according to varying types of stimuli. Pacifiers connected to electronic equipment can record babies' sucking patterns (which vary according to peaceful or stressful stimuli). Eye tracking devices and computers are available to interpret this and much more data from the infant prior to birth.

It is a matter of popular knowledge that there are many ways in which tranquilizers and premedications given to the mother during delivery effect the neonate's initial weight gain and his response to nursing and early learning tasks (Brazelton, 1970; Lester, Als & Brazelton, 1982). Intrauterine conditions of subclinical malnutrition, frequent infection and even mild hypoxia of high altitude are powerful influences in the neonate's behavior (Brazelton, 1972; Scott, 1976). Brazelton (1977) listed the following variables as strongly influencing the performance of the neonate: unexpectedly prolonged intervals between pregnancies, maternal height, and socioeconomic group. In addition, this researcher (1982) reported that "infants born to older mothers of high parity demonstrated poorer social interactive skills. . ." Physiologically inadequate intrauterine environment is known to effect later performance on behaviors related to activity and alertness (Stott,1973; Rutt & Offord, 1971). Infants from a deficient uterine period lacked energy for relating to the social and inanimate environment (Brazelton, Koslowski, & Tronick, 1977).

While concrete laboratory evidence is lacking at the present, the indications are that maternal emotions, both during pregnancy and immediately after, have a long term impact on the baby (Sontag, 1966). Indications of such prenatal stress were observed in newborns dying soon after birth due to peptic ulcers, thought to have developed because the mother was under severe stress during the last trimester of her pregnancy.

Gadpaille (1975) is persuaded that the mother's emotional states can be communicated to the fetus she is carrying. "A fetus is subject to all the same biochemical influences as its mother whenever she is under stress" (Gadpaille, 1975, p. 25). This author cites experiments with laboratory animals indicating that the adrenal glands of the fetus also respond to the stress of the mother.

When pregnant rats were subjected to high levels of stressful conditions during the critical period of sexual differentiation, the males born to them were rendered permanently less able to perform normal male sexual behavior, and more prone to respond to female behavior (Gadpaille, 1975, p. 26).

Hofer (1981), dealing with animal experiments, states:

Prenatal exposure to alcohol, methadone, heroin, major tranquilizers, barbiturates, and amphetamines, all have been shown to produce long-term effects on the behavior of off-spring when juvenile or adult, weeks and months after the intrauterine period of exposure to these substances.

Stott (1973), as a result of a prolonged study, reports cautiously that stresses involving severe, continuing personal tensions - in particular, marital discord - were closely associated with child morbidity in the form of ill health, neurological dysfunction, developmental lag, and behavior disturbance. Sameroff(1975) states essentially the same thing. Both Stott and Sameroff are cautious and warn against jumping to dogmatic conclusions concerning cause and effect in every case. Of significant interest to the hypnoanalyst is the observation by Sameroff and Stott as well as by Hofer that potential adult behavior may be influenced by prenatal trauma or stress when followed later in life by subsequent stressful conditions. We would define this as the ISE and the SPE, perhaps followed by further SIE's.

There are indications, though not proof, that the father's role in providing a stable and secure environment, is a factor in the mother's emotional state, which in turn influences the fetus (Coppolillo, 1976). Stott also dealt with this (1973). In addition Huttunen and Niskanen (1978), Finnish researchers, theorize on the basis of data gathered during World War II, that grief-stricken mothers who lost their husbands during the third to fifth months of pregnancy or the ninth and tenth months produced off-spring with some form of psychiatric disorder. Both of these periods may be critical in the fetal brain development. Thus maternal stress, resulting from marital strife or loss of the father in one of these crucial periods, may be a source of trauma adversely affecting the fetus.

Further, it is clear that events that occur in utero alter the physiological mechanisms that provide for emotional activity. Boyden (1974) reviewed the animal experiments on the effects of stress. He found that pregnant mothers who were highly stressed provided offspring with high anxiety and aggression levels.

Gray (1971) found that the emotional response of an animal could be radically altered by stressing its mother while pregnant. The adrenal activity of animals was increased when their mother was highly stressed while pregnant, causing them to be more emotional.

Sex hormone levels during intrauterine life have been found to have a radical effect. In rodents, genetic males have been feminized by the deprivation of androgen or the injection of an anti-androgenic substance during prenatal development. This causes the external genitalia to be feminized and leads them to perform sexually as females upon reaching adulthood (Goldman, 1978; Goy, 1968; Money & Schwartz, 1978).

In just the opposite way, genetic female rodents, who are treated with androgen prenatally, will display male adult sexual behavior. They mount females and attempt intromission and they are much more aggressive, in general, than females. Further, exposure to prenatal or neonatal testosterone will render them permanently acyclic (Goldman, 1978; Money & Schwarts, 1978). This effect has also been demonstrated in mice, guinea pigs, ferrets, dogs, hamsters, sheep and Rhesus monkeys (Baum, Gallagher, Martin and Damassa, 1981; Erskine & Baum, 1982; Goldman, 1978; Goy, 1968; Money & Schwartz, 1978).

The suggestion of this material is clear. Activities that alter the hormone levels of the mother, also alter the hormone function of the fetus and thereby alter the emotions and behavior of the individual during growth. Stress raises androgen and adrenalin levels of the mother which increases the masculinization, aggression and anger levels and general emotionality level of the developing infant. (Cf. also Ward, 1972.)

We are not left with evidence only from rodents. Pillard (reported by Spezzano, 1981) observed that human adults burn up testosterone during the stress of combat. If stress on the pregnant human mother burns up testosterone her fetus needs, the basic substrata of male sexual behavior will simply not exist.

The preceding, and similar data, are taken into account in the concept of the Initial Environmental Experience (IEE). Lewter (1981) makes a strong case for consideration of the intrauterine experience as a predetermining factor in the Initial Sensitizing Event. His point is, that, while the ISE is a specific experience at a point in time, one must consider the general impression which the infant receives in utero for a period of time also. That experience may be pleasant and favorable or unpleasant and traumatic. This preconditioning is a powerful influence on how the infant gets its start in the world.

The intrauterine experience involves both a psychological and physiological union with the mother. The nature of this union, for good or ill, is recorded as the first impression of existence on that infant. This is a pre-ISE experience and is geared to the basic need of survival. Survival is equal to life. Lewter effectively makes his point as follows:

Once the IEE is established, any threat to this basic survival formula, coupled with any predisposing limitations, the organism can be expected to become sensitized by the threat. Utilizing the hypnotic regression we can explore the intrauterine experience where the organism experiences both physiological and psychological union. This union is often recorded as survival=life and a condition that spells trouble in an outside world if threatened

There are many ways to view this sense of survival (life); several ways follow: (1) if the intrauterine experience is unpleasant, the safe and secure survival formula is in existence before the unpleasantness, which may result in the WZ syndrome and schizophrenia; (2) if the intrauterine experience is unpleasant, the unpleasantness is equated to safe and secure survival, the organism must then maintain unpleasantness to survive. This could support the need to resist getting "well, "and spark the need to "silence" anyone who touches these normally repressed fears; and (3) the intrauterine experience and union is ultimate intimacy -- perfect belonging must come to an end at birth. Thus a chance to continue life becomes a traumatic experience for the infant. Some people may elect to remain in the womb emotionally, mentally, spiritually,

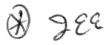

although their physical body is delivered; or some individuals will spend a lifetime attempting to return to the womb or build a substitute.

One such example would be a womb of fat constructed by the obese.

Lewter's thesis is that understanding the IEE concept goes beyond the ISE which may see the ACT of birth as an initial trauma. This theory postulates that there is a state of being prior to the trauma that is recorded in the infant's psyche and helps to form the initial survival messages. These in turn influence future symptomotology.

The Birth Process

The potential emotional threat of the birth process has been a subject of discussion since Freud. Various psychoanalysts have theorized on the subject but there has apparently not been a consensus on actual therapeutic procedure which is dependable in verifying specific events and effectively treating them. A possible exception would be some psychoanalysts and Primal Scream Therapists.

Of course the possibilities of birth trauma physically have long been known and physicians have been dealing with such by increasingly effective procedures. It is the relationship between physical birth trauma and specific emotional disorders of later life that have eluded psychotherapists.

Some of the more frequent birth trauma are the following. Caesarean section (Ponder, 1970), severe asphyxia (Scott, 1976), timing of cord clamping (Theorell, Prechtl, Blair, & Lind, 1973), effects of prolonged labor (Keith & Norval, 1950), drug and chemical risks (Browit Grodin, & Manning, 1972; Schwarz & Yaffe, 1980), and any form of abnormal parturition (Erickson, 1981; Little, 1961) - even premature or delayed birth.

Such trauma can result most impressively as a physical death threat and emotional identity confusion, as well as other afflictions such as chronic head aches and other bodily pain, breathing problems such as asthma, and generalized ego confusion related to being accepted or rejected, security and insecurity, and such like. Such feelings underlie a multitude of possible symptomatic expressions.

The Neonate

I wish to stress that all of this research, not only the report at the New York meeting, but research that has gone on since that time indicates that the infant's nervous system is much more advanced at the time of birth than was previously thought possible.

Due to research in the last five years, newer and more advanced questions are being asked concerning the fetus and neonate. These have to do with how infants process what they see and hear. "What do infants judge to be similar or different?" "How much can they remember?" "What can they predict?" It is possible by using a variety of highly specialized methods to determine a great deal more about infant development and to study the various kinds of brain function.

Of particular interest to those who are concerned with prenatal and birth trauma and influence, are the following reports. Meltzoff and Moore (1977) in doing research with newborns one hour after birth observed a pronounced difference in the babies who were born to mothers who received no medication during labor and delivery, (except local anesthetics) and those babies who were born to mothers by Caesarean section and/or had received heavy medication during the delivery process. (See also Ponder, 1970.)

Physiologists and psychologists, some twenty-five years ago, insisted that newborns could not see more than the difference between light and dark and that babies were too absorbed by their insides to react very much to the outside world during their first three months after birth. This is in sharp contrast to the present indications that infants are able to imitate facial gestures by the age of two weeks and that six month old babies use some kinds of rules to sort out sounds. Held (1979b) observed that the infants' binocular vision undergoes a sudden jump between 16 and 21 weeks of age. This means that at an age when babies were previously thought to see very little, they have the ability to see differences in the distance between objects.

Bower, Dunkeld, and Wishart (1979) found that, contrary to previous observations, infants 18 - 26 days old can discriminate between real objects and pictures of objects.

In addition to the foregoing evidence of the fetus and neonate's sensitivity and response to the environment, more research is demonstrating that the infant, during the first weeks of life, is much more alert than previously thought possible. There are indications of surprising muscular agility and dexterity for the newborn which had not previously been observed. For example, Dunkeld and Bower (1980) have found that infants between 13 and 27 days old possibly have an unlearned ability to pick up information about change of position in the third dimension. Spelke (1976, 1981) observing the perceptual explorations of infants 4 months old, noted that they learn auditory-visual relationships even when the object appeared in a different location. This suggests sound-object learning rather than space or response learning. Neonates have been observed to defend themselves against intrusive, negative stimuli and seek to control interfering motor and autonomic responses that they may attend to important social and nonsocial stimuli (Als, Tronick, Lester & Brazelton, 1977).

A system for assessing the complicated face-to-face interactions of infant to adult has been devised by Tronick, Als and Brazelton (1980) whereby combinations of behaviors are categorized. Findings show that infant's responses are: protest, avoid, monitor, set, play, and talk.

Piaget found that infants in the first eight months would not remove a cloth or a cup from off a toy. The conclusion was that with them it was "out of sight, out of mind." Bower and Wishart (1972) disagree, finding that this age infant reached out to obtain an object that had been made to go out of sight by switching off the light, leaving the infant in total darkness. Another traditional view has been modified by Bower, Broughton, and Moore (1970) who demonstrate that in judgment situations the infant's vision dominates touch. Traditionally it has been taught that "touch teaches vision" in ontogeny. Bower, in another study (1966) suggested that "infants (aged 4 - 6 weeks) can in fact register most of the information an adult can register but can handle less of the information than adults can. . ."

I have cited these examples to the point of tedium (and there are many more) in an effort to impress on the reader that researchers in the field of infant development, having discovered ways of securing information from their subjects, are unveiling every year new evidence that the newborn is not just a "blank tablet waiting to be written upon" as John Locke is reported to have described it. And certainly it is a far cry from the medical textbook of 1963 which took the position that the newborn could not fix its eyes or respond to sound, and that conscious awareness does not exist in the newborn as it does in an older child.

For the analyst who is concerned about the period of infancy and particular influences on personality formation, there is mounting evidence of the infant's awareness of the relationship with parents. The interaction between parents and their infants is such that the infant influences the behavior it receives back from the parent (Brazelton, 1978; Brazelton & Als, 1979; Tronick, Als, & Brazelton, 1977, 1980). Fathers are not exempt from influence on the infant's behavior. Spelke, Zelazo, Kagan, & Kotelchuck (1973) observed that infants from low-father-interaction families were most upset when alone at the time a stranger came in the room. They also became bored most rapidly with nonsocial stimuli. Infants who were least fearful with the stranger came from high-father-interaction families and displayed the greatest interest in inanimate stimuli, smiling in response to it.

Another example of the revision of knowledge regarding the infant's learning capacity is in the ability to imitate adult movements. Piaget maintained that infants develop the ability to imitate adults around the end of the first year. Experiments by Meltzoff and Moore (1977) demonstrate that infants imitate facial gestures of adults as early as two weeks of age.

The point of the foregoing details is this: the prenatal environment, the birth experience and the early postnatal environment make a profound impression on the infant, who is sensitive, receptive, and easily impressed with conditions which are other than optimum. If, later in life, traumatic relationships or experiences occur which in some way may be linked with the birth experiences (in that person's perception), consequences in the nature of an emotional problem will likely follow.

Patricia Goldman-Rakic sums up the current situation regarding research in the field of infant development and cognition:

We've only just begun to uncover the neuromechanisms involved in development. If there's ever going to be some interaction between neuroscience and the theoreticians it will be in research on infants. (Quoted in Pines, 1983, p. 53.)

The careful scholar is going to be cautious about drawing dogmatic conclusions from the data presented in the foregoing pages; however, neither should the clinician be so reluctant to wait for laboratory evidence that he or she hesitates, in treating patients, to take into account that there are mounting indications that the Initial Sensitizing Event can take place prior to birth, at birth, or in the period immediately following birth. Of course, there will be variables which alter conditions. Early trauma may be subsequently neutralized by stabilizing conditions in the environment, while relatively minor stresses, pre- or postnatally, may be aggravated subsequently by severe conditions, resulting in symptoms.

Early Mechanical Memory

In addition to the physiological explanation for early impressions made upon the fetus and neonate, as alluded to in the foregoing pages, there is another possible explanation, that of "early mechanical memory." This may

have been a "grasping at straws" by psychotherapists of earlier days when the physiology was not well known or understood. On the other hand, those theorizing in this area may have been prophetic.

Melanie Klein, an outstanding psychoanalyst who has made major contributions to the field of human behavior, pushes back the major dynamics of ego and superego development to the first year of life (Monroe, 1955). As a result of studying countless cases, she observes that passive sucking gives way to active biting by around 6 months as the child does something about its anxieties. The infant is not just a mechanical object in the first months of life. It is an active, thriving bundle of human feelings and responses. Without modern electronic devices to aid in her studies, Klein observed that the infant has a rudimentary appreciation of objects. It is dominated by organs and biological processes which the child recognizes from its own experience. And beyond this, Klein sees what appears to be recognition of dim phylogenetically determined images of the principle organs of feeling for itself: the penis, vagina, and somehow senses the general idea of the fusion of coitus and childbirth. Here Klein sees evidence of recognition of the breast of the mother, its own feces and urine, genitals, process of incorporation and expulsion, presence and absence of the mother, etc. All of these elements compose the infant's world and impressions made by means of these elements are the source of mechanical impressions which last throughout life.

The theory of phylogenetic memory, simply stated, is that impressions are somehow made by, on, or through the genes and are passed from one generation to the next, perhaps on a par with some animal instincts. This kind of a "memory" would be inherited. This is not the place for a discussion of this theory in detail. It can be researched in the writings of Melanie Klein and those who have followed in her school of thought.

The theory of mechanical memory is closely akin to the above. This theory is that impressions are somehow made on the cells of the body, perhaps even at specific locations of the body, and they remain. Dr. Itamar Yahalom (1975), child psychoanalyst at the Reiss-Davis Child Clinc, Los Angeles, proposed that the child has images based on simple touch, for example, the nipple of the breast in its mouth makes an impression that stays with the infant. Perhaps there is a kind of chain reaction made on the soma cells which is somehow retained into adulthood. Dr. Yahalom's wide experience in the field of child study coordinates with what Klein has proposed. There are others who would agree.

Our own opinion, based on the preceding theories and on a myriad of

[handwritten: Has anyone done this in a flotation tank or in a water bed?]

age regressions to birth, is that the person in a medium or deep trance is in a condition much like the fetus in the prenatal and neonate state.

The fetus, floating in the amnionic fluid, is in a position and condition to receive stimuli and impressions in a peculiar manner. Because it is surrounded by fluid, there would be a blending of auditory and sensory stimuli. When one is under water in a swimming pool or a lake, and there is a noise of a weight dropping on the bottom of a pool or the sound of a boat motor, one "feels" the sound on the body as well as "hears" it with the ears. Sound waves and shock waves pass through the fluid and register on the body as well as the ears. Bear in mind that the fetus has been in the fluid long enough that the skin would be extremely sensitive to the environment, not toughened by exposure or age. Furthermore, the nerves of the upper epidermis, being directly related to the emotional state, would further contribute to a registering of environmental stimuli as emotional impressions. Thus it can be said that the mind of the fetus is in a free floating (!) lethargic condition, open and receptive to influence and suggestion from the environment. And because of the part the body plays as a sensory organ, it stands to reason that registration takes place on and in the soma cells. Consequently, recall of events, having taken place at this early period, would involve these vague impressions that are somehow "recorded" on the body as well as the mind.

There is another aspect that should be stressed at this point. The symbiotic relationship of the mother and the fetus or neonate bears some similarity to the relationship between the hypnotist and the patient. The rapport develops into a transference of a particular sort. Borrowing a technical term from theology, I would call it a synergistic relationship.

In theology, the synergistic concept is that the Holy Spirit cooperates with the human will in the regeneration of man. This kind of cooperation or mystical union of man (in need of regeneration - a spiritual birth) with the Spirit of God, results in man's change. This change is not just in a modification of behavior, but a change in the heart (mind, emotions) and thus the entire life is altered. The synergistic concept involves an unbalanced relationship. In theology the more powerful and influential element is the Spirit of God and the weaker and more receptive element is man, who is altered and benefits from this spiritual fusion. Likewise in the hypnotic relationship the patient or subject is the more receptive element who agrees to the therapeutic relationship and expects to be benefited there from. In the fetal/neonate relationship with the mother, obviously the

[handwritten: Water bed w/ motion + weighted blanket]

228

infant is the weaker of the two and stands to be the more greatly influenced by the relationship.

In all three of the above levels of relationship, the fusion or affiliation involves the unconscious, a deep, permanent or semi-permanent change made by a dominant element upon the passive/receptive partner.

Perhaps something akin to this is what Chertok (1982) had in mind when describing the "primary relationship":

Not much is known about relational life at the very first stages of development. The only certain thing is that it begins very early - some authors even believe that the fetus records the mother's responses. How does communication circulate? Through which channels? Should one speak of this in terms of excitation and discharge? Are the baby's feelings at first articulated around the pleasure/pain pole as Freud tended to think? Or does man, at the very outset, have at his disposal a set of biologically determined responses? It can merely be observed, that for the maturation of the organism, a certain amount of excitation, produced by the "other" triggers off the necessary processes. At this stage, the "other" is not yet perceived as an object. He is part and parcel of the subject's sensory-motor field.

Chertok, in this challenging paper (1982) further provokes thought by this statement:

But the fact nonetheless remains that unconscious processes are both psychological and physiological, and that the articulation of the two levels is still fairly unfamiliar to us.

He goes on to say that hypnosis "represents a psychobiological crossroads. . . in effect, becoming another approach to the hidden side of the unconscious."

Those clinicians who have regressed patients back to birth in the process of hypnoanalysis have seen the recall, frequently to the patient's surprise, based on a vague, gut feeling of the intrauterine environment, the birth canal, strangulation, twisting, one or another part of the body emerging first, feelings of being held tightly or loosely, sensations of light, heat, cold etc. Emotions of the post-birth environment include the presence or absence of certain ones, being welcomed or rejected, an awareness of the condition of the mother or other siblings present at the time. We have had experience with a number of patients who have been intently aware of the threat of death to a twin or to the mother, or to oneself.

Thus, in one form or another, there are indications that impressions may be made on the fetus or neonate that remain imbedded on the mind and/or on the body to such an extent that emotions or behavior are influenced later in life. Admittedly, much is speculative, but as years go by there is more experimentation that gives credence to much that has been labeled as "theoretical." But for all of the impressions that may be registered on the mind and/or body of the neonate, how may the therapist and patient gain access to such information? The process of hypnotic age regression not only opens the doors to this stored body of events, but at the same time lends credence to the theory that the information from this early period is indeed "remembered" and available. Raikov (1982), as a result of experiments, tersely states the case for age regression to birth in these words:

Can some memory traces of infantile experiences persist in the nervous system? This registration and persistence would be present at an "unconscious" level, until reactivated in hypnotic regression. . . The memory structure can be assumed to consist of three parts: a, the usual memory, b, an unconscious memory of the kind revealed in high dreams and in some physiological processes, and c, preconscious memory, in which the infant registers or reflects reality without the ability to understand what is reflected.

The Process of Age Regression to Birth

There are several prerequisites to keep in mind in planning an age regression to prebirth or birth experiences. First, the therapist must be confident. If there is doubt, the subject most likely will sense this and not respond. Secondly, the therapist should plan for creating an emotional experience. This would involve the use of metaphors, visualizations and even sound effects which create a mood completely separating the subject from the here and now. I prefer to use sound effects and visualization of a rocket journey, stating that there is a theory that the farther out in space one goes, the further back in time one goes. Thus, on this journey, one is going back to the time of one's beginning. The use of earphones and a sound effects tape as an adjunct, combined with a vibrating chair, make this procedure effective. We use a tape of a jet taking off, then fade into sound effects used on the ASTRAL SOUNDS tape (1981). We visualize the engines dropping off and cut off the vibration of the chair or couch at that time. Then the quieter astral sounds are used while describing peacefully floating in space. The final stage pictures the subject in the peace and quiet of the uterus, fully protected and nourished.

At this time we use the sound effects of the intrautero heart beat (Murooka,1974) in order to further create the mood. In our opinion, the fetus heard this sound long enough in the beginning, that replaying it under these circumstances triggers, by association, the recall of events that took place at that time, if, indeed, the events made an impression. If those events were traumatic enough at the actual time of pregnancy and delivery, an impression most likely registered. If pregnancy and birth were routine, in most cases, no impression was made that would be recalled. We stress to the patient to get in touch with a gut feeling, no matter how vague, and describe it. Occasionally one will say weakly, "I don't remember." I reply, "I don't want you to remember. Give me your FEELING or IMPRESSION from the gut." I find that creating a vivid setting, stimulating a mood, and asking for a feeling comes nearer starting the process than any other procedure. Once the patient "gets in touch" and starts the process, usually there is a flowing of feeling tied in with events. Frequently, there is dramatic abreaction and I, the therapist, feel I am there, privileged to share in a primordial scene of the most fundamental importance to my patient.

The value of making an emotional setting for the pre-birth experience is in recreating the "state dependent learning" situation described by Rossi (1986). When the emotions are sufficiently stimulated in a similar fashion to what they were at birth, the impressions or "memories" of that occasion are brought back. This is because the total physical condition peculiar to that original occasion provokes a replay of impressions made on the mind and body at that time. This has been called the "law of association."

It should be said that even though we have good reason to suspect the prebirth or birth experience to be of therapeutic significance, and thus find the solution in this age regression, not every patient responds as one could wish.

There are those patients who have no impressions whatsoever of the prenatal or birth experience. Others have some impressions, but I have the feeling, sometimes, that the patient is either role playing or projecting to that period, perhaps to accommodate me. However, even at this, there is an emphasizing of the patient's pattern of behavior or mode of operation in life, whereby the imagined or projected concept of the prenatal conditions or birth process takes place, like the waking dream (Epstein, 1981), at a different level of reality than that of the concrete world. Even this experience can be beneficial therapeutically. It is based on the principle underlying the projective test.

Clinical Examples

One has to be cautious, as Stott emphasizes (1973), and not jump to unwarranted conclusions regarding cause and effect. There are so many variables that one should not conclude that every time a pregnant mother has what appears to be a traumatic period of time, say, with abuse from an alcoholic husband, that this means that the fetus is, in some way, marked. One pregnant mother may be particularly sensitive and have a very pronounced response, with a surge of insulin, which in turn would effect the fetus adversely. Another mother is not as sensitive and would take the abuse in stride, consequently, with little or no surge of insulin to the fetus. Other variables such as sex, race, timing etc. (cf. Stott, 1972, p.195) would keep this pattern of prenatal and birth trauma inconsistent. Such variables, perhaps, account for the variation in the experimental reports on both humans and animals. Due to the very nature of the subject of prenatal influence, truly scientific experiments cannot be made. . . at least at this time.

This does not mean that the clinician must wait on the experimental psychologist to come up with laboratory evidence, properly duplicated, demonstrating that every time certain external events take place that the fetus will be effected in a certain pathological way, in order to treat effectively a patient whose ISE appears to be prebirth or birth trauma. Ultimately the clinician is faced with a pragmatic approach, viz., "What will it take to get this patient relief or cured?" When the phraseology, word association test responses, symptoms, or other behavior (verbal or non-verbal) indicate to the sensitive therapist that the ISE took place either before birth, at birth, or soon thereafter, he or she should do an age regression to birth and check it out. Indeed, in my opinion, the innumerable examples of such age regressions, and the way in which patient and therapist successfully deal with them, are strong indications (if not "evidence"), that many forms of trauma made indirectly and directly upon the fetus or neonate account for much psychopathology. This is called by Stott the concept of congenital vulnerability (1972, p.194). The following are some examples of patients who were congenitally vulnerable and suffered an ISE during this period.

Mr. D.P., age 37. This man obviously suffers the aftereffect of cerebral palsy, by his manner of gate, other motor activity, speech etc. He is a professor of sociology at a small southern college. His throat had a tendency to close on him and choke off his breath at moments which were tense for one reason or another (i.e. threatening). In his analysis, I thought on more than one occasion, I had found the Initial Sensitizing Event for his symptom, but to no avail. Such events turned out to be Symptom Intensifying Events. In the process of analysis I had worked backward through his life looking for the original trauma which was the precursor of his present problem and still had not found the source. It occurred to me that birth was the logical possibility. In a hypnotic age regression to birth the patient spontaneously drew up in the fetal position and said nothing. He then began to twist, appearing very awkward, he choked, coughed and caught his breath in such a manner that I thought he might have a spasm. His chin was drawn down on his chest, at another point his head was thrown back grotesquely. After he calmed down and the twisting movement stopped, I told him he could express to me what he had felt. He said he felt he had been strangled and thought he would die; finally he came out of darkness into light. Obviously his current symptoms were recurring in the classroom when he perceived a threatening situation; such was analogous to the first threatening situation of his life in which the response was essentially the same.

Mr. F. V., age 40, FAA employee, controller in radar direction in Air Transport Clearance. As in the previous case, this man was thrown into a threatened position in his work and reacted with anxiety. The presenting symptom was also a kind of choking sensation, being extremely conscious of excessive saliva upon which he feared "I might choke." In looking for the Initial Sensitizing Event I took the patient back to birth. He began to twist and squirm, but talked as he did so and told me in a weaker than usual voice what he felt. I expected that he was caught in the umbilical cord - exactly so. It was obvious that he was a breach birth. He said, "I get the sensation like it's someone else - like I'm observing it...yet I feel a hand under my left arm, left knee and right foot. My right arm isn't out. Its being doubled back toward my body (?) I feel a little pain in my right arm."

A note I wrote was: "Rt arm drawn up tight - head droop. Left arm out straight - tense - rt. leg flexed. Rt. arm stretched out straight above head."

Now comes the umbilical cord problem. Patient continues: "Restriction across throat (arms stretched above head). It's still across there . . . across throat. . . . Left arm pressure. . . Cord from left ear up under chin . . . sore place . . . left side of neck . . . numbness in right shoulder . . . I'm breathing freely. Feel like I'm resting now. Slight sensation of lump at adams apple. . . feel slight pressure on left ear. . ."

The patient referred to his body as twisting involuntarily to conform to something, he did not know what. But this was not the whole story. He improved after this event, but was not over his symptom. I was disappointed, but realized there must be something else. We repeated the birth experience. This time there was the sensation of being held tightly against his body (!). He felt constricted. He smelled milk, he salivated. . .the impression left him. I wished for more details, but they were not forthcoming. I speculated that he got more milk than he could swallow at one time and probably choked on it. This was associated closely with the previously described choking experience, pain in the right arm, being restricted, etc. Later it became clear that his arm apparently had been broken in birth and it was bound to his body. Further scenes came to mind of being held against his mother's body, arm bound tightly and unable to move when choking on too much milk. It was never clear whether milk was from the breast or bottle.

There is an interesting postscript to this particular example. After this information appeared as an article in *Medical Hypnoanalysis* (1984. 5, 1) a physician (Stephen W. Cobb, M.D., Gyn. Dallas, TX) observed that a person without experience in delivering births could not describe such realistic gestures by imagination. Such a birth experience had to be an authentic reproduction.

Mrs. B. M., age 39, housewife, mother. Presenting symptom: anxiety about driving her car, going places alone. She lives in a small town and goes to another nearby town to do her major shopping. While this has always been a task it was becoming more difficult for her when she, in desperation, came for help lest she be too confined to do her shopping.

During the analysis, an age regression brought to light a time of fright when she was watching some men dig a well (for water). She became frightened when she thought, "I would hate to get caught in that - I'd get stuck and couldn't get out." Now, why would she think that? I expected her to go on with the story and tell how she did in fact fall in and panicked and this would be the ISE. Not so. She didn't fall in and her re-living of the event ended right there. There was nothing in this that would appear traumatic to me, but it was to her. Why?

I thought of the birth canal and regressed her to birth. During the experience she related how she was not ready to be born. She was premature at 8 months. (I later checked with her mother who told me she almost miscarried.) She further described perfectly the environment of the uterus, saying she could feel it: "The feeling I have is. . . if I were in that environment I'd want to get out. . . I have the feeling of something. . .of smothering. I feel like my hands are tied. I feel the need for air. . . ."

The following cases are presented because of some variation in the birth experience. The first one illustrates two pronounced variations. One in the kind of reception the infant felt and later a revelation which explained years of subsequent abuse.

Mrs. J.S., age 30, housewife and mother. Presenting symptoms complex. Originally came for marriage counseling, later divorced which brought on anxiety, inferiority, inadequacy as mother and the like. I regressed her to birth in more than one unsuccessfulul effort, but because I was convinced, due to other information coming from her, that birth had something to do with the Initial Sensitizing Event, I kept on at times when I felt she was in a deep trance. After the first successful birth regression she related: "I'm given to my mother. She's cold like a snake. Then I'm afraid. I just cry. I don't feel like I'll survive. I'm afraid for my life 'cause she's so cold. . . . She won't let father love me. He doesn't know how. He just stands off and won't do anything. Later on he thinks I don't care about him. It was my mother who said I was supposed to be a boy. Maybe it didn't matter to him . . . ."

Mrs. S. had the Death Complex all of her life. She accepted the idea of death very soon after birth. Melanie Klein and others refer to the early death instinct associated with aggression. In this case it was associated with the frustration and rejection of the mother who was "cold like a snake." The mother continued throughout early childhood to try to make her into a boy. The hypnotic images Mrs. S. saw of herself as a child were those of having her hair in pigtails, wearing jeans and playing always with boys. Emotionally she had no vagina and no uterus. Her body was neither typically feminine nor masculine. Early in therapy her breasts were small, body lithe and trim.

There is more to the record of Mrs. S., who has been a patient for a long time. Later, in another age regression to the prenatal period, she came to realize she was not conceived by her mother's husband, but by an unknown lover. In session by session off and on over a period of several years, many events of abuse by her mother's husband, including sexual abuse before the age of six, have come to light. Fortunately, after an interval of several years, Mrs. S. is a beautiful and successful professional woman and well adjusted to life. She continues to grow by self-improvement in a most effective way.

Another case, (Mrs. J.A.), illustrates how, in a vivid way, the word association test revealed that the ISE was the birth experience. Among many other responses were the following:

FEAR: death
LIFE: death

LIVE: die

AT THE END OF THE ROAD: life

AS A CHILD: I died. Therapist: "When?" (pause) When I was born (pause) that doesn't make sense.

I WAS NEAR DEATH WHEN: I was young. . . its real hard to. . .real tight. . . I can't move. . . I've just gotta move...

IF I LOSE: I choke

CONFINEMENT: tight

Needless to say the birth experience was significant to this patient.

The following example illustrates the principle of sensing the acquisition of a soul at the time of the first breath (see Register, 1981).

Ms. Z.C., age 32, unemployed. Ongoing phobia of both life and death, including compulsive behavior. Her description of her birth as follows:

"Anxious - clostrophobic - bored - floating. (Long pause.) Now lethargic. . . like being suffocated. . . like something closing in on you. Get away from what's dropping. Get out and get away. I feel dropping... One minute floating, the next pushed, shoved. Sick at stomach, falling, dropping?. . . Feel afraid. . that's it. Makes me sick. . . (series of words about being compelled to go somewhere) . . . Now nothing to breathe (series of short desperate pants) . . . lungs hurtng (quick inhalation). Get breath. . .feel good. . . jaws. . .such a relief. . .breathe like it fills your soul. . . sends energy out to your limbs. . . electric impulses out to toes, arms, above my naval. Some white light spread out when breath comes in.

One more example which is unusual. Mrs. A., age 41, brought in the following poem soon after a regression to birth. A note appended stated: "I didn't compose this. I felt it."

Quietly I lie in the water-bed
Without a thought in my head
But to move lazily now and then
And curl and stretch and lie still again.

But there's something bidding me awake,
This languorous feeling to forsake,
Bidding me twist and struggle free
Of the quiet comfort holding me.

Bands are binding, propelling me
Towards something I cannot see.

**And there is pain the first I've ever known
As I am gripped by a will not my own.**

**My confused mind backward turns.
My tortured body backward yearns.
But I'm cast screaming into the earth
And know surely the hour of my birth.**

Deductions

Obviously these are the briefest of notes on these interesting patients. Other examples could be given. With each of these patients the reliving of the birth experience in hypnosis was a turning point in the therapy. Here are the points most pertinent to this subject.

Note that in each case, when the birth experience is relived, the patient describes vividly in sensuous terms. The recall in words is based on "feelings" associated with some specific part or organ of the body. It is as if an indelible impression were made upon that very spot, like the ear, throat, Adam's apple, arm, etc. In each of these cases the birth trauma was, in fact, a threat to the life of the infant. In adulthood, when there was an emotional threat, there was a response with a symptom similar to the response physically at birth. It was as if the part of the body which felt the deep impressions at birth was now reactivated to have the same feelings again, like playing an identical record over again. This is particularly obvious in examples one and two. With patient number three, it is analogous. Some impression, left vaguely on her mind, was that it was not the right time for her to "go out" or else something sinister would happen. There was the vague childhood impression of being caught in the stricture of the well, when just looking at it aroused a feeling of fear which could not be described or explained.

It is our opinion that the woman in example number four (original DX probably "borderline") would have committed suicide if it had not been for leaving her two children. She says, "I was never shown how to love." The varied symptomotology in adulthood, and the lack of femininity (in childhood), are the direct result of birth trauma, or more precisely, post-birth trauma, when she was rejected by her mother the very first time she was presented to her.

Conclusions

Several authorities have speculated on how early an infant's memory functions and in what manner. It must not function in the same manner during the first year of life that it does as the infant matures, but this does not preclude recall of some kind. It has been posited that impressions are somehow made on the body cells and that a "Mechanical Memory" functions with an automatic response originating in the body.

Five case studies have been presented exhibiting in hypnosis a vivid recall of birth trauma. These examples have all the earmarks of authentic recall of actual (or felt) events. The after-effects (presenting symptoms) coincide with the trauma. After abreaction in reliving the event of trauma, there was a marked and obvious remission of (some) symptoms and a release of anxiety, at least to some degree in all of the them.

Such consequences and descriptions lend credence to the hypothesis, that in the first months of existence (intrauterine and post-natal), traumatic experiences make a deep impression of some kind on the infant. In many such cases the impression is to such an extent that it is possible later in life to recall the trauma in two ways, viz., 1) by the occurrence of symptoms centered on the previously affected organs as a result of threatening events; 2) by re-living the original event through hypnosis.

♣Chapter co-authored with the author's son and partner, John A. Scott, Jr.,Ed.D., and appeared originally in Medical Hypnoanalysis, 1984, 5, 17-33.

Chapter 8

SUMMARY, CONCLUSIONS, RECOMMENDATIONS

A Case Study Example

The best illustration of how this method of psychotherapy works will be seen with actual examples of patients and their treatment. The following case study has been selected because in it principles of the procedure are brought out in a typical way. It is truly "text book example." Of course every patient has his/her own peculiarities, but there also are some similarities with each client. The following example incorporates most of the basic principles of the treatment procedure.

There are some minor alterations of details of the patient information in order to disguise the identity of the patient. But the essential elements of the person are accurate. The personal thoughts that I had as we went along in the case history and wrote down with a red pen, but kept to myself, are reported here thus: (*Italics in parentheses*). A "long pause" is abbreviated by "*l.p.*"

A Case of Panic: Mr. F. B.

Mr. B. (Frank, age 50) changed jobs. He had a managerial position as an accountant in manufacturing and improved his position and income when he went to work as an executive vice-president for another manufacturer. I saw him within a few weeks of his job change.

Background: Mr. B. had seen a doctor of internal medicine months before I saw him and was taking Xanax for panic and occasionally Tagomet (Rx) for his stomach, and had been doing so for one and a half years. I asked him what his problem was, and. he replied, "I get tense and start to smother. If I don't have my medicine, I get a numbness in my hands, light-headed and dizzy. I've done a lot of thinking trying to figure out what triggers this. Mostly its due to stress, not eating properly. I deal with issues above the normal line of duty. (*He actually doesn't. He thinks he does.*) I used to go all day long and not eat more than coffee and snack. (*Heroics?*). Now I have to have something on my stomach. When I first went to Dr. G. early in 1991 with stomach problems, I had an ulcer or acid build up. I decided it was a stomach related problem. Headaches accompanied it. Normally the attack had come before or by 9:00 or 10:00 a.m. I once woke up in the middle of the night shivering. Later I was burning up....My wife has taken me to the hospital several times when I thought I was having a heart attack....This goes back 20 years. I've worked hard all my life."

"My wife was trying for pregnancy. I traveled. I had a fear of death. Panic starts out of the wild blue. I get tense, start smothering, hyperventilate. I have to have something to get out of it. I'm having both nervousness and panic one or two times a week. It gets a little worse. I think about it more. I'm too preoccupied with it. Its hard to keep my mind off of it. My job at the DEF Co. became more stressful. There were upper management changes and they put more work on us. I started talking to the ABC Co. I'm a perfectionist, or want to be a perfectionist, in my job. I wanted a new adventure in carving out a pl and be sure I did a good job, pleasing to everybody..."

I concluded that Mr. B. had the Walking Zombie Syndrome and the Ponce De Leon Syndrome, among other problems, and began to go through the case history form for further details.

Duration of illness? "Stomach problems began in 1986-87. Panic was several years ago and I did not know it was panic, 1987-88."

What would you do if you were cured that you cannot do now?

"Let me live a normal life, which I'm not living now. Last January (4 months earlier) I was smothering and didn't know why it happening." (He started to work for the ABC Co. 3 months before this. His new boss is a woman.) "I'm preoccupied with a fear of symptoms lately.

Present occupation and duties? "Executive vice president. Work with a variety of people all day, trouble shooting."

What would you rather do? "Own a golf course and play golf."

Past history. "As a baby I got a penicillin shot and had allergic reaction. They rushed me to the hospital." There was a drowning experience in the 6th grade. Migraine head aches since 1987. Ulcers maybe since 1986/87. Dyspnea with panic attacks. Hyperemesis, same period last few years. In the 3rd grade (8 y/o) there was a tonsillectomy in which an ether mask was used." He's basically a "Type A" personality. On that check list he responded with: "always fanatic about schedules;" "Yes" in quest for numbers, multiphasic activity, guilty when relaxing, no time for aesthetics (except with kid's sporting activities).

Family history. Father worked hard, never accomplished anything. He drank up what he had. Not much relationship with him as a child. Harsh discipline. Mother was very loving, caring, but meted out strict discipline. Pt. (Patient) had to run home from school due to daddy's drinking. He was the middle of five boys. Older brother was killed in a car wreck when Pt. was 15 years old. (= *1964, WZS*)

Sex history. Sexual curiosity expressed with neighbor girl in 3rd grade. Caught, stern rebuke, embarrassed. Started intercourse by 15 with schoolmate. Almost engaged by 21, but the girl's family didn't approve of him because of his poor background (father alcoholic). (*Self-conscious, ID*). Sexual relationship with wife twice a month. Feels he's intruding when he asks for it. Frequently premature ejaculation. Wife orgasms but not often. "I don't think my wife feels good about her body." Sex life not satisfactory. Would be better if he had more time for it and if he didn't have to initiate it 90% of the time. Not many signals that she enjoys it. While trying to get his wife pregnant the first time (resulted in birth of a girl) he said, "I had a nervous condition of fear of dying." (strange! WZS)

Psychological history. Had nightmares in the third grade. Traumatic incidents: brother Billy's accident when Pt. was 15 y/o (*WZS*). Accident in family car in 4th grade. Grandmother lived with them and died when Pt was in 10th gde. Thought about suicide years ago when had nervous condition (*shift position*). Most disturbing emotional experience: (*S-sigh-eyes down*): "It's hard to distinguish. There were two of them. One when my brother died and when dad died. (*2 deaths, WZS*)

Religion. Ultra conservative church. "I was fearful of God. I changed churches and went with girl friend to another fundamental church." Regarding guilt, little confusion with the change of churches. Was an officer in one church and then left because of church problems. "I couldn't take it any more. I used to be real active. I was hurt to some degree by people who claim to be Christian and then do things in a non- Christian way."

Anything you haven't told me? "I came from a very poor family. In elementary school the better-to-do kids would sneer at me. My girl friend's parents didn't accept me, and there were some Christians who didn't accept me."

THE BRYAN WORD ASSOCIATION TEST

In this report, rather than list every single response on the test, I will give the patient's. responses that are more pertinent to understanding the basis for the ensuing treatment procedure. Note that by the time the test is completed the essence of his analysis is apparent. On the actual printed history form, green and red lines go from one response to another so as to connect the responses which are directly related to a common subject. Here I will give the related responses together in the same paragraph. The theme "quantities equal to the same quantity or to equal quantities are equal to each other" is the foundation for this connection of thought subjects. This is a very important principle in evaluating this test. The unconscious mind of the patient. has them connected and by the words used shares this association with you, the therapist. This test was given the fourth and fifth hours of therapy. The first two hours were taking the case history. The third was giving the initial hypnotic induction. The patient. was hypnotized and the principles of how to take this test were given. The replies are as follows. In each response the stimulus word(s) from the test come first in front of a colon (:). Patient's response is in quotation marks.

Life: "death". Death: "burial". Live: "die". "Why am I alive?" When Andy died: "I died". (*WZS. Start to cry. Cry. Violently cry.*) I asked if he wanted to tell me more about his brother's death. Here is an example of a spontaneous age regression. A rule of thumb is when the patient. is ready to abreact, that's the time to do it - even if it is out of sequence with the treatment plan.

Patient's words: "The last night (*l.p.*) Andy and I were together the last night. He had bought a new car (new to him). He was so proud of it. He was going to the next town to see his girlfriend and asked me to go. He seldom did that. I thought it was great. We went to the next town but his girl was not at home. So we returned home where he showed off his new car. It was a good night. We enjoyed it.

"We went home and went to bed. It was a small house and we slept together. Andy got up the next morning to go to school. Dad's car wouldn't start so Andy jumped him off of his car. It was winter. Andy came back in the house to get me up to catch the school bus. He left. (*Start to cry*). A few minutes later there came a knock on the door: 'There's been an accident up the road.' It was Andy. I had a younger brother and sister and I was responsible for getting them up, getting breakfast and getting them off to school. (Mother and daddy both worked). I left them to see about the accident. I got there. He was unconscious. I was afraid he was going to die. It was a two car accident. The ambulance came (*crying strongly*). They took the other guy first. He just had a broken jaw. They waited on another ambulance to come for my brother. I had to worry about trying to get my brother to a safe place. I needed to go with Andy and I couldn't go." [I observe how tense the situation is. I also want to keep the emotion up for a complete abreaction] (*Pt. shakes his hands, then fists, l.p.*) I say, "So what did you do?"

Patient continues: "I had a neighbor go for my brother and sister and we went to Grandma's, who lived in town. (*Not clear*). I told them, then we all went to the hospital. Some of our relatives worked at the hospital. A cousin gave us reports on Andy and the surgery. It was a head injury. There was talk about giving him blood. I was scared. I didn't know my blood type...and then he died. (*Sigh!... Sigh!...I want to ask for more detail, such as "Your thoughts?" But will wait till another time. Plan to return to this incident.*)

I ask: "At what point did you become aware that you died with him?" (l.p.). "I don't know. Why did he have to die? He was so young. I feel sick at my stomach."

(For a brief period we talked. I took his mask off)

Patient softly and reflectively said, "I feel like all the life has gone out of me."

I replied positively, "Of course. You said you died when Andy died. You've just relived it" Since our time is up I give him calming and peaceful suggestions and reassurance that we are making progress. He left saying there was "tingling" in his hands and he was a little light headed. I didn't refer to "panic." I just give some positive suggestions that these feelings would pass.

At the next session we did more on the Word Association Test. Some pertinent responses were: Failure: "never". My greatest fear is: "failure." My biggest failure: "is not here...I uh,...it doesn't make sense." The deacons were accused of: "Failure."

My father, Henry: "Loved me." Depressed: "Mother." Dominate: "Parents". My greatest need: "is being wanted." My mother made me feel: "inadequate." My mother thought I was: "guilty." My mother, Eva: "stays depressed." Unwanted: "me". Affection: "never." As a poor family in childhood: "I was deprived." A problem with my new job: "is authority." As a child I felt: "Needless."

I ask myself: "why I am alive." When I almost drowned I thought: "life was over." Need: "life." Why: "am I alive?" Car accident: (*blank - no response; I observe "block"*.)

I get nervous: "whenever I make love." Most of the time: "I feel helpless." When I make love: "It feels great." If only: "I knew" [I ask "what?" "Clarify"] He: "How to satisfy..."

I ask, "Your wife?"

Response: "yes"

My greatest need: "is being wanted." My greatest fault: "is worrying too much." Guilt: "Within". Pleasure: "Sex." Punishment: "Rejection."

I have given some detail on the WAT in order to demonstrate how much can be gained during this period of time. This is a very effective tool for learning more of the unconscious processes. You will readily note some inconsistencies that he struggled with. I revealed some of his responses to him as the subject came up during the following course of therapy. But I usually do not summarize the WAT until making the Personal Tape summary. But it is helpful to call the patient's attention to some responses when making interpretations or bringing out a certain point.

HYPNOANALYTIC THERAPY SESSIONS

At the beginning of the next session patient. stated that he had reported for work, but then took off to walk by the lake. Tension developed, so after a while he took a Xanax. I hypnotize him and we do an Age Regression back to the time of his first panic attack.

"I'm 27 years old and work at the DEF Co. as supervising accountant. I'm sitting at my desk after lunch. I had a smothering feeling...a tingling... hyperventilate. . .I nearly pass out."

I ask, "What happened this morning?"

"I can't recall. I had a lot of work to do. I had been off a few days. I cut my leg mowing the yard. They took several stitches. I was behind at work."

I ask questions for further clarification.

"I'm not fulfilling my obligation. There could be problems. Numbers are not getting into the system right. The job is not getting done. Upper management will not like it."

I ask, "That's the bug-a-boo?"

"I guess so .Yeah."

I say: "Hold on to that feeling. Go back through the years to an earlier time, the first time you had that same feeling ...failure at your job, or what was expected of you."

"When I was a Senior in high school (18 years old). I was working 40 hours a week. The pressure got to me. I had an attack at school - almost a panic attack. I was light-headed, nervous, muscles jumping. I want to release all the tension in me. I released by four guys holding me down (friends). I had some kind of fit. I let go all my tensions. A big guy had a hard time holding my right hand down. Those were good days."

I ask: "Why were you working 40 hours a week?"

"My parents moved to a neighboring town and I stayed here to graduate. I needed money to live on and for my car. I had to work. I lived with my older brother."

I ask him to hold on to that feeling and go to an earlier experience where he had that same feeling.

"I'm 17, practicing football. In practice I got real hot. He gave a bunch of us breaks. I'm sitting with my helmet on. We're not allowed to take them off. I blacked out. I couldn't see but I could hear. I feel a numbness, a tingling and I couldn't breathe. They took me to the dressing room and helped me get dressed. Coach wanted me to get a doctor's check-up. But I'm from a poor family and I couldn't afford it. So I quit football. I felt miserable."

"Because you're poor and couldn't get a check up, so you couldn't play football for this cause," I ask.

"I hated not being a part of the team and one of the guys. It was self-esteem."

(In notes to myself I observe intensifying events to the WZS and that there was a sense of failure. Furthermore here was more evidence of an Identity Problem.)

At the beginning of the next session he reported that he had been more at peace, more relaxed, not majoring on anything. He had reflected on his childhood, panic, school. He had had an overview of where we are and what's taking place. "I feel like I'm tired. I was going to ride my bike a while and I felt exhausted." I explained that he probably was emotionally tired.

After this brief conference I hypnotized him and played two tapes, one on the value of a positive mental attitude, the other on conquering self (PMA 1 + GS 10).

At the beginning of the next session he reported that he slept better last night than he had in a long time. In the hypnotic period I attempted an Age Regression back to birth, but there was no visible response. This may indicate that there was nothing unusual or traumatic about the birth. It could also mean that we were unable to break the time/memory barrier at this time. However, we were able to get a response to the early penicillin allergic reaction. I observe to him that, "Your body has remembered this reaction. In this you have gasped for breath, felt light-headed, chest and stomach affected. Those feelings in infancy have been carried over into adulthood. There was the threat of death, hyperventilation, excitement in the rushed trip to the hospital." This is likely the Initial Sensitizing Event to the WZS.

While we are in this early stage of childhood at a good level of hypnosis, I take him to the tonsillectomy at eight years old. There were several factors in this event which were significant. He hated the suffocating feeling he got from the mask over his face. At this point he abreacted with quick breathing and fright. He hated being tied down so that he couldn't move. There was no help. His parents weren't there. He could see lightning flashes and couldn't do anything about it. He was angry because he didn't want to be there and there was a feeling of panic. He stayed drowsy, slept a lot and his throat hurt. He faded in and out all of the time.

I asked if he could see that his last panic attack was similar to this event, that it was like a repetition.

I took him to another trauma in childhood. This was the nightmares of the third grade.

He reported seeing a scary movie where a body changed from an ape to a human by **a blood transfusion**!

I called attention to the fact that here was a deeply placed fear of a blood transfusion. He was afraid of a blood transfusion at the time of Andy's surgery, but didn't know why. The doctor said that Frank was the best one to give a transfusion to Andy but he was afraid to do it. This movie and nightmares are the reason. During the earlier age regression he did not state that he refused the transfusion. He confessed it at this time.

"This explains your refusal," I said.

"Yes" (*Tears, crying*).

He continued: "Our bed room was separate from the rest of the house.

It was old. There was a breezeway in between us and the others. I didn't want to be out there. I was afraid. I was afraid every night when I went to be out there. I was afraid the same thing would happen to me that happened in that movie."

I pointed out how this deeply impressed his mind with fear and this continued to influence him. He continued to give himself Negative Hypnotic Suggestions over a period of time and this deepened his sense of fear and insecurity. Then gradually over a period of time the event itself slipped into the background. Then I impressed him with the fact that that event was long ago and far away. As a child it would be normal to get a wrong impression from a movie like that. And of course he would feel guilty for refusing the transfusion. The possibility of a transfusion was a serious threat. But as an adult he could and should discard that impression along with other outgrown childish concepts. With that false impression gone, the fear would also dissipate.

Next we dealt with the family car accident. Several family members were in the car. An older brother was driving too fast. The car flipped over, a door came open, scared, going upside down, car hits bank, screaming, hollering, people try to get out, dad pulls free (he's drinking), brother pinned under the door. "I'm standing by the door. Gas is leaking. I feared an explosion before daddy could pull my brother free. We go to the hospital. Dad had a broken leg. Brother was in the operating room a long time. Doctors said they did everything they could. We didn't know whether he would live. His jaw was broken in two places, ribs were broken and he had internal injuries. I was afraid he would die, but he didn't."

I point out that this further intensifies the experience as a "death like" experience. He felt he was in the presence of death.

I ask him to go to the next death-like experience. This is a swimming experience at eleven or twelve years old. There was a family picnic on a river bank. He doesn't know how to swim. He slips off of a rock and goes under suddenly. The water is cold. Immediately he thinks he'll die. He comes up, but there is nobody there to help him. He yells as he goes under again. He's choking, smothering, there's no air. I interject: "Like when you had the ether mask over your face?"

"Yes. It seems like eternity. Somebody reaches down and pulls me up. I get out coughing and gagging. I felt so helpless, afraid. I panicked."

"At the threat of death?" I asked.

"Right".

(*This is another symptom intensifying event.*)

Grandmother's death is another death experience at about the same period in his life. When he was in the sixth grade his beloved grandmother fell and broke her hip. Then she had a stroke in the hospital and never revived. He mused, "I didn't understand why she had to die. She seemed so young... and she loved her grandkids." While softly crying he said, almost inaudibly, "... at the funeral. I didn't want her to die. I wanted her to live forever. . . she fixed the best pinto beans and corn bread. She was soft-spoken and a very good person."

The following is a technique that is effective to use in most situations like this. It is a procedure to help the client find closure and resolution at a death. I asked the patient. to picture himself with his grandmother in the hospital and that he had a chance to have a last conversation with her. "See her right there. You are with her. You touch her hand and you hear her say, 'It's time for me to go. I must tell you good-bye."

Tears streaming down his face, he mournfully says, "I don't want you to go gra'ma."

I observe a frightened, lonely, little boy losing the most important person in his life. "You can hear her say she must go on; that she loves you, and that she will see you one day on the other side. What else do you want to tell her? Speak to her."

"I love you gra'ma. Don't go. . ."

At this point reference is made to grandfather's death. He died of stroke. He also had skin cancer for many years. He had kept to himself, so the patient. did not have much of a relationship with him. All the same, here was another death in the family. And this death, like grandmother's, was another Symptom Intensifying Event.

As this long session came to a conclusion I played two tapes. One was WZS 1 describing the Walking Zombie Syndrome. This describes how there is an Initial Sensitizing Event which set the client up for an acute awareness of death and this is followed by another event (or perceived event) as a death-like experience or a threat of death to one's self or close relative or friend. Then the consequences of this are felt unconsciously and/ or consciously which results in a response in mood by the person going through it. The symptoms usually are depression and all that goes with it. Change in dress, relationships, sleep habits, eating habits, working habits, attitude toward life and death. In other words the waking diagnoses is what is described in DSM IIIR (IV) as depression. However, some patients respond with a reaction to morbidity by increased activity. I describe this with the metaphor of a person about to drown, how with the threat of death there is a frantic struggle to survive.

It is gratifying to see an authority like Eigen recognizing and describing the Walking Zombie Syndrome, albeit he uses another name, viz., "Psychic deadness." In an interview he stated:

"Psychic deadness can take many forms from a variable numbing of self to a more chronic self-anesthesia. In extreme forms it can approach total loss of self-feeling. The cases I write about involve more than emptiness and loss of meaning, although these may be involved. The sense of deadness is a feeling in its own right and spans diagnostic categories.... I describe a man who coasted through life feeling well enough, but as time went on, he became progressively plagued by a background deadness. He was tormented by something missing -- he was missing. A dead spot was where he ought to be." (Eigen, 1996).

This "progression" Eigen refers to is what we would call the Symptom Intensifying Events. I, personally, am convinced that most people who are diagnosed as "depressive" in one or more of its many forms have as an underlying diagnosis the Walking Zombie Syndrome. They usually are grieving for their own death!

In this case I played a second tape titled, WZS 2, in which there is assurance that the person lived and continues to live. That those experiences are in the past and now is the time to come alive and enter in the challenge of the present to the fullest, to really participate in life etc.

At the beginning of the next session, the patient stated he had a hard morning. His stomach had bothered him and he felt some dizziness at his temples. He stated matter-of-factly, "I got upset and nervous today, but not with the tingling feeling in the back of my head like before. Tension is relieving." He had been asked to make a trip with some co- workers on business, but he was afraid to go.

I wanted to get the "death experiences" out of the way so went back to the relationship with his father and his death. He was very slow to respond to my encouragement to return to childhood. He stated it was hard to picture anything; his dad wasn't around much. No one scene came to mind. "I can just see him being there occasionally. Most of the time I saw dad he was drinking. I always wanted to be around him, but he never was available. If he was there and wanted to go the kids were too little. We took a trip together when I was 20 years old. I never had much time with him. He and mother fussed a lot. He treated us children about the same. I hated their fussing. Why couldn't they get along? Mother kinda liked to fuss. He'd fuss back at her and then drink. I think that's what drove him to drink."

I responded with this observation: "I've known situations which appeared to be similar. The wife fusses a lot, does not want sex. The husband goes to drink in order to divert himself away from sexual frustration. It may have been that way with him."

Patient. continued, "As the years went on it got worse. Dad spent his money on booze and mother was obligated to pay the bills and keep things together. I have mixed emotions about it. Both were at fault. It continued about the same way."

At this point I interrupted to summarize some of what we had learned so far. Due to his father's drinking and distance, "You missed getting a wholesome relationship with your father. A boy needs a male to identify with during the period of latency to help prepare him for manhood. You didn't get it.

"You were susceptible to a series of death experiences which would have affected anyone to some degree. But you did not have enough experience to fortify yourself to be strong enough to cope with that many situations. Your father's weakness deprived you of having a strong male to pattern after. This deprivation, combined with the death experiences, has resulted in restricting your emotional growth and development. There is a boy inside of you that has not finished growing up yet. It is possible that in your relationship with your wife that it is the boy inside that has not been able to take the lead in your relationship with her, especially your sexual relationship."

Frank continued: "Later in life he worked for me a while at DEF until six months before he died. He got lung cancer and went downhill fast. He was a big man and suddenly became thin." Patient becomes emotional now and describes how the last two weeks of his father's life the children took turns sitting with him as he wasted away. Once patient was called from the golf course to the hospital and observed how his father suffered. His father told him he was going to go. Patient said, "No, hang in there." Then walked out and cried. Then he said, "Growing up I was taught that boys and men don't cry. It was a sign of weakness."

There was a pause and then he continued, "I don't like fussing, hollering, yelling. I'd seen it growing up. Where do you let all that frustration out?" By now he was shouting loudly.

I snapped back, "Play golf!"

Then my wife complains, "Too much time playing golf."

I describe the Ponce De Leon Syndrome and how a characteristic of this is that one vacillates, is unsure of oneself, is uncertain and can't decide. He can see that he has this syndrome.

In describing the death of his father he states, "It's 2:00 a.m. and all the others have left. I was there with dad. . . I dozed off. He started gargling (!) a little; he was choked. I asked for suction for his throat. I watched him breathe. I dozed a few minutes. Then I woke up and didn't hear him breathing. I jumped up, looked, touched, buzzed. No pulse. He'd died at 4:00 a.m. while I was asleep." He was crying fully now.

I calmly said, "You were in the same room when he died. That's good. He died in peace. That's good."

Patient interrupts, "I'm getting numb. My hands are going numb; all are hurting."

Once again I asked him to have a last conversation with his dad by picturing talking to him alone after the others had left. He has this conversation stating he loves his father. I picture his father saying, I go to meet Andy on the other side."

I conclude the session by comforting and encouraging him and then play FM 13, which is about the ideal relationship of a boy with his father during the period of 7 to 12 or 13 years old.

At this time in the therapy I had a conference with his wife, Anne. She is a nice looking lady, in her mid-forties, blonde, medium length hair, wearing shorts. Immediately I could tell she is not expressive, but was eager to cooperate, stating firmly, "Anything to help my husband get over this." She went on to say that they had been married 22 years and that his panic attacks started 21 years ago. Several times they had been up in the middle of the night to take him to the emergency room with what he called a "heart attack."

"Frank never talks about anything that bothers him. He bottles it up inside him. We have a daughter the same way. . . Frank was better for several years. I assured him it was just panic. But he saw it differently. I blamed him getting worse on his job change. I'm conservative. I don't like job changes. He was afraid of failure at his new job. He never talks. He'll listen to me, but he can't share. . . Over the years I've lost patience with him. He gets mad if I tell him what I think. Occasionally he'll say, 'This attack is different from the last time.' Once he had panic and called me at work and I refused to come see to him. He's never forgiven me for that. He was down. That really hurt. . .I feel like I have three children (*includes Frank!*). I'm pulled. He feels the children get more attention than he does.

But he's supportive of the children in their activities. We were married over five years before we had children. During that time he got all the attention. He's a wonderful father."

Inquiry into her background revealed that she was the youngest of several children, having a brother immediately older than she. Her father wasn't around much and her mother was strong and didn't work outside the home. She was close to her mother and identified with her, and is the person from whom she got her nurturing and leadership traits. From the beginning Frank has leaned on her and she has gotten tired of it.

Their sex life was neither very good nor very bad. She has orgasms if he will share in foreplay and not ejaculate prematurely. She said that at times he complained of his penis burning. She feels most of the time she initiates sex, whereas Frank told me she almost never does. She continued, "He's seemed weak at times and I think he doesn't feel like it. When he doesn't last long this frustrates him."

When I asked summarily, "Is your sex life satisfactory?", she responded, "Its not right."

In my next session with Mr. B. I planned to continue with investigating any further death-like experiences. I was curious about his reference to having death feelings when he was trying to impregnate his wife the first time. After saying at the beginning of the regression, "I can't get to anything," he was able to get in touch with those early feelings. For some reason he had a fear of dying and strongly felt he was too young to die. At that time he said he developed stomach and chest pains. He went to several doctors and was told he had a nervous stomach. Again he stated that he wasn't sure that he was ready to die. Clearly he had the WAS at that time.

A few years after the pregnancy issue, he and his wife started going to church. There had to be some adjustment because he was changing denominations and this was a difficult decision. Then after changing there was some conflict among the leaders of that church and his feelings were hurt. Still, going back to church reduced his conscious fear of dying. He later became a leader and teacher in a new congregation.

We can see from the report of Mr. B's wife and from his insecurities, strong evidence of his immaturity (PD.).

In a good hypnotic state, an Age Regression to the relationship with his mother revealed the following: "I see mama always working around the house trying to take care of us children."

I comment: "You're observing her?" (*His respiration increased noticeably*).

He responded hesitantly: "Very few times I can ever. . . I don't know if I've ever been with mama alone as a child."

"You're not alone with her?"

"Sometimes she had a job. During hard times she'd get a job if she could. Us boys always had to take care of the house. Mama was very strict that everything be done on a daily basis."

I asked how he felt about that.

"I couldn't be a kid for having to work at home. For a while the only way we could go to a movie was on Wednesday night with milk carton tops. Then I started selling newspapers for ten cents. I got three cents profit. I got up to 50 each Wednesday and made $1.50. As a 10 year old I was proud. I could occasionally go to the show on Saturday afternoon. But I still had the chores or housework to do. She threatened if I didn't do the job. When she whipped us, we had to cut the switch. If we cut it too small, we went back and got another one. Sometimes you wanted to be a kid and not do the chores. . . but you got a whipping."

I responded: "Frank I'll share with you what I have heard you say. You just told me you were punished for being a kid. You were being conditioned to do all work and no play. Your experiences for being able to play as a child were reduced greatly. You learned if you didn't work you suffered consequences (punishment). This has led to a compulsion to over-work which in turn has produced stress and neglect of recreation. Note that recreation really means to **re-create**. You were learning that if you didn't please her with your work you would be punished. The first woman in your life conditioned you to certain feelings and expectations of yourself. These same feelings are being automatically applied in one way or another to the next two women in your life, namely your wife and your new boss. You were also learning if you crossed the line, that is, disobeyed, you'd be punished. You missed getting a soft, warm, intimate, loving relationship with your mother and this has consequences down to the present."

I further explained the process of the working of the mind and behavior on the basis of cause and effect. And concluded with positive suggestions that next week he would be calmer and the fears would lessen. I then played tape FM 4 on a boy's oedipal needs in the relationship with his mother at four, five, six and seven. I explained that this described an ideal relationship and no family reached the ideal, but here was what he missed and it resulted in slowing down his emotional maturation and influenced his relationship with women. Furthermore, his failure to get some of the child's needs like play time, affected his attitude toward work and recreation. All of this contributed to his "Type A" personality type.

It goes without saying that in a situation like this the therapist needs to know how much interpretation to make to that particular patient. One can reveal too much and overload the patient. Or one can give too little and stretch out the time therapy takes. It isn't always easy to walk this tight rope.

When Mr. B. returned he reported that he had had two spells. He observed that he triggered one by taking a quick breath. But he "got a hold of it and thought to be calm and cool and it settled down."

I then gave suggestions to make a plan to start tapering off of Xanax. And that by the strength of his own mind with self-hypnosis he should give himself the feelings that he expected to receive by taking the prescription.

In an effort to help him see more of his Identity problem, we did an Age Regression back to childhood to clarify his inferiority.

In the second grade his family lived in an old house on a mountain outside of town. He describes it thus, "There are large cracks in the floor and walls, and water comes from a creek. We go get it to wash and to drink. It's cold in the winter"

I inquire as to his thoughts and feelings about this.

"I didn't understand why we had to get water from a creek. It was a chore. We had to go down the hill and back. I was embarrassed about where we lived. We had no visitors. When I got on the school bus, I didn't have good clothes like the other kids had. We lived there only one year. We moved a lot. Mother and daddy would get behind on the rent and so we were forced to move.

"I was in the eighth grade before we had an inside bath and running water. At school in lots of cases I didn't have lunch money or paper and pencil or a tablet to write with. I was embarrassed. I didn't understand why I didn't have what others had, like new clothes and shoes. I didn't have a book satchel. At times the kids may have made fun of me.'

'When I played ball in the eighth and ninth grades, I can't recall my family ever being there to watch me. I always had to get a ride. Maybe my parents didn't care.'

'In the ninth grade I got a steady job and from then on I can buy for myself. I worked at the Dairy Mart at night and cooked hamburgers. Before I had inferiority and no self-esteem. If my parents ever picked me up, it was in an old, rough, auto. What we had, everybody else had a lot better."

I observed, "Then you had to quit football because you didn't have enough money for a physical check-up."

He continued, "I went back to work more. There were no sports at all my senior year. I had to work fulltime. I was out of a lot (of school activity). I had no part with the crowd of my peers. I wasn't in sports. I started work at a plant at 3:00 p.m. and worked till 11:00. Got to bed at 12:30 or 1:00 a.m. and had to be at school at 8:00."

I talked with him about how much of these feelings he brought with him into adulthood. I observed that he missed getting a healthy relationship with his parents, as well as missing a lot in social adjustment at school. This resulted in a lack of confidence and self-assurance. Also the poverty of his family affected his self-concept.

I further observed, "This squelched your emotional growth because you were deprived of emotional nourishment. This was no fault of your own. Neither can we blame your parents because we don't know what their problems were. It was an unfortunate situation. **But you can largely make up for it**."

I concluded the session by playing tape PDL 1, which describes the syndrome and explains immaturity in simple terms that the patient can understand. There is a child locked within who frequently influences your thought, speech and action.

I then established his "PDL level." While the client is still hypnotized, I deepen the level by giving suggestions and invite him to see this image.

> Picture yourself completely surrounded by darkness. In a few moments I am going to say the word NOW loudly and snap my fingers. At that time a number will flash on out there in the darkness like a neon sign coming on. That number will be the age of the child deep within you. That number will come from within. Do not plan it. Give it no thought. It will come to you on the spur of the moment.
> Just focus on my voice. Deeper, deeper. . .
> NOW (snap fingers into the microphone).

Frank's immediate response was "11." I told him this figured. Very soon we will start helping that boy grow through the stages of pre-adolescence and adolescence into manhood and thus help him to some degree make up for lost time.

At the next session Frank brought in two brief dreams. Each was on a small piece of scratchpad paper. On one were these words: *CHASE SOME FOLDER OF.*

Consciously, before hypnosis, Frank knew nothing else about the dream. But, as is the case with many clients when hypnotized, much of the dream returns to mind. In this case Frank described the dream this way. "There are three of us chasing a girl. It could be my brothers. Not co-workers. She has a folder. She has a picture of herself in the folder. We stopped her and opened up the folder. There was the picture. It seems like in a way I'm the girl. And yet I'm chasing her. The picture is me."

I explain that many times the patient plays more than one role in the dream. Characters change places and even change gender. I observe to him, "You are carrying a picture of yourself. You also are chasing yourself."

Frank interrupts, "It could be a game."

"Observe, Frank, you are chasing yourself. Could this be a kind of frustration? You're seeking to discover more about yourself, who you are."

Frank: "That makes sense. The folder has information about myself, who I am."

Perhaps this symbolizes the work we're doing in this therapy. Getting the full knowledge is elusive.

The second dream is as brief as the first one. It says, GRANNY'S HOUSE OAK TREE POND. I introduce it by asking to dream the dream again and tell me what's happening.

"As a child I enjoyed going to Granny's house, about 4 or 5 years old, and playing. It was a fun house to visit. There was a big oak tree by a pond. Granny told us to go play by the pond where it was quiet and peaceful. I had a feeling of love and care."

I asked if it wasn't a relief from his own house.

"I think so. She was probably the only adult who cared. We shared some moment of time - and love."

I asked when Granny died.

He answered, "I was either in the fifth or sixth grade."

He became very pensive and after a pause said, "Granny used to go around the house singing all the time. She'd get the kids together and tell ghost stories."

Here were some good times from childhood and such times were redeeming factors in his life.

In order to keep the therapy as brief as possible, we focused most of the sessions on reconstructing the events and relationships of the patient's life which were traumatic or were deficits, and therefore negative. But in the reconstruction, in order to reframe the negative life experiences, we desire to have a core of positive events or relationships upon which to build. This is similar to the principle the dentist uses to construct a cap. There must be a basic core of the tooth upon which to reconstruct. The plan in the latter part of the psychotherapy regimen is to help the patient go back in hypnosis and visualize a better childhood, and in so doing emphasis can be made on those memories which have even a faint hint of something positive, like a brief, loving relationship with a grandparent.

I considered this juncture a good place to summarize in outline form the major points of the analysis. I played tape number SPS 17 in which I explain the triple allergenic theory of how the problem developed. In Frank's case I give the Initial Sensitizing Event, the Symptom Producing Event and a Symptom Intensifying Event with each of the underlying diagnoses, vis., the WZS, the PDL syndrome and the ID problem.

The reason I give this preview is so that the client can begin to see the cause and effect procedure of his/her problem and this begins to take the mystery out of the whole situation. After reflecting on this for a few days, the whole summary is easier to grapple with. Furthermore, the entire analysis summary can be quite complicated in some cases. So hearing it a stage at a time makes it easier to comprehend.

At this point I have conducted 15 sessions, although a few of them were 2 hours or so in length. During this time I talked with Frank almost daily by phone. He lives a distance away from me. He reported having some tense times and would take Xanax once or twice a day irregularly. His worst times were when he took his kids out of town to a basketball tournament. He had to go to the car and stretch out and rest. He also had a few weak spells at work.

At the next session Frank came in saying he was "not so good." Over the week end he had gone with his children to another tournament out of town. He had to take his prescription twice. There was to be a ball game at 5:00 p.m. . At 4:00 he started getting nervous. He stated, "The games excite me, so I took a pill at 4:00. The gym was real cold and the game was delayed. I got chilled and went to the car. I started trembling. In spite of the heater, I had uncontrollable shaking. I stayed in the car during the ball game. I told my son I wasn't feeling good.'

'The kids were supposed to go back for games Sunday. My legs have been weak lately. I was talking to a guy and felt anxiety 45 minutes before the game. I slept in the car a while.'

'After we returned home I tried to exercise. When I walked around the block I felt weak and dizzy. My appetite is gone. I ate the best last night I've eaten in two weeks. I had diarrhea some.'

'There's nothing really happening to excite me. I have anxiety at the games. I told Anne, 'This is part of it. I feel uncomfortable around a lot of people. It didn't used to have effect on me. Fear of anxiety built up in me. I stay cold most of the time. My blood is restricted, just not flowing. For a week now I have a mild type of head ache.''

I responded cheerfully, "That's good. Your unconscious mind is automatically summarizing your condition. Notice that you're referring to **travel in your car, your children are the same age you and Billy were when he was killed, there is a sporting event which you can't seem to tolerate, a crowd of people you are avoiding perhaps because they might make fun of you, and you summarize the emotions you felt when earlier foundation events took place.** This demonstrates that we're putting together the analysis of your problems effectively."

I then took a kind of inventory with these questions:

"Are you doing your self-hypnosis?"

"Some, not as much as I should, two or three times a day."

I continued: "How about exercise?"

"I try to walk around the block one and one-tenth miles exhausts me."

"What about personal recreation?"

"Nothing. I have no desire to play golf. If I get time off, I sleep and rest, just tired."

I asked about last intercourse.

He brightened up somewhat, "Two nights ago. That's much better, improved considerably. Intercourse four times since I saw you last. My wife feels much better. She seems more understanding, so am I."

"How are you functioning at work?"

He lost his enthusiasm immediately. "I have some dizziness. I'm light headed at work, but this is improvement over what it was."

My private thoughts at this point were these. It happens sometimes that summarizing the contributing causes brings back the emotions to some extent that accompanied those events when they first took place. In other words, the patient may feel worse momentarily. At other times there is relief and the patient immediately feels better. He was so delicate, I felt it best to summarize his problems in stages. It probably was a good call.

Sometimes when a patient hopes and expects to get better at a certain time, but doesn't or even feels worse, I give this metaphor:

"If a person goes to a physician complaining of an abdominal pain, immediately the doctor begins to feel around over the abdomen. When the patient yells in pain the doctor observes, 'You appear to have appendicitis.' The pain has identified the source of the problem - the vermiform appendix. So it is similar many times with emotional pain. In recreating certain events the pain is felt. That's a sign of accuracy." In Frank's case his going to his car could have more than one explanation. One might expect first an unconscious retreat to the womb. But in this case we had already done an age regression back to birth and got no results. If I had had the luxury of time, and he did not get well, I would have endeavored several times to take him back to birth expecting to get some abreaction, producing an Initial Sensitizing Event. But this was not the case this time. There may have been no unconscious factor in going to the car, but I suspected there was because his car is very prominent in his life and always has been. I haven't listed all of the events in his life associated with his car yet.

All the same, I felt this was the time to do his complete "P Tape" summary. I had made a written outline, which I planned to follow. I went back over all of my notes and put the analysis together in a logical and understandable way, clarifying the cause and effect relationship of the contributing events and relationships to his symptomatology.

P-TAPE FRANK B.

Now, Frank, we're going to summarize the analysis which we have been working on. Keep in mind we are not here to judge anyone or criticize or blame anyone. We're here to understand you and your life a little better.

We're going to be reviewing the traumatic events and relationships in your life which have contributed to your problem and there were a lot of unfortunate circumstances over which you had no control. But I want to emphasize that there is much more that's positive about you and your life than there is that's negative. It's just that for purposes of understanding your problems, we need to dwell on those unhappy and painful events.

Now, when you came to me, among other things you complained of these symptoms. You said, "I get tired and start to smother. If I don't take medicine I get numbness in my hands, light headed, dizziness.'

I've done a lot of thinking trying to figure it out, what triggered it. Mostly undue stress, not eating properly. I've been to the doctor many times. I used to go all day long and not eat more than coffee and a snack. I noticed head aches also accompanied it. I have it before 9 or 10 or in the middle of the night'.

'By the time I was a senior in high school I worked 40 hours a week and took a full load. I had some nervous conditions before that. When my wife was trying for pregnancy I had a fear of death."

The Word Association Exercise, among other things, revealed the following: The subject of death was on your mind in many ways. For example you said, "Why am I alive?" "When my father died, I died." "When Billy died, I died." You also had a profound fear of failure and stated that the greatest obstacle to your happiness was failure.

You showed you were very concerned about your own personhood. You had several great needs, namely to be loved, wanted, to feel adequate. You often felt helpless, that you had no balls, no response, deprived, etc.

"I concluded that underlying all of these and other symptoms you had the Walking Zombie Syndrome, the Ponce De Leon Syndrome and Identity Problem. Here is how these syndromes developed.

The Walking Zombie Syndrome

ISE Penicillin shot in infancy caused threat of death, fear and made an impression on your body which your body remembered.

SPE T & A at 8 y/o. Ether mask, threat of death, panic, anger.

SIE Third grade, TV show of changing of ape to human by blood transfusion.

SIE Fifth grade, car accident, flipped over. Brother injured.

SIE 11 y/o Drowning experience, breathing, choking, fright.

SIE Sixth grade, grandmother's death, deep impression.

SIE Andy's death, grief guilt, deep impression.

SIE Grandfather's death.

SIE 17 y/o Practicing football, blacked out, numb, tingling, couldn't breathe.

SIE 18 y/o Sr. hi. schl. Fatigue brought into the syndrome, tension.

SIE 27 y/o at DEF - hyperventilate, tingling, smothering, work stress brought into the syndrome.

SIE's Panic attacks off and on since then.

SIE Job change to ABC, work for a woman boss

The Ponce De Leon Syndrome

ISE The childhood period, deficient relationship with parents. Lack of a relationship with father, missed male traits of maturity. Relationship with mother, missed closeness, love, intimate relationship. Lack of play as a child and with children.

SPE 8y/o Start of WZS inhibited growth process

SIE's Further restricting childhood experiences, embarrassing experiences in front of peers at school. Threats and whippings from mother, coercion to work harder; you wanted to be a kid like the others and couldn't. This prevented you from coming normally and naturally through the stages of childhood development.

The Identity Problem

ISE Childhood feeling of inferiority, self-consciousness. Embarrassed about where you lived. Kids made fun of you. Felt unwanted, needless. Mother made you feel unwanted and inadequate, concept of no balls.

SPE Had to quit football because of no money for check-up. You hated not being a part of the team, as one of the guys.

SIE Insecure and uncertain about job at DEF.

SIE Insecure about job at ABC, uncertain and fearful relationship with female boss.

Conclusion

Now you understand why you came to have the panic attacks. These events are all behind you now and your childhood understanding and interpretations are no longer applicable. Regarding the WZS you will come to feel more and more alive and be able to participate in the main stream of life.

Regarding the PDL syndrome, the growth process will continue and vicariously you will go through the stages of growth that all children do and will pick up traits and characteristics of each stage that you may have missed originally.

In going through this process your feelings about yourself will improve, and you will feel the natural dignity that God intended you to have as a human being.

Now there will be a pause while you reflect on these thoughts and contemplate the new era in your life which is beginning now.

Comments

When I go over the P Tape outline to the patient, I record it at that time. I tell the client that this will be replayed for him/her frequently till they are completely familiar with all of it and that it will no longer elicit from her/him the emotion that used to be there. As this is taking place the panic symptoms will decrease in intensity and disappear entirely.

I also emphasize that we are now in the Reinforcement Stage of therapy and that this strengthening process will become more intense. If improvement has not started by now, it will start. If it has already started (as it had with Frank), it will continue more rapidly. This confidence is important at this juncture to the patient.

When or if the patient comes into the office with reports of symptoms, I take it in stride, remarking that this happens, that the body got in the habit of responding with certain biochemical influences and this habit will decrease, but the patient will have to cooperate and work at it by the continual use of self-hypnosis and other processes which I shall mention, like applying the mirror technique, etc.

Therapy Continues with Frank B.

Because of Frank's difficulties with his mother **and** the feeling of occasional fear with his new female boss, I helped him visualize a more favorable relationship in childhood with his mother. We capitalized on her devotion to the children, her own hard work, and the fact that she did so well under adverse circumstances. But he also visualized how he wished her to be based on what I described of his basic oedipal needs. Later I asked him what his present view of his relationship with his mother was. He replied, "It's good. Mother giving time, care and concern (long pause). No problems." Furthermore he observed that his withdrawal from his wife was typical of the 12 or 13 year old boy. Then as he develops masculine confidence he draws closer.

In succeeding sessions I impressed his mind with tapes on the stages of growth through adolescence to masculine maturity. I emphasized the accompanying traits of the respective age level and the accomplishments that typically should be made at that time. Each stage of childhood development is built upon the foundation of the previous accomplishments.

Two or three sessions later he gave this report: "I'm doing great. Have good days at work, all smooth..."

I encourage him to keep a healthy diet, improve his exercise program, plan personal and family recreation, improve his total relationship with his wife (including sex education), and participate at church. He had to be cautioned several times on putting himself down too much. I used a sermon tape on human dignity several times, how that we are created in the image of God and have His Spirit in us and that we have a reason for existence and a mission to accomplish.

One session he came in and said that he took off at noon to do some errands. He went to get his car washed and while there he got a jack hammer effect in his neck and head. I had him go back and relive the incident in hypnosis and here is what came out.

"I pull into the car lot and get out of the car. I stand there in the sun..."

I interject, "Freeze the action right there. What's going through your mind?"

"I think I fear I'll have an attack. I'm breathing normal, not excited. I guess I think, 'What if I have an attack? What will take place?' There again my car's being washed. I can't get in it and drive away. I'll have to wait for it to be out. If I did have an attack - What?" (Pause.)

I ask, "Then the attack started?"

"I saw some guys I knew and talked to them and looked at their cars. The tension eased."

I challenged him, "You're right there, outside. What if you have an attack and can't get in your car and escape?"

He answered, "I'll be helpless, anxious, no control, fear."

I ask him to bridge back to an earlier time in childhood when he had the same set of feelings.

Immediately he responded, "It all goes back to the tonsillectomy. I was afraid. I was strapped down."

I ask quickly, "Do you have freedom?"

"None, no way of escape (*tonsillectomy. l.p.*) Suffocation, and dying. Like I was in another world with lightening bolts. I couldn't understand. Nobody to help me."

I observe, "You had that same feeling when you were away, or out of town. You can't escape death." I then rationalize the T & A procedure. "This was a routine operation with most children in bygone years. There is nothing critical about it. But your **interpretation** of the event is scary

263

based on lack of support from family and other frightening and insecure experiences. See it differently. It's over and you are now a grown man, etc. Now separate the gym from the operating room and the car wash from the operating room."

Frank responded with this, "Now I feel embarrassment. I know it shouldn't happen and it probably won't happen. But still there is a little 'if'. So it makes me uncomfortable to be around friends who don't know about my condition. I'm embarrassed that it might come on."

I encourage him, "It is ninety percent unlikely to happen. Give yourself a positive suggestion that you will remain **Calm, Cool, Collected and Composed.** Remember the four 'C's'. Now I'm going to prove it to you. Let's go get in your car."

We get in his car and I ask him to drive to the busiest mall that is close to us. We go to a new Super Walmart. It is mid-afternoon and the parking lot is crowded. I tell him I am going to let him out and I am going to drive off in his car and leave him there. In hypnosis I tell him he is to go in the store and walk around, being aware of all of the people, and he is going to notice the four 'C's' in his mind and that he will enjoy being there. I will leave in his car and pick him up at the front in about 15 minutes.

At this point I may not have been as confident as I sounded or as he was. But we carried it out without a hitch. He got in the car smiling at his accomplishment.

There were a few bobbles after this at home and at work, but he continued to improve and get stronger. The course of therapy, like true love, is not always straight. His wife reported to me once that he got to golfing compulsively, recreation was a chore, he looks for a quick fix, and still thinks he might get trapped. I told her not to listen to it, to reject his negative suggestions and replace them with positive expectations.

While in hypnosis I give him ego strengthening suggestions including traits and characteristics of leadership and good management. I had a connection to casually inquire about his behavior and attitude at work. The report was that more than one of his co-workers had noticed an obvious improvement in his presence and demeanor at work. Of course they did not know why.

I had him report again to his doctor and get directions for further decreasing his medication. This took place and I continued to give him hypnotic suggestions for confidence. I insisted that he continue with his regimen of self-hypnosis, exercise, healthy eating, recreation, family relationships, sex, etc.

His visits with me tapered off and faded into occasional phone calls to check with him. The panic attacks stopped. His total life continued to improve. It has been two years since we completed therapy. Recently I called to check on him. He has had no further symptoms. His "boss-lady" reports he is doing much better as a leader and manager.

CONCLUSION

I give the case of Frank B. as an example of the usual course of therapy and to illustrate some of the common issues and procedures that are useful in most therapy situations. This was a successful treatment program. With patients who come to our office with panic attacks, we have a higher success rate than ninety percent. There are other disorders that have the same high expectations of success. Of course there are other more serious disorders which could be given as examples where the success rate was less than ninety percent. This procedure is particularly effective with Anxiety, Depression, PTSD, and Panic. The procedure is effective with borderline conditions, but as one would expect, that is long-term therapy. I avoid treating Schizophrenic and Psychotic patients where possible.

Most all of the Age Regressions were planned while taking the case history. His trauma with the football team was a surprise and following the emotional bridge led to another one or two significant incidents. This shows the value of taking a detailed history at the beginning. But it also shows the value of asking the client to follow a set of emotions back to a previous time when he/she felt the same way. The principle here is state dependent memory, wherein a memory is attached to a biochemical state of the body. When the chemical conditions are repeated, the memory returns. (See Rossi, 1986.)

Medical Hypnoanalysis has been demonstrated to be effective by its use by members of the American Academy of Medical Hypnoanalysts. Further instruction in this method is offered by this Academy. Such instruction is available through semi-annual seminars and by a residency training program.

At the begining of this book I stated that perhaps this is a therapy whose time has come. The need for quick, yet thorough treatment has been proved to be of the utmost importance. The time is now!

APPENDIX A

CASE HISTORY FORM

case no. date phone(s)
patient's name
home address
city state zip
occupation employer
business address
city state telephone
age birthplace sex s.w.m.sep.d.
r.p. occupation
business address
city state telephone
home address
city state telephone
next of kin relationship
occupation
address of kin   telephone
referred by occupation
address of referee telephone
medical insurance
diagnosis for insurance or reference:

I. PRESENT ILLNESS:

a. Body language and appearance
b. What medicines, drugs, or alcohol have you had today?

c. Date of last physical and doctor

d. Patient's story
   (Life in general) On a scale of 1-10 where are you now?

e. Is there any area about which you would rather not be questioned?

f. Duration of Illness
g. Conditions causing variation in illness

h. What you would do if cured you cannot do now? Illness stops from doing what?
i. Outline of Rx already tried
j. Present occupation Like Disklike
k. What would you rather do?

II. PAST HISTORY:

Deathly illness or accident?
a. Childhood diseases: Measles Mumps Chicken Pox Whooping Cough Scarlet Fever
Vaccinations: Small Pox Diphtheria Polio Typhoid Aid Test
Other diseases: Malaria Pneumonia Obesity Drowning
Diabetes
Rheumatic Fever Tuberculosis HFAA Migraine Heart
Disease Hypertension
Enuresis Alcoholism or DA? Emaciated Thyroid Weight (Fluctuate?)
Ulcers
Epilepsy Nephritis Tonsillitis Nervous Breakdown Serious Infection
Serious Flu Menstrual Problems Gonorrhea Syphilis
Insomnia Sweating
Cancer Burns Accidents Clitis Hemorrhoids Dyspnea
Hemorrhage
Hyperemesis Other

Who do you like or take after?

b. Surgery and/or hospitalizations

No. Operation Year---Age Remarks

1.
2.
3.
4.
5.

c. Mental States Exam
Interpersonal relationships Suicidal
Affect/Suicide
Thought processes
Speech
Ideation
Perception
Orientation and Memory
Hallucination/Insight

III. FAMILY HISTORY

a. CA TBC Mental Diabetes Ht Disease EAHF
Rheumatis/Arthritis} Goiter Obesity Nephritis Epilepsy
Allergies Alcoholism
b. Where was childhood spent? Happy or unhappy
childhood?
c. What was happy and what was unhappy?
d. Father: Name Age _____Health _____Occupation

e. What sort of person is he? (Relation to patient)

Nickname
f. Mother: Name Age
_____Health _____Occupation
Nickname
g. What sort of person is she? (Relation to patient)

h. Father and mother: (Relation between, rows, etc.)

i. Step-parents: Name   Age   Heath
j. Brothers and Sisters   Age   Personality type, Values, Health,
Information, Etc.

1.
2.
3.

k. What do you know about your mother's pregnancy with you and birth?

1. Mother's age when pregnant with you? Married?

IV. SEXUAL HISTORY

a. Early sexual incidents (With child, with adult, fears, threatened, caught, punishment
etc.)
b. Puberty age Source of sex knowledge

c. Masturbation: (Began? Incident? Same sex? Opposite? Now? Fantasy then, now? Use of vibrator, other aids?)
d. Pre-marital intercourse
e. Homosexual:
f. Animal
g. Have you ever engaged in prostitution?

h. Frequency of IC Have you ever climaxed?

i. Do you climax? Under what conditions?

j. Positions
k. Frequency of masturbation? Birth control
l. Fantasies
    ORAL   SEX POTENTIAL
m. Cunnilingus?   Fellatio?
n. Enjoy?   Enjoy?
o. With Whom?   With Whom?
p. Reasons   Swallow?
q. Is your sex life satisfactory
r. Extra Marital -- Variety? (Who, When, Where, Names, Dates, Places, Reasons,
Feelings, Fantasies, Groups, Pains, Swaps, Orgies

Has spouse had EMIC?

s. Traumatic incidents (Rape, Groups, Guilt, Sex habits, sex contacts with relatives)

t. Impotence, frigidity and nymphomania

u. Remarks

v. Is there any sexual or other incident you haven't told that you think I really should know?

w. Number of pregnancies (Had or Caused) Children

Sterility

Miscarriages Abortions Date Married

x. Pregnancy   List

Planned? M-F Name(AB.?) Birth Date Trauma, Delivery, Anoxia, Cord Feeding (B. B)

1.

2.

3.

V. PSYCHOLOGICAL HISTORY:

a. Nervous habits before going to school, sleepwalking, nightmares, frightened repeatedly, etc.

b. Age in school (Happy or not, if not, Why)

c. Educational level (Why)

d. Teachers (Names, ages, and relationship with)

e. Traumatic incidents (Accidents, Deaths, Illnesses, High Fevers, Operations, Embarrassing Moments, Emotional

Incidents, Dating Experiences)

VI. HABITS: Alcohol Coffee Other Beverages

a. Drugs Tobacco Meals: Reg.? Bal.? Sleep

Bowel Movements Exercise

b. Abnormalities?

c. Nervous Habits?

Nail Biting _____Thumb Sucking _____Stuttering

Hives _____Tics,_____ Twitches, _____Sniffles

Grind Teeth _____Speech Problems _____Other

VII. PRESENT SOCIAL HISTORY:

a. What do you think people say behind your back that you don't like?

b. If you could change one thing about yourself, what would it be?

c. On what do you spend your money and on what do you like to spend it?

d. How do you spend your time and how would you like to spend it?

e. Single: Why?

f. Attitude toward opposite sex

g. For any reason have you ever thought it would be desirable to eliminate your sex drive? (Even temporarily?)

h. Social life, (Friends, Hobbies, Interests)

i. What are the occupations of your relatives and friends?

j. Have you ever thought about suicide?

Have you ever attempted suicide? _____ Describe and list

k. Have you ever been in service? (Which Branch? Where? Seen Action?)

1. Have you ever been arrested? _____ How many times? _____

Charges?

Reduced from? _____ Convicted?_____ Sentences?   Dates

etc.

Have you ever thought about suing anybody? or ever been sued?

m. How and where living? (Wife, relations, on own, relations with people)

n. Have you ever had serious marital difficulties? (If so, give details on page 11, 12)

o. What is the most disturbing experience of your life?

VIII RELIGION: (Religious, Political, Psychological beliefs)

(Church affiliation, What is God like?)

a. Have you lived in accord with your childhood teaching?

b. Are you in accord with your church doctrine?

c. Are you living in accord with your own religious beliefs?

d. Is there anything you feel guilty about?

Is there anything you have not yet told me, which you think I really should know?
Traumatic Incidents?
e. Therapy goals
f. What do you know about hypnosis?

IX. MARITAL HISTORY: (Dating history -- Describe mate)

Engagements Courtship (Ages, Lengths, Breakups, etc.)

Marriages
Age Marriage Date Spouse's age, name Separation-Date-Cause Divorce-Date-Cause
1.
2.
Remarks (Children of)
Has spouse been married before?
Children?
b. For what reason did you get married? (Was this a forced marriage without love?)
c. What is there of lasting value on which your marriage rests?

d. When did marital difficulties of a serious nature start?

e. How would separation or divorce affect the family?

f. Whom do you know in your family or close acquaintances that is unhappy like yourself?
g. How do you communicate with spouse?
h. What subject do you fight about?
i. What would spouse like for you to change?

j. What would you like for your spouse to change?

k. Do you want to make your marriage a success?

1. Have you thought of separation or divorce?
m. How do you get along with in-laws?

APPENDIX B

INITIAL PROTECTIVE SUGGESTIONS

by
William J. Bryan, Jr., M. D.

These are permanent suggestions, routine, permanent suggestions given to every patient and these suggestions will take complete and thorough effect on you, mind, body and spirit. They will sink into the deepest part of your subconscious mind, never to be removed, sealing themselves permanently, stamping themselves indelibly on every single cell of your brain and your body. The first suggestion is, you will never be able to be hypnotized by anyone but a qualified practitioner. You will never be able to be hypnotized by anyone but a qualified practitioner.

Second, you will never be able to be taken advantage of in any way while in the state of hypnosis. You will never be able to be taken advantage of in any way while in the state of hypnosis.

Third, you will never be able to be hypnotized unless you want to be hypnotized. You cannot be hypnotized against your will, or without your consent. You will never be able to be hypnotized unless you want to be hypnotized. You cannot be hypnotized against your will, or without your consent.

Fourth, you will never be able to be hypnotized while you hold the wheel of an automobile in your hands, while operating any moving machine or in any situation in which it might be dangerous to you. You will never be able to be hypnotized while you hold the wheel of an automobile in your hands, while operating any moving machine or in any situation which might be dangerous to you.

Fifth, should you be hypnotized and should an emergency situation arise which requires your immediate attention, you would immediately become wide-awake, clear headed, refreshed and alert and handle the situation capably and more efficiently than you would otherwise. Should you be hypnotized and should an emergency situation arise which requires your immediate attention, you would immediately become wide-awake, clear-headed, refreshed and alert and handle the situation capably and efficiently.

Six, should you feel that you need any other suggestions to protect you while in the state of hypnosis these suggestions are given to you and take full and complete effect upon you, just the same as if I had said them. If you feel that you need any other suggestions to protect you while in the state of hypnosis these suggestions are given to you and take full and complete effect upon you, just the same as if I had said them.

Seven, in addition to the six protective suggestions I have given you, from this moment on, whenever I say the one word, "sleep", to you, under these circumstances, you will immediately drop into a deep, deep hypnotic trance. Even deeper than the one you are in now. Your eyes will close, all your muscles will completely collapse and you will continue to go even deeper and deeper with every breath you take, until I wake you up. Now it is only when you want to be hypnotized and only when I say the word, "sleep", as a command and only when I or one of my associates say the word "sleep". For the word "sleep" in ordinary conversation will neither disturb you nor produce a hypnotic trance. You cannot be hypnotized by accident. With your permission and at my command, all your muscles will completely let go and collapse and you will continue to go deeper and deeper and deeper with every breath you take, in a deep state of hypnotic relaxation.

While under hypnosis the following suggestions will apply to you. While under hypnosis the following suggestions will apply to you. First of all, you will always hear every suggestion I give to you. You must hear every suggestion I give to you. Every suggestion I give to you will be in harmony with your desires for improvement. You will always hear every suggestion I give to you. You must hear every suggestion I give to you. Every suggestion I give to you will be in harmony with your desires for improvement. All your defenses and inhibitions and resistances to therapy are completely dissolved while in the hypnotic trance. All your defenses and inhibitions and resistances to therapy are completely dissolved while in the hypnotic trance.

APPENDIX C

THE BRYAN WORD ASSOCIATION TEST

The following test shows the stimulus words in the left column. The replies by the patient are shown on the right. What the therapist thinks to himself is in italics in parentheses. The spontaneous comments made to the patient are given in capital letters in parentheses.

1. Jones John
2. Sweet Coke
3. Smith M
4. Soft   bed
5. George daddy
6. Bell   church
7. Alive M
8. Father daddy
9. Sugar sweet
10. Mother M
11. Problem weight
12. Fear money
13. Life (l.p.) living
14. Gertrude me
15. Anxiety nervous
16. Green grass
17. Death me
18. John husband
19. White snow
20. Love happiness

21. Overweight me
22. Desire happy
23. Blue me
24. Hate me
25. Bill (p.) brother
26. Red fire
27. Live happy
28. Mouth face
29. Sex all time
30. Bite eat
31. Teeth chew
32. Tongue mouth
33. Jean (2nd C.) girl
34. Vagina body
35. Clitoris (l.p.) body
36. Exciting (l.p.) happy
37. Uncle Willie uncle
38. Penis John
39. Please help me
40. Lovely pretty

41. Boys men
42. Suck no
43. Breast body
44. Need Bill
45. Belief religion
46. Doctor doctor
47. God Creator
48. Hypnosis peace
49. Treatment   rest
50. Climax stop
51. My F, George is a good worker
52. Anger mad
53. When I lose my weight (FINISH) I'll be happy
54. Depressed   me
55. My M., Alice is my friend
56. Hostility anger
57. Why am I like this
58. Horrible me
59. My H., John *(hesitantly)* don't ... love ... me
60. Homosexual boys
61. Who am I
62. How can I be happy
63. I think of myself as fat
64. I became fat
65. Basically bad *(self-hate* - 161)
66. Younger Kay
67. Dark night
68. A good figure Kay is someone small
69. Escape fear
70. Abortion baby
71. Dominate rule
72. Baby Kay
73. Guilt (p. uh) adultery (own guilt & punishment)
74. Pleasure brother
75. Punishment my weight (* *case -184)
76. If only I could lose my weight I would be happy
77. There must be an end
78. Why can't I be like I'm supposed to be
79. Every single time (p.) I go to bed (*finish*) John studies
80. My marriage is not happy
81. My greatest fear is losing everything
82. My greatest desire is to be happy
83. My greatest need is to be happy
84. My greatest fault is eating
85. I'm afraid when (sl.p.) of what John will say
86. I hold back   everything
87. Men are to me dirty
88. At the end of the road death
89. Underneath it all good
90. When I make love my mind's not with it
91. As long as I'm overweight I'm unhappy
92. I really care about my kids
93. I really desire happiness
94. Women are to me friends
95. My greatest talent/ability is nothing
96. My biggest failure marriage
97. I was near death when uhuh *(quiet)* Bill *(emotion)*
98. The greatest obstacle to happiness is my weight
99. Its so easy to eat
100. I resent John

101. If I were thin I'd look good (yeah & appealing to men)
102. I ask myself (S) why I let myself go
103. The one thing I need most is happiness
104. 20 years from now I'll probably be dead
105. The warmth of your lips makes me feel good
106. Most of all I want to be happy and little
107. I thought I was being punished when M. got sick
108. If I really let go uh(grunt) l.p.) I'd probably leave
109. Submit (nod) substitute
110. Touch feel
111. Pride (purse lips) mine
112. Virgin body
113. Pain death
114. Marriage mistake
115. Lips Bill
116. Kiss Bill
117. Prick pin
118. Rapid fast
119. Dick (p) Jane
120. Pussy (p) woman
121. Fuck slang word
122. Cock Bill
123. Feel touch
124. Peter man
125. Balls man
126. Character personality
127. Between my legs (p) hair
128. In the hole wrong
129. Party crowd
130. Screw Bill
131. Response answer
132. Cunt mine
133. Come climax
134. Semen Bill
135. Swallow saliva
136. Cheat adultery
137. Lie (s) me
138. Steal thief
139. Divorce *(s-nod head "no")* not right
140. I feel like I'm somebody when I'm with Bill
141. Children mine
142. Virtue I don't know
143. Kindness Bill
144. War that's what I have
145. Affection   Bill
146. Adultery   me (cf. 73)
147. Black light
148. Scream scared
149. Where will it get me
150. Warm (s) feeling loved
151. An extra marital affair *(disgust)* is adultry
152. Food I eat (?) my past time
153. Home my home
154. Kind Bill
155. Gentle Bill
156. When my B. had a tumor I thought I was being punished (75)
157. Masturbate play with yourself
158. Nurse baby
159. Freedom   peace
160. Frigid myself
161. Confidence I don't have any (cf. 65,58)
162. Funeral death
163. Prostitute girl
164. Narcotics drugs

165. Confinement jail
166. Trust belief
167. Authority John
168. Dirty sex
169. What's going to happen to me (due to guilt)
170. When I'm on top I reach a climax (*can enjoy it - 160*)
171. If I knew I'd never be punished (*grunt*) I don't know
172. If I knew I'd never be caught I guess I'd keep seeing Bill
173. My deepest thoughts tell me I do wrong
174. Lying down relaxing
175. Please don't leave me
176. On my back relax
177. When I'm nude I'm terrible
178. Tests like this huh make you think
179. I sinned when I had the affair with Bill. I still want to be with Bill

180. Believe me if I say where I've been (WHERE?) with Bill (WHEN) today
181. When fire breaks out hot
182. I enjoy being with Bill
183. At the very bottom of it all it worries me (*guilt*)
184. I'm just tired of being so fat. G. calls me fat all the time.
185. I feel best when I talk with Bill or see him - feel so relaxed
186. When I feel clean I take a bath
187. I'll be well when I lose my weight and be happy
188. I consider myself fat
189. Next time I marry I don't know if I would again or not
190. I'm the type of person who (S) wants to have a family do things together - and enjoy life

BIBLIOGRAPHY

Ackerman, N. (1954). The diagnosis of neurotic marital interaction. *Social Casework*, 4, 139-147.

Ackerman, N. (1958a). The family approach to marital disorders. In H. Greenwald (Ed.), *Active psychotherapy*. New York: Basic Books.

Ackerman, N. (1958b). *The psychodynamics of family life*. New York: Basic Books.

Adams, W.J.(1972). Utilizing the interpersonal relationship concept in marriage counseling. In H. L. Silverman (Ed.), *Marital therapy*. Springfield, IL: C. C. Thomas.

Albert, G. (1972). Are marriage counselors qualified to counsel? In H. L. Silverman (Ed.), *Marital therapy*. Springfield, IL: C. C. Thomas.

Alexander, F., & French, T. M. (1946). *Psychoanalytic therapy*. New York: Ronald Press.

Als, H., Tronick, E., Lester, B. M., & Brazelton, T. B. (1977). The Brazelton neonatal behavioral assessment scale. *Journal of Abnormal Child Psychology*, 5,215-231.

Ambrose, G. & Newbold, G. (1958). *A handbook of medical hypnosis*. Baltimore: Williams & Wilkins.

Anastasi, A. (1968). *Psychological testing*. New York: Macmillan.

Anderson, H. H. & Anderson, G. L. (1951). *An introduction to projective techniques*. New York: Prentice-Hall.

Annis, L. G. (1978). *The child before birth*. Ithaca, NY: Cornell University.

Ard, B. N. (1969). Assumptions underlying marriage counseling. In B. N. Ard & C. C.

Ard (Eds.), *Handbook of marriage counseling*. Palo Alto, CA: Science and Behavior Books.

Ard, B. N. & Ard, C. C., (Eds.) (1969). *Handbook of marriage counseling*. Palo Alto, CA: Science and Behavior Books.

Araoz, D. L. (1981). Negative self-hypnosis. *Journal of Contemporary Psychotherapy*, 12, (1), 45-5 1.

Araoz, D. L. (1985). *The new hypnosis.* New York: Brunner/Mazel.

Arey, L. B. (1974). *Developmental anatomy.* Philadelphia: W. B. Sanders.

Assagioli, R. (1965). *Psychosynthesis.* New York: Hobbs, Dorman.

Bach, G. R. & Deutsch, R. M. (1970). *Pairing: how to achieve genuine intimacy.* New York: Avon.

Bachrach, L. L.(1975). *Marital status and mental disorder: An analytical review.* Rockville, MD: U. S. Department of Health, Education and Welfare.

Bader, E., & Pearson, P. T.(1988). *In quest of the mythical mate.* New York: Brunner/Mazel.

Bailes, F. (1971). *Your mind and you.* Marina Del Rey, CA:DeVorss.

Bakan, P. (1978). Dreaming, REM sleep and the right hemisphere: a theoretical integration. *Journal of Altered States of Consciousness*, 3, 285-307.

Balog, J. (1985). Expanding the five "R's" of hypnotherapy. Paper presented at the semi-annual meeting of the Society of Medical Hypnoanalysts, Memphis, TN, April.

Bandura, A. (1976). New perspectives on violence. In V. C. Vaughn, III, & T. B.

Brazelton (Eds.), *The family - can it be saved?* Chicago: Year Book Medical Publishers.

Barber, T. X. (1958). The good hypnotic subject. *Science Digest*, 43, 36-41.

Barber, T. X. (1984). In A. A. Sheikh (Ed.), *Imagination and healing.* Farmingdale, NY: Baywood.

Bardill, D. R. (1966). A relationship focused approach to marital problems. *Social Work*, 11,70-77.

Barnett, E. A. (1980). Hypnoanalysis and the negative birth experience. *Medical Hypnoanalysis*, 1, 68-74.

Barnett, E. A. (1981). *Analytical hypnotherapy.* Kingston, Ontario:Junica.

Baron, S. (1960). Levels of insight and ego functioning in relation to hypnoanalysis. *International Journal of Clinical and Experimental Hypnosis*, 8, 18-35.

Barten, H. H. (1971). *Brief therapies.* New York: Behavioral Publications.

Barth, K. (1957). *The word of God and the word of men.* New York: Harper.

Baum, M. J., Gallagher, C. A., Martin, J. T., & Damassa, D. A. (1982). Effects of testosterone, dihydro-testosterone or estradiol administered neonatall, on sexual behavior of female ferrets. *Indocrinology*, 111, 773-780.

Bean, F. D., & Kerchoff, A. C. (1971). Personality and perception in husband-wife conflicts. *Journal of Marriage and the Family*, 33, 351-359.

Bellak, L. (1955). An ego-psychological theory of hypnosis. *International Journal of Psycho-Analysis*, 36, 375-378.

Berg, C. (1941). War in the mind: a case book of a medical psychologist. London: Macaulay Press.

Berman, E. M., & Lief, H. I. (1975). Marital therapy from a psychiatric perspective: An overview. *American Journal of Psychiatry*, 132, 583-592.

Bernard, J. (1975). Note on changing lifestyles: 1970-1974. *Journal of Marriage and the Family*, 37, 582-593.

Berne, E. (1966). *Games people play.* New York: Grove Press.

Bernheim, H. (1888). Die suggestion und ihre heilwirkung. (Trans. by S. Freud.) Leipzig: F. Deutche. Cited by Conn, J. H., Hypnosynthesis. *Journal of Nervous and Mental Disease*, 1949, 109, 9-24.

Bertalanffy, L. Von. (1968). *General Systems Theory.* New York: Braziller.

Bick, C. (1981). Hypnoanalysis and some of its effects. *Medical Hypnoanalysis*, 2, 13-19.

Bieber, I. (1980). *Cognitive psychoanalysis.* New York: Jason Aaronson.

Bier, W. C., (Ed.) (1965). Marriage: *A psychological and moral approach.* New York: Fordham University Press.

Blanck, G., & Blanck, R. (1974). *Ego psychology theory and practice.* New York: Columbia University Press.

Blatt, S. J. (1975). The validity of projective techniques and their research and clinical contribution. *Journal of Personality Assessment*, 39, 4, p.327.

Boas, C. V. (1962). Intensive group psychotherapy with married couples. *International Journal of Group Psychotherapy*, 12, 142-153.

Bonelli, P. M. (1980). Smoking therapy: A composite approach. *Medical Hypnoanalysis*, 1, 163-167.

Boswell, L. K. (1949). The initial sensitizing event of emotional disorders. *Journal of Nervous and Mental Disease*, 109, 9-24.

Boswell, L. K. Jr. (1961). The initial sensitizing event of emotional disorders. *Journal of the American Institute of Hypnosis*, 2(1), 13-22.

Boswell, L. K., Jr. (1966). The Bryan electronic automated robot hypnotist. *Journal of the American Institute of Hypnosis*, 7(3), 27-30.

Bowen, M. (1978). *Family Therapy in Clinical Practice*. New York: Jason Aronson.

Bower, T. G. (1966). The visual world of infants. *Scientific American*, 215, 80-92.

Bower, T. G. (1972). Object perception in infants. *Perception*, 1, 15-30.

Bower, T. O., Broughton, J. M., & Moore, M. K. (1970). The coordination of visual and tactual input in infants. *Perception and Psychophysics*, 8, 51-53.

Bower, T. G., Dunkeld, J., & Wishart, J. 0. (1979). Infant perception of visually presented objects. *Science*, 203, 1137-1139.

Bower, T. G. & Wishart, J. G. (1972). The effects of object on motor permanence. *Cognition*, 1, 165-172.

Bowers, M. K. (1974). *Hypnosis for the seriously curious*. San Francisco: Brooks/Cole.

Bowers, M. K. & Brecher, 5. (1955). The emergence of multiple personalities in the course of hypnotic investigation. *Journal of Clinical and Experimental Hypnosis*, 3, 188-199.

Boyden, S. V., (Ed.) (1974). *The impact of civilization on the biology of man*. Toronto: University of Toronto Press.

Braman, 0. R. (1982). *The oppositional child*. Guam Main Facility: Isle of Guam Publishers.

Bramwell, J. M. (1921) *Hypnotism: its history, practice, and theory*. London: Rider.

Brazelton, T. B. (1970). Effect of prenatal drugs on the behavior of the neonate. *American Journal of Psychiatry*, 126, 126 1-1266.

Brazelton, T. B. (1972). Implications of infant development among the Mayan Indians of Mexico. *Human Development*, 15, 90-111.

Brazelton, T. B. (1973). Effect of maternal expectations on early infant behavior. *Early Child Development & Care*, 2, 259-273.

Brazelton, T. B. (1977). The behavior of nutritionally deprived Guatemalan infants. *Developmental Medicine & Child Neurology*, 19, 3 64-372.

Brazelton, T. B. (1978). The remarkable talents of the newborn. *Birth and the Family Journal*, 5, 187-191.

Brazelton, T. B. (1982). Perinatal circumstances and newborn outcome among the Gusii of Kenya: assessment of risk. *Infant Behavior and Development*, 5, 11-32.

Brazelton, T. B. & Als, H. (1979). Four early stages in the development of mother-infant interaction. *Psychoanalytic Study of the Child*, 34, 349-369.

Brazelton, T. B., Koslowski, B., & Tronick, B. (1977). Neonatal behavior among urban Zambians and Americans. *Annual Progress in Child Psychiatry & Child Development*, 665-6 76.

Breger, L. (1968). Motivation, energy, and cognitive structure in psychoanalytic theory. In J. Marmor (Ed.), *Modern psychoanalysis*. New York: Basic Books.

Breger, L., Hunter, I., & Lane, R. W. (1971). *The effect of stress on dreams*. New York: International Universities Press.

Brenman, M. (1949). Dreams and hypnosis. *The Psychoanalytic Quarterly*, 18, 45 5-465.

Brenman, M. & Gill, M. M. (1947). *Hypnotherapy*. New York: International Universities Press.

Breuer, J. & Freud, S. (1939). *Studies in hysteria*. Boston: Beacon Press, 1939.

Breuer, J. & Freud, S. (1955). (Ueber den Psychischen Mechanismus hysterischer ph Eaenomaene. Neurol. Centralbl. 4 and 43 (1893). Vide: Ges Schriften von S. Freud, Vol. 1, mt. Psychoanalyt. Verlag. Leipzig-Vienna-Zurich, p. 7-24. Cited by Stokvis, B. Hypnosis and psychoanalytic method. *Journal of Clinical and Experimental Hypnosis*, 3, 253-255.

Brill, A. A. (Ed.). (1938). *The basic writings of Sigmund Freud*. New York: Modern Library.

Broderick, C. (1975). Power in the governance of families. In R. E. Cromwell & D. H. Olson (Eds.), *Power in families*. New York: John Wiley & Sons.

Brown, D. P. & Fromm, E. (1986). *Hypnotherapy and hypnoanalysis*. Hillsdale, N.J.: Lawrence Eribaum Associates.

Brown, W. (1921). *Psychology and psychotherapy*. London: Arnold.

Brown, W. A., Grodin, J., & Manning, T. (1972). Prenatal psychological state and the use of drugs in labor. *American Journal of Obstetrics and Gynecology*, 113, 598.

Bryan, D. (1928). Book review. *International Journal of Psychoanalysis*, 9, 265-266.

Bryan, W. J., Jr. (1960). Editorial. *Journal of the American Institute of Hypnosis*, 1, (1), 1.

Bryan, W. J., Jr. (1961a). Treatment of alcoholism. *Journal of the American Institute of Hypnosis*, 2,(1), 38-50.

Bryan, W. J., Jr. (1961b) The walking zombie syndrome. *Journal of the American Institute of Hypnosis*, 2(3), 10-18.

Bryan, W. J., Jr. (1961c). The walking zombie syndrome. *Journal of the American Institute of Hypnosis*, 3(3), 10-18

Bryan, W. J., Jr. (1962). More about zombies. *Journal of the American Institute of Hypnosis*, 3(4), 41-43.

Bryan, W. J., Jr. (1963). A history of hypnosis. *Journal of the American Institute of Hypnosis*, 4(1), 27.

Bryan, W. J., Jr. (1964a). Hypnosis and smoking. *Journal of the American Institute of Hypnosis*, 5(2), 17-37

Bryan, W. J., Jr. (1964b). Ponce de Leon syndrome. *Journal of the American Institute of Hypnosis*, 5(1), 34-43.

Bryan, W. J., Jr. (1965a) The use and abuse of hypno-aids. *Journal of the American Institute of Hypnosis*, 6(4), 31-42.

Bryan, W. J., Jr. (1965b). Comparative analysis of a killer. *Journal of the American Institute of Hypnosis*, 6(2), 16.

Bryan, W. J., Jr. (1966a). Turning losers into winners. *Journal of the American Institute of Hypnosis*, 7(2), 30.

Bryan, W. J., Jr. (1966b). Sex, strangling, and sadism. *Journal of the American Institute of Hypnosis*, 7(4), 10-22.

Bryan, W. J., Jr. (1967a). Reprint from San Diego County Medical Society bulletin, July 1967. *Journal of the American Institute of Hypnosis*, 8(4), 46.

Bryan, W. J., Jr. (1967b). Hypnosis and homosexuality, part 3. *Journal of the American Institute of Hypnosis*, 8(3), 31-43.

Bryan, W. J., Jr. (1969a). A new hypnotic technique in treating patients who feel guilty about breaking the Mosaic Law. *Journal of the American Institute of Hypnosis*, 10(3), 110-115.

Bryan, W. J., Jr. (1969b). Problem clinic. *Journal of the American Institute of Hypnosis*, 10(2), 88.

Bryan, W. J., Jr. (1969c). Problem clinic. *Journal of the American.Institute of Hypnosis*, 10(1), 33-41.

Bryan, W. J., Jr. (1969d). Moral and theological problems in hypnoanalysis. *Journal of the American Institute of Hypnosis*, 10(4), 161-168.

Bryan, W. J., Jr. (1969e). *Hypnosis and fire. Journal of the American Institute of Hypnosis*, 10(1), 17-19.

Bryan, W. J., Jr. (1969f). Problem clinic. *Journal of the American Institute of Hypnosis*, 10(2), 88-90. (f)

Bryan, W. J., Jr. (1970). Symptomatic hypnosis in primary and secondary osteoarthritis. *Journal of the American Institute of Hypnosis*, 11(3), 128.

Bryan, W. J., Jr. (1971a). *The chosen ones*. New York: Vantage Press.

Bryan, W. J., Jr. (1971b). Survival today, tomorrow and forever. *Journal of the American Institute of Hypnosis*, 12(3), 135-138.

Bryan, W. J., Jr. (197 Ic). Anorexia Nervosa. *Journal of the American Institute of Hypnosis*, 12(4), 1 92-193.

Bryan, W. J., Jr. (1971d). Problem clinic. *Journal of the American Institute of Hypnosis*, 12(4), 194. (d)

Bryan, W. J., Jr. (1971). Postgraduate course No. 1000. *Journal of the American Institute of Hypnosis*, 12, (2), 95-96.

Buber, M. (1937). *I and thou*. Edinburgh: T. & T. Clark.

Buber, M. (1955). *Between man and man*, Boston: Beacon Press.

Bucher, W. W., & Carrol, J. (1962). Ordinal position and conformity. *Journal of Abnormal Psychology*, 65, 13 1-139.

Buckley, R. W. (1950). The treatment of post-traumatic syndrome by hypnotic analysis. *Journal of Nervous and Mental Disease*, 111, 122-138.

Burks, J., & Rubenstein, M. (1979). *Temperament styles in adult interaction: Applications in psychotherapy*. New York: Brunner/ Mazel.

Burstein, I., Kinch, R. A. & Stern, L. (1974). Anxiety, pregnancy, labor, and the neonate. *American Journal of Obstetrics and Gynecology*, 118, 195.

Bychowski, G. (1956). Interaction between psychotic partners. In V. W. Eisenstein (Ed.), *Neurotic interaction in marriage*. New York: Basic Books.

Calderone, M. S. (1972). Sex-education in the United States: A fresh look. In H. L. Silverman (Ed.), *Marital Therapy*. Springfield, IL: C. C. Thomas.

Carrington, W. L. (1961). *The healing marriage*. Greatneck, NY: Channel Press.

Carter, Y., & Glick, P. C. (1976). *Marriage and divorce: A social and economic study*.

Cambridge, MA: Harvard University Press.

Cartwright, D. 5. (1955). Success in psychotherapy as a function of certain actuarial variables. *Journal of Consulting Psychology*, 19, 357-363.

Cases, P. C., & Duttes, J. E. (1962). Birth order as a selective factor among volunteer subjects. *Journal of Abnormal Psychology*, 64, 302.

Chaves, J. F. (1968). Hypnosis reconceptualized: an overview of Barber's theoretical and empirical work. *Psychological Reports*, 22, 587-608.

Cheek, C. B. & LeCron, L. M. (1968). Clinical hypnotherapy. New York: Grune & Stratton.

Chertok, L. (1968). The discovery of transference. *International Journal of Psycho-Analysis*, 49, 561-576.

Chertok, L. (1 978a). Editorial, *Journal of Nervous and Mental Disease*, 166, 231-233.

Chertok, L. (1978b). The unconscious in France before Freud: premises of a discovery. *Psychoanalytic Quarterly*, 47(2), 192-208.

Chertok, L. (1982). The unconscious and hypnosis. *The international Journal of Clinical and Experimental Hypnosis*, 30, 95-105.

Chertok, L. & Kramarz, P. (1959). Hypnosis, sleep and electroencephalography. *Journal of Nervous and Mental Disease*, 128, 227-238.

Chessick, R. D. (1985). *Psychology of the self and the treatment of narcissism*. Northvale, N.J. :Jason Aronson.

Clinebell, H. J. (1966). *Basic types of pastoral counseling*. New York: Abingdon.

Cole, S. (1978). Teenage Girls. Unpublished manuscript prepared for Newsday, SUNY at Stony Brook, 1976. In T. J. Paolino, Jr., and B. S. McCrady (Eds.), *Marriage and Marital Therapy*. New York: Brunner/Mazel.

Conn, J. H. (1949a). Hypno-synthesis. *Journal of Nervous and Mental Disease*, 109, 9-24.

Conn, J. H. (1949b). Hypnotic relaxation and analysis. In R. H. Rhoades (Ed.), *Therapy Through Hypnosis*. New York: Citadel Press, pp. 194-212.

Conn, J. H. (1953). Hypnosynthesis III. Hypnotherapy of chronic war neuroses with a discussion of the value of abreaction, regression and revivification. *Journal of Clinical and Experimental Hypnosis*, 1 ,(1), 29-43.

Conn, J. H. (1960). The psychodynamics of recovery under hypnosis. *International Journal of Clinical and Experimental Hypnosis*, 8, 3-15.

Conn, J. H. (1982). The nature of magnetic treatment. *Journal of the American Society of Psychosomatic Dentistry & Medicine*, 29,(2), 44-53.

Cookerly, J. R. (1974). The reduction of psychopathology as measured by the MMPI clinical scale in three forms of marriage counseling. *Journal of Marriage and the Family*, (36,) 332-335.

Cooper, D. (1970). *The death of the family*. New York: Random House.

Coppolillo, H. P. (1976). The transitional phenomenon revisited. *Journal of the American Academy of Child Psychiatry*, 15, (1), 36-48.

Corriere, R. & Hart, J. (1977). *The dream makers*. New York: Funk & Wagnalls.

Costello, C. G. (Ed.) (1970). *Symptoms of psychopathology*. New York: John Wiley & Sons.

Cox, M. (1978). *Structuring the therapeutic process: Compromise with chaos*. New York: Pergamon Press.

Cronbach, L. J. (1949). *Essentials of psychological testing*. New York: Harper & Row.

Cuber, J. F. (1965). Three prequisite considerations to diagnosis and treatment in marriage counseling. In R. H. Kiemer (Ed.), *Counseling in marital and sexual problems*. Baltimore: Williams & Wilkins.

Dalal, A. S. (1966). An impirical approach to hypnosis: an overview of Barber's work. *Archives of General Psychiatry*, 15, 151-157.

Davanloo, H., (Ed.) (1978) *Basic principles and techniques in short term dynamic psychotherapy*. New York: SP Medical and Scientific Books.

Davanloo, H., (Ed.) (1980). *Short-term dynamic psychotherapy*. New York: Jason Aronson.

Davitz, L. L. (1981). Baby Hunger. *McCalls*, 109 (Nov.), 10.

Davitz, L. L. (1982). Baby Hunger - discussion. *McCalls*, 109 (Jan.),8.

Delgado, J. M. (1969). *Physical control of the mind*. New York: Harper.

Dement, W. (1960). The effect of dream deprivation. *Science*, 131, 1705-1707.

Dempster, W. N. (1964). Birth order and need affiliation. *Journal of Abnormal Psychology*, 68, 535-537.

DesLauriers, A. M. (1971). Ego psychology and the definition of behavior disorder. In H. E. Rie (Ed.), *Perspectives in Child Psychopathology*. New York: Aldine-Atherton.

Dicks, H. V. (1967). *Marital tensions*. New York: Basic Books,

Dixon, N. F. (1971). *Subliminal perception: the nature of a controversy*. London: McGraw-Hill.

Dowling C. (1981). *The Cinderella complex*. New York: Summit.

Draguns, J. G., Haley, E. M., & Phillips, L. P. (1968). Studies of Rorschach content. *Journal of Projective Techniques and Personality Assessment*, 32, 1, p. 26.

Dunkeld, J. & Bower, T. G. (1980). Infant response to impending optical collision. *Perception*, 9, 549-554.

Edmonston, W. E., Jr. (1981). *Hypnosis and Relaxation*. New York: John Wiley.

Ehrenreich, G. A. (1951). The influence of unconscious factors in hypnotizability. *Bulletin of the Menninger Clinic*, 15, 45-58.

Eidelberg, L. (1956). *Neurotic choice of mates*. In V. Eisenstein (Ed.), *Neurotic interaction in marriage*. New York: Basic Books.

Eisenberg, L. (1976). Youth in a changing society. In V. C. Vaughn, III, & T. B. Brazelton (Eds.), *The family - can it be saved?* Chicago: Year Book Medical Publishers.

Eisenbud, J. (1937). Psychology of headache. *Psychiatric Quarterly*, 11, 592-619.

Ellis, A. (1962). *Reason and emotion in psychotherapy*. New York: Lyle Stuart.

Ellis, A., & Harper, R. A. (1961). *A Guide to Rational Living*. Englewood Cliffs: Prentice Hall.

English, O. S. & Foster, C. J. (1951). *Fathers are parents too*. New York: Putham's Sons.

English, O. S. & Pearson, G. H. (1963). *Emotional problems of living*. New York: W. W. Norton.

Epstein, O. (1981). *Waking dream therapy*. New York: Human Sciences Press.

Erickson, G. D. & Hogan, T. P. (Eds.) (1976). *Family therapy*. New York: Aaronson.

Erickson, M. H. (1933). The investigation of a specific amnesia. *British Journal of Medical Psychology*, 13, 143.

Erickson, M. H. (1937). Development of apparent unconsciousness during hypnotic reliving of a traumatic experience. *Archives of Neurology and Psychiatry*, 38, 1282.

Erickson, M. H. (1 938a). The use of automatic writing in the interpretation and relief of a state of acute obsessional depression. *Psychoanalytic Quarterly*, 7, 443.

Erickson, M. H. (1938b). A study of clinical and experimental findings on hypnotic deafness (I). *Journal of General Psychology*, 19, 127-150.

Erickson, M. H. (1939a). Experimental demonstration of the psychopathology of everyday life. *Psychoanalytic Quarterly*, 8, 338.

Erickson, M. H. (1939b). Induction of colorblindness by a technique of hypnotic suggestion. *Journal of General Psychology*, 20, 61-89.

Erickson, M. H. (1945). Hypnotic techniques for the therapy of acute psychiatric disturbances in war. *American Journal of Psychiatry*, 101, 668.

Erickson, M. H. (1958). Naturalistic techniques of hypnosis. *American Journal of Clinical Hypnosis, 1, 3-8.*

Erickson, M. H. (1959). Further techniques of hypnosis - utilization techniques. *American Journal of Clinical Hypnosis*, 2, 3-21.

Erickson, M. H.(1960/l980). Breast development possibly influenced by hypnosis: Two instances and the psychotherapeutic results. In E. Rossi (Ed.), *The collected papers of Milton H. Erickson on hypnosis. II. Hypnotic investigation of sensory, perceptual and psychophysical processes.* New York: Irvington.

Erickson, M. H. (1966). Experiential knowledge of hypnotic phenomena employed for hypnotherapy. *American Journal of Clinical Hypnosis*, 8, 299-309.

Erickson, M. H. (1981). *Risk factors associated with complications of pregnancy, labor, and delivery.* St. Louis: C. V. Mosby Co..

Erickson, M. H. & Kubie, L. S. (1938). The use of automatic drawing in the interpretation and relief of a state of acute obsessional depression. *Psychoanalytic Quarterly*, 7, 443-466.

Erickson, M. H. & Kubie, L. S. (1939). The permanent relief of an obsessional phobia by means of communications with an unsuspected dual personality. *Psychoanalytic Quarterly*, 8, 471-509.

Erickson, M. H. & Kubie, L. S. (1941). The successful treatment of a case of acute hysterical depression by a return under hypnosis to a critical phase of childhood. *Psychoanalytic Quarterly*, 10, 583-609.

Erickson, M. H. & Kubie, L. S. (1940). The translation of the cryptic automatic writing of one hypnotic subject by another in a trance-like dissociated state. *Psychoanalytic Quarterly*, 9, 51.

Erickson, M. H., Rossi, E. L., & Rossi, S. I. (1976). *Hypnotic Realities.* New York: Irvington.

Erskine, I. S. & Baum, M. J. (1982). Plasma concentrations of testosterone and dihydro-testosterone during perinatal development in male and female ferrets. *Indocrinology*, 111, 767-72.

Esman, A. H. (1968). Marital psychopathology: Its effects on children and their management. In S. Rosenbaum & I. Alger (Eds.), *The marriage relationship*. New York: Basic Books.

Etzioni, A. (1977). Science and the future of the family. *Science*, 196, 487.

Ferenczi, S. (1926). *Further contributions to the theory and technique of psychoanalysis.* London: Hogarth.

Ferrara, S. J. (1981). The use of tapes as an adjunct in hypnoanalysis. *Medical Hypnoanalysis*, 2, 105-110.

Finch, S. M., & Cain, A. C. (1968). Psychoanalysis of children: problems of etiology and treatment. In Judd Marmor (Ed.), *Modern psychoanalysis*. New York: Basic Books.

Fisher, C. (1953). Studies on the nature of suggestion Part II. *Journal of the American Psychoanalytic Association*, I, 406-437.

Fisher, C. (1960). Introduction. *Psychological issues*, 2, 1-40.

Fisher, L. (1976). Dimensions of family assessment: A critical review. *Journal of Marriage and Family Counseling*, 2, 367-376.

Fiske, D. W. (1975). A source of data is not a measuring instrument. *Journal of Abnormal Psychology*, 84, 20-23.

Flegenheimer, W. V. (1982). *Techniques of Brief Psychotherapy*. New York: Jason Aronson.

Forer, L. (1976). *The birth order factor.* New York: David McKay.

Foulkes, D. (1966). *The psychology of sleep.* New York: Charles Scribners.

Frankl, V. E. (1965). *The doctor and the soul.* New York: Alfred Knopf.

Frenczi, S. (1926). Theory and technique of psycho-analysis. (Compiled by J. Rickman,

Translated by J. I. Suttie et. al.) In E. Jones (Ed.), *The International Psycho-analytical Library*, Vol. 11. London: Hogarth Press.

Freytag, F. F. (1959). *The hypnoanalysis of an anxiety hysteria*. New York: Julian Press.

Freud, S. (1910). On the universal tendency to debasement in the sphere of love. *The standard edition of the complete psychological works of Sigmund Freud* (Vol. 11). London: Hogarth Press.

Freud, S. (1938). *The basic writings of Sigmund Freud*. (A. A. Brill, Ed.). New York: Modern Library.

Freud, S. (1949a). *Collected papers*. London: Hogarth Press and the Institute of Psychoanalysis.

Freud, S. (1 949b). *A general introduction to psychoanalysis*. (J. Riviere, trans.), New York: Perma Giants.

Freud, S. (1 953a). On psychotherapy. *The standard edition of the complete psychological works of Sigmund Freud* (Vol. 7). London: Hogarth Press.

Freud, S. (1 953b). *A general introduction to psycho-analysis*. (J. Riviere, trans.). New York: Permabooks.

Freud, S. (1957). On narcissism. In J. Strachy et. al *The standard. edition of the complete psychological works of Sigmund Freud* (Vol. 14). London: Hogarth Press.

Freud, S. (1960). Basic Principles of Psychoanalysis. (A. A. Brill, Ed.). New York: Washington Square Press.

Freud, S., & Breuer, J. (1959). On the psychical mechanism of hysterical phenomena. *Collected Papers* (Vol. 1). New York: Basic Books.

Freytag, F. F. (1959). *The hypnoanalysis of an anxiety hysteria*. New York: Julian Press.

Fried, E. (1980). *The Courage to Change*. New York: Brunner/Mazel.

Fromm, E. (1965). Spontaneous autohypnotic age regression in a nocturnal dream. *International Journal of Clinical Hypnosis*, 13, 119-131.

Fromm, E. (1970). Age regression with unexpected reappearance of a repressed childhood language. *International Journal of Clinical Hypnosis. 18, 79-88*.

Fromm, E., & Shor, R. E. (Eds.) (1979). *Hypnosis: Developments in Research and New Perspectives* (2nd ed). New York: Aldine.

Frosch, J. (Ed.). (1951). *The Annual Survey of Psychoanalysis*. New York: International Universities Press, 2.

Fross, G. (1969). Audio analgesia in dentistry. *Journal of the American Institute of Hypnosis*, 10,(1), 5-9.

Frumkin, L. R., Ripley, H. S., & Cox, G. B. (1978). Changes in cerebral hemispheric lateralization with hypnosis. *Biological Psychiatry*, 13, 741-750.

Fry, W. F., Jr. & Salameh, W. A. (1987). *Handbook of humor and psychotherapy*. Sarasota, FL: Professional Resource Exchange, Inc. P.197

Gadpaille, W. J. (1975). *The cycles of sex*. New York: Charles Scribner's Sons.

Galin, D. (1974). Implications for psychiatry of left and right cerebral specialization. *Archives of General Psychiatry*, 31, 572-583.

Galin, D., Diamond, R. & Branff, D. (1977). Lateralization of conversion symptoms: more frequent on the left. *American Journal of Psychiatry*, 34, 578-580.

Garzzaniga, M. 5. (1970). *The bisected brain*. New York: Appelton-Century-Crafts.

Gear, M. C., Liendo, E. C. & Scott, L. L. (1983). *Patients and agents*. New York: Jason Aaronson.

Gebrke, S., & Moxom, J. (1969). Diagnostic classifications and treatment techniques in marriage counseling. In B. N. Ard & C. C. Ard (Eds.), *Handbook of marriage counseling*. Palo Alto, CA: Science and Behavior Books.

Geovacchini, P. (1965). The classical approach. In B. Greene (Ed.), *The psychotherapies of marital disharmony*. New York: Macmillan.

Gill, M. M. (1948). Spontaneous regression on the induction of hypnosis. *Bulletin of the Menninger Clinic*, 12, 41-48.

Gill, M. M. (1951). Ego psychology and psychotherapy. *Psychoanalytic Quarterly* 20, 62-71.

Gill, M. M. & Brenman, M. (1947). Treatment of a case of anxiety hysteria by an hypnotic technique employing psychoanalytic principles. *Bulletin of the Menninger Clinic*, 143, 7, 163-171. Reprinted in Brenman & Gill (1947).

Gill, M. M., & Brenman, M. (1959). *Hypnosis and related states*. New York: International Universities Press.

Gill, M. M. & Menninger, K. (1946). Techniques of hypnoanalysis, a case report. *The Bulletin of the Menninger Clinic*. 10, 110-126.

Gilman, L. (1958). *Insomnia and its relation to dreams*. Philadelphia: Lippincott.

Gindes, B. C. (1951). *New concepts of hypnosis.* New York: The Julian Press.

Glasser, W. (1965). *Reality therapy - a new approach to psychiatry.* New York: Harper & Row.

Goldfried, M. (1977). Behavioral assessment in perspective. In J. D. Cone & R. P. Hawkins (Eds.), *Behavioral Assessment: New Directions in Clinical Psychology.* New York: Brunner/Mazel.

Goldfried, M. R., & Sprafkin, J. N. (1976). Behavior personality assessment. In J. T. Spence, R. C. Carson, & J. W. Thibaut (Eds.), *Behavior approaches to therapy.* Morristown, NJ: General Learning Press.

Goldman, B. D. (1978). In J. B. Hutchinson (Ed.), *Biologic determinants of sexual behavior.* New York: John Wiley & Sons.

Goldstein, D., & Lamer, K., Zuckerman, S., & Goldstein, H. (1977). *The dance-away lover.* New York: Ballentine.

Goleman, D. (1976). Why the brain blocks daytime dreams. *Psychology Today*, March, 68-70.

Goleman, D. (1977). Split-brain psychology: fad of the year. *Psychology Today*, Oct., 89f.

Gordan, J. E. (1967). *Handbook of Clinical and Experimental Hypnosis.* New York: MacMillan.

Gottschall, L. D. (1969). Psychopathology of religious disorders. *Journal of the American Institute of Hypnosis, 10*,(3), 119-121.

Goy, R. W. (1968). In R. P. Michael (Ed.), *Indocrinology and Human Behavior.* London: Oxford University Press.

Gravitz, M. A. & Gerton, M. I. (1984). Origins of the term hypnotism prior to Braid. *American Journal of Clinical Hypnosis*, 27, 2, October.

Gray, J. A. (1971). *The psychology of fear and stress.* London: Wiedenfeld & Nicholson.

Greene, B. L. (1970). *A clinical approach to marital problems: Evaluation and management.* Springfield, IL: C. C. Thomas.

Green, C. E. (1974). "I know I'm dreaming" - the lucid dream. In R. L Woods & H. B.

Greenhouse (Eds.), *The New World of Dreams.* New York: Macmillan.

Green, M. R., Uliman, M., & Tauber, E. S., (1968). Dreaming and modern dream theory. In J. Marmor (Ed.), *Modern psychoanalysis.* New York: Basic Books.

Greenhouse, H. B., & Woods, R. L. (Eds.) (1974). *The new world of dreams*. New York: Macmillan.

Greenson, R. R. (1975). *The technique and practice of psychoanalysis*. New York: International Universities Press.

Grinker, R. R. & Spiegel, J. P. (1943). *War neuroses in North Africa. The Tunisian campaign*. New York: Josiah Macy Foundation.

Gruenewald, D. (1982). A psychoanalytic view of hypnosis. *American Journal of Clinical Hypnosis.* 24, 185-190.

Gurman, A. S. (1971). Group marital therapy: clinical and empirical implications for outcome research. *International Journal of Group Psychotherapy,* 21, 174-189.

Gurman, A. S. (1973). The effects and effectiveness of marital therapy: a review of outcome research. *Family Process,* 12, 145-170.

Gurman, A. S. (1978). Contemporary marital therapies: Critique and comparative analysis of psychoanalytic, behavioral and systems theory approach In T. J. Paolino, Jr. & B. S. McCrady (Eds.), *Marriage and Marital Therapy*. New York: Brunner/Mazel.

Gurman, A. S., & Kniskern, D. P. (1978). Research on marital and family therapy: Progress, perspective and prospect. In S. L. Grafield & A. E. Bergin (Eds.), *Handbook of Psychotherapy and Behavior Change: An Empirical Analysis* (2nd ed.). New York: Wiley.

Hadfield, J. A. (1919). *Psychology of power*. New York: Man.

Hadfield, J. A. (1920). Hypnotism. In H. Crichton-Miller (Ed.), *Functional nerve disease*. London: Frowde.

Hadfield, J. A. (1940). Treatment by suggestion and hypnoanalysis. In E. Miller (Ed.), *The neurosis in war*. New York: Macmillan.

Hafner, R. J., (1986). *Marriage and mental illness*. New York: Guilford Press.

Haley, J. (1963). Marriage therapy. *The Archives of General Psychiatry,* 8, 2 13-234.

Hambidge, G. (1959). The Simultaneous Psychoanalysis of Marriage Partners. Paper read at meeting of the American Psychoanalytic Association, Philadelphia.

Harper, R. A. (1960). Marriage counseling as a rational process-oriented psychotherapy. *Journal of Individual Psychology.* 16, 192-207.

Harper, R. A. (1959). *Psychoanalysis and psychotherapy*. Englewood Cliffs, NJ: Prentice-Hall.

Harris, T. A. (1969). *I'm OK--You're OK*. New York: Harper & Row.

Harrower, M. (1958). The measurement of psychological factors in marital maladjustment. In V. W. Eisenstein (Ed.), *Neurotic interaction in marriage.* New York: Basic Books.

Hartman, B. J. (1966). Uncovering hypnoanalytical techniques. *Journal of the American Institute of Hypnosis,* 7,(3), 41-43.

Hartman, B. J. (1967). Dreams and hypnoanalysis. *Journal of the American Institute of Hypnosis, 8,* 27-29.

Hartman, B. J. (1968). Automated desensitization in conjunction with the B.E.A.R. hypnotist. *Journal of the American Institute of Hypnosis, 9,* (3), 9-12.

Headley, L. (1977). *Adults and their parents in family therapy.* New York: Plenum Press.

Hefez, A. (1973). Neurosis and manage - a phenomenological analysis of disturbed married couples. *Israel Annals of Psychiatry and Related Disciplines,* 11, p. 8 1-90.

Heiman, M. (1956). The problem of family diagnosis. In V. W. Eisenstein (Ed.), *Neurotic Interaction in Marriage.* New York: Basic Books.

Held, R. (1979a). Development of visual resolution. *Canadian Journal of Psychology,* 33, (4), 213-221.

Held, R. (1979b). Infant visual acuity is underestimated because near threshold gratings are not preferentially fixed. *Vision Research,* 19, (12), 1377-79.

Helmreich, R. L. (1968). *Birth order effects.* Naval Research News. Washington, D. C.: Office of Naval Research. 1-6.

Herod, J. W. (1982). A review of Senoi dream principles: adaptation to hypnoanalysis. *Medical Hypnoanalysis,* 3, 96-107.

Hiebert, W. J., & Stahmann, R. F. (1977). Commonly recurring couple interacting patterns. In R. F. Stahmann & W. J. Hiebert, (Eds.), *Klemer's Counseling in Marital and Sexual Problems.* Baltimore: Williams & Wilkins.

Hilgard, E. R. (1977). *Divided consciousness: multiple controls in human thought and action.* New York: Wiley.

Hilgard, J. R. (1979). *Personality and hypnosis.* Chicago: University of Chicago Press.

Hofer, M. A. (1981). *Roots of human behavior.* San Fransisco: W. H. Freeman.

Holzman, J. *Authentic sound effects* (Vol. 2). New York: Elektra records.

Hoopes, M. H., & Harper, J. M. (1987). *Birth order roles & sibling patterns in individual & family therapy.* Rockville, MD: Aspen Publishers.

Hull, C. L. (1933). *Hypnosis and suggestibility.* New York: Appleton-Century.

Hunter, R., & Macalpine, I. (Eds.). (1963). *Three hundred years of psychiatry 1535-1860.* London (New York): Oxford University Press.

Huntington, R. M. (1958). The personality-interaction approach to the study of the marital relationship. *Marriage and Family Living,* 20, 43-46.

Jacob, T. (1975). Assessment of marital dysfunction. In M. Herson & A. S. Bellack (Eds.), *Behavioral assessment: A practical handbook.* New York: Pergamon Press.

Jacobs, B. L. (1976). Serotonin: The crucial substance that turns dreams on and off. *Psychology Today,* March, 70-71.

Jacobson, E. (1956). Interaction between psychotic partners. In V. W. Eisenstein (Ed.), *Neurotic interaction in marriage.* New York: Basic Books.

Jacobson, N. S. (1977). Problem solving and contingency contracting in the treatment of marital discord. *Journal of Consulting and Clinical Psychology,* 45, 92-100.

Jacobson, N. S. (1978). A review of the research on the effectiveness marital therapy. In T. J. Paolino, Jr., & B. S. McCrady (Eds.), *Marriage and marital therapy.* New York: Brunner/Mazel.

Janet, P. (1925). *Psychological healing.* New York: Macmillan.

Johnson, D. (1961). *Marriage counseling: Theory and practice.* Englewood Cliffs, NJ: Prentice-Hall.

Jones, E. (1961). *The life and work of Sigmund Freud.* New York: Bask Books.

Joyce, V. (1985). The play of illusion on an opening to the future of the self reflections of a religious clinician occasioned by rereading "the future of an illusion". In EM. Stern (ed.), *Psychotherapy and the religiously committed patient.* New York: Haworth Press.

Joynes, J. (1976). *The origins of consciousness in the breakdown of the bicameral mind. Boston:* Houghton Mifflin.

Kaplan, H. S. (1974), *The new sex therapy.* New York: Brunner/Mazel.

Kaplan, L. J. (1978). *Oneness and separateness: From Infant to individual.* New York: Simon & Schuster.

Kearns, W. (1985). *Reaping the harvest.* Menninger Perspective, 1, 24.

Keith, H. M. & Norval, M. A. (1950). Neurologic lesions in the newborn; preliminary study, role of prolonged labor, asphyxia and delayed respiration. *Proceedings of the Staff Meetings of the Mayo Clinic*, 25, 11-13.

Keller, D. H. (117). A psychoanalytic cure of hysteria. *Institution Quarterly*, 8, 78-82, Springfield, IL.

Kemper, T. (1966). Mate selection and marital satisfaction according to sibling type of husband and wife. *Journal of Marriage and the Family*, 28, 346-349.

Kernberg, O. (1974). Barriers to falling and remaining in love. *Journal of the American Psychoanalytic Association*, 22, 486-511.

Key, W. B. (1973). *Subliminal seduction.* New York: Signet.

Key, W. B. (1976). *Media sexploitation.* New York: Signet.

Kimber, J. A. (1969). Psychologists and marriage counselors in the United States. In B. N. Ard & C. C. Ard (Eds.), *Handbook of Marriage Counseling.* Palo Alto, CA: Science and Behavior Books.

King, N. (1987). *The first five minutes.* New York: Prentice Hall. *P.197, 198*

King, P. D. (1957). Hypnosis and schizophrenia. *Journal of Nervous and Mental Disease*, 125, 481-486.

Klaus, M. H., & Kennell, J. H. (1976). Parent to infant attachment. In V. C. Vaughn, III and T. B. Brazelton (Eds.), *The family - can it be saved?* Chicago: Year Book Medical Publishers.

Kleitman, N. (1957). Cyclic variations in EEG during sleep and their relation to eye movements, bodily motility, and dreaming. *Electroencephalography and Clinical Neurophysiology*, 9, 673-690.

Kleitman, N. (1963). *Sleep and wakefulness* (Rev. ed.). Chicago: University of Chicago Press.

Klemperer, E. (1954). Changes in body image in hypnoanalysis. *Journal of Clinical and Experimental Hypnosis*, 2,(2), 157-162.

Klemperer, E. (1961). Shortest distance therapy in hypnoanalysis. *International Journal of Clinical and Experimental Hypnosis*, 9, 6 3-77.

Klemperer, E. (1968). *Past ego states emerging in hypnoanalysis.* Springfield, IL: Charles C. Thomas.

Klimek, D. (1979). *Beneath mate selection and marriage.* New York: Von Nostrand Reinhold.

Kline, M. V. (1953). Freud and hypnosis: A critical evaluation. *British Journal of Medical Hypnotism*, 4,(3), 2-11.

Kline, M. V. (1955). *Hypnodynamic psychology*. New York: The Julian Press.

Kline, M. V. (1958). *Freud and hypnosis*. New York: Matrix House.

Kline, M. V. (1960). Hypnotic age regression and psychotherapy: clinical and theoretical observations. *International Journal of Clinical and Experimental Hypnosis*, 8, 18-35.

Kline, M. V. (1963). *Clinical correlations of experimental hypnosis*. Springfield, IL: Charles C. Thomas.

Kline, M. V. & Schneck, J. M. (1951). Hypnosis in relation to the word association test. *Journal of General Psychology*, 44, 129.

Korchin, S. J. (1976). *Modern clinical psychology*. New York:Basic.

Krich, A. (1967). Active strategies in marriage counseling. In. H. Greenwald (Ed.), *Active psychotherapy*. New York: Atherton Press.

Kroger, W. S. (1977). *Clinical and experimental hypnosis*. Philadelphia: Lippincott.

Kroger, W. S., & Fezler, W. D. (1976). *Hypnosis and behavior modification: Imagery conditioning*. Philadelphia: Lippincott.

Kubie, L. S. (1939). A critical analysis of the concept of a repetition compulsion. *International Journal of Psychiatry*, 20, 3 90-402.

Kubie, L. S. (1943). Manual of emergency treatment for acute war neruoses. *War Medicine*, 4, 582-598.

Kubie, L. (1956). Psychoanalysis and marriage. In V. Eisenstein (Ed.), *Neurotic interaction in marriage*. New York: Basic Books.

Kubie, L. S. (1957). Induced hypnogogic reveries for the recovery of repressed data. *Bulletin of the Menninger Clinic*, 1 943b, 7, 172-182. Also in R. H. Rodes, (Ed.), *Therapy through hypnosis*. New York: Citadel Press.

Kubie, L. S. (1961). Hypnotism, a focus for psychophysiological and psychoanalytic investigations. *Archives of General Psychiatry*, 4,40-54.

Laing, R. D., & Esterson, A. (1970). *Sanity, madness and the family*. Baltimore: Penguin Books.

Landis, J. T., & Landis, M. G. (1963). *Building a successful marriage* (4th ed.). Englewood Cliffs, NJ: Prentice-Hall.

Laner, M. R. (1976). The medical model, mental illness, and metaphoric mystification among marriage and family counselors. *Family Coordinator*, 25, 175-181.

Lasin, H. (1964). Frigidity. *Journal of the American Institute of Hypnosis*, 5, (3), 21.

Lear, M. (1972). Save the spouses, rather than the marriage. *New York Times Magazine*, August 13, 12-28.

LeBoyer, F. (1975). *Birth without violence*. New York: Alfred Knopf.

LeCron, L. M., & Bordeaux, J. (1947). *Hypnotism today*. New York: Grune & Stratton.

Lederer, W. J., & Jackson, D. D. (1968). *The mirages of marriage*. New York: Norton.

Lemon, K. (1990). *Growing up firstborn*. New York: Bantam-Doubleday.

Leslie, G. R. (1964). Conjoint therapy in marriage counseling. *Journal of Marriage and Family Living*, 26, 65-71.

Lester, B. M., Als, H., & Brazelton, T. B. (1982). Regional anesthesia newborn behavior: a reanalysis toward synergistic effects. *Child Development*, 53, 687-692.

Lester, D. (1966) Sibling position. *Journal of Individual Psychology*, 22, 204-207.

Lewis, C. S., (1944a). *The problem of pain*. New York: Macmillan.

Lewis, C. S., (1944b). *The case for Christianity*. New York: Macmillan

Lewith, G. (1985). Why do people seek treatment by alternative medicine? *British Medical Journal*, 290.

Lewter, N. C. (1981). Initial environmental experience: a powerful tool for psychotherapy and hypnotherapy. *Medical Hypnoanalysis*, 2, 157-160.

Ley, R. (1980). An archival examination of an asymmetry of hysterical conversion symptoms. *Journal of Clinical Neuropsychology*, 2, 1-9.

Lifshitz, K. & Blair, J. H. (1960). The polygraphic recording of a repeated hypnotic abreaction with comments on abreactive psychotherapy., *Journal of Nervous and Mental Disease*, 130, 246-2 52.

Ligon, E. M. (1938). *The psychology of Christian personality*. New York: Macmillan.

Lillienfeld, A. M. & Pasamanick, B. (1955). The association of maternal and fetal factors in the development of cerebral palsy and epilepsy. *American Journal of Obstretics and Gynecology*, 70, 93-101.

Lindner, R. M. (1944). *Rebel without a cause*. New York: Grune & Stratton..

Lindner, R. M. (1951). Introduction. In B. C. Gendes, *New concepts of hypnosis*. New York: Julian Press.

Lindner, R. M. (1957). Hypnoanalysis. In R. H. Rhodes (Ed.), *Therapy through hypnosis*. New York: Citadel Press.

Link, H. C., (1938). *The return to religion*. New York: Micmillan.

Little, W. J. (1961). On the influence of abnormal parturition, difficult labour, premature birth, and asphyxia neonatorum of the mental and physical condition of the child especially in relation to deformities. *Lancet*, 2, 378-380.

Lyndon, C. B., & Lyndon, B. H. (1967). Counseling for family living. In B. N. Ard & C. C. Ard (Eds.), *Handbook of marriage counseling*. Palo Alto, CA: Science and Bahavior Books.

Mace, D., & Mace, V. (1974). *We can have better marriages*. Nashville, TN: Abingdon.

Machotka, P. (1967). Delineation of family roles. *American Journal of Orthopsychiatry, 37*.

Mahler, M. S., Pine, F., & Bergman, A. (1975). *The psychological birth of the human infant*. New York: Basic Books.

Mahler, M. S., & Rabinovitch, R. (1956). The effects of marital conflict on child development. In V. Eisenstein (Ed.), *Neurotic Interaction in Marriage*. New York: Basic Books.

Malan, D. H. (1976). *The frontier of brief psychotherapy*. New York: Plenum Press.

Malone, T. P. & Malone, P. T. (1987). *The art of intimacy*. New York: Prentice Hall.

Mann, J. (1973). *Time-limited psychotherapy*. Cambridge, MA: Harvard University Press.

Mangus, A. R. (1957). Role theory and marriage counseling. *Social Forces*, 35, 200-209.

Marcel, G., (1950). *The mystery of being*, (2 vols.) London: Harvil Press.

Margolin, G. (1977). A multilevel approach to the assessment of communication positiveness in distressed marital couples. *International Journal of Family Counseling*, 6, 81-89.

Martin, P. A. (1976). *A marital therapy manual*. New York: Brunner/Mazel.

Maslow, A. H. (1950). Self-actualizing people: A study of psychological health. In W. Wolff (Ed.), *Personality symposium no. 1*. New York: Brune & Stratton.

Masserman, J. H. (1941). The dynamics of hypnosis and brief psychotherapy. *Archives of Neurology and Psychiatry*, 46, 176-179.

May, R., Angle, B., & Ellenburger, H. (Eds.) (1958). *Existence*. New York: Basic Books.

Mazor, N. (1951). An experimental study of the hypnotic dream. *Psychiatry*, 14, 265-277. See also Frosch, 1951.

McDonald, A. P. (1967). Birth order effects in marriage. *Journal of Marriage and Family*, 656.

McDonald, R. E. (1968). The role of emotional factors in obstetrical complications (a review). *Psychosomatic Medicine*, 30, 222.

McNeil, T. & Weigerink, R. (1971). Behavioral patterns and pregnancy and birth complication histories in psychologically disturbed children. *Journal of Nervous and Mental Disease*, 152, 315-324.

McPhail, F. L. & Hall, E. L. (1941). A consideration of the cause and possible late effect of anoxia in the newborn infant. *American Journal of Obstetrics and Gynecology*, 42, 686-701.

Meares, A. (1958). *Marriage and personality*. Springfield, IL: C. C. Thomas.

Medved, D. (1989). *The case against divorce*. New York: Donald I. Fine.

Mehler, J., Bertoncini, J., Barrier, M. & Jassik-Gerschenfeld, D. (1978). Infant recognition of mother's voice, *Perception*, 7, 491-497.

Meissner, W. W. (1978). The conceptualization of marriage and family dynamics from a psychoanalytic perspective. In T. J. Paolina, Jr. & B. S. McCrady (Eds.),

Marriage and Marital Therapy. New York: Brunner/Mazel.

Meltzoff, A. N. & Moore, M. K. (1977). Imitation of facial and manual gestures by human neonates. *Science*, 198, 74-78.

Menninger, K. (1942). *Love against hate*. New York: Harcourt, Brace & World.

Menninger, K. (1985). Psychiatry's unsolved riddle. Menninger *Perspective*, 16, (2), 3-7.

Millikin, L. A. (1961). Hypnotherapy in arthritis. *Journal of the American Institute of Hypnosis*, 2(1), 5.

Mischel, W. (1968). *Personality and assessment*. New York: John Wiley & Sons.

Mischel, W. (1971). *Introduction to personality*. New York: Holt, Rinehard & Winston.

Missildine, W. H. (1963). *Your inner child of the past*. New York: Simon & Schuster.

Mittelmann, B. (1956). Analysis of reciprocal neurotic patterns in family relationships. In V. Eisenstein (Ed.), *Neurotic Interaction in Marriage*. New York: Basic Books.

Money, J. & Schwartz, M. (1978). In J. B. Hutchison (Ed.), *Biologic determinents of sexual behavior*. New York: John Wiley & Sons.

Monroe, R. L. (1955). *Schools of psychoanalytic thought*. New York: Holt, Rinehard & Winston, 211-215.

Montagu, A. (1956). Marriage: A cultural perspective. In V. Eisenstein (Ed.), *Neurotic interaction in marriage*. New York: Basic Books.

Morris, D. (1977). *Manwatching*. New York: Harry N. Abrams.

Morris, J. K. (1965). *Marriage counseling*. Englewood Cliifs, NJ: Prentice-Hall.

Moss, C. S. (1967). *The hypnotic investigation of dreams*. New York: John Wiley.

Moss, D. M. (1977). Three levels of mate selection and marital interaction. *Journal of Religion and Health*, 16, 288-303.

Mowrer, O. H. (1961). *The crisis in psychiatry and religion*. Princeton, NJ: Von Nostrand.

Mowrer, O. H. (1964). *The new group therapy*. New York: Von Nostrand.

Mudd, E. H., Stone, A., Karpf, M. J., & Nelson, J. F. (1958). *Marriage counseling: A casebook*. New York: Association Press.

Munroe, R. L. (1955). *Schools of psychoanalytic thought*. New York: Holt, Rinehart & Winston.

Murooka, H. (nd) *Lullaby from the womb* (recording #ST- 11421). Los Angeles: Capitol records, Inc.

Murphy, W. F. (1955). *The clinical interview* (2 vols.). New York: International University.

Murray, M. A. (1957). *The Splendor that was Egypt*. London: Sidgwick & Jackson.

Nadelson, C. C. (1978). Marital therapy from a psychoanalytic perspective. In T. J. Paolino, Jr., & B. S. McCrady (Eds.), *Marriage and Marital Therapy*. New York: Brunner/Mazel.

Nathan, P. E. (1981). Symptomatic diagnosis and behavioral assessment: A synthesis. In D. H. Barlow (Ed.), *Behavioral assessment in adult disorders*. New York: Guilford Press.

Nelson, R. O., & Barlow, D. H. (1981). Behavior assessment: Basic strategies and initial procedures. In D. H. Barlow (Ed.), *Behavioral assessment in adult disorders*. New York: Guilford Press.

Nemiah, J. C. (1973). *Foundations of psychopathology.* New York: Jason Aaronson.

Newman, O. (1976). The search for a new form of extended family. In V. C. Vaughn, III, & T. B. Brazelton (Eds.), *The family - can it be saved?* Chicago: Year Book Medical Publishers.

Niebuhr, H. R. (1963). *The responsible self.* New York: Harper & Row.

North, E. E., Jr. (1985). Psychiatry's unsolved riddle. *Menninger Perspective,* 16, (2), 3-7.

O'Connell, D. N., Shor, R. E., & Orne, M. T., (1970). Hypnotic age regression: an empirical and methodological analysis. *Journal of Abnormal Psychology Monograph,* 76, 3, Pt 2.

O'leary, K. D., & Turkewitz, H. (1978). Marital therapy from a behavioral perspective. In T. J. Paolino, Jr., & B. S. McCrady (Eds.), *Marriage and Marital Therapy.* New York: Brunner/ Mazel.

Oates, W. E. (1973). *The psychology of religion.* Waco, TX: Word

Olmstead, A. T. (1923). *History of Assyria.* New York: Charles Scribners.

Orne, M. 1. (1971). The simulation of hypnosis: why, how, and what it means. *International Journal of Clinical and Experimental Hypnosis,* 19, 183-210.

Ornish, D. (1990). *Dr. Dean Ornish's program for reversing heart disease.* New York:Random House.

Paloutzian, R. F. (1975). The role of emotional feelings: A social psychological perspective and case study. *Journal of Psychology and Theology.*

Paolino, T. J., Jr., (1978). Marital therapy from a psychoanalytic perspective. In T. J.

Paolino, Jr., & B. S. McCrady (Eds.), *Marriage and marital therapy.* New York: Brunner/Mazel.

Parlour, R. R. (1961). A psychoanalytic psychiatrist is introduced to hypnosis. *Journal of the American Institute of Hypnosis,* 2,(4), 10.

Pascal, B. (1958). *Pascal's Pensees.* New York: E. P. Dutton.

Paul, N. L. (1976). Effects of playback on family members of their own previously recorded conjoint therapy material. In G. D. Erickson & T. P. Hogan (Eds.), *Family Therapy.* New York: Jason Aaronson.

Phillips, E. L. & Wiener, D. N. (1966). *Short-term psychotherapy and structured behavior change.* New York: McGraw-Hill.

Pine, F. (1985). *Developmental theory and clinical process*. New Haven: Yale University Press.

Pines, M. (1982). Baby your incredible. *Psychology Today*, (Feb,), 48-52.

Piotrowski, Z. A., & Dudek, S. Z. (1956). Research on human movement response in the Rorschach examinations of marital partners. In V. Eisenstein (Ed.), *Neurotic Interaction in Marriage*. New York: Basic Books.

Pittman, F. (1989). *Private lies*. New York: W. W. Norton.

Platonow, K. I. (1933). On the objective proof of the experimental personality age regression. *Journal of General Psychology*, 9, 190.

Plutchik, R. (1967). Marriage as dynamic equilibrium: Implications for research. In H. L. Silverman (Ed.), *Marital counseling*. Springfield, IL: C. C. Thomas.

Poetzl, O. (1960). The relationship between experimentally induced dream images and indirect vision. *Psychological Issues*, 2,41-120.

Ponder, C. B. (1970). Respiratory distress in the newborn infant due to blood aspiration in infants delivered by caesarian section. *American Journal of Obstetrics and Gynecology*, 106, 711-717.

Prachaska, J. & Prachaska, J. (1978). Twentieth century trends in marriage and marital therapy. In T. J. Paolino, Jr., & B. S. McCrady (Eds.), *Marriage and Marital therapy*. New York: Brunner/Mazel.

Pruyser, P. W. (1968). *A dynamic psychology of religion*. New York: Harper & Row.

Pulver, S. E. & Eppes, B. (1963). The Poetzl phenomenon: Some further evidence. *Journal of Nervous and Mental Disease*, 136, 527-534.

Raginsky, B. B. (1961). The sensory use of plasticine in hypnoanalysis. *International Journal of Clinical and Experimental Hypnosis*, 9, 233.

Raikov, V. L. (1982). Hypnotic age regression to the neonatal period: with comparisons with role playing. The International Journal of Clinical and Experimental Hypnosis, 30, 108-115.

Regensburg, J. (1956). Application of psychoanalytic concepts. In V. Eisenstein (Ed.), *Neurotic Interaction in Marriage*. New York: Basic Books.

Register, R. L. [Pen name for John A. Scott, Sr.] (1981). When does life begin? *Medical Hypnoanalysis*, 2, 141-151.

Rhodes, R. H. (1957). Hypnosis: what it is and what it does. In R. H.

Rhodes (Ed.), *Therapy Through Hypnosis*. New York: Citadel Press.

Riddell, W. G. (1970). Severe ulcerative colitis and hypnotherapy. *Journal of the American Institute of Hypnosis*, 1l,(3), 113-114.

Rie, H. E. (1971). *Perspectives in child psychopathology*. New York: Aldine-Atherton.

Ritzman, T. A. (1982a). The identity problem. *Medical Hypnoanalysis*, 3,5-18.

Ritzman, T. A. (1982b). Depression and the nature of God. *Medical Hypnoanalysis*, 3, 129-139.

Ritzman, T. A. (1983). Pain as an assurance of life. *Medical Hypnoanalysis*, 4, 23-30.

Ritzman, T. A. (1984). Stress and the birth experience. *Medical Hypnoanalysis*, 6, (2), 51-56.

Roche Laboratories. (1966). *The anatomy of sleep*. Nutley, NJ: Hoffman-LaRoche.

Rogers, C. R. (1951). *Client-centered therapy*. Boston: Houghton-Mifflin.

Rogers, C. R. (1977). *On personal power, inner strength and its revolutionary impact*. New York: Delacourte Press.

Rogers, F. M. (1976). Television and the family. In V. C. Vaughn, III, & T. B. Brazelton (Eds.), *The family - can it be saved?* Chicago: Year Book Medical Publishers.

Rossi, E. L. (1986). *The psychobiology of mind-body healing*. New York: W. W. Norton.   P. 101

Rossi, E. L. & Cheek, D. B. (1988). *Mind-body therapy: Methods of ideodynamic healing in hypnosis*. New York: W. W. Norton.

Rotter, J. B. (1951). Word association and sentence completion methods. In H. H. Anderson & G. L. Anderson (Eds.), *An introduction to projective techniques*. New York: Prentice-Hall.

Rubin, Z. (1972). Lovers and other strangers: The development of intimacy in encounters and relationships. Paper presented at the Annual Convention of the American Psychological Association, Honolulu, September, 1972.

Rubenstein, D. & Timmons, J. (1978). Depressive dyadic and triadic relationships. *Journal of Marriage and Family Counseling*, 4, 13-23.

Rue, J. J., & Shanahan, L. (1978). *Daddy's girl, mama's boy*. New York: Signet.

Rutledge, A. L. (1969). Male and female roles in marriage counseling. In

B. N. Ard & C. C. Ard (Eds.), *Handbook of marriage counseling.* Palo Alto, CA: Science & Behavior Books.

Rutt, C. N. & Offord, D. R. (1973). Prenatal and perinatal complications in childhood schizophrenic women. *Journal of Nervous and Mental Disease*, 157, 191-199.

Sacerdote, P. (1974). Grow thin with hypnotic dreams. In R. L. Woods & H. B. Greenhouse (Eds.), *The new world of dreams.* New York: Macmillan.

Sager, C. J. (1976). *Marriage contracts and couple therapy.* New York: Brunner/Mazel.

Samaroff, A. J. (1975). Early influences on development fact or fancy? *Merril-Palmer Quarterly of Behavior Development*, 21, 4.

Satir, V. (1969). Family communication and conjoint family therapy. In B. N. Ard & C. C. Ard (Eds.), *Handbook of marriage counseling.* Palo Alto, CA: Science and Behavior Books.

Saul, L. J., Laidlaw, R. W., Nelson, J. F. Ormsby, R., Stone, A., Eisenberg, S., Appel, K. E., & Mudd, E. H. (1953). Can one partner be successfully counseled without the other? *Marriage and Family Living*, 15, 5 9-64.

Schachter, 5. (1959). *The psychology of affiliation.* Stanford, CA: Stanford University Press.

Schafer, R. (1967). *Projective testing and psychoanalysis.* New York: International Universities Press.

Schilder, P. & Kauders, O. (1927). *Hypnosis.* New York: Nervous and Mental Disease Pub. Co..

Schneck, J. M. (1953). *Hypnosis in modern medicine.* Springfield, IL: Charles C. Thomas.

Schneck, J. M. (1954a) *Studies in scientific hypnosis.* Baltimore: Williams & Wilkins.

Schneck, J. M. (1954b). A Hypnoanalytic investigation of psychogenic dyspnea with the use of induced auditory hallucinations and special additional techniques. *Journal of Clinical and Experimental Hypnosis*, l,(l), 80.

Schoen, R., & Nelson, V. E. (1974). Marriage, divorce and mortality: Life table analysis. *Demography.*

Schwarz, R. H. & Yaffe, S. J. (Eds.), (1980). *Drug and chemical risks to the newborn.* New York: A. R. Liss.

Scott, H. (1976). Outcome of severe birth asphyxia. *Archives of Disease of Childhood*, 51, 7 12-716.

Scott, J. A., Jr. (1981). Conjoint marital therapy and hypnoanalysis: A comparative study, *Medical Hypnoanalysis*, 2, 32-37.

Scott, J. A., Sr. (1975). Early mechanical memory. *Journal of the American Institute of Hypnosis*, 16,(4), 179-196.

Scott, J. A., Sr. (1977). Hypnoanalysis in marital therapy. American Institute of Hypnosis Seminar on Hypnoanalysis, Las Vegas.

Scott, J. A., Sr. (1978). Hypnoanalysis in marital therapy. Semi-Annual Meeting, Society of Medical Hypnoanalysts, Houston.

Scott, J. A., Sr. (1979). Hypnoanalysis in marital therapy. National Convention of the National Alliance for Family Life, San Francisco.

Scott, J. A., Sr. (1980a). Hypnoanalysis in marital therapy. Semi-Annual Meeting, Society of Medical Hypnoanalysts, Las Vegas.

Scott, J. A., Sr. (1980b). Problem clinic. *Medical Hypnoanalysis*, 1, 139-140.

Scott, J. A., Sr. (1981). [Under pen name of R.L. Register] When does life begin? *Medical Hypnoanalysis*,2, 141-15 1.

Scott, J.A., Sr. & Scott, J.A., Jr. 1984. Age Regressions to Birth. *Medical Hypnoanalysis*, 5, (1), 17-33.

Scott, W. C. (1946). Book review of R. M. Lindner, Rebel without a cause. *The International Journal of Psycho-Analysis*, 27, 166f.

Sears, R. R., Maccoby, E. E., & Lavin, H. (1957). *Patterns of child rearing.* New York: Harper & Row.

Segalowitz, S. J. (1983). *Two sides of the brain.* Englewood Cliffs, N.J.: Prentice Hall.

Shaywitz, S., Cohen, D. & Shaywitz, B. (1980). Behavior and learning difficulties in children of normal intelligence born to alcoholic mothers. *Journal of Pediatrics*, 96, 978-981.

Sheppard, S. A. (1967). Depression - a case report. *Journal of the American Institute of Hypnosis*, 8,(3), 21-23.

Sheppard, S. A. (1970). Hypnosis in the diagnosis and treatment of mental illness, part one. *Journal of the American Institute of Hypnosis*, 11 ,(4), 189-193.

Sheppard, S. A. (1971). Hypnosis in the diagnosis and treatment of mental illness, part two. *Journal of the American Institute of Hypnosis*, 12,(l), 40-43.

Shostrum, E. & Kavanaugh, J. (1971). *Between man and woman.* Los Angeles:Nash.

Sifneos, P. (1979). *Short-term dynamic psychotherapy.* New York: Plenum.

Siegel, B. S. (1988). *Love, medicine, and miracles.* New York: Harper & Row.

Silverman, H. L. (1972). *Marital therapy.* Springfield, IL: C. C. Thomas.

Skinner, B. F. (1953). *Science and human behavior.* New York: Macmillan.

Skynner, A. C. (1976). *Systems of family and marital psychotherapy.* New York: Brunner\Mazel.

Sluzki, C. E. (1978). Marital therapy from a systems theory perspective. In T. S. Paolino, Jr., & B. S. McCrady (Eds.), *Marriage and Marital Therapy.* New York: Brunner/Mazel.

Sontag, L. W. (1966). Implications of fetal behavior and environment for adult personalities. *Annals of the New York Academy of Science,* 134, 782-786.

Sontag, L. W. & Newberry, H. (1940). Normal variations of fetal heart rate during pregnancy. *American Journal of Obstetrics and Gynecology,* 40, 449-452.

Spanos, N. P. (1970). Barber's reconceptualization of hypnosis: an evaluation of criticisms. *Journal of Experimental Research in Personality,* 4, 241-258.

Spazzano, C. (1981). Prenatal psychology. *Psychology Today,* (May, 49-57.)

Spelke, E. (1976). Infants' intermodal perception of events. *Cognitive Psychology,* 8, 553-560.

Spelke, E. (1981). The infants acquisitions of knowledge of bimodally specified events. *Journal of Experimental Child Psychology,* 31, 279-291.

Spelke, E., Zelazo, P., Kagan, J. & Kotelchuck, M. (1973). Father interaction and separation protest. *Developmental Psychology,* 9, 83-90.

Spelt, D. L. (1948). The conditioning of the human fetus in utero. *Journal of Experimental Psychology,* 38, 338-346.

Spiegel, J. P., & Bell, N. W. (1959). The family. In S. Arieti (Ed.), *American handbook of psychiatry.* New York: Basic Books.

Stahmann, R. F., & Hiebert, W. S. (Eds.) (1977). *Klemer's counseling in marital and sexual problems.* Baltimore: Williams & Wilkins.

Standley, K., Soule, B., & Copans, S. A. (1979). Dimensions of prenatal anxiety and their influence on pregnancy outcome. *American Journal of Obstetrics and Gynecology,* 135, 22.

Steger, M. (1951). Hypnoidal psychotherapy. New York: Froben Press.

Reviewed in *Journal of Nervous and Mental Disease*, 1952, 115, 464-465.

Stein, C. A. (1964). Displacement and reconditioning technique for compulsive smokers. *International Journal of Clinical and Experimental Hypnosis*, 12, 2301.

Steinglass, P. (1978). The conceptualization of marriage from a systems theory perspective. In T. J. Paolino, Jr., & B. S. McCrady (Eds.), *Marriage and marital therapy*. New York: Brunner/Mazel.

Stekel, W. (1974). Every dream is a confession. In R. L. Woods & H. B. Greenhouse (Eds.), *The new world of dreams*. New York: Macmillan.

Stern, E. M., (1985). *Psychotherapy and the religiously committed patient*. New York: Haworth Press.

Stewart, H. (1970). Book review. E. Klemperer, Past ego states emerging in hypnoanalysis. *International Journal of Psycho-Analysis*, 51, 89.

Stierlin, H. (1977). *Psychoanalysis and family therapy*. New York: Jason Aaronson. Stone, A. (1953). Can one partner be successfully counseled without the other? A symposium. *Journal of Marriage and Family Living*, 15, 59-64.

Stokvis, B. (1955). Hypnosis and psychoanalytic method. *Journal of Clinical and Experimental Hypnosis*, 3, 253-255.

Stotland, E. (1971). *Empathy and birth order*. Lincoln, NB: University of Nebraska Press.

Stott, D. H. (1972). The congenital background to behavior disturbance. In M. Roff, L. N. Robins & M. Pollack (Eds.), *Life history research in psychopathology*, (Vol. 2). Minneapolis: University of Minnesota Press.

Stott, D. H. (1973). Follow up study from birth of the effects of prenatal stresses. *Developmental Medicine and Child Neurology*, (Dec.), 15, (6), 770-787.

Stoyva, J. M. (1974). The effect of hypnosis on night dreams. In R. L. Woods & H. B. Greenhouse (Eds.), *The New World of Dreams*. New York: Macmillan.

Strecker, E. A. (1946). *Their mother's sons*. Philadelphia: Lippincott.

Strecker, E. A., & Lathbury, V. 1. (1956). Their mother's daughters. Philadelphia: Lippincott.

Strong, A. H. (1947). *Systematic theology* (Vol. II). Philadelphia: Judson.

Strupp, H. H. (1968). Psychoanalytic therapy of the individual. In Judd Marmor (Ed.), *Modern psychoanalysis*. New York: Basic Books.

Stuart, R. B. (1969). Operant-interpersonal treatment for marital discord. *Journal of Consulting and Clinical Psychology*, 33, 675-682.

Stuart, R. B. (1971). *Trick or treatment*. Champaign, IL: Research Press.

Stuart, R. B. (1976). Operant-interpersonal treatment for marital discord. In D. H. Olson (Ed.), *Treating relationships*. Lake Mills, IA: Graphic Press.

Stuart, R. B. (1980). *Helping couples change*. New York:Guilford.

Sullivan, H. S. (1953). *The interpersonal theory of psychiatry*. New York: Norton.

Sutton-Smith, B., & Rosenberg, B. G. (1970). *The sibling*. New York: Holt, Rinehart, & Winston.

Szasz, T. S. (1960). The myth of mental illness. *American Psychologist*, 51, 15, 113-118.

Szasz, T. S. (1965). *The ethics of psychoanalysis*. New York: Basic Books.

Taylor, J. W. (1956). Relationship of success and length in psychotherapy. *Journal of Consulting Psychology*, 20, 332.

Terman, L. M., Bettenweiser, P., Ferguson, L. W., Johnson, W. B., & Wilson, D. P. (1938). *Psychological factors in marital happiness*. New York McGraw-Hill.

Theorell, K., Prechtl, H. F., Blair, A. W. & Lind, J. (1973). Behavioral state cycles of normal newborn infants; a comparison of the effect of early and late cord clamping. *Developmental Medicine and Child Neurology*, 15, 597-605.

Thiessen, H. C. (1949). *Lectures in systematic theology*. Grand Rapids: Eerdmans.

Thomas, A., Chess, S., Birch, H. O. (1968). *Temperament and behavior disorders in children*. New York: New York University Press.

Thomas, A., Chess, S., Birch, H. G. Hertzig, M. & Korn, S. (1963). *Behavioral individuality in early childhood*. New York: New York University Press.

Thompson, C. (1950). Psychoanalysis: evolution and development. In John Frosch (Ed.), *The Annual Survey of Psychoanalysis*, 1, 501.

Tillich, P. (1951). Systematic Theology (Vol. I). Chicago: University of Chicago.

Tillich, P. (1957). *The courage to be*. New Haven: Yale.

Toman, W. (1969). *Family constellation*. New York: Springer.

Tournier, P. (1965). *The adventure of living*. New York: Harper & Row.

Tronick, E. O., Als, H., & Brazelton, T. B. (1980). Monadic phases:

A structural descriptive analysis of infant-mother face to face interaction. *Merril-Palmer Quarterly*, 26, 3-24.

Tronick, E. O., Als, H., & Brazelton, T. B. (1977). Mutuality in mother-infant interaction. *Journal of Communication*, 27, 74-79.

Tsoi-Hoshmand, L. (1976). Marital therapy: An integrative behavioral-learning model. *Journal of Marriage and Family Counseling*, 2, 179-191.

U. S. Department of Commerce, (1972). Bureau of the Census. *Statistical abstract of the United States*, 63-64.

U. S. Department of Health, Education and Welfare, Public Health Service, (1977). *Vital and Health Statistics*, Divorces, Series 21, No. 34.

Van Pelt, S. J. (1962). An answer to asthma. *Journal of the American Institute of Hypnosis*, 3,(2), 7-12.

Volgyesi, F. A. (1967). General medicine radically altered by modern medical hypnosis. *Journal of the American Institute of Hypnosis*, 8,(2), 46-49.

Wachtel, E. F., & Wachtel, P. L. (1988). *Family dynamics in individual psychotherapy*. New York:Guilford Press.

Wagner, M. K., & Bragg, R. A. (1970). Comparing behavior modification approaches to habit decrement - smoking. *Journal of Consulting and Clinical Psychology*, 34, 258.

Ward, I. (1972). Prenatal stress feminizes and demasculinizes the behavior of males. *Science*, 175, 82-84.

Watkins, J. (1949). *Hypnotherapy of war neuroses*. New York: Ronald Press.

Watson, A. S. (1967). The conjoint psychotherapy of married partners. In B. N. Ard & C. C. Ard (Eds.), *Handbook of marriage counseling*. Palo Alto, CA: Science and behavior Books.

Weiss, R. L. (1978). The conceptualization of marriage from a behavioral perspective. In T. J. Paolino, Jr., & B. S. McCrady (Eds.), *Marriage and marital therapy*. New York: Brunner/Mazel.

Wickramasekera, I., (Ed.) (1976). *Biofeedback, behavior therapy and hypnosis*. Chicago: Nelson-Hall.

Williams, J. (1974). Stimulation of breast growth by hypnosis. *Journal of Sex Research*, 10.

Windle, W. F. (1967). Asphyxia at birth, a major factor in mental retardation: 280 suggestions for prevention based on experiments in monkeys. *Psychopathology of mental development*. Springfield, Ill: Thomas.

Winch, R. (1952). *The modern family*. New York: Holt, Rinehart, & Winston.

Winch, R. (1963). *The modern family*. New York: Holt, Rinehart, & Winston.

Winch, R. (1967). Another look at the theory of complementary needs in mate selection. *Journal of Marriage and the Family*, 29, 756-762.

Wingfield, H. E. (1920). *An introduction to the study of hypnotism*, (Ed. 2). London: Balliere, Tindall & Co. R. B. (1940). Scientific hypnotism. Boston: Christopher Pub. House. Reviewed by Sandor Lorand, *International Journal of Psycho-Analysis*, 21, 242, 243.

Winnicott, D. W. (1958). *Collected papers: through pediatrics to psychoanalysis*. London: Tavistock.

Winnicott, D. W. (1965). *The family and individual development*. New York: Basic Books.

Wolberg, L. R. (1945). *Hypnoanalysis*. New York: Grune & Stratton.

Wolberg, L. R. (1948). *Medical hypnosis* (2 vols.). New York: Grune & Stratton. P. 193

Wolberg, L. R. (1964) .*Hypnoanalysis*. New York: Grune & Stratton.

Wolberg, L. R. (1967). *The technique of psychotherapy*. New York: Grune & Stratton.

Wolberg, L. R. (1971). *Medical hypnosis* (2 vols.). New York: Grune & Stratton.

Wolberg, L. R. (1980). *Handbook of short-term psychotherapy*. New York: Thieme-Stratton.

Wolf, B. & Rosenthal, R. (1948). *Hypnotism comes of age*. New York: Bobbs Merrill.

Wolpe, J. (1973). *The practice of behavior therapy*. New York: Pergamon Press.

P. 227 → Yahalom, I. (1975). Lecture at Riess-Davis Child Clinic sponsored by the California Graduate Institute, Los Angeles, July.

Yalom, I. (1975). *Theory and practice of group psychotherapy*. New York: Basic Books.

Yang, R. K., Zweig, A. R., Douthitt, T. C., & Federman, E. J. (1976). Successive

relationships between maternal attitudes during pregnancy, analgesic medications during labor and delivery, and newborn behavior. *Developmental Psychology*, 12, 6.

Zenkin, J. (1948). Book review of L. M. LeCron & Jean Bordeaux, Hypnotism today. *Journal of Nervous and Mental Disease*, 108, 354.

Take acupressure face
lift class in Nov. 2015 from
Infinity.. Script them
for Hypoacupuncture face
lift.
Add the work of Ashley?
(holding points on the head
one day workshop at Infinity)
Use of Jon Gabriels
script to tighten loose
skin as part of it!

When + where can you be most
you? How do you know you
like that?.

CPSIA information can be obtained at www.ICGtesting.com
Printed in the USA
LVOW07s1749011015

456528LV00003B/597/P